Albert R. Jonsen is Professor of Ethics in Medicine and Chairman, Department of Medical Humanities, University of Washington School of Medicine. He is co-author of a standard work on medical ethics. He was a member of the National Commission for the Protection of Human Subjects of Biomedical and Behavioral Research and of the President's Commission on the Study of Ethical Problems in Medicine.

Stephen Toulmin is Avalon Foundation Professor of the Humanities at Northwestern University, and was before that a member of the Committee on Social Thought at the University of Chicago. He is the author of *The Return to Cosmology* (University of California Press, 1982), and many other books in philosophy.

p.14
p.19
p. 312 - 313
p. 316

D1319889

The Abuse of Casuistry

The Abuse of Casuistry

A History of Moral Reasoning

Albert R. Jonsen

Stephen Toulmin

UNIVERSITY OF CALIFORNIA PRESS

Berkeley · *Los Angeles* · *London*

University of California Press

Berkeley and Los Angeles, California

University of California Press, Ltd.

London, England

Library of Congress Cataloging-in-Publication Data
Jonsen, Albert R.
   The abuse of casuistry.
   Includes index.
   1. Casuistry. I. Toulmin, Stephen Edelston.
II. Title.
BJ1441.J66   1988   171'.6   87-14307
ISBN 0-520-06063-6 (alk. paper)

Printed in the United States of America

1 2 3 4 5 6 7 8 9

Contents

Preface		vii
Prologue: The Problem		1
PART I. BACKGROUND		21
1.	Theory and Practice	23
2.	The Roots of Casuistry in Antiquity	47
3.	Cicero: Philosopher, Orator, Legislator	75
PART II. THE PRECURSORS		89
4.	Christian Origins	91
5.	The Canonists and Confessors	101
6.	The Theologians	122
PART III. HIGH CASUISTRY		137
7.	Summists and Jesuits	139
8.	Texts, Authors, and Methods	152

PART IV. THREE SAMPLES OF CASUISTRY   177

9.   Profit: The Case of Usury   181
10. Perjury: The Case of Equivocation   195
11. Pride: The Case of the Insulted
     Gentleman   216

PART V. THE CRISIS   229

12. Casuistry Confounded: Pascal's Critique   231
13. The Achievement of Casuistry   250

PART VI. THE FUTURE OF CASUISTRY   267

14. After *The Provincial Letters*   269
15. Philosophy and the Springs of Morality   279
16. The Revival of Casuistry   304
17. Epilogue: Conscience and the
     Claims of Equity   333

     Appendix   345

     Notes   355

     Name Index   405

     Subject Index   409

Preface

The occasion that led to the writing of this book exemplifies its thesis. From 1975 to 1978 the authors collaborated in the work of the National Commission for the Protection of Human Subjects of Biomedical and Behavioral Research, which was set up by the United States Congress in 1974. One outcome of this work was a casuistry (or moral taxonomy) for distinguishing acceptable from unacceptable ways of involving humans as subjects in medical or behavioral research. As the commission's work approached its end we compared notes, and found that we were independently struck by aspects of its methods and results that were hard to account for in terms of current ethical theory. The time had come (it seemed to us) to reconsider the older "case methods" of confessional and pastoral theology, which relied on Aristotle's analysis of moral practice in the *Nicomachean Ethics* and which have their parallels in the moral practice of Judaism and Islam.

The historical research needed to pursue our argument was supported by a grant from the U.S. National Endowment for the Humanities, #RO79/14660. One of the authors (A.R.J.) did much of this historical research at the Woodstock Library, Georgetown University, and at the Bodleian Library of Oxford University. At the Woodstock Library Fr. Henry Bertels and Br. Thomas Marshall were unfailingly helpful, though they had no way of knowing whether we intended to praise or vilify their Jesuit predecessors. The research at Oxford was made possible by a year of sabbatical leave from the University of California, and was fortuitously made more pleasant and fruitful by election as a temporary member of Christ Church.

This year was so fruitful because a fine Pascal scholar who provided invaluable guidance, Alban Krailsheimer, is a member of that college and because two of the geniuses of casuistry in the Anglican tradition were also at "the House"—Robert Sanderson, Bishop of Lincoln and Regius Professor of Case Divinity (1587–1663), and Kenneth Kirk, Bishop of Oxford and Regius Professor of Moral Theology (1886–1954). Whether or not these venerable casuists helped to guide the work, this author owes thanks to the dean, canons, and students of Christ Church for their hospitality and intellectual stimulus. Gratitude is also owed to Alexander Murray of University College, Oxford, Anthony Keary of Baliol, and to R. M. Hare of Corpus Christi College for useful advice in the fields of history and moral philosophy. Fr. John Mahoney, S.J., read this text; had his own *The Making of Moral Theology* (Oxford, 1987) been in print, it would have influenced our book.

Another fortuitous event attended the preparation of this book. Much of the writing of the historical chapters was done at Villa Serbellone, built by Cardinal Nicolo Sfondrata in 1540, the very year in which Pope Paul IV approved the establishment of the Society of Jesus. Sfondrata was raised to the cardinalate by that pope, and it is pleasing to think that they blessed the writing of this book at the villa. In any case, thanks are owing to the Rockefeller Foundation for granting A.R.J. a month's stay at the Rockefeller Study and Conference Center which now occupies the Villa Serbellone at Bellagio, Italy. At Oxford and at Bellagio, Mary Elizabeth Jonsen was an irreplaceable amanuensis. Finally, the influence of many Jesuit teachers is acknowledged. They revealed the intellectual and moral benefits of sound and honest casuistry.

The other author (S.E.T.) owes the opportunity to complete his share in this joint work, in part to the Guggenheim Foundation and the University of Chicago for supporting a year of research leave, and in part to the Getty Trust, which made it possible for him to spend the year 1985–86 as a scholar at the Getty Center for the History of Art and the Humanities at Santa Monica, California. Mary McBay and Steve Nelsen made valuable contributions to the research for this book. Particular thanks are given to Kurt Forster,

Herbert Hymans, and their colleagues at the center; as well as to the University Research Library at the University of California, Los Angeles; and, above all, to Vicky Jo Varner, whose wizardry with the Apple Macintosh played so large a part in the production of the final manuscript.

Finally, we both wish to add a word of thanks to Jack Miles of the *Los Angeles Times*, formerly of the University of California Press, whose help and encouragement gave us special strength in planning this book at a critical stage in the project.

San Francisco, California   *A. R. Jonsen*
Evanston, Illinois   *S. E. Toulmin*

Prologue: The Problem

In the course of the 1984 American presidential campaign, Geraldine Ferraro, the first woman to be nominated vice-presidential candidate by a major political party, was challenged to state her position on abortion. She declined to endorse a simple, still less an extreme position on either side of the dispute about the morality of abortion. She repeatedly stated that she was personally opposed to abortion but believed that it should be a matter of choice and supported the rights of women to make their own decisions.[1]

This response stirred a debate that echoed from the American campaign trail to the halls of the Vatican. One Catholic bishop called Representative Ferraro's position "absurd, dangerous . . . not a rational position."[2] A leading American prelate, Archbishop O'Connor of New York, declared that a Catholic could not "in conscience" vote for a candidate who explicitly supported abortion, by refusing to work for the reversal of its present legal status.[3] In response, a group of Catholic theologians, priests and nuns sponsored a full-page advertisement in the *New York Times*[3] proclaiming that "a diversity of opinion regarding abortion exists among committed Catholics"; claiming by way of partial evidence that "a large number of Catholic theologians hold that even direct abortion, though tragic, can sometimes be a moral choice"; and resting their position on "adherence to the principles of moral theology such as probabilism, religious liberty and the centrality of informed conscience." Their proclamation elicited from the Vatican a swift and fiery thunderbolt. The Sacred Congregation for Religious and Secular Institutes immediately demanded retraction and threatened those who refused with dismissal from their religious congregations. In the view of the Vatican authorities, "the only legitimate Catholic position" was that expressed in the statements of popes and the hierarchy, to the effect that "direct termination of prenatal life is morally wrong in all instances."

To many Americans—Catholics as well as others—this dispute among a lay Catholic politician, the Vatican hierarchy, and the group of American nuns, priests, and theologians was essentially a political debate or, at best, one more reprise of a continuing conflict between dogmatic theologians and pragmatic politicians. Yet behind the contemporary debate, with all its topicality and newsworthiness, there lies a deeper intellectual conflict between two very different accounts of ethics and morality: one that seeks eternal, invariable principles, the practical implications of which can be free of exceptions or qualifications, and another, which pays closest attention to the specific details of particular moral cases and circumstances. Much of the current abortion debate has been carried on in terms that appeal to certain supposedly universal principles, from which the participants deduce practical imperatives that they regard as applying invariably and without exception. Yet even in the passages here quoted from the nuns' *New York Times* advertisement we can discern the influence of an older, long-respected method for the practical resolution of moral issues: namely, the method known traditionally as "casuistry." What this method was, how it came to reach its peak in the sixteenth and seventeenth centuries, and why it so largely fell into intellectual disrepute from the mid-seventeenth century on are the questions we shall be addressing in the central chapters of this book.

Clearly this debate among Geraldine Ferraro, the Vatican authorities, and the American nuns was not purely intellectual in content. There was also an institutional element to the dispute: a tussle between ecclesiastical authority and personal conscience. In this context the appeal of the nuns to "the centrality of informed conscience" may naturally be read as stating a very American bent to question authority and think independently: as such it forces to the

surface some difficult questions about the legitimate scope and reach
of individual opinion and spiritual discipline within an organized
religious denomination. Within such a community, what scope
properly belongs to ecclesiastical authority and personal conscience,
respectively? And over what aspects of the moral life are the individual members of such a Church entitled to insist on exercising
their own individual consciences?

These matters of internal discipline within the Catholic church are
not, of course, open to general public debate: There outsiders have
no standing to argue. They may privately regard the Vatican statement as having been precipitate and ill-considered, as it was apparently issued without prior consultation with the American Catholic
bishops, or even with the Papal Nuncio to the United States. They
may also regret the harshness of its language as dashing hope for a
more open ecumenical debate between Catholics and others and as
putting in doubt the sincerity of earlier Vatican promises to work
toward Christian unity. In the last resort, however, the authority
and power of the Vatican to forbid either Catholic laypeople (such as
Geraldine Ferraro) or members of the religious orders (such as the
nuns) from expressing opinions about contentious moral issues is an
internal affair for Catholics.

Still, outsiders are certainly free to comment about the intellectual
points at issue among Representative Ferraro, the nuns, and the hierarchy of the Church. The terms in which the public debate about
such ethical issues as the moral permissibility of abortion is carried
on concern all parties, Catholics and non-Catholics alike. And at this
point, the exchange between the Vatican authorities and the
American religious only added further complexity to an already confused discussion. For though we all understand more or less what is
meant by phrases such as "religious liberty," "informed conscience,"
and "morally wrong in all instances," technical terms such as *probabilism* (about which we will say more later) are quite unfamiliar to
most contemporary readers.

In one respect the current debate about the morality of abortion
bears on its face the hallmark of much present American thought,
not merely about ethics but also about law and public policy.
Activists on both sides of the abortion debate have looked for
universal laws and principles, which they could then nail to their
respective masts; and their insistence on framing those principles in
unqualified and universal terms, wherever this was possible, has

done much to make the whole debate irresoluble. In former times there were always those who could discuss the morality of abortion temperately and with discrimination: acknowledging that here, as in other agonizing human situations, conflicting considerations are involved and that a just, if sometimes painful, balance has to be struck between different rights and claims, interests, and responsibilities. That temperate approach underlay traditional common-law doctrines about abortion, long before the first statutory restrictions were enacted in Britain and America, in the years from 1803 on. It was also the approach adopted by the United States Supreme Court in the classic case, *Roe v. Wade*; and, most important, it is the approach taken by Thomas Aquinas, whose position is closer than is generally recognized to that of the common law and the Supreme Court. (Aquinas acknowledges that the balance of moral considerations necessarily tilts in different directions at different stages in a woman's pregnancy, with crucial changes beginning around the time of "quickening."[5])

Despite this temperate and discriminating tradition, the public rhetoric of the abortion controversy has increasingly come, in recent years, to turn on "matters of principle." The more this has happened, the less temperate, less discriminating, and above all less resoluble the debate has been. Too often the resulting argument has boiled down to pure head-butting: an embryo's unqualified and unconditional "right to life" being pitted against a woman's equally unqualified and unconditional "right to choose." Those who insist on arguing out the abortion issue on the level of high theory and general principle thus guarantee that on the practical level the only possible outcome is deadlock.

In the resulting confusion, people who support neither of the extreme positions can only wring their hands. The more principles become slogans and are nailed to the mast, the more the fanatics on both sides are driven to frustration or even to violence, and the harder it is to see how any effective resolution is possible. So in framing the questions for analysis in this book, we shall at the outset avoid taking sides over the substantive points at issue in the abortion debate. Instead, we shall begin by stepping back and asking, How can such contentious moral issues be resolved at all? What kinds of resolutions do they lend themselves to? Pitting contrary ethical principles against one another quickly becomes fruitless, so we must look elsewhere for arguments that show more promise of providing a way out. If we go beyond the bare assertion of general principles, what alternative possibilities are open to us?

We might, for instance, try approaching the issue from the direction of sociology. In a striking book Kristin Luker has illuminated the actual course of the abortion debate by relating the moral and intellectual positions adopted by activists on each side ("pro-life" and "pro-choice") to their respective life plans, personal commitments, and levels of education.[6] As her research demonstrates, female pro-choice activists turn out predominantly to belong to professional class families, to have a higher-than-average level of education, and to be themselves in paid employment: of the leading female pro-choice activists in California whom Luker interviewed, 94 percent were in the paid labor force. By contrast the corresponding female pro-life activists came in most cases from blue-collar working-class families, had stopped their education early, and were committed to being wives and mothers: fewer than 2 percent turned out to be in the paid labor force. Furthermore these deep differences between activists on the two sides reflect basic choices made quite early in life. Having opted in their teens on the one side for further education and independent professional lives and on the other for familial dependence and the satisfactions of maternity, the two groups can hardly be expected to be hospitable to each other's arguments. Given the deep differences between their respective "world-views" and "value systems," (Kristin Luker concludes) we cannot be surprised that they end up talking past each other.[7]

Luker's sociological insights are fascinating and helpful as far as they go, but they can hardly be the end of the matter. By deliberately concentrating on the attitudes of activists, she was confessedly paying attention to the zealots in this debate; and in any such divisive argument zealots are the people least open to reason. So if we are to understand in what kinds of terms such contentious moral issues can be discussed fruitfully and with some hope of resolution, we must set the zealots aside and look at the manner in which the people in the middle might argue the case.[8]

THE TYRANNY OF PRINCIPLES

Why is the zealot's concentration on universal and invariable principles so damaging? And how can we escape from the practical deadlock to which that emphasis condemns us?

These questions are particularly worth posing because of the underlying assumption that an ethical position always consists in a code of general rules and principles. That assumption is not confined to moral zealots. Much more widely, people at large tend to talk as though "ethical principles" or "moral rules" were *exhaustive* of ethics: that is, as though all that moral understanding requires is a commitment to some code of rules, which can be accepted as authoritative. On this view the practical problems of the moral life can be dealt with simply and finally by recognizing—or choosing—the particular code of rules that one will accept as having authority over one's thoughts and actions. Correspondingly, the central problem in philosophical ethics is simply to explain what makes certain kinds of rules count as "moral" rules as contrasted with, say, the rules that govern sports or games, the rules for prudent investing, or the rules of social etiquette.

As we shall see again and again in what follows, this approach to ethics drastically oversimplifies the discussion of moral issues, and that oversimplification does more than anything to generate the kind of standoff that is apparent in the abortion debate. On one side are those who see some one particular set (or "code") of rules and principles as correct, not just now and for them but *eternally and invariably.* Having made that commitment, they then regard anyone who does not share that code as "morally blind" and so undeserving of respect. (Such dogmatism leaves little room for honest, conscientiously based differences of moral opinion.) On the other side are those who reject as unwarranted all attempts to define so unique and eternal a body of ethical principles binding on peoples at all times and in all cultures. Yet as an alternative to that dogmatic position, people in this second group see no possibility except to allow every nation, culture, and period to decide on and live by its own code, worldview and "value system." As the example of Kristin Luker indicates, social scientists are particularly attracted to this position. So (it seems) once we accept rules and principles as the heart and soul of ethics, no middle way can be found between absolutism and relativism.

The damage to our ethical thinking which follows from this exclusive emphasis on universal invariable rules is not confined to the theoretical level. It causes difficulties in practice also by skewing our perception of the moral problems that arise in the actual circumstances of life. For if we fight off this bewitchment by the dream of an ethical algorithm—a universal and invariable code of procedures capable of providing unique and definitive answers to all our moral questions—it quickly becomes clear that even the best set of rules or principles cannot by itself satisfy our expectations. Taken by themselves, the *general* rules and maxims that play a part in people's ethical deliberations are only rarely matters of serious dispute. We scarcely need to be reminded about the viciousness of (for example) willful cruelty: in practice these things are typically "beyond question." If I go to the store to pick up a cauliflower for dinner, similarly, the fact that I am expected to offer money in exchange—that is, to buy the cauliflower rather than merely appropriating it—is a truism from both the legal and the moral point of view. This situation can hardly be said to give rise to a moral *issue*, still less a moral *problem:* the case is too clear and simple, too nearly paradigmatic to be in any way problematic or open to doubt.

On the contrary, it is just those situations that are *not* covered by appeal to any single simple rule that begin to be problematic; and in just those cases our concern to act rightly gives rise to genuinely moral "questions" and "issues."

> If I go next door and borrow a silver soup tureen, it goes without saying that I am expected to return it as soon as my immediate need for it is over: that is not an issue and gives rise to no problem.
>
> If, however, it is a pistol that I borrow and if, while it is in my possession, the owner becomes violently enraged and threatens to kill one of his other neighbors as soon as he gets back the pistol, I shall find myself in a genuinely problematic situation. I cannot escape from it by lamely invoking the general maxim that borrowed property ought to be returned promptly.

The latter case is problematic in a way in which the former is not because the obligation to return borrowed property here *conflicts with* the obligation to avoid being a party to violence or homicide.

Nor are the shortcomings of simple isolated rules apparent only in cases in which two different rules conflict and so point us in contrary directions. Even a simple rule may leave us in genuine doubt in situations to which it applies only *marginally or ambiguously.*

> If I go to the pet store and bring home a tortoiseshell tomcat or a collie puppy, it is taken for granted that I will ensure that it is fed and cared for rather than abandoned to fend for itself. Once again, this is both legally and morally "beyond question."

> But if a child goes out to the pond with a jam jar of water and comes back with frogs' eggs in the jam jar, it is not equally obvious that general maxims about the rights of innocent life and the need to avoid cruelty to animals have the same unambiguous force as before.

We understand general maxims—whether about lending and borrowing, cruelty to animals, avoiding violence, or the rights of innocent life—because, and to the extent that, we are familiar with the central unambiguous kinds of cases (the "paradigmatic" cases) that those maxims are commonly understood to cover. Hanging onto the silver soup tureen without saying a word, or simply not troubling to feed your new puppy, are things that plainly "put you in the wrong." Such actions are not necessarily inexcusable; yet at the very least they call for some explanation. By contrast, if I decide to hang onto the borrowed pistol until its owner has simmered down, or if the child fails to nurture the frogs' eggs it collected from the pond, those actions are not "in question" in quite the same way. The fact that every moral maxim, rule, or other generalization applies to certain actual situations centrally and unambiguously but to others only marginally or ambiguously, makes the latter situations just as problematic in their own way as the situations in which different rules or maxims come into conflict.

To put the central point in a nutshell, once we move far enough away from the simple paradigmatic cases to which the chosen generalizations were tailored, it becomes clear that no rule can be entirely self-interpreting. The considerations that weigh with us in resolving the ambiguities that arise in marginal cases, like those that weigh with us in balancing the claims of conflicting principles, are never *written into* the rules themselves. In dealing with real-life moral problems, which so often turn on conflicts and ambiguities of these two types, we are forced to go behind the simple rules and principles themselves and see what underlies them.

Another true story will underline the point. A well-known television news magazine program presented a tragic case:

> A handicapped young woman had difficulties with the local Social Security office. Her social security payments were insufficient to cover her rent and food, so she started a telephone answering service, which she operated through the telephone at her bedside. The income from this service was itself less than a living wage, but it made all the difference to her situation. When the local Social Security office heard about this source of additional income, however, it withdrew the cor-

responding part of her benefits. In addition, it ordered her to repay some of the money that she had been receiving in the meanwhile: the fact that she had not told them about the additional income led to her being classified as a case of "welfare fraud."

Initially the television team made its film segment about her case merely to show how inflexible the administration of social security could be. Unfortunately (the reporter then explained), between the making and the showing of the segment, the young woman had taken her own life in a fit of despair. By way of personal comment the reporter added, "There should be a *rule* to prevent this kind of thing from happening."

Notice that the reporter did not say, "The local Social Security office should be given more discretion to *waive*, or at least *bend*, the existing rules in hard cases." What he suggested was, "There should be an additional rule, so as to prevent such inequities happening again in the future." Justice, he apparently believed, is ensured only by establishing an adequate system of rules; and injustice in the administration of those rules can be prevented only by adding *more* rules. Yet what is called for in a case like this is not multiplication of further rules the inflexible application of which will only end by creating still more hard cases. Surely the issue is rather one for the exercise of wisdom, discretion, and discernment in enforcing the rules we already have. In morality, as in law and public administration, the assumption that all practical decisions need to rest on a sufficiently clear and general system of invariable rules or principles has, from a theoretical point of view, a certain attractiveness. But in the actual business of dealing with particular real-life cases and situations, such rules and principles can never take us more than part of the way. The real-life application of moral, legal, and administrative rules calls always for the exercise of human perceptiveness and discernment—what has traditionally been referred to as "equity"—and the more problematic the situations become, the greater is the need for such discernment.

Accordingly, several of the questions that will recur in the course of this book will have to do with "rules": in particular with their nature, functions, and limits. Those questions include, for instance, the following:

1.   What force and function do rules or principles truly have, either in the moral life or in the practice of the law?

2. What social and historical circumstances make it natural and
    appropriate to discuss moral and legal issues in the language of
    rules and principles?
3. Why do our contemporary discussions of ethics and law so of-
    ten become preoccupied with rules and principles?
4. May we not do better to look for the central issues about justice
    and morality in other directions?

Far from rules playing an exclusive or even an indispensable part in
law and ethics (we shall discover), they have a limited and condi-
tional role. The current vogue or habit of regarding "codes of rules"
as capturing the heart of the matter is the outcome of certain powerful but not uniquely important developments in the social and intellectual history of the last three hundred years. If looked at in a
longer historical perspective, rules of law and principles of ethics
turn out in practice always to have been balanced against counter-
weights. The pursuit of Justice has always demanded both law and
equity; respect for Morality has always demanded both fairness and
discernment. If we ignore this continuing duality and confine our
discussion of fundamental moral and legal issues to the level of
unchallengeable principles, that insistence all too easily generates—or becomes the instrument of—its own subtle kind of tyranny.

But is there a real alternative? Our answer in this book will be
yes. Human experience long ago developed a reasonable and effective set of practical procedures for resolving the moral problems that
arise in particular real-life situations. These procedures came to be
known as "casuistry" and those who employed these procedures
professionally were "casuists.") In its own quiet way this traditional
method of discussion still contributes to our ways of thinking about
moral issues through the practical advice of priests and ministers,
psychologists and agony columnists. (At their best such agony
columnists as Ann Landers are capable casuists.)

Yet however indispensable it is in practice, the whole enterprise of
casuistry lost its theoretical respectability and its good name some
three hundred years ago. Since that time the nature and claims of
the casuists' method have been widely and deeply misunderstood;
as a result most modern readers assume that casuistry is as dead or
disreputable as astrology. So before we can even begin to show how
a reapplication of older casuistical procedures still serves us well in
dealing with our own vexed ethical issues, we must first do some-

thing to clear those misunderstandings out of the way. We shall therefore have to start by explaining the historical origins and exemplifying the practical merits of the classical enterprise of casuistry, especially as it was practiced during its peak century between A.D. 1550 and 1650.

THE DISREPUTE OF CASUISTRY

Few intellectual activities have been more reviled than casuistry; yet few practical activities are (we shall argue) more indispensable. Ever since the French mathematician and philosopher Blaise Pascal attacked the Jesuit confessors of Paris in his *Provincial Letters*, in the mid-seventeenth century, attempts to base a general account of ethics on the analysis and classification of "cases" and "circumstances" have been objects of disrepute, both among educated laypeople and among scholars, especially academic philosophers. In their eyes moral judgments can be securely grounded only by relating them back to universal principles; and any morality of circumstances and cases seems doomed (as Pascal declared) to serve as an invitation to excuse the inexcusable.

Many factors have combined to keep this disrepute alive. These days we rarely even hear the word "casuistry" uttered; and when we do, its use tends to be disparaging. The *Oxford English Dictionary* defines casuistry quite accurately as

> that part of ethics which resolves cases of conscience, applying the general rules of religion and morality to particular instances in which circumstances alter cases or in which there appears to be a conflict of duties.

But the *OED* goes on to comment that the word's use was "apparently at first contemptuous"; and the accompanying entry for the word "casuist" adds the remark, "often with sinister application." The very form of the word *casuistry* in fact embodies a slur: the telltale ending –*ry* marks it as belonging to a well-known family of dyslogistic terms that refer to the disreputable use of different arts, and includes also "Popery" and "wizardry," "sophistry" and "harlotry." (The German language contains a similar family of -*rei* words, e.g. *Schweinerei*.) It finally becomes clear that the original sense of the word *casuistry* was intended critically when we note that the *OED*'s first relevant citation—"cages for gnats . . . tomes of casuistry"—comes from Pope's *Rape of the Lock,* published in 1725 (i.e., more than fifty years *after* Pascal's polemic).[9]

Another *OED* citation reads,

> Casuistry destroys by distinctions and exceptions all morality, and effaces the essential difference between right and wrong.

A third quotes the definition of casuistry offered by the *Penny Cyclopedia* (1836): "the art of quibbling with God." The word *casuistry* thus refers primarily to the *ignoble* use of the casuists' art, just as "sophistry," "wizardry," and the like refer to the ignoble use of those other arts. Current embarrassment might be eased if we set aside the intentionally scornful word "casuistry," and put some alternative term in its place; "case ethics" (say), or "casuistics," on the model of the French *casuistique* and the German *Kasuistik.* Using such an alternative form would not defuse Pascal's attack entirely, but it might help to avoid begging the crucial question: whether *all*—or only *some*—uses of case reasoning in ethics are ignoble, evasive, and disgraceful. Faced with an unthinking abuse of casuistry, indeed, the wisest course may be to react as the Society of Friends did, when onlookers mockingly called them *Quakers:* by ignoring the implicit reproach and treating the prejudicial word "casuistry" as a neutral term of art, like "dentistry" and "chemistry."

Among academic philosophers, the last century has seen the disrepute of case morality only deepen. Henry Sidgwick's book, *The Methods of Ethics* (1874), launched moral philosophers in a new direction, shifting their focus from the particular concrete issues of practical life toward the more abstract general issues of ethical and "meta-ethical" theory. So by the mid-twentieth century, Ethics (regarded as a part of academic philosophy) scarcely addressed the practical issues and specific circumstances that confront human agents in their actual moral lives, and preferred to concern itself with formal analyses, definitions, and other generalities, all of them being issues that presumably apply across the whole of ethics and are neutral as between moral judgments of particular kinds.

Given this background of scorn and abuse, it is no surprise to find a late-nineteenth-century critic writing,

> Without doubt, few words in history are as infamous as *casuistry:* it is certainly a peculiar task to attempt its rehabilitation.[10]

That peculiar task is precisely the goal of this book. Of course, our wish is to rehabilitate not the *word* "casuistry" but rather the *art* to which it disparagingly refers: the practical resolution of particular moral perplexities, or "cases of conscience." That art has had a long and honorable history in the ethics of the Western cultural tradition; and it would barely need rehabilitation but for two historical episodes: (1) Pascal's savage and brilliant attack on the Jesuits, about whom he said (echoing Tertullian), "one knows not whether to laugh or weep at them,"[11] and (2) the rejection of an ethics of cases and circumstances by more recent writers on moral philosophy.

Our book thus has a double aim. On the positive side, we shall show that the casuists' art has a legitimate and central part to play in practical ethics, of a kind that makes it relevant to ethical theory also. On the negative side, we shall consider how casuistry fell into its current disrepute: what defects in its practice prompted Pascal's original attack, and what subsequent misconceptions have led philosophers to deny "case ethics" any respectable intellectual pedigree.

This enterprise is not an antiquarian one. When properly conceived (we claim), casuistry redresses the excessive emphasis placed on universal rules and invariant principles by moral philosophers and political preachers alike. Instead we shall take seriously certain features of moral discourse that recent moral philosophers have too little appreciated: the concrete circumstances of actual cases, and the specific maxims that people invoke in facing actual moral dilemmas. If we start by considering similarities and differences between particular *types* of cases on a practical level, we open up an alternative approach to ethical theory that is wholly consistent with our moral practice.

In the last few years, discussions of specific circumstances and cases have at last returned to favor. This has happened almost inadvertently as a by-product of the current preoccupation with professional ethics, notably medical ethics. Writing about the current revival of interest in "moral dilemmas," as "cases of conscience" are nowadays called, one reviewer of Sissela Bok's book *Lying* said,

> Her book is an example of what might be termed the "new casuistry," in which moral philosophers examine specific cases . . . against the claims of a set of moral arguments.[12]

The reviewer compared it with another "distinguished example of the new casuistry, Michael Walzer's *Just and Unjust Wars*." (We note,

with some irony, that few professional moral philosophers today
recognize either Sissela Bok or Michael Walzer as members of their
guild.) The reviewer commended both books for their "ability to
convey the high moral stakes involved in their respective struggles"—struggles that emerge not only in the life of the professions
but also from the policies and choices of government and business.
We can follow these in the daily papers: "Is first use of nuclear
weapons ever morally permissible?" "Should the foreign policy of
the United States pursue the defense of human rights with vigor, or
should it rather negotiate quietly?" "Ought our college to invest in
companies doing business in South Africa, or should it divest itself
of such stocks and shares?" The arguments surrounding such questions as these are the matter of the new casuistry; but the philosophical disrepute into which "case ethics" has fallen means that the
forms and methods proper to such arguments are not widely discussed or understood. That is our concern here.

Meanwhile in the practical quandaries of everyday life, the use of
case analysis continues uninterrupted. Friends and colleagues, psy-
chotherapists and agony columnists, parents and children, priests
and ministers: anyone who has occasion to consider moral issues in
actual detail knows that morally significant *differences* between cases
can be as vital as their *likenesses*. We need to respect not only the
general principles that require us to treat similar cases alike but also
those crucial distinctions that justify treating dissimilar cases differently. One indispensable instrument for helping to resolve moral
problems in practice, therefore, is a detailed and methodical map of
morally significant likenesses and differences: what may be called a
moral taxonomy.

In one respect, of course, such practical considerations mean more
to moral theologians than to moral philosophers. By vocation theologians have to keep in touch with concrete pastoral concerns as
much as with abstract intellectual issues, and they are less ready to
scorn the discussion of specific cases and particular circumstances.
After Pascal, as much as before, Catholic pastoral practice has kept
alive the analysis of morality in terms of similarities and differences.
A small stream of casuistry also survived in the Protestant and
Anglican traditions. In Judaism the analyses of contemporary moral
issues to be found in a periodical such as *Tradition* build upon a discipline that goes back continuously to antiquity. About casuistical

discussion in practical contexts we may therefore say: "Everybody depends upon it, even though few people say so explicitly."

Of course, like all other practical arts, the art of analyzing moral issues in terms of cases and circumstances is capable of being either put to good use or misused; and in the latter event one can fairly do as Pascal did in drawing attention to abuses of the art and condemning them. With this point in mind we can restate the central puzzle that Pascal's argument raises for us: that of identifying the central thrust of his attack as he actually presented it. His position can be read in either of two ways. On the one hand, if it were true that seventeenth-century French Jesuits were unduly tender toward those of their penitents who were wealthy or highborn, then Pascal was right to criticize them for their *partiality*. But if that were the only issue raised by his polemic, his criticisms would have applied only to *mis*uses of the case method in ethics and would have had no general relevance to casuistry or case ethics as a whole. On the other hand, the educated public of Pascal's own time read *The Provincial Letters* as discrediting not just *bad* casuistry but *all* casuistry: as they saw matters, the distinction between "good" casuistry and "bad" was a distinction without a difference.

Historically speaking, it is not fully clear even now which is the correct reading of Pascal's intentions. Sometimes he seems to be writing from within the casuistical tradition, as a "rigorist" objecting to the "laxism" of his contemporaries. At other times the sweep of his argument carries him right outside the whole tradition and implies that all casuistical reasoning alike is deceptive or compromising. Blaise Pascal himself died young and in much distress of mind, so it is possible that he never finally chose between these two views. In any case the ambiguity had a powerful use as rhetoric. First, Pascal painted a horrendous picture of the ways in which sloppy and dishonest use of the case method had corrupted the casuists of his time. That done, he was in a position to suggest, without proving it, that this corruption was an inescapable feature of the casuistical method itself.

For the purposes of our argument, we cannot afford to leave that ambiguity unresolved. To make our project wholly clear, our *sole* aim is to argue a case for the former, more discriminating position. The practical choice (we shall argue) is not between a high-minded ethics of pure principle and an inevitably debased morality of cases and circumstances: it is between *good* casuistry, which applies general rules to particular cases with discernment, and *bad* casuistry, which does the same thing sloppily. Certainly, as anyone must concede, case reasoning in ethics can be misused; but when well directed, the art of casuistry remains the single most powerful tool of practical analysis in ethics. As a result the crucial question about casuistry is *not* the question whether we are to use it at all; rather, it is how to tell its acceptable uses from its genuinely disreputable *misuse, or abuse*.

The rhetorical insults traditionally heaped on case ethics by its critics are therefore justified only when the method is misused. For this reason the title we have chosen for our book is drawn from the writings of the distinguished Anglican casuist, Kenneth Kirk; it embodies a deliberate play on words:

> The *abuse* of casuistry is properly directed, not against all casuistry, but only against its *abuse*.[13]

THE LOCUS OF MORAL CERTITUDE

A final autobiographical remark will explain how the present authors came to collaborate on this "peculiar task" of rehabilitating casuistry. The decision was one result of a shared experience, which gave us both a striking first-hand experience of what "the new casuistry" holds in store for moral reflection and discussion, and compelled us to think about its methods. In 1974 the United States Congress passed legislation to set up the National Commission for the Protection of Human Subjects of Biomedical and Behavioral Research; and between early 1975 and mid-1978 this commission conducted hearings and deliberations and published a series of reports and recommendations. One of the present writers was a member of the National Commission, the other worked with it as a staff member and consultant.

The commission was established in the aftermath of the Supreme Court's controversial abortion ruling in *Roe v. Wade*, in response to press reports about certain dubious experiments on human fetuses performed in Scandinavia and about scandalous experiments conducted on rural black men in Tuskegee, Alabama. Its primary charge was to review the federal regulations about research with an eye to the protection of the "rights and welfare" of those persons who were involved as research subjects in either biomedical or behavioral investigations, but its mandate went far beyond the remedy of particular abuses. The commission was also required to study the ethical issues arising in scientific research using vulnerable research subjects of different sorts—prisoners, children, and the mentally disabled, in addition to human fetuses—and to develop general statements of ethical principle to serve as a guide in the future development of biomedical and behavioral research.

In pursuing this work the commissioners soon found it necessary to develop their own detailed "moral taxonomies" for classifying the morally significant similarities and differences between the various kinds of research. The research ethics for different groups of vulnerable subjects, on which their subsequent recommendations were based, thus evolved in a case-by-case manner. Less by deliberate historically informed choice than under the urgent press of practical concerns the commissioners adopted a *casuistical* mode of thinking. Why did the case method carry conviction and so often allow them to reach agreed recommendations, despite all their other differences? In answering that question we shall get our first hint about how to overcome the objections to "casuistry" raised by moral philosophers and others.

Again and again the commission's deliberations displayed the same unforeseen feature. The eleven commissioners had varied backgrounds and interests. They included men and women; blacks and whites; Catholics, Protestants, Jews, and atheists; medical scientists and behaviorist psychologists; philosophers; lawyers; theologians; and public interest representatives. In all, five commissioners had scientific interests and six did not; and before they started work, few onlookers expected them to have much basis for agreement, either about general moral principles or about the application of these principles to particular problems. On hearing the composition of the commission one respected commentator reportedly said, "Now we shall presumably see matters of eternal principle decided by a six-to-five vote!" All the same, things never worked out that way in practice. At no time in its activities did the commission's opinion divide cleanly along a line between scientists and laypeople; nor did the other differences of background have anything resembling their expected effect on the practical discussions. Quite the contrary: so long as the commissioners stayed on the taxonomic or casuistical level, they usually agreed in their practical conclusions.

Even when the commissioners disagreed, furthermore, the nature and extent of their disagreement were always quite clear. Faced, for example, with marginal or difficult issues, some members were inclined to take a somewhat more conservative view, whereas others were more liberal. ("What are we to say about research involving six-year-old children? Ought they to have all the same protections as infants? Or do they already have some capacity to understand and give assent to research procedures involving no more than minimal risk?") Serious differences of opinion began to appear only when individual commissioners went beyond the stage of formulating practical proposals and explained their individual *reasons* for participating in the collective recommendations. At this point, at last, differences of background that lay dormant during the case-by-case discussions sprang back to life. The Catholic members of the commission gave different reasons for agreeing from the Protestants, the Jewish members from the atheists, and so on. Even when, as a *collective*, the commission agreed about particular practical judgments, the *individual* commissioners justified their readiness to join in that consensus by appealing to different "general principles."

At the time this outcome appeared philosophically paradoxical. Members of the commission were largely in agreement about their specific practical recommendations; they agreed what it was they agreed about; but the one thing they could not agree on was *why* they agreed about it. So long as the debate stayed on the level of particular judgments, the eleven commissioners saw things in much the same way. The moment it soared to the level of "principles," they went their separate ways. Instead of securely established universal principles, in which they had unqualified confidence, giving them intellectual grounding for particular judgments about specific kinds of cases, it was the other way around.

The *locus of certitude* in the commissioners' discussions did not lie in an agreed set of intrinsically convincing *general* rules or principles, as they shared no commitment to any such body of agreed principles. Rather, it lay in a shared perception of what was *specifically* at stake in particular kinds of human situations. Their practical certitude about specific types of cases lent to the commission's collective recommendations a kind of conviction that could never have been derived from the supposed theoretical certainty of the principles to which individual commissioners appealed in their personal accounts. In theory their particular concrete moral judgments should have been strengthened by being "validly deduced" from universal abstract ethical principles. In practice the general truth and relevance of those universal principles turned out to be *less* certain than the soundness of the particular judgments for which they supposedly provided a "deductive foundation."[14]

Yet need this outcome really have seemed paradoxical? How one answers that question will depend on how one answers a more fundamental question: "What *kind* of understanding of human conduct does Ethics provide?" On the one hand, for some 2,500 years there have always been those who regarded ethics as a topic for *theoretical* discussion: a kind of "moral geometry" that makes particular ethical perceptions more intelligible by showing how they exemplify rules or laws that are both *more general* and also capable of being known with *greater certainty.* This first view treats ethics as a science, which gives a coherent and systematic account of human conduct of a kind that our unsystematized moral perceptions can only hint at.

On the other hand, from the very beginning there have been other thinkers who challenged the adequacy of this first approach. Aristotle, for instance, questioned whether moral understanding lends itself to scientific systematization at all, and his arguments show that he was already aware of those features of moral judgment and conduct that were so puzzlingly evident in the course of the National Commission's work. Far from being based on general abstract principles that can at one and the same time be universal, invariable, and known with certainty (he argued), ethics deals with a multitude of particular concrete situations, which are themselves so variable that they resist all attempts to generalize about them in universal terms. In short, Aristotle declared, ethics is not and cannot be a science. Instead, it is a field of experience that calls for a recognition of significant particulars and for informed prudence: for what he called *phronesis,* or "practical wisdom."

For their practical purposes, then, the members of the National Commission trusted their collective perceptions about what was at stake in particular types of "biomedical and behavioral research" more than they trusted the universal principles of any particular ethical theory. So long as they did so, nothing in their procedures was intrinsically paradoxical. It showed only that they understood the differences between "theory" and "practice"—that is, between the demands of scientific understanding and those of practical good sense; and in this they displayed a capacity for "practical wisdom" that Aristotle would have applauded.

In the chapters that follow we shall begin by exploring more deeply the implications of this distinction between science and prudence, intellectual theory and practical understanding. Taking this as our point of departure, we may then venture out to meet the attacks on casuistry and case ethics with greater confidence; and we can even go over to the counterattack. For (it turns out) the arguments by which Blaise Pascal and his successors have brought the enterprise of casuistry into disrepute contain, in turn, their own fundamental flaw, one that Aristotle would have recognized, only to deplore. Even now, we shall argue, the rejection of case ethics is a lingering expression of the intellectual dream that, after all, ethics may yet be transformed into a universal theoretical science. And that (we shall see) is precisely what, from the outset, Aristotle's distinction between *episteme* and *phronesis*, or between scientific understanding and practical wisdom, was designed to undercut.

PART I

Background

1

Theory and Practice

In the public debate about moral issues such as racial equality and abortion, deeply felt convictions struggle against an ambiguity the locus of which is not hard to identify. We inherit two distinct ways of discussing ethical issues. One of these frames these issues in terms of principles, rules, and other general ideas; the other focuses on the specific features of particular kinds of moral cases. In the first way general ethical rules relate to specific moral cases in a *theoretical* manner, with universal rules serving as "axioms" from which particular moral judgments are deduced as theorems. In the second, this relation is frankly *practical*, with general moral rules serving as "maxims," which can be fully understood only in terms of the paradigmatic cases that define their meaning and force.

The modes of argument associated with each approach are familiar provided that we consider them one at a time. When we discuss specific cases of conscience in concrete detail and practical terms, aside from the abstract theoretical arguments of moral theology and philosophical ethics, we understand either mode of reasoning well enough. But if we ask how these two kinds of arguments relate together, we find ourselves at a loss.

How far and in what respects do general ethical doctrines carry weight when we deal with specific moral problems in complex practical situations?

Conversely, how far and in what respects can one rely on particular perceptions about specific situations when criticizing general doctrines in ethical theory?

Nowadays the received view is that particular moral decisions simply apply universal ethical rules to particular cases; while moral decisions are sound to the extent that they are validly deduced from such rules:

In this situation, such an action would be murder;
Murder is invariably and universally wrong;
So, acting in that way would be inescapably wrong.

The least we can do to reply to this view is to argue, first, that it oversimplifies a far more complex practical relationship and, second, that the "applying" and "deducing" which moral reasoning is said to involve are quite mysterious, unless we show in detail *just how* appeals to "universal principles"—whether framed in religious, philosophical, or everyday terms—help to resolve moral quandaries in practice. Certainly the experience of the National Commission casts some doubt on this view. So long as the commissioners discussed specific cases, their consensus showed how far they shared moral perceptions in practice: the moment they turned to consider the theoretical principles that underlay those particular perceptions, they lacked a similar consensus. How, then, can it be said that the particular judgments about which they evidently *agreed* were, all alike, "deduced from" universal principles about which they openly and plainly *disagreed*?

THE CLASSICAL ACCOUNT

The relevance of general matters of abstract theory to the specific problems of concrete practice may be obscure in ethics; but it has never been obscure *only* in ethics. So let us start by asking how this general relationship was originally analyzed in antiquity, and then see what light this classical account still throws on current issues.

The first explicit account was developed by the philosophers of classical Athens. Their prototype of "theoretical" reasoning was *geometry*. There the starting point was a few general statements the meaning of which was clear and the truth of which was beyond question: from these were derived, by formal deduction, conclusions that were neither obvious nor self-explanatory. Starting from elementary definitions and statements about lines and angles, surfaces and solids, for instance, one might prove the famous theorem of Pythagoras, that

> the area of a square constructed on the longest side of a right-angled triangle is equal to the sum of the areas of squares constructed on the two shorter sides;

or the far more surprising result attributed to Plato's student, Theaetetus, (who died tragically early) that

> only five ways exist of fitting together equilateral plane figures, e.g., triangles, squares or pentagons, so as to form regular convex solids.[1]

The rigor of geometry was so appealing, indeed, that for many Greek philosophers formal deduction became the ideal of *all* rational argument. On this view an opinion can be accepted as "knowledge," or an argument as truly solid, only if it is related deductively ("necessarily") to clear and obvious initial principles. So, it seemed, the whole of geometry might follow necessarily from an unquestioned set of definitions and general statements; and these were subsequently organized into canonical form, as the "axioms" of Euclidean geometry. In due course, too (the hope was), other sciences would find their own unquestioned general principles to serve as their starting points, in explaining, for example, the natures of animals, plants, and the other permanent features of the world.[2]

If this were only done, all true sciences would be able to argue with the same necessity as geometry. When the scientist (geometer, zoologist, or whatever) works with clear and self-evident theoretical principles, his certainty of their truth will outweigh all his opinions about the particular facts he uses to explain them. He will grasp the definitions of "equilateral plane figure" and "regular convex solid" with more certainty than he can ever have about Theaetetus' theory of the five regular convex solids. Indeed, all sciences with well-formulated principles share this feature: their general principles are better understood, and known with greater certainty, than any of the specific conclusions they are used to explain.

How far, on this classical account, does the scope of "theory" reach? Not all of our knowledge, Aristotle argued, is of this sort; nor do we have this theoretical kind of certainty in every field.[3] In *practical* fields we grasp particular facts of experience more clearly, and have more certainty of their truth, than we ever do about the general principles that we may use to account for them. As an illustration, he cites the everyday belief that chicken is good to eat (i.e., nourishing).[4] Knowing *that* chicken is good to eat, he argues, is one thing, but knowing *what makes it* good to eat is quite another. Practical experience assures us of the initial fact quite apart from any subsequent nutritional explanation. What makes chicken good to eat is perhaps the fact that it is a light meat: that being so, a scientific explanation will read,

> Chicken is a light meat; light meats are easy to digest; so chicken is easy to digest. That is why it is good to eat.

But the true explanation may be quite other, or even unknown. Still, however uncertain the explanation remains in theory, the gastronomic fact that chicken is good to eat is not, in practice, seriously in doubt. Direct human experience testifies to it in advance of any explanation.

How is it that in such cases we are surer of the facts to which experience testifies directly than we are of the general principles that explain them? Why is the relationship between principles and instances here apparently reversed? The reason (Aristotle adds) is that we have left the realm of Theory for that of Practice.[5] In the realm of Practice, certitude no longer requires a prior grasp of definitions, general principles, and axioms, as in the realm of Theory. Rather, it depends on accumulated experience of particular situations; and this practical experience gives one a kind of wisdom—*phronesis*—different from the abstract grasp of any theoretical science—*episteme*. On Aristotle's account this reversed relationship between principles and cases is typical of those fields of knowledge that are by nature "practical" rather than "theoretical."[6]

The realm of the practical included, for Aristotle, the entire realm of *ethics*: in his eyes the subject matter of moral reflection lay within the sphere of practical wisdom rather than theoretical comprehension. We return to this point in the next chapter, where we shall look at the *Nicomachean Ethics* in more detail. For the moment (one may remark), if Aristotle was right about this, the reversed locus of certitude in the deliberations of the National Commission should have been expected![7]

The classical account of Theory and Practice involved three further distinctions. In theoretical fields such as geometry, statements or arguments were *idealized*, *atemporal*, and *necessary*:

1. They were "idealized" in the following sense. Concrete physical objects, cut out of metal in the shapes of triangles or circles, can never be made with perfect precision, nor can the metal sheets from which they are cut stay perfectly flat, so that they exemplify the truths of geometry only approximately. The idealized "straight lines" and "circles" of geometry, by contrast, exemplify such truths with perfect exactness.
2. They were "atemporal" in the following sense. Any geometrical theorem that is true at one time or on one occasion will be true at any time and on any occasion. Pythagoras did not "prove" some temporal concrete fact that just happened to be true in his particular time but a permanent relationship that held good "universally." So there was no question of his theorem *ceasing* to be true at some later time.
3. Finally, theoretical arguments were "necessary" in a twofold sense. The arguments of Euclidean geometry depended for their validity both on the correctness of the initial axioms and definitions and on the inner consistency of the subsequent deductions. Granted Euclid's axioms, all of his later theorems were "necessary consequences" of those initial truths. If any of the theorems were questioned, conversely, this implied either that their starting point was incorrect or else that the steps taken in passing to the theorems were formally fallacious.

In all three respects, practical statements and arguments differed from theoretical ones by being *concrete, temporal,* and *presumptive.*

1. They were "concrete" in the following sense. Chickens are never idealized entities, and the things we say about cooking make no pretense to geometrical perfection. A particular chicken may be "exceptionally delicate," but it is never "only approximately [still less, ±0.05%] a chicken." Thus the truth of practical statements rests on direct experience: abstraction or idealization do not protect them from experiential challenges.
2. They were "temporal" in this sense. The same experience that teaches what is normally the case *at any time* also teaches what is the case *only sometimes.* (Chicken is edible all year round, but game birds are stringy if taken out of season.) Truths of practical experience thus do not hold good "universally" or "at *any* time": rather, they hold "on occasion" or "at *this or that* moment"—that is, usually, often, at most always.
3. Finally, practical arguments were "presumptive" in this sense. Chicken is normally good to eat, so a particular chicken just brought from the store is "presumably" good to eat. In unusual cases that conclusion may be open to rebuttal: the chicken in question may have been left too long in summer heat and gone

bad. The presumptive conclusion is, however, open to doubt "in point of fact": no one is denying the initial generalization, or questioning the formal validity of the presumptive inference. Still, if we depart far enough from the "normal" or "typical" cases, reasonable conclusions based on the soundest presumptive arguments may, in practice, be upset.

All three crucial features of the classical account were connected. Statements in geometry were atemporal, and its arguments necessary, just because they did not refer to familiar objects such as metal plates and chickens but to idealized entities such as *the circle* and *the triangle*. By contrast, practical statements were temporal and the corresponding arguments presumptive simply because they referred to actual events, agents, and objects, particular circumstances, and specific places and times. When telescoped together, these distinctions had another, unhelpful effect. They turned the original contrast of Theory with Practice into an outright divorce. So the "atemporal" world of intellectual reflection and certain knowledge was set apart from the "temporal" world of practical actions and corrigible opinions; and the timeless insights of intellectual theorists were esteemed above the workaday experience of the practical craftsman. Eventually the "atemporality" of Theory was even interpreted as implying that its subject matter was Immutable and its truths Eternal, and it became associated with the unchanging *celestial* world. Meanwhile the temporality of Practice was equated with Transitoriness and linked to the changeableness of *terrestrial* things. With this divorce the "immortal" world of universal theoretical principles was separated from the "mortal" world of particular practical skills and cases.[8] The ripples caused by this equation have been influencing Western thinking ever since.

THE CLASSICAL ACCOUNT AND ITS
MODERN RELEVANCE

How far is this account of Theory and Practice still relevant today? Certainly skeptics can find reason to ignore it. Nobody today credits Euclidean geometry with the universal absolute truth it promised 2,500 years ago: the mathematical creation of non-Euclidean geometries brought to light an unlimited range of axiom systems, each of which generates a consistent sequence of theorems. Nor does anyone today suppose that the theories of natural science share the formal certainty of geometrical theorems, whether Euclidean or non-Euclidean; still less that they are as abstract as Greek geometry. Over the last two hundred years, in fact, scientists have given up trying to "prove" their theoretical principles self-evidently true; rather, they now take pride in being "empirical" philosophers. So at a time when science and technology are interacting so closely, we can no longer suppose that an unbridgeable intellectual gulf divides the theoretical insights of science from the practical procedures of the arts, crafts, or industry.

The divorce of Theory from Practice is thus a thing of the past, and no purpose is served by reviving it. As an analytic contrast, however, we cannot ignore the *distinction* between them, for two distinct reasons. First, the problem of matching principles (e.g., ethical principles) to cases (e.g., moral cases) affects all fields of human experience in which general rules are invoked to support practical decisions that require specific actions affecting the personal circumstances of individual human beings. In clinical medicine and civil engineering, economics and politics, quite as much as in ethics, the universality of general principles must still be squared with the particularity of specific decisions.

Issues of public administration, law, and medicine (as of ethics) thus become truly problematic just at the point at which rules, laws, and other theoretical generalizations apply ambiguously or marginally, or at which alternative rules or principles point in contrary directions and have to be arbitrated between. Three sample scenarios will illustrate the point:

> An elderly widow comes to the Social Security office, claiming that she has been wrongly deprived of her old-age pension payments. On investigation it turns out that the contributions her immigrant husband paid before his death were barely sufficient to qualify her for a pension at all.

> A patient comes to a physician's office with an unusual combination of fever and pallor, earache and bronchial congestion. The doctor is in doubt whether this is an unusually severe case of the current influenza or whether it indicates, rather, the far more dangerous onset of a more serious disease—for example, meningitis.

> A plaintiff testifies in civil court that she injured herself on a defective stairway, which her landlord negligently left unrepaired. Another tenant testifies, to the contrary, that the staircase was not badly maintained and alleges that the plaintiff was drunk at the time of the fall.

What is involved in dealing with such problems? All three issues involve matters of judgment, which arise out of initially ambiguous or marginal situations where no "universal principle" can settle the matter once and for all. In real life practical issues of these kinds are resolved by looking at the concrete details of particular cases. Are there, after all, weighty reasons of equity to allow the widow's claim to a pension, treat the sick patient on the basis of the less probable but more threatening diagnosis, or award the injured tenant damages in spite of her possible contributory drunkenness? At the end of the day we simply have to decide in which direction the strongest demands of administrative equity, the most pressing medical indications, or the testimony of the most credible witnesses finally point *in this case*.

Once this practical judgment is exercised, the resulting decisions will (no doubt) be "formally entailed by" the relevant generalizations, but that connection throws no light on the grounds by which the decisions are arrived at, or on the considerations that tilt the scale toward one general course of action rather than the other. What such decisions involve can be explained only in *substantive* and *circumstantial* terms. The demands of administrative equity, the significance of alternative diagnoses and therapeutic indications, or the probative weight of contrary witnesses: all of these raise questions of rational substance, not logical form, and particular decisions (say, to prescribe a treatment designed to deal with the likely influenza while guarding against a possible meningitis) call for substantive balancing of the foreseeable risks and prospective benefits of alternative actions, with an eye to the detailed circumstances of the actual situation.

The analytic contrast between Theory and Practice is important for a second reason: the classical account implied both that theoretical statements can make universal claims which hold good at any place or time *only* if they are as idealized as the axioms or theorems of Greek geometry, and that theoretical arguments lead to necessary conclusions *only* if they are cut off from concrete objects and practical experience. By our standards both implications are exaggerated; but each of the classical contrasts in itself can still throw light on the current practice of the sciences: notably, on the contrasted ways in which intellectual problems arise *within* theories (when general ideas are dealt with in their own terms) and *outside* them (when those general ideas are applied to specific cases, or in particular circumstances).

In scientific theory today general ideas are no longer divorced from actual objects, yet they are still "idealized" in a weaker sense: they refer directly only to preselected objects, which exemplify them precisely enough to be relevant to the theory. In practical professions such as medicine, by contrast, the procedures are "concrete" in a similarly weakened sense: they apply equally to every case that presents itself, and every instance is equally relevant for practical purposes. To physicists engaged in refining gravitation theory, the motions of planets and earth satellites are of direct interest, whereas the fluttering of a falling sheet of paper is not. Astronomical movements and falling papers both exemplify gravitation, but planets and satellites provide straightforward and unadulterated cases of gravitation in action, in a way that fluttering papers do not. Even if we recorded a sheet of paper's falling precisely, using a high-speed cinema camera, the gravitational aspects of that event cannot in practice be separated from the effects of air currents and other outside influences. Being directly interested in exact theoretical issues and general ideas, physical scientists thus learn from planetary movements in a way they cannot learn from falling sheets of paper: in a physicist's eyes (so to say) the fluttering papers "do not count." So the standing of the physical sciences as exact, idealized, and theoretical disciplines is purchased only at a price. They are "exact and idealized" because they are highly *selective*: they pay direct attention only to circumstances and cases that are "abstracted" (i.e., selected out) as being relevant to their central theoretical goals.

In the same weaker sense, practical fields such as law, medicine, and public administration deal with concrete actual cases, not with abstract idealized situations. They are directly concerned with immediate facts about specific situations and individuals: general ideas concern them only indirectly, as they bear on the problems of those particular individuals. Unlike natural scientists, who are free to decide in advance which types of situations, cases, or individuals they may (or need not) pay attention to, physicians, lawyers, and social service workers face myriad professional problems the moment any client walks through the door. They may end up by referring some of those clients to other, more appropriate professionals, but they cannot choose to ignore them or their problems. Where scientists study specific cases for any light they can throw on general theoretical ideas, members of the service professions, conversely, study general ideas for any help they can give in dealing with specific practical cases.

The intellectual claims of scientific theory today may no longer refer beyond the familiar changing world of temporal experience, but in their own way scientific principles are still "atemporal": covering *all* relevant cases, *anywhere*, at *any* time. Conversely, the practical goals of the service professions are still, in the corresponding sense, "temporal": focusing on *specific* cases and *particular* occasions. A physicist lecturing about high-energy particle theory may refer both to observations made last week at the Stanford Linear Accelerator Center and to events that supposedly took place long ago, soon after the cosmological Big Bang. Because his concerns are not specifically tied to particular times or places, there is nothing incongruous in his discussing both in the same terms. The fundamental question for him is, "What phenomena are shared at all times, in all contexts?" and the *universality* of theory makes all times and places equivalent. Conversely, what matters most to the practicing lawyer or physician is the *particularity* of the problems facing this individual client or patient here and now: his professional duty is to find out the unique features of the present client's particular problems.

This contrast, between the *atemporal* focus of scientific theory and the preoccupation of legal and medical practice with the *here and now*, is a crucial difference between "theory" and "practice" as those terms are now understood. Scientists study particular events occurring here and now primarily for the light they can throw on universal atemporal theories: practitioners appeal to universal atemporal theories chiefly for the help they may give in dealing with practical problems arising here and now. So, far from reflecting any opposition between Theory and Practice, the varied concerns of scientists and practitioners complement one another.

Another feature of the analytic contrast between Theory and Practice concerns the solidity of argument in each. Within scientific theories today arguments are no longer accepted on a priori grounds alone, but they are still "necessary" in a less ambitious sense. So long as any scientific conclusion follows from theoretical principles strictly, that inference is valid formally quite as much as substantively. Conversely, when practical arguments go beyond the scope of any formal theory their conclusions are "presumptive" in a similar sense. Their soundness depends not on formal validity alone but on the richness of the substantive support for any general ideas they use and the accuracy with which any particular case has been recognized and classified.

Clinical physicians and medical scientists, for instance, may have occasion to discuss the same bacterial infections in either of two ways. They may do so in *general theoretical terms:*

When an acute bacterial infection is treated with a suitable antibiotic agent, the multiplication of the bacteria is checked and the body's immune system fights the infection off quickly; but when the infection is not so treated, the bacteria multiply unchecked and the immune system takes longer to overcome the infection. Administration of an appropriate antibiotic is thus an effective therapy for such infections.

Given that the index of an antibiotic's effectiveness is the speed with which it helps the body throw off infection, the relationships presented in this argument are indisputable and even "demonstrative." As it stands, however, this argument does not tell us how bacterial infections can be identified in practice, or what antibiotics are effective against which infections. Thus even in clinical contexts, theoretical arguments are detached from the details of actual experience.

Alternatively, a physician may report, as follows, on the *condition of an individual patient*:

This patient displayed typical symptoms of a bacterial infection, and initial laboratory tests showed streptococci in the blood. After a week of anti-streptococcal antibiotics, however, there has been no significant improvement.

Further tests are required, to determine if the first lab tests were incorrect or incomplete, and other bacteria were masked by the streptococci; or if we are here faced with a new strain of streptococci, which calls for the use of different antibiotics. While this is being checked out, the patient should continue to rest, take plenty of fluids, and give the existing treatment the best chance of working.

In this second case the solidity of the argument depends not on the formal validity of the inference but on ensuring that the present case is described as completely and accurately as practical purposes demand. As always, the presumption that the patient's condition would improve in a week or so is open to disappointment, but that failure casts no shadow on the general soundness of the corresponding argument. ("That is how things typically go," we may say, "but you meet the odd case that turns out differently.") So the original argument was either "off the point," as the infection was not what the lab results suggested, or else it was an occasion to identify a new strain of antibiotic-resistant streptococci. Either way, the issue is *substantive*: the relevance of our general ideas to the actual facts of this situation, and the failure of the initial presumption points the physicians toward fresh substantive discoveries.

Taken in its revised form, the classical contrast between Theory and Practice captures two points that are still important. To begin with, the word "arguments" has two functionally distinct senses, formal and substantial. Theoretical arguments are chains of proof, whereas practical arguments are methods for resolving problems. In the first, formal sense, an *argument* is a "chain" of propositions, linked up so as to *guarantee* its conclusion. In the second, substantive sense, an *argument* is a network of considerations, presented so as to *resolve* a practical quandary. Taken in these two contrasted senses, "arguments" operate in quite different ways and have different kinds of intellectual merits. They conform to different patterns and must be analyzed in different terms.

Theoretical arguments are structured in ways that free them from any dependence on the circumstances of their presentation and ensure them a *validity* of a kind that is not affected by the practical context of use. In formal arguments particular conclusions are deduced from ("entailed by") the initial axioms or universal principles that are the apex of the argument. So the truth or certainty that attaches to those axioms *flows downward* to the specific instances to be "proved" (fig. 1).[9]

The universal starting point . . .

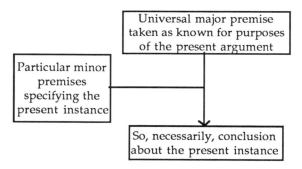

. . . underpins the particular end point

Fig. 1
Theoretical Argument

In the language of formal logic, the axioms are *major premises*, the facts that specify the present instance are *minor premises*, and the conclusion to be "proved" is deduced (follows *necessarily*) from the initial premises.

Practical arguments, by contrast, involve a wider range of factors than formal deductions and are read with an eye to their occasion of use. Instead of aiming at strict entailments, they draw on the outcomes of previous experience, carrying over the procedures used to resolve earlier problems and reapplying them in new problematic situations. Practical arguments depend for their power on how closely the *present* circumstances resemble those of the earlier *precedent* cases for which this particular type of argument was originally devised. So, in practical arguments, the truths and certitudes established in the precedent cases *pass sideways*, so as to provide "resolutions" of later problems (fig. 2).

The outcomes of experience . . .

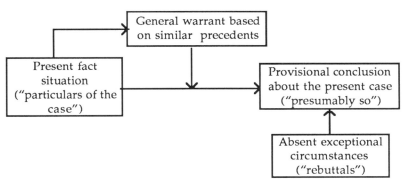

. . . serve to guide future action

Fig. 2
Practical Reasoning

In the language of rational analysis, the facts of the present case define the *grounds* on which any resolution must be based; the general considerations that carried weight in similar situations provide *warrants* that help settle future cases. So the resolution of any problem holds good *presumptively*; its strength depends on the similarities between the present case and the precedents; and its soundness can be challenged (or *rebutted*) in situations that are recognized as *exceptional*.[10]

Further, the contrast between Theory and Practice, in its current form, departs from the classical formula in one crucial respect. It no longer involves an outright divorce, or professes to separate intellectual grasp of "unchanging entities" from technical know-how about "changeable objects." Instead, it regards all the scientific and technological disciplines as ranged along a *spectrum*. Some of these come close to the theoretical extreme whereas others are basically practical; but all of them are in one or another respect both intellectual and technical, and each combines theoretical analysis and practical technique in its own distinctive way.

At one extreme, some branches of mathematics still aspire to the classical ideal of geometry. Their goal is full "axiomatization," by which theorems are linked into a single "deductive system," or piece of cohesive intellectual knitting. Moving along the spectrum, the branches of physics that have cosmological ambitions (e.g., particle physics or unified field theory) still refer in practice to concrete objects and situations and so are dependent on laboratory experiment and astronomical observation. The disciplines of biology lie further along the spectrum: biological theory does not aspire to the abstractness or universality of physical and chemical theory: rather, biologists select a specific "subject matter" and objects of study, using taxonomic keys and other identification techniques.[11]

Finally, toward the practical end of the spectrum are those activities the preeminent concern of which is to *change* the world rather than to *understand* it. Prime among these is clinical medicine: here we shall pay closest attention to the ways in which general physiological explanations, on the one hand, and clinical knowledge of particular cases, on the other, blend in the course of clinical practice. As we shall find, this provides a powerful model to use for analyzing the manner in which "theoretical" and "practical" considerations blend in the field of ethics as well.

CLINICAL MEDICINE AS A PRACTICAL ENTERPRISE

No professional enterprise today is closer to moral practice, or better exemplifies the special character of "practical" inquiries, than clinical medicine. Clinical practice, for a start, shares the emphasis on the certitude of direct experience that was for Aristotle a mark of the *practical*. Recall his appeal to the dietary virtues of chicken. We do not need a nutritional theory, he argues, in order to be sure that chicken is nourishing: on the contrary, it is only because we know from experience that chicken is in fact nourishing that the question, "What *makes* it that way?" arises at all. Clinical experience, likewise, gives physicians solid assurance of well-founded knowledge about health and disease, in advance of all explanations from biochemists and other scientists.[12] That practical knowledge, too, may be a point of departure for new scientific questions: for example, just because we already know that aspirin does in fact relieve headaches, we can go on to ask the scientific question, "*How* does it relieve them?"

Medicine blends theory and practice, intellectual grasp and technical skill, *episteme* and *phronesis*, in its own characteristic manner. It spans the spectrum of Theory and Practice, from the general theories of biomedical science at one extreme to the particular procedures of clinical practice at the other. In doing so it illustrates the complex and subtle ways in which theoretical and practical knowledge bear on each other. At one extreme, medicine overlaps into the natural sciences. Research in physiology and other biomedical fields aims to refine our general ideas (specifically, our general ideas about health and disease) quite as much as research in any other science. The central core of medicine, however, comprises practical procedures designed not to explain health and disease in theory but to treat illnesses and restore health, as a matter of practice. These procedures are the medical profession's collective property: though general in form, they comprise general practical skills (*technai*, in Aristotle's terms) rather than belonging to theoretical science (*episteme*). At the other extreme are the skills that are the individual physician's personal property. A doctor's skill in handling his patients' medical problems demands not only knowledge about the general practical techniques of diagnosis and therapy but also specific and particular kinds of clinical understanding. The central question for him is always, "Just what specific condition is affecting this particular patient, and just what should we do about it, *here and now*?"

In this last respect clinical knowledge requires what Aristotle calls "prudence" or *phronesis*: practical wisdom in dealing with particular individuals, specific problems, and the details of practical cases or actual situations. A working doctor does not rely only on a general understanding of diseases (nosology) and their treatment (therapeutics). A knowledge of medicine in general may be of no practical value in the absence of two more particular skills: the ability to recognize any particular patient's problems, as they present themselves here and now, and also to be able to treat them promptly and responsively, as they take their course.

Clinical medicine is thus *scientific* only in this sense: that the treatment of disease nowadays relies heavily on the generalized scientific knowledge developed by generations of research physicians and biologists. In other respects it is no more scientific today than it has ever been. The specificity of the ailments with which the working physician deals, and the individuality of the patients who suffer them, mark clinical medicine as falling squarely in the realm of practice, not theory. Often enough theory and practice intersect in clinical medicine today; yet with such different goals, they also at times conflict. A brief scenario will show how easily this can happen.

> An elderly woman is admitted to hospital suffering from half a dozen of the ailments common in old age. The admitting physician finds it hard to tell which of her signs, symptoms, and complaints are the effects of which ailment.

So far, so good: in such a situation the prudent physician concentrates on clinical management of the patient's immediate discomforts rather than making a heroic attempt to "cure" underlying conditions that do not lend themselves to full scientific understanding. But at this point a further complication arises:

> The attendant physician who takes the patient's history is not a primary care internist, ready to deal with all her problems as he finds them, but a research scientist in gerontology, who is professionally interested only in selected aspects of geriatric disease.

Now the contrast in goals and methods between scientific theory and clinical practice surfaces and may cause problems. From the standpoint of a research physician who views the patient's illness with theoretical eyes, her current medical condition may be of no scientific relevance. It may be so hard to sort out her multiple ailments and study them separately that for gerontological purposes her case has no more relevance than the falling of sheets of paper had for the purposes of gravitational research. The gerontologist faces a conflict of duties: as a clinical practitioner, his responsibility is to care for the patient in any way her condition requires, but as a scientist he has no direct interest in spending time on cases that do not promote his research. The usual division of labor in a research hospital may give him a way out of his conflict: he may refer the patient to a primary care internist who is concerned with her clinically, not scientifically, so freeing himself to look out for other patients whose medical conditions are more significant for science.

How, then, can we best characterize the relations between theory and practice in contemporary medicine? Is all clinical medicine—the reflective use of medical judgment in dealing with the specific conditions of particular patients—simply "applied biomedical science"? To answer that question either with a plain yes or with a flat no is equally misleading. Certainly major theoretical elements from the biomedical sciences lie behind modern clinical practice. But biology does not bear on clinical medicine in any simple or direct (let alone formal) way: their interrelations are substantive and subtle.

On the one hand, the rights or wrongs of any clinical procedure, as a way of treating a particular patient's current condition, is never simply or formally "deducible from" the general principles of biological theory: no strict deductive links hold between them. Where the mechanisms of the disease that a particular patient presents are scientifically understood, the practitioner can properly draw on that understanding as intellectual background to his clinical decisions. But clinical knowledge does not automatically give out at the point where biology runs out of steam. If a case does not fall clearly within one or another of the classes of disease of which we have a full scientific grasp, the clinical tasks of diagnosis and treatment are less open to theoretical understanding, but they are no less typical elements of clinical practice. Just at this point modern medicine reverts to its earlier status, as an inherited craft or "mystery"; and as such, it is the current phase in a practical tradition the origins of which are much older than those of modern biological science. On the other hand, just because general biomedical theories and particular clinical decisions are not linked by a medical "geometry," there is no reason to despair of the substantive "rights and wrongs" of clinical decisions. Even without a rigorous theoretical basis, clinical judgments are not (as some would argue) the personal hunches or expressions of taste with which individual doctors respond to each practical situation in turn. The guarantees of medical objectivity do not, in practice, depend only on formal theoretical entailments: the strongest support for agreeing to a clinical diagnosis or a therapeutic proposal comes from substantive medical evidence.[13]

There is, of course, a germ of truth in the "personal" view. In a given case, when the doctor accepts a scientific theory or clinical procedure, his decision is not a mere hunch or matter of taste, but typically it does remain a matter of *personal judgment*. What is the subject matter of this judgment? When a doctor reviews a medical history and pattern of symptoms, what exactly does he "perceive"? We can define the object of clinical judgment more clearly if we think of this clinical perception as a kind of *pattern recognition*.

In clinical diagnosis the starting point is the current repertory of diseases, injuries, and disabilities for which descriptions exist in the medical literature. When instances of these conditions are encountered, on trauma ambulances or hospital wards, they are the teaching material required to help students or interns recognize the "presentation" of these conditions. Formally a medical condition is defined by the classical description, and this is a useful guide in identifying diseases that are met comparatively rarely. But a description is clinically fruitful only when it is based on perceptive study of actual cases, and it is practically effective only if paradigmatic cases exist to *show* in actual fact what can otherwise only be *stated*: namely, the actual onset, syndromes, and course typical of the condition. Given this *taxonomy* of known conditions and the paradigmatic cases that exemplify the various types, diagnosis then becomes a kind of perception, and the reasons justifying a diagnosis rest on appeals to analogy. As new cases present themselves for examination the physician collects details from each patient's history, his own immediate observations, and the results of laboratory tests and uses these facts to "place" a particular patient's condition in one or more of the recognized "types." Forced to choose among alternative diagnoses, he must decide how close (or analogous) the present case is to each of the possibilities. This diagnostic question may have only one answer: any diagnosis of a patient's diarrhea, say, may be ruled out, other than a *Salmonella* infection. But it is often necessary to take two or more possible diagnoses seriously; while on occasion physicians may be faced by complex combinations of distinct pathological conditions.

In marginal and ambiguous cases clinicians who are equally skilled and conscientious may share their information fully and have the best wills in the world; yet through "reading" the same history and symptoms differently, they may offer different diagnoses and treatment proposals for one and the same case. When this happens no conclusive evidence or arguments need be available to choose between their "readings"; but this does not mean that their judgments are subjective or uncheckable. Quite the contrary: as the patient's condition unfolds, the consequences of the rival views will show up in fact, making it clear just how "objectively" serious the differing implications of those judgments really were.

With or without an explicit scientific foundation, then, the heart of clinical practice and training comprises a taxonomy of medical conditions. Medical students and interns in training are shown cases that exemplify the constellations of symptoms, or "syndromes," typical of these varied conditions. In this way they learn what to look for as indicative of any specific condition and so how to recognize it if it turns up again on a later occasion. The key element in diagnosis is thus "syndrome recognition": a capacity to *re*-identify, in fresh cases, a disability, disease, or injury one has encountered (or read about) in earlier instances. In this respect clinical knowledge of particular cases is like the field botanist's mastery of botanical taxonomy, which permits him to identify a new specimen, first, say, as a monocotyledon, then as a member of the amaryllis family, finally as belonging to a South American genus, possibly *Alstroemeria*. Given the respective missions of botany and clinical medicine, the initial steps in both cases are to identify the samples at hand: for this purpose the indispensable tools are a rich enough taxonomy and experience in syndrome recognition.

Clinical medicine's central reliance on the taxonomy of illness also explains why the pattern of reasoning by which physicians link symptoms with diseases typically relies on *arguing from analogy*. The conclusions of diagnostic arguments usually embody three linked components.

1. A pattern of signs and symptoms ($s_1, s_2, s_3 \ldots$) is cited which apparently includes enough of the distinctive elements of condition *a* rather than, say, *b* or *c* to warrant a presumptive diagnosis.

2. These similarities are judged close and distinctive enough to justify using treatment procedures appropriate to condition *a*.

3. The possibility of exceptions is guarded against by agreeing that the provisional diagnosis will be reconsidered in case further symptoms turn up ($s_7, s_8, s_9 \ldots$) that are possible signs of the rarer conditions, *d, e,* or *f*.

The relations between a diagnostic conclusion and the evidence on which it is based (symptoms, onset, etc.) are precisely those typical of practical reasoning rather than theoretical proof. First, the conclusion is related to the evidence by *substantive* rather than formal connections. Second, the conclusion follows as a *rebuttable* presumption, not as a necessary entailment. Finally, the inference from the evidence to the conclusion is not timelessly valid, regardless of context, but thoroughly *circumstantial*: dependent on detailed facts about the circumstances and nature of the particular case. For this reason all diagnostic conclusions are tentative and open to reconsideration if certain crucial symptoms or circumstances have been overlooked or the later course of the illness brings important new evidence to light.

CASUISTRY AND DIAGNOSTICS

Medicine is a useful model for the analysis of moral practice in several respects. Clinical medicine is prototypically "practical" both in Aristotle's sense of the term and also in contemporary usage; so the leading features of clinical practice help us to put flesh on Aristotle's schematic statements about the differences between "practical wisdom" and "theoretical understanding." In moral as in medical practice, the resolution of practical problems draws on a central taxonomy of type cases, and the pattern of argument by paradigm and analogy is once again at work. Last but not least, when medicine is practiced conscientiously as well as skillfully, it becomes a prototypically *moral* enterprise. A doctor who diagnoses correctly and who prescribes successfully behaves meritoriously, not merely because his actions are *effective* but equally because, given his relationship to the patient, these kinds of actions are *appropriate*: that is, they fulfill his *duty* as a physician—so much so that one might even regard clinical practice as a "special case" of moral conduct generally.

It should not be surprising, therefore, if many features that mark off clinical medicine from more theoretical enterprises hold good for other kinds of moral conduct. So as we study the history of case morality—notably the "high casuistry" of late medieval and early modern Europe—we shall bear in mind the casuists' assumption that morality does indeed lie in the realm of practice, not theory, and remember what consequences this distinction implied for those who knew their Aristotle. Before we return to the question of how universal ethical principles relate to specific moral judgments in particular cases and embark on our account of the development of casuistry since antiquity, we should stop and pose the question, "How far do the patterns of practical reasoning employed in everyday moral life, and explicitly recognized in the casuistical tradition, share the crucial features of medical practice?"

Our examination of medicine brought the following key features of clinical practice to light:

1. The merits of clinical decisions are related to the theories of biomedical science, not by any strictly formal entailments but in more indirect, substantive ways.
2. The crucial points of clinical reference are the diseases, disabilities, and injuries contained in the current taxonomy of pathological conditions.
3. Diagnostic reasoning proceeds analogically, using medical taxonomy as a source of paradigm cases to which all comparisons refer back.
4. Clinical inferences and conclusions—being substantive and timely, not formal and atemporal—are presumptive, rebuttable, and open to revision in the light of fresh evidence.
5. Clinical arguments—being presumptive, not necessary—always leave room for conscientious physicians to reach different diagnostic opinions about marginal and ambiguous cases.

All these features of medical theory and clinical practice suggest parallel questions about ethical theory and moral practice.

To begin with the general relationship between theory and practice, our central problem about the relevance of universal ethical principles to particular moral decisions, is more easily resolved if we take the example of medicine seriously. The deadlock between ethical dogmatists, whose absolute principles admit of no exceptions, and moral relativists, who see no room for anything but local custom and individual taste, is inescapable only so long as we remain on the theoretical level; but in practical medicine this deadlock is easily resolved. The suggestion that particular clinical decisions are either necessary entailments of theoretical biology or else personal whims of individual physicians collapses the moment we recognize what indirect and lengthy chains of argument link clinical decisions back to, for example, biochemistry. As we shall now see, by taking a practical view of ethics we can again avoid the unpalatable choice between a strict "moral geometry" and the appeal to "personal preferences."

To begin with the relevance of *taxonomic* procedures to ethics, this was clear enough when the National Commission dealt with the ethics of human experimentation. One crucial factor in the commission's ability to agree on recommendations about specific types of cases was its reliance on a moral taxonomy by which kinds of human experimentation were first distinguished, then treated differently. Given that a taxonomic procedure is effective in this one moral situation, may it not be equally effective in resolving other kinds of moral problems? To what extent, for example, is research with children similar to research with the mentally infirm? The other parallels between practical reasoning in medical and moral contexts are no less apparent. If the practical analysis of moral issues means working with a taxonomy of moral cases and circumstances, it is also natural to use *analogical reasoning* to bring new and problematic types of cases into the classification system that summarizes the agreed resolutions of earlier, less problematic cases. So it need be no surprise that, like a modern clinician's diagnostic methods, the procedures that casuists have used to resolve moral problems appeal to understood and agreed *paradigms*, or *type cases*, from which they survey their way analogically to less understood, still disputed issues.

Judgments about moral issues, arrived at in the concrete circumstances of a practical case, can no more be abstracted from their detailed circumstances than can medical judgments about the present condition of individual patients. Clinical inferences and conclusions about particular cases are never necessary or contextless, always *presumptive* and *revisable* in the light of further experience, and there is no reason why matters should be any different in the moral realm. We may reasonably expect the same resistance to dogma, and the same kind of openness to experience, in practical case morality, as we rightly demand in case medicine or in case law.

One final parallel between morals and medicine deserves to be underlined. All detailed clinical inferences are presumptive; so clinical judgments about a patient's condition, and about the prognosis for his recovery, are never final. Honest and conscientious doctors may therefore read marginal or ambiguous cases differently, without being open to criticism. Surely the same is true more generally, of moral as well as medical judgments. If absolute agreement is too much to ask in the technical context of clinical medicine, must not the moral realm, too, leave room for honest and conscientious *differences of opinion?*

This question is neither idle nor empty; it has hidden subtleties to which we shall return. We may be prepared for differences of moral opinion between honest and conscientious individuals in *marginal and ambiguous* cases, for instance, but this in no way means that similar differences of opinion are admissible in *all kinds* of cases. Arguing from paradigm cases about preservation of life and telling the truth, the casuists, as we shall see, allowed no room for conscientious disagreement about cases of, say, willful cruelty to innocents or purely selfish deceit. In their eyes the locus of "conscience" was the class of cases over which the moral distinctions were still obscure, turned on marginal interpretations of the relevant considerations, or were so balanced between contraries that no accepted reading of the current taxonomy yielded a conclusive answer. So between the individual judgments required in ambiguous cases and the personal preferences of the moral relativists lie a million miles of distance. Like disagreements between careful physicians, again, serious differences of view among moral individuals may also lead to substantively different conclusions; and when this happens, these conclusions may teach us something about the "practical wisdom" of the individuals involved.

Yet when all these qualifications are taken into account, it is still true that moral arguments can no more lead to final and definitive conclusions than do the parallel arguments in clinical medicine. In both fields the best we can do is appraise the particular situation in which we find ourselves with the highest degree of clinical perceptiveness we can bring to the situation. But our judgments are always made at particular times, on the basis of the given facts and observations, and so are often "timely" and "context dependent." They remain, that is, *substantive* and *practical*, with all the fallibility and revisability that these terms imply.

Comparing practical morality with medicine, as we are doing here, is not original. St. Augustine, for instance, described morality as a discipline "which is a medicine of the mind."[14] Many thinkers in the European tradition of casuistry, at whose work we shall look in later chapters, had an eye for the similarities between clinical and moral perception, and often drew explicit parallels between the tasks of moral advisers or confessors on the one hand and those of medical practitioners on the other. In the year 1215, for instance, the decrees of the Fourth Lateran Council, which required all Christians to confess their sins to a priest annually, compared these responsibilities:

> The confessor should be discreet and careful in the manner of experienced physicians . . . diligently inquiring about the circumstances of the sin and the sinner, whereby he can learn what sort of advice to offer and what remedies to employ, making diverse attempts to heal the ailing person.[15]

Nor is the basic pattern of reasoning by paradigm and analogy unfamiliar to those who know the tradition of casuistry at first hand. Writing about the methods of casuistry in his study, *Conscience and Its Problems*, Bishop Kenneth Kirk, the Anglican scholar and moralist from whom the title of this book is borrowed, acknowledges the role of taxonomy in case reasoning, whether in ethics or elsewhere. *Mutatis mutandis*, indeed—Bishop Kirk's statements about "casuistical method" might be read in a medical sense; and as such they sound very like an account of the steps required to identify and describe a new "clinical entity" in medicine. At any rate, his words may serve as a summary of the points about practical reasoning that we shall keep in mind as we explore the history and implications of the casuistical tradition:

> Casuistry is a process of applying old illustrations to new problems, to discover when the new corresponds to the old in its essential features, so that the same principle will cover both. The more we collect valid illustrations of each particular principle, the less room for doubt there will be about its applicability in normal circumstances; and the more hope there will be of reaching a definition so inclusive as to make further examination of instances superfluous. Then the law will be defined in relation to hitherto unforeseen areas in the map of conduct. Every such conquest of the hitherto undefined is in fact an achievement of casuistry.[16]

2

The Roots of Casuistry in Antiquity

The contrast noted in the first chapter, between the abstract grasp of idealized scientific theories and the concrete mastery of practical situations, was not easily formulated in Western cultural history. The scholars who discussed this distinction took a long time to define it in detail, and some of its aspects are in dispute even today. Looking back to the world of antiquity, we do not find its implications for ethics immediately recognized; nor do we find a full system of "case morality" explicitly presented in classical times. The crystallization of Christian casuistry, and the case method for deciding moral issues that was its practical core, appeared only after the year 1000 A.D. Yet casuistry grew from roots in the ideas and practices of not one but three earlier cultures: the ideas of Greek philosophy, the judicial practices of Roman Law, and the traditions of rabbinical debate that developed within Judaism. The elements that the casuists took from these earlier cultures did not come to them as ready-made building blocks. Rather, there were fragmentary hints and adumbrations of what might be done; and in each case the methods and achievements of the casuists were significant advances on those of their forerunners.

We begin our account of the historical background by looking in turn at these three sets of origins, bringing the story down to the time of Cicero and the early years of Imperial Rome.

ATHENS, ROME, AND JERUSALEM

Let us start at Athens in the fifth and fourth centuries B.C., in the time of Plato and Aristotle. Aristotle argued that a general unitary theoretical approach to ethics did not illuminate the practical problems of human conduct in specific cases and situations, but neither he nor later Greek philosophers presented anything like a full-scale casuistry. At most, by distinguishing practical or prudential wisdom from theoretical or intellectual knowledge as they did, they laid foundations on which moral theologians and philosophers later built.

Why, then, were the Athenian philosophers in no position to develop a true "case morality"? The reasons were as much institutional, or social, as they were logical or doctrinal. The patterns of social and professional life needed to promote such a development never existed in classical Athens. For a start, matters of personal conduct and character were the shared concern of all citizens, not the specialized concern of any particular group of scholars or teachers. Socrates never professed to be a "learned doctor" with a special claim to intellectual or moral authority. He was not a professional theologian or a rabbi but merely one citizen among others who had reflected seriously about questions his fellow citizens often begged. The Athenians accordingly recognized no élite circle of professional "ethicists" as being better equipped than other people to argue out a taxonomy of right and wrong modes of conduct. Instead—at least among full citizens—ethical discussion had the same egalitarian, democratic character it has in the United States today.[1]

In discussing the character and conduct of their fellow citizens, too, classical Athenians disregarded some distinctions that many people in a modern liberal society regard as indispensable: notably those that mark "moral" issues off from "legal" and "political" ones. When a question arose, for instance, whether an individual citizen was qualified for public office, the procedures for settling it respected certain formal rules, but the substance of the resulting debate was never legalistic. It was argued before a jury of as many as fifteen hundred citizens, and the orators who solicited the jurors' votes invoked any argument that might move them, whether it was (by our standards) legal, moral, or political. In classical Athens anything was grist for this mill: no one for a moment would have accepted the present American practice of rejecting political nominees as "unfit for office" only if they are proved to have broken an actual law. As a candidate for public office, a citizen of Athens might be held up to admiration or contempt for reasons of many different kinds—his sexual habits as a young man, his present reputation, the seeming implications of his political views for the future of the city—or for all of these reasons at the same time.[2]

In short, the Athenians did not insist on the distinctions that we regularly draw between law, ethics, and politics, and procedural distinctions to which we are accustomed were unknown to them.[3] Aristotle's books on politics and ethics substantially overlap, and neither book demarcates a third, distinct field of *law*: in a broad sense, Aristotle argues, ethical issues also belong to "politics," for they have to do with the ways in which people live together in *poleis*—that is, cities, communities, and other collectivities. This is not to suggest that classical Greeks *failed* to recognize distinctions they should have found self-evident. In homogeneous and compact societies such as the Greek city-states, the differences between law and morality are never as clear as in larger, more mixed ones. So rather than asking why classical Athens lacked some modern distinctions and procedures, historians of ethics should look and see when, where, and for what reasons it later became important to refine the procedures of law, morality, and politics in ways that *demanded* such distinctions.

The Athenian philosophers faced one further problem. As traders and travelers, Athenians were better informed than many Greeks about people with cultures, languages, and ideas different from their own—for example, the Persians to the east and the Egyptians to the south. This familiarity posed troubling problems about cultural diversity, together with the ambiguities about ethics that such diversity always brings. From the time of Hecateus and Herodotus, cultural differences were a standing challenge to the moral and intellectual self-confidence of the Hellenes in general and the Athenians in particular.[4] This problem was most pressing in theology and ethics: as Xenophanes put the point, with the help of a striking image,

> If oxen and horses had hands, or could create works of art like those made by men, horses would draw pictures of gods like horses and oxen of gods like oxen, and they would make the bodies of the gods in accordance with the form that each species itself possesses.[5]

How, then, can rational discussions about moral and religious issues avoid "cultural relativism"—that is, the conclusion that each community is entitled to its own ethical and theological beliefs—or transcend the differences between the ideas of different cities, peoples, or cults? In such matters are the local, temporary traditions of particular groups of human beings the only measure? Is each human community free to take this measure in its own way? Or can one frame more general, timeless arguments, which can go behind these variations and yield more authoritative, enduring, and universal positions?

These questions formed one significant starting point of the Greek philosophers' search for "philosophical foundations" of ethics, and for "universal principles" in which the foundations might be expressed. From the outset, the philosophers' pursuit of principles was undertaken on three levels at once and involved other issues besides ethical ones. On an abstract, ontological level, they hoped to go behind the innumerable and changing objects and events that are evident in day-to-day experience ("the Many") and identify the basic constituents of a cosmic order, either as a single enduring entity ("the One") or at least as some limited set of permanent entities ("Elements"). Against this unity, the flux of human experience was a transient shadow play.[6] For some this project was the fulfillment of an intellectual, even a "scientific" hope: the idea that the "mixture" and "separation" of enduring elements will explain all the phenomena of nature foreshadowed in later physics. For others, the underlying ambition was more clearly religious; and its role in fifth-century Greece represents a distant echo of Buddhism and other Oriental religions of the same period.

On another, more empirical level the search for principles was directed at accounting for natural phenomena, or "appearances." Given the puzzling movements followed by, for example, the stars and planets, could a system of material or mathematical constructions be devised that allowed one to work out the precise details of those movements? If that could be done, a successful ontology might serve as the basis for an intelligible system of cosmology also.[7]

For the Greek philosophers, then, the problem of finding general and enduring "principles" to serve as a rational foundation for ethics was to be tackled as part of a larger intellectual enterprise. Theoretically, they discussed moral philosophy alongside, and in the light of, planetary geometry ("saving appearances") and ontology ("the One and the Many"); and the ways in which different writers attacked those other issues affected their approach to ethics, too. Here we shall not be much concerned with the ontological aspects of Greek moral philosophy, although we shall see how the philosophers' ideas about ethical and political theory reflected their ideas about astronomy and geometry. In the *Republic*, for instance, Plato used the astronomers' geometrical ideas about planetary motion to encourage a hope that a similar formal theory might apply to human societies. By discovering the "universal principles" of political theory, might we not give human *social* order as rational a basis as that which geometry gives to the *natural* order of the Heavens? If so, law (*nomos*) and custom (*ethos*) could follow the example of nature (*physis*), and the cultural diversity of moral beliefs and political practices would find an underlying theoretical unity by being rooted in formal geometry.

This whole debate, of course, lay within the realm of abstract theory. In practice, the speculative arguments of Plato and Aristotle had little effect on the exercise of moral decision in fifth- or fourth-century Athens. Instead moral thought and practice continued to operate in time-honored ways, appealing to traditional standards, received maxims, and customary patterns of life. Looking for evidence about Athenian moral ideas in the philosophers, accordingly, we may be misled by the fact that Greek philosophical texts on the whole, have survived better than direct records of live moral debates and deliberations. So in order to reconstruct the practical beliefs current in classical Athens, we must resort to inferences, using as starting points evidence from Greek literature (e.g., poetry and drama), surviving records of law court proceedings (e.g., the speeches of Demosthenes), and any other collateral evidence available—for example the images preserved on contemporary pottery.[8] From these sources we may infer what maxims and proverbs, wise saws and modern instances were familiar to the audiences at plays by, say, Aristophanes and Sophocles, what rhetorical appeals orators might rely on to make a client look admirable or an opponent contemptible, and what kinds of personal conduct were recognized as typical, or emblematic, of men and women from different professions and social classes.[9]

Still, there is little sign in all this that their fellow Athenians regarded Aristotle and Plato as serious moral teachers, or that the philosophers did more than accept a "common-sense" Athenian understanding of practical morality as a source of abstract reflections about ethics. On the contrary, Socrates himself became the target of Aristophanes' satire. Learned philosophers are not necessarily seen by their contemporaries as people with a profound *phronesis*.

Socrates taught all who came to listen to him in the marketplace; but once it entered the Academy, philosophy became "academic."

Culturally and socially, early Rome was a very different place from fifth-century Athens. The Romans began as they went on: a highly practical people with a strong sense of social hierarchy and a marked respect for religious authority. Though they mastered the practical techniques of farming and road building, for example, they never developed their own original systems of abstract thought; and even in their artistic tastes, they showed their preferences for practical activities and country life. Horace's *Odes* idealized his rural retreat in the Sabine Hills, and Virgil was applauded for his long poem, the *Georgics*, in which he showed off his acquaintance with such farming matters as the nurture of honey bees. When moved by theoretical curiosity, whether philosophical or scientific, the Romans turned to the Greeks for instruction; and after they annexed Greece in the second century B.C., most of higher education and professional services at Rome were provided by men of Greek origin or training.

The ways in which moral issues were handled in Rome during the classical period were correspondingly unlike those current in Athens at the same time. Given their traditions, the citizens of early Rome respected the collective wisdom in moral matters, quite as much as in technical ones, as embodied in people of experience; and they developed institutions that took advantage of this wisdom. Initially the City was small and relatively homogeneous, and its members shared well-established ideas of justice, fairness, property, and propriety. In conception and application alike their moral and legal ideas were much more similar to Henry Maine's "customary law" than they resembled John Austin's "positive law." They derived their binding force chiefly from the shared recognition of the community: formal adjudication was required only when ambiguous or marginal situations arose, and on such occasions the Romans turned for decisions to the College of Pontiffs.

In their primary role the pontiffs were priests of the Roman State religion: they administered and transmitted a cult that served the social and political order of the City, as Shinto has done more recently in Japan. Being the guardians of the City's traditions, they had judicial duties too: they were trusted, in particular, to apply their judgments wisely when problems arose about the exact application of accepted moral and legal ideas. (The dividing line between the *legal* and the *moral* was, once again, not wholly clear.) For its first three hundred years, indeed, Roman law comprised no systematic body of rules or generalizations, which went beyond the bounds of accepted good sense.[10] Unlike modern judges, Roman pontiffs were required only to render decisions: they did not have to give reasons or cite well-established "rules" as justifying their adjudications. In a word, their task was not to argue: it was to pontificate.[11]

How, we may ask, was this possible? Can a system of law operate without rules, reasons, and the binding force of precedents? For us today, the legal apparatus so much involves formal "rules" and "laws" that the idea of "a law without rules" may appear paradoxical. At this point, therefore, we should bear in mind the social circumstances of early Rome. In Rome as in other small homogeneous communities, the function of "adjudication" was more arbitral than regulatory: a matter less of "laying down the law" by framing legal generalizations than of mediating disputes and resolving ambiguities. Like labor arbitrators today, judges in such communities were less bound by precedent than are modern judges. Typically a Roman pontiff resolved problems in which the practical application of the traditional consensus was unclear, and the balance of interests between the parties was too fine to be settled except by the judgment call of a disinterested and trusted arbitrator.

In genuinely marginal cases all that any arbitrator can do is take the detailed circumstances of the current dispute under advisement and then decide that, all in all, it is more equitable (i.e., *fairer*) to tilt the scale to one party rather than the other. All that he can do, in a word, is exercise his *discretion*. In modern usage his rulings will turn on considerations of "equity" rather than issues of "law" in the strict sense. (Here we may recall what Aristotle said about the need for *phronesis*, not *episteme*, in arriving at concrete decisions in particular situations.) Such rulings do not require one merely to apply general legal rules, since in truly marginal cases the available "rules" are not decisive. Rather, it relies on the exercise of judicial discrimination in assessing the delicate balance of facts at issue in a particular case. Thus "pontificating" did not, as modern colloquial usage may suggest, involve laying down the law in a dogmatic and ungrounded way. Rather, it was a matter of resolving marginal disputes by equitable arbitration, which is what their fellow citizens trusted "pontiffs" to do.

This state of affairs did not last. After a while the cases coming up for arbitration by the pontiffs began to display certain shared features, and this led to the formulation of new statutes (*leges*). Many of these had to do with questions about the right to inherit property: in what cases might a householder's illegitimate children by, say, a concubine or a slave girl share in his estate alongside the children of his acknowledged wife? Long before the first imperial codification, therefore, Roman law began to develop a general apparatus of *regulae*, or rules. Five different sets of factors helped strengthen this new reliance on rules.[12]

As the City grew the caseload increased beyond a point that the pontiffs could handle alone, so less experienced judges were brought in to resolve some of the disputes. These others did not enjoy the same implicit trust that the pontiffs did, so their rulings had to be "regularized." Again, with the rise of lawyering as a profession, law schools were set up and *regulae* were articulated for teaching purposes. Since it relied on the personal character and reputation of the individual pontiffs, "discretion" was not easy to teach: legal instruction meant moving over to formal rules and more teachable skills in arguing. Third, Rome acquired an empire, and foreign peoples came under the City's authority. Because those other peoples already had their own bodies of customary law, which had to be harmonized with the body of Roman law, it was necessary to establish a concordance between the "rules" of these different bodies of law.[13] Fourth, the demands of imperial government meant the growth of a bureaucratic civil service, and this (as always) developed its own regular operating procedures. Finally, the academic discussion of Roman law was increasingly pursued in the context of, and in terms taken from, Greek philosophy. Cicero was a highly skilled practicing attorney, but he was also a serious philosopher impressed by the Stoic idea of the *logos*, or "universal reason."

The resulting proliferation of rules and laws led to significant changes in judicial practice. First, two distinct groups of issues were functionally differentiated. On one side are issues that can be decided by applying *general* rules, or laws, according to the maxim, "Like cases are to be decided alike." On the other side are issues that call for discretion or discernment, with an eye to *particular* features of each case, according to the maxim, "Significantly different cases are to be decided differently." (This distinction is the ancestor of the modern contrast between legal and equitable jurisdiction, or Law and Equity.) Second, when the Emperor Constantine consolidated imperial power in Byzantium, he brought Equity under his direct control and, as a matter of policy, restricted the exercise of discretion to his personal court and chancellor. From then on, in the public arena judges had the thankless task of applying general "rules of law" with minimum room for discretion. Only when the resources of law were exhausted might a citizen who felt unjustly treated appeal to the emperor, in his capacity as "father of the fatherland" (*parens patriae*), to exercise clemency or equity. Politically, this division of labor might be advantageous to the emperor, but at the same time it sowed the first seeds of a suspicion that the Law is one thing but Justice is quite another.[14]

The move from the College of Pontiffs to the Emperor Constantine was thus a significant change. So long as Rome remained a small town with a homogeneous population, the pontiffs could serve both as priests of the national cult and as impartial arbitrators of moral or legal disputes. In the latter role their activities were arbitral and equitable rather than narrowly "legal." Once Rome was an empire with a full court system and a bureaucratic state machine, judicial activities became more legal than arbitral, and the judges lost their equitable jurisdiction. Equity became the preserve of the emperor, who was now referred to not just as *parens patriae* but also as *pontifex maximus,* or "supreme pontiff"—a title later taken over by the Pope as the spiritual head of the Roman Catholic Church. More recently, since the political decline of the monarchy destroyed the earlier purpose of the separation, most Anglo-American jurisdictions have undone Constantine's division and have merged both legal and equitable functions in the same courts. Yet it is still usually the case that equitable remedies can be sought only in cases in which legal remedies are unavailable or unworkable. In this respect the dead hand of the Emperor Constantine still rules us from the grave.

Judaism handled issues of moral practice in ways intermediate between the egalitarianism of the classical Athenians and the elitism of the Roman pontificate. Athenians acknowledged the moral wisdom of particular individuals and listened to them with special respect; but this respect was earned and recognized on a personal basis and no formal authority attached to it. Athens had no college of pontiffs, as Rome did, with an institutional duty to make decisions in difficult moral or legal cases: instead, the entire body of citizens formed its own deliberative assembly, which dealt with public issues on a collective basis. Judaism combined elements of Athenian participation and Roman authority.

The term "Rabbinic Judaism" is used to describe the "mode of Judaic religion created by the Rabbis of the early centuries of the Common Era and eventually embodied in the laws and doctrines of the Talmud . . . continuing essentially in its classic forms from its very beginnings to the present day."[15] The traditional religion of the Hebrew people centered on two sacred realities: the Temple of Jerusalem in which the One True God was worshipped, and the Torah, or Law, spoken by God through Moses to the People and expressed in the first five books of the Hebrew Bible (or Pentateuch). The Pentateuch contains 613 commandments governing the daily religious and secular life of the people: these were known as the "Written Law." According to tradition Moses also delivered to the people a detailed interpretation of the Written Law known as the "Oral Law."

From the fifth century before the Common Era, teachers (known as *Sopherim*, "scribes," or Men of the Book) expounded the Written and Oral Law, explaining its meaning and relevance as guides for the life of the Jewish people. This activity, continuing up to the second century of the Common Era, produced codifications of the Oral Law (Mishnah), which were given authoritative form by Rabbi Judah the Prince at the end of the second century. The Mishnah comprises 63 treatises collected into six orders and covering different aspects of life: prayer, holy days, marriage, civil and criminal law, temple ritual, and ceremonial purity.

Once redacted into the Mishnah, these codes in turn became the basis for commentary and explanation. Two main schools developed—one in Palestine and one in Babylonia—and there flourished down to the sixth century. Each of these centers of Torah study produced a Talmud (literally, a "teaching"), which collected the scholars' discussion of the Mishnah; and these two Talmuds, particularly the Babylonian Talmud, have been objects of commentary and sources of application by successive generations of rabbis to the present day.

In this rabbinical tradition, learned commentators have explained the texts; judges have issued rulings; famous rabbis have answered requests for interpretation. As the Jewish people dispersed throughout Europe, Africa, and Asia during the Middle Ages these activities continued and were carried on within quite different cultures. Jewish belief and practice were preserved and adapted to meet a variety of new needs and circumstances; and as a result an immense body of literature was created. This literature, the intellectual tradition behind it, and the dedication to live according to its letter and spirit comprise *Halakhah*. Literally derived from the verb "to go," it is "the way" in which the people of Israel are to walk, the path each Jew and the nation are to travel, "and Thou shall show them the way wherein they are to go."[16] *Halakhah* is the expression of the moral and religious duties that encompass and give spiritual meaning to Jewish life. *Halakhah* is the casuistry of Rabbinic Judaism.[17]

Since the Middle Ages, ten or a dozen Jews have formed a *schul* large enough to debate some disputed issue and reach a collective point of view. The special reputations that individual rabbis held for moral discernment gave their opinions special weight and authority; and the task of a *schul* debate was often to assemble the relevant views of the authoritative rabbis and weigh their opinions against one another. Of course, if a current problem raised novel issues, previous rabbinical views were not always wholly "to the point." But the discussion could bring earlier opinions to bear on a current problem by using them as landmarks from which to "triangulate" the way to a resolution of the special problems in a novel case. Indeed, the method and substance of *schul* discussions about moral issues well exemplify the "clinical" character of concrete diagnostic reasoning in the spheres of ethics and law. In the Judaic tradition, then, the egalitarian wisdom of the people and the elitist authority of the rabbis coalesced into a mode of moral reasoning between the Roman and the Athenian.

Historically the rabbinical debate was more than a simple precursor of Christian casuistry. The two traditions were created and refined in parallel, and rabbinical procedures are, to this day, used as means of adjudication in Jewish congregations or synagogues, as well as in, for example, the informal tribunals that monitor professional conduct in the international diamond business.[18] Yet one may hesitate to see the Jewish debate about *Torah* as a prime example of "moral casuistry," as the rabbinical debate always focused on the obligations to which Jews are subject *as Jews*. The Jewish law codifies the special duties associated with Judaism using a taxonomy whose basic units are the six hundred and thirteen paradigmatic examples and maxims found in the Pentateuch. When cases arise that involve also non-Jews, they are not seen as subject to the full panoply of 613 duties: but only to the nine broader human obligations that form the so-called Code of Noah.[19] So it is not for nothing that Torah is spoken of as a system of "law,"—that is, as the possession of a particular human community—rather than a system of "morality" making equal claims on all human beings. In this respect, Judaism differs from Roman law and Christian moral theology, both of which inherited the universalizing ideals of Alexander and late Hellenism.

More than three hundred years before the Apostle Paul taught that there was "neither Jew nor Gentile, neither bond nor free"[20] but that all human beings equally are objects of God's love and care, Alexander of Macedon swept away the particularisms of the different nations. For him, there was "neither Hellene nor Barbarian": his Empire was a universal one. which gave citizenship to Greeks and Indians, Persians and Egyptians; and the Roman Empire inherited this ambition also.[21] So, in classical antiquity, similar moral taxonomies took shape in different contexts, and were used in different ways. In Judaism, for example, rabbinical decisions were prospective, discussing whether it would (or would not) be lawful to perform an action of a given kind. By contrast, Christian confessors gave retrospective judgments about whether it had (or had not) been sinful to perform an action. But this contrast had little effect on the practical content of their teachings.

The distinctive feature of ethical thought among the classical Greeks was their attempt to find in philosophy an intellectual basis for moral practice. At first, Greek philosophical theories did not directly affect the Jewish Law; but they did influence Roman legal ideas, and through them the traditions of the Western Church within which "casuistry" took shape. At this point, therefore, we shall look and see how the ethical theories of Greek philosophy came to grips with the demands of moral practice, until they were finally taken over by the lawyers and orators of the Roman world.

FROM GEOMETRY TO RHETORIC

When Plato and Aristotle set out to compare and contrast the value of the main kinds of *knowledge*—theoretical comprehension of abstract arguments in the sciences, practical command of general craft techniques, and the prudential wisdom that is required to handle particular legal problems or medical cases—they had different stakes in the philosophical debate. Faced with a generation of Athenians whose ways of thinking he regarded as confused, short-sighted, and pragmatic, Plato made a case for the virtues of general theory and theoretical argument (*episteme*), and downplayed the significance of technical reasoning (*techne*) and practical wisdom (*phronesis*). When Aristotle developed his mature ideas a generation later, he took the merits of theory for granted, and tried to give a fairer, less partisan account of other varieties of knowledge.

In their backgrounds and affiliations, the two men shared so much that many of their views overlapped; it is a mistake to think of them as radically opposed. However, about ethical theory and moral practice, Aristotle's final views moved far away from those of his master; and, if we juxtapose their positions, we can perhaps see how Aristotle's account of practical wisdom in resolving particular concrete problems (*phronesis*) pointed ahead to new, more effective methods of dealing with issues in law, politics, ethics and rhetoric, in a way that Plato's geometrical account of "the Good" never could. Notably, we shall see why (in his eyes) moral practice responds to a rhetorical or "temporal" account of ethical reasoning better than it can ever do to a purely formal or "timeless" account.

Most important for Plato himself was the ethical and political significance of his ideal of abstract universal theory. For the Greek city-states, the last part of the fifth century B.C. was a time of war, political crisis, and moral doubt: this is evident from the tragedies of Aeschylus and Sophocles, as well as from the Platonic dialogues. Aeschylus showed his sorrow at the deterioration of older religious and aristocratic ideals; Sophocles was perplexed about the competing moral claims of the *polis* and the family; Euripides displayed a wider uncertainty about the existence of any discernible moral order. Given this climate of conflict and skepticism (as it seemed to Plato) people approached moral issues opportunistically, or even cynically, with an eye on nothing but the worldly interests of those involved. At the beginning of the *Republic*, Thrasymachus argues that the only question that really counts in politics is, "Who is the strongest? Who can best get his way, by persuading, cajoling, or if necessary forcing other citizens to serve his interests?"

As against this tough-minded or "realistic" attitude to politics, Plato had Socrates present a case for believing that political affairs can be studied in impartial intellectual terms, leaving aside all questions of strength or wealth in favor of collective interests and universal goals. In the long run, he claimed, it is possible to fashion a *polis* with the same kind of stable, permanent, intelligible order that we find in nature, specifically in astronomy. The most powerful weapon against cynicism is, therefore, the conviction that political problems can be decided by appeal to general principles, rather than force, or "clout." In a stable, rationally ordered state, discussions of policy will focus not on the special interests of individuals or groups, but on matters of universal concern: in modern terms, for example, issues of environmental protection, rather than just paying off the tobacco farmers.

In this situation Plato's indignation was primarily directed at the school of teachers known as "Sophists." As professional teachers of rhetoric, Sophists could find a ready audience in the turbulent Athenian democracy, by helping those who presented their arguments most persuasively to take advantage of the prevailing moral agnosticism. The Sophists' program relied largely on teaching techniques for setting out opposing arguments on public issues, with a seeming implication that either side could be held with equal confidence. The leading sophist Gorgias' last book, *Double Arguments*, showed how this technique can reinforce the belief that nothing truly general can be said in ethics, so that there is nothing left to be considered apart from particular cases and situations. According to Gorgias, there was no "absolute" justice. Actions toward enemies, e.g., were basically different from actions toward friends. Cheating, lying to or stealing from enemies is not merely permissible, it is just; and it may even be just to deceive a friend, if it is done for his own good. In the ethics of the Sophists, the key notions were the "right time" and "opportune moment." Justice was manifest only in concrete situations: so the fundamental obligation was "to say or refrain from saying, to do or refrain from doing, the right thing at the right time."[22]

The Sophists thus put great weight on the *timeliness* of acts. Their word for "opportune occasion" (*kairos*) was a rhetorical term of art: a speaker must recognize from his audience's reactions the right moment (*kairos*) to introduce a fresh point. It was a technical term of art in medicine, too: a doctor must recognize when a constellation of signs and symptoms calls for a new method of treatment. It was used in theory of poetry, referring to the moment when the hearer recognizes the intimate connection between two images. From the theological viewpoint, too, people encounter situations in which even immoral actions seem providential, if well timed: as Aeschylus says, "Sometimes the God recognizes a value even in the opportune use of falsehoods." Finally, Aristotle uses the same term for the "timely" circumstances of any action.[23]

The doctrine of "opportune time" had (for Plato) a corrosive effect on the very idea of moral reasoning. Rightly or wrongly, the Sophists' teaching—like cultural relativism and the extreme forms of "situation ethics" today—suggested that moral issues must be judged afresh on every occasion, from scratch, and that no common features mark off certain types of actions, cases, and situations from others as *opportune* for respecting the customary "rules of conduct." Fairly or unfairly, Plato depicts Gorgias as boasting that a mastery of rhetoric provides the greatest of human goods—namely, the ability to persuade, and thereby enables the individual to rule over others in his City.

Socrates' own response was a view of moral wisdom as being an inward and decisively personal assurance about the foundations of moral action, rooted in the agent's self-knowledge. Socrates did not reject the Sophists' idea of "opportunity": he merely insisted that even one who acts "opportunely" achieves true virtue only by acting out of adequate self-understanding. Plato went much further than this, reinterpreting and enlarging on Socrates' ideas, notably in the *Republic*. In Plato's inspired city few citizens had any occasion to recognize the Ideal Form of the Good: only the "guardians" could undergo that experience, and were intellectually equipped to play a part in the city's affairs as rational rulers, judges, and legislators. In his famous image of the Cave, Plato imagines that the Guardians have withdrawn from the world of everyday affairs and come through dialectic to recognize the Ideas and Truths that human affairs exemplify only partially. Returning from their encounter with abstract general Ideas, they find the messy complexity of human life bewildering:

> They appear awkward and ridiculous, with their eyes still dazed and unaccustomed to the darkness, whenever they are compelled in a court or a forum to dispute over the shadows of justice . . . . wrangling over [alternative] conceptions of justice with men who have never beheld Justice itself.[24]

Soon the Guardians' experience of timeless truths and eternal entities sets them apart from their fellows as an élite equipped to deal with moral and political issues in a way that the generality of the citizens cannot.

Thus, Plato undercut completely the ethical significance of timely, "opportune" action. In his account the true object of moral knowledge was not what actions have to be performed *in time* but, rather, how ideas are related in a theoretical world of *timeless* reality. In his determination to defend the rationality and objectivity of ethics against the agnosticism and relativism that he saw the Sophists encouraging, he subordinated practical awareness of specific facts about particular situations to a firm intellectual grasp of universal ethical principles. He countered the Sophists with so complete an absolutism that he ended by giving no guide to practical action, even to those who mastered his theory thoroughly. For Socrates, moral competence is rooted in self-knowledge: its assurance lies in simple but unshakable convictions of rightness, and is directed toward the particular demands of the present moment. Plato converts a capacity for moral discernment into an unwavering vision of eternal universal Truth. Socrates claims that the merest slave boy carries in his mind the innate capacity he needs to learn geometry, and uses this as an image of how all human beings arrive at a clear grasp of morality: Plato, going further, presents moral knowledge as a sub-species of formally demonstrable, or "geometrical," knowledge and ends by treating Ethics (in the phrase of Spinoza) as a theoretical Science *modo geometrico demonstrata*.

Plato's account was thus as far as could be from taking the claims of "case ethics" seriously. Yet his view of moral knowledge has been strongly influential throughout the centuries, especially among philosophers: it is also one origin of a view very fashionable today, which places at the center of the public debate about moral issues unqualified appeals to general "matters of principle." This basic strategy, of demanding *generality* above all else, has led Plato's successors to treat ethical theory, like all other branches of philosophy, as a field that aspires to the abstract exactitude which Theaetetus and his colleagues had achieved in the field of geometry. So conceived, all the varied "goods" or ends of human action were just subspecies of a single timeless and universal Good; and if only our grasp of this universal Ideal Good were fully complete, that insight should enable us to solve all moral problems definitively and with mathematical certainty. Anything *universal* that was true of the Form of the Good, must deductively—in conformity to the demands of logical necessity—be true, surely, of any *particular* "good" also.

About this last conclusion, Plato's most talented pupil had serious reservations. How, Aristotle asked, can the vision of an abstract, universal, and entirely general "Form of the Good" give us specific guidance when we really need it—that is, in moral practice? Though he began as Plato's pupil, Aristotle's mature views were less grandiose and all-embracing than his master's: both his views about practical reasoning in general, and specifically his ethical ideas.[25]

By Aristotle's time, the sheer novelty of geometrical theory had worn off, so the special virtues of *episteme* never prevented him from paying serious attention to reasoning of other kinds. Nor were the broader social and cultural stakes as weighty for him as they had been for Plato a generation earlier. Emerging from wars with Persia and Sparta successful but exhausted, Athenians became reconciled to the prospect of Macedonian domination; and Aristotle himself did not mind acting as the young Alexander's private tutor. Nothing stopped him, accordingly, from taking a moderate position, which was less hostile to the "timely" and the "opportune" than Plato's had been, and calculated to redress the balance between the theoretical sciences and other more practical types of knowledge.

One central question presented itself for his consideration:

In what respects and for what purposes are exact theories and geometrical reasoning "to the point"?

Not everything philosophers recognize as "knowledge" can be captured in abstract universal terms; nor does all of human experience rely on the same rational methods. Rather than look for *completely* general, universal, and permanent truths in all areas alike, philosophers should be satisfied to discover, in each field of experience separately, the *most general*, universal, or permanent truths the nature of that field admits. If the relevant modes of reasoning in fields like medicine turn out not to be abstract and timeless but dependent on time, occasion, and circumstances, so be it!

This change, from Plato's philosophical agenda to Aristotle's, is particularly important for ethics. Early in the *Nicomachean Ethics*, for instance, Aristotle wrote,

The same exactitude is not to be looked for in all fields of knowledge, any more than in all kinds of crafts. It is the mark of an educated mind to expect just that exactitude in any subject that the nature of the matter permits. For it is unreasonable to accept merely plausible arguments from a mathematician, and to demand formal demonstrations from an orator.[26]

So he laid the groundwork for a detailed analysis of the different fields of knowledge, according to their varied subject matters, the different types of problems they raise, and the kinds of reasoning that are appropriate in resolving such problems.

To begin with, Aristotle defined *theoretical* knowledge of two kinds, both of which relied on formal, demonstrative, or "analytic" arguments. In sciences the subject matter of which was abstract and immediately intelligible (e.g., geometry), the validity of arguments rested wholly on the meanings of the terms employed; but that was not the only kind of "theory." In such natural sciences as botany and zoology, analytic reasoning would once again be possible, if one could assume that the actual real-life animals or plants available to us in the real world fall into permanent, well-defined "natural types" each with its own distinctive character or "essence." To the extent that the world comes to us already divided up into "genera" and "species," and hybrid, intermediate forms are the exception, not the rule, one could bring analytic arguments to bear not only on formal definitions and abstract ideas but on concrete matters of fact as well.

In Aristotle's day, of course, Darwin's theory of organic evolution was more than two thousand years in the future, and there was no reason to doubt that zoology and botany could be exact, demonstrative sciences, quite as much as, for example, astronomy. Still, the need to assume the existence of "essences" in the natural sciences limited the scope of theoretical knowledge and analytic reasoning. Indeed, the *absence* of any such preexisting divisions in the subject matter of Ethics—the fact that the circumstances and cases that human conduct deals with *do not* come neatly packaged in "natural kinds"—is precisely what prompted Aristotle to deny that ethics can be a science: that is, a field for "universal and eternal" principles and quasi-geometrical argumentation.[27]

As against theoretical sciences such as geometry and zoology, Aristotle classified "practical" knowledge into two distinct kinds. On the one hand, there were *generic* ways of getting things done: these he called *technai*. (We still refer to them as "techniques"; i.e., the concern of technicians or other technical experts. The generic task of radiologists, for example, is to take and interpret X-ray photographs of patients sent for examination.) On the other hand, there was the understanding of *specific* kinds of cases: what he called *phronesis*. This practical knowledge concerned concrete situations the nature and complexity of which were unknown beforehand: it dealt with them not by merely reapplying predetermined generic techniques but by recognizing what combinations of actions are appropriate to complex or ambiguous situations. Radiologists are "technicians" because the nature of their tasks is defined in advance; clinical physicians have no specific predefined tasks because their responsibility is to deal perceptively and in a timely way with whatever medical needs any particular patient may have, in response to all eventualities, as and when they may occur. This second kind of "practical" knowledge, Aristotle says, is exemplified in the capacity to deal with the *moral* demands of life in perceptive and timely ways, as and when they arise. This puts ethics into the realm of *phronesis*, "prudence," or "practical wisdom,"[28] rather than into that of *episteme*, or "science."

What, then, was at issue for Aristotle when he challenged the view that ethics can be a science? Timeless, intellectual grasp of scientific ideas and arguments, he says, differs from timely, personal wisdom about moral or practical issues in three crucial respects:

First, they differ in universality or particularity. The things about which we frame scientific theories have timeless, universal natures and are as they are "necessarily"; but it is quite different with those things that are the concern of practical prudence.

> Whatever we know in a "scientific" way holds good generally; but with things that are variable by nature there is no way of knowing how they will be, once they are beyond the range of observation.
> Unlike scientific knowledge, which rests on formal demonstration, things whose basic principles are open to variation do not lend themselves to demonstration . . . . Hence, practical prudence (*phronesis*) is not the same as scientific knowledge (*episteme*).[29]

He continues, "Prudence involves not only general rules: it must also take into account particular facts, since it is concerned with practical activities, which always deal with particular things."[30]

Second, scientific ideas and practical issues differ also in what we called the "locus of certitude" in each kind of knowledge. With scientific knowledge that certitude lay in a grasp of theoretical principles; in practical issues, certitude arises from knowledge of particulars.

> Where anyone bases his certitude about something on correspondingly certain principle, he knows about it in a scientific way; for,

unless the certitude of his principles is greater than that of the conclusion he bases on them, his knowledge will be a matter of mere happenstance . . . .

That is why people who lack a grasp of general ideas are sometimes more effective in practice . . . Since *phronesis* is practical, it requires understanding of both kinds: knowledge of particular facts even more than a grasp of generalities.[31]

Finally, the two kinds of knowledge differ in their ultimate court of appeal. In a fully developed science, all the elements in its arguments are governed by the basic "universal principles" to which they can be led back by way of explanation, and from which they can be derived by formal deduction. In the realm of practical knowledge the situation is quite different.

In this respect, *phronesis* and *episteme* are opposed. The intellect masters the basic definitions of a science, which are not further demonstrable [and argues from these definitions]; but *phronesis* deals with the "ultimate particular" (*to eschaton*), and this is an object of perception (*aisthesis*) rather than *episteme*.[32]

How, then, do we "perceive" these ultimate particulars?

Not by normal sense perception, to be sure; but in the kind of way we recognize that the triangle (say) is an ultimate element (*eschaton*) in mathematics.[33]

In ethics as in mathematics we have an "eye" for paradigmatic or type cases: in both fields there is no appeal behind this experience. In unambiguous ("paradigmatic") cases we can recognize an action as, say, an act of cruelty or loyalty, as directly as we can recognize that a figure is triangular or square. Faced with examples of either kind, people of experience "know them when they see them": given that perception, no further "deductive proof" is needed that a triangle is triangular, or an act of cruelty is cruel.[34]

By emphasizing the differences between *episteme* and *phronesis* Aristotle circumvented the relativism of the Sophists without falling into the exaggerated absolutism of Plato's refutation, and so restored the balance between them. Issues of practice call for *phronesis,* not *episteme,* so that ethical decisions and judgments are unsuited to rigorous "proofs" based on appeals to universal, invariable, or "axiomatic" principles. Instead they involve reasons, principles, and certainties of a distinct and distinctive kind. Plato's appeal to a universal, unique, and eternal Form of the Good, represented in all particular, varied, and transient "good things," only concealed the *unlimited diversity* of ethical problems and situations:

> Matters of practical conduct have nothing invariable about them, any more than matters of health. This is true of ethics in general, and it is true even more of moral issues arising in particular cases. These are not a scientific or professional matter: rather, as in medicine or navigation, they require human beings to consider what is appropriate to specific circumstances (*tous prattontas*) and to the specific occasion (*pros ton kairon*).[35]

The appeal to a single universal, abstract Form of the Good is, thus, of no help to human beings in dealing with actual concrete problems of moral practice in different circumstances or situations.[36]

The ethical ideas presented in Aristotle's *Nicomachean Ethics* were intended to be "practical and attainable by human beings" and to keep in touch with the practical realities of human life and conduct. This meant acknowledging and coming to terms with three distinctive features of Ethics and ethical judgments:

1. the absence of "essences" from the world of human affairs and ethical deliberation;
2. the "opportune" character of all timely choices and actions;
3. the "circumstantial" dependence of every ethical judgment on the detailed fact situation involved in that particular case.

Aristotle never denied that *any* general considerations are relevant to ethics, as the more extreme Sophists reputedly did. In his view, practical reasoning in ethics no more lacked general premises about the nature and lessons of human experience than medicine lacks general premises about the natures and courses of different diseases. He was no more willing than Plato to undermine the paradigmatic status of those general moral ideas—kindness and cruelty, loyalty and betrayal, trust and deceit—that are intelligible to all "prudent and understanding persons."

Still, it was less easy to see just how these general ideas match the kaleidoscopic variety of actual situations. Bare intellectual mastery of the theoretical implications of general ideas and universal principles is one thing: recognizing what specific ailment is involved in a patient's current medical condition, or what specific moral obligation a practical situation gives rise to, is quite another. So "prudent understanding" calls for the kind of experienced eye that can perceive all the relevant contingent facts about the particular situation in question.[37]

To this extent Aristotle concedes the Sophists' central claim: that ethical situations are not limited to any "fixed species" but come in an unlimited variety of permutations and combinations. In natural sciences such as botany and zoology the populations studied are limited to the existing "essences"; in ethical, medical and similar areas of human experience there are no fixed patterns. In ethics as in clinical medicine practical understanding rests not on "theory" alone but on recognizing just what general moral notions are relevant to varied situations as they arise in practice.

As Aristotle saw, the essential variety in human situations had one further consequence. The demands of justice go beyond the rules of law. Justice can be done in practice only if *nomos*—rule-governed "law"—is supplemented by *epieikeia*—or "equity," i.e., a reasonable and practical application of general legal rules:

> A law is always a general statement, yet there are cases which it is not possible to cover in a general statement. . . .
> This does not make [the general statement] a *wrong* law: the error is not in the law, nor in the legislator, but in the nature of the case, the stuff of practical conduct being essentially variable. When the law lays down a general rule, and a later case arises that is an exception to the rule, it is then appropriate, where the lawgiver's pronouncement was too unqualified and general, to decide as the legislator himself would decide if he were present on this occasion. . . .
> The essential nature of "equity" is thus to correct the law in situations where it is defective on account of its generality. . . . Like the leaden rule used by builders on Lesbos, which is not rigid but can be bent to the shape of the stone, a ruling is thus made to fit the circumstances of the particular case.[38]

A prudent, understanding judge or agent can never treat universal laws or principles as absolute or invariable. There is always room for discretion in asking how far general rules, as they stand, apply to particular fresh cases, however marginal and ambiguous, and how far they should be waived or bent (like a builder's leaden ruler) to respect the exceptional character of novel situations.

In dealing with exceptional cases the task is not just to know when equity demands that an exception be made. It is necessary to go further and ask exactly how—in just what other terms—the legislator would have reformulated the general rule if he had been cognizant of this specific kind of situation. The experience of bringing our corpus of laws, rules, and principles to bear on a sequence of ambiguous and marginal cases is thus an occasion to refine the current statements of those laws, rules, or principles and make them more discriminating.

At this point Aristotle is hovering on the verge of adopting a "casuistical" approach to moral and legal problems, but he does not pursue further the implications of this conclusion. At most he hints at some crucial features of a "case method" in law and ethics, which in due course became the possession first of medieval canonists and theologians, who used it in building up a critical taxonomy of moral categories, and later of Anglo-American common lawyers, who used it to develop and criticize inherited notions about tort, contract, and other main categories of the law.

Aristotle provided much of the groundwork needed for this step, but he never took it for himself. If we look in his writings for any systematic list of what things human experience finds "good and bad" or "right and wrong," we shall find no such classification. If anything, like the Sophists, he tends to exaggerate the variability of actual situations, and makes them appear more kaleidoscopic than he need have done. He does not discuss what kinds of things are good or right, appropriate or obligatory, in abstract and general terms: only what is good or right, appropriate or obligatory *for an agent of a specific kind*, acting *on an occasion of a particular sort*, in a situation that involves *other people of equally specific kinds*. He is not seeking to develop a full scale moral taxonomy: rather, he is concerned to show how the moral deliberations of specific agents depend on their social, political, and personal status, and on the spirit in which they act.

One part of Aristotle's *Nicomachean Ethics* alone, namely, books VIII and IX, resembles a "casuistical" analysis at all closely. There Aristotle draws a series of distinctions between different personal relationships, or kinds of *philia*. (W. D. Ross's edition of the *Ethics* actually calls these books "a casuistry about friendship."[39]) The standard translation of the Greek word *philia* into the English word "friendship" is misleading; in modern colloquial English, being "friends" is only one of many relationships we have with other people. The Greek term *philia* can refer, equally, to other relationships:

for example, between shopkeeper and customer, father and son, husband and wife, officer and private, or physician and patient. True, it is correct to render *philos* as "friend" when, for example, Aristotle argues that *philia* in its highest form is achieved only as between two large-spirited people (*anthropoi megalopsychoi*) who come from similar social backgrounds. But his aim in these books is not to define what we call "friendship" today: he is quite as much concerned with the variety of other kinds of personal relationship (*philia*) and with the different ways in which the conduct that is appropriate in dealing with other people depends on the nature of one's *actual* relationship with them.

Evidently, different relationships involve different obligations. Within his consulting room a practicing gynecologist may properly do things to a patient that would be highly objectionable, or even legally actionable, if done by anybody else or in some other situation. Again, actions that may be appropriate by a father to his son might be found intolerably bossy as between personal friends or colleagues. Indeed, the very arts of human conduct that children master while growing up ("learning how to behave") are concerned with just such differences: as we may say, "You just don't act like that" toward your grandmother, your school principal, or your bridge partner, as the case may be.

Still, Aristotle's aim was not to develop a classification of kinds of *philia* that was to be comprehensive. The basic contrast, for him, was between personal relationships entered into with different general intentions, or in different spirits—as a way of getting pleasure, for the sake of self-improvement, or for the other partner's good—and he did not spell out all other differences in any detail. In this respect as in others, Aristotle ends by giving an account of Ethics written by an Athenian citizen and gentleman for his fellow citizens and gentlemen of Athens. He takes it for granted that any educated and experienced citizen of Athens knows what actions are appropriate within any given relationship and befit a father or juror, soldier or friend, without needing him to catalogue these duties.

By making moral judgment a matter of *phronesis* not *episteme*, and placing ethics squarely in the realm of the practical, Aristotle took moral philosophy a long way from its starting point in Platonic "theory." On his account, ethical problems can be solved rationally only by going beyond abstract and universal terms and paying attention to specific circumstances: this had not been so obvious to people who viewed Ethics from the theoretical, Platonist standpoint. If Aristotle were right, sound and certain moral judgments about real-life situations are not reached by relying on uncriticized "intuitions" of universal and invariable Truths or of eternal and abstract Forms. Instead the relevance of such generalities must always be criticized in the light of the detailed facts of the particular situation.

In the long run this point was to have influential consequences. In the first place, it led to a bifurcation of the intellectual debate, as a result of which practical disciplines such as law and medicine came to be discussed in concrete, contextual terms, with only passing glances at matters of philosophical theory. From this time on a whole string of writers appears whose philosophical concerns are, in this sense, "practical" not "theoretical." This genealogy links Hermagoras of Temnos, the third-century teacher who turned Aristotle's view of practical wisdom into a theory of rhetoric, with Cicero in Rome, and so, by way of the medieval schools, with such modern figures as Adam Smith and Thomas Jefferson. These genealogical links are not merely a matter of speculative guesswork about vague "influences": they had a solid intellectual basis. Any account of moral or practical wisdom as *phronesis* carried the procedural implication that the first step in handling such issues is to identify the situation in which the act in question is (or is to be) performed, and this idea became the central insight of all subsequent "practical philosophy."

Early in book III of the *Nicomachean Ethics*, Aristotle lists the features of a situation that have to be considered in order for the moral standing of any action to be properly judged. Only when all these "circumstances" have been specified, with an eye to the actual situation, is it clear what *kind* of "action" is being considered; and only then can the action be soundly appraised.

> To enumerate these circumstances: they are (i) "Who did it?" (ii) "What was done?" (iii) "To what (or in what context) was it done?"; and, in appropriate cases, (iv) "Using what (e.g., an instrument)?" (v) "To what end (e.g., as an act of lifesaving)?" and/or (vi) "In what manner (e.g., gently or violently)?"[40]

This list of factors, or "circumstances," was the first of many such lists and, as we shall see, assumes great significance in the eyes of the canonists, casuists, and common lawyers.

Aristotle's emphasis on the need for *phronesis* in ethics meant, in addition, that practical issues are to be discussed and deliberated about not in "geometrical" but in "rhetorical" terms. The task for moral reasoning is not to construct a self-consistent or formally valid "proof." Formal proofs call for intellectual precision of a kind that that even the brilliant youth can display; but moral wisdom is the province of human beings who are rich in experience.

> The young may be experts in geometry, mathematics and other similar branches of knowledge. . . . *Phronesis* requires a knowledge of particular cases, which comes from experience, which a young man does not possess, since experience is the fruit of years.[41]

Over practical issues, the task is to make a case that is capable of carrying conviction with "prudent and understanding men": that is, people whose experience has equipped them to appreciate and weigh the significance of the details of particular cases.

Even though moral deliberation is not "theoretical"—axiomatic or geometrical—it can nonetheless be rational or reasonable in its own "practical" way. So the practical philosopher's long-term task is to show what kinds of procedures reasonable human beings use in facing problems, exchanging opinions, advancing relevant considerations and arriving at well-argued resolutions of their problems, in substantive or practical, rather than formal or theoretical terms. Substantive arguments carry weight, for instance, only when they are *to the point*—that is, relevant to the matter currently under discussion: even a rigorous formal demonstration is an obstacle to understanding if produced in a context in which it is beside the point. A moral argument is reasonable, again, only if it addresses questions that are relevant and appropriate to its particular circumstances and specific issues. (In Aristotle's terms, only if it is "topical.") So, in an innocent sense of a despised word, moral arguments are "rhetorical." This does not mean that they move their audiences by irrelevant appeals to their tastes, prejudices, or material interests. It means only that they engage their hearers' current preoccupations, address the actual concerns, and take into account their particular backgrounds: in the language of the Quakers, "speaking to their condition."

In this innocent sense physicians have different "rhetorical" occasions for explaining their opinions about a case to each other, to a patient's family, to the patient himself, and (perhaps) to a learned society, the jury in a law court, or a newspaper reporter. Any doctor who knows his business will then report his views and explain his reasons for holding them in different terms on each occasion. These rhetorical adjustments are not deceitful, prejudicial, or misleading as the familiar, dyslogistic notion of "rhetoric" implies: rather, the physician is ensuring that his explanation is forceful and intelligible, given the particular listeners' specific interests and backgrounds. In the older, less antagonistic sense such "rhetorical" adjustments are responses to the varied circumstances in which the physician speaks.

Ethical arguments carry weight with the "prudent and under-standing" only if their conclusions rest on general truths that the hearers find convincing. For Aristotle moral generalities (or "universals") were based on the wisdom of experienced human beings, and so he examined the manner in which such arguments operate in a treatise whose relevance to Ethics is not obvious to moderns—namely, the *Rhetoric*. He was, of course, vividly aware of the abuse of rhetorical methods, which Plato had excoriated in his attacks on the Sophists. Yet, as he said at the beginning of the *Rhetoric*, that abuse was not inevitable: "What makes a man a Sophist is not his rhetorical ability but his moral purpose" and rhetorical ability may well be used to good purpose.

Aristotle presents rhetoric as a combination of logic and ethics—the chief aim of which is to persuade people about the right and the good.[42] It is concerned with recommendations about actions to be pursued or avoided, with the justification or condemnation of actions already performed, and with the allocation of praise or blame to past actions, with an eye to the future. Rhetoric thus deals with questions about benefit or harm, justice or injustice, and human worth, and in one respect its methodology is similar to that of ethics: both subjects finally rest on appeals to "ultimate particulars" or "paradigm cases." Given this convergence of ethics and rhetoric, he concludes, his treatment of rhetoric must refer to ethics, at least in a summary fashion; so he inserts into the argument of the *Rhetoric* a digest of books I–IV of the *Nicomachean Ethics*.

As he demonstrates in the *Rhetoric*, the function performed in formal or analytic reasoning by "syllogisms" is taken over, in ethics and rhetoric, by analogous arguments, that he calls "enthymemes." Enthymemes establish their particular conclusions presumptively or probably (not "necessarily"): they appeal, for example, to matters of common knowledge, general maxims, or "signs"—what a detective calls "clues"—or by referring to historical events, fictional stories, or other well-known "examples" (*paradeigmata*). As a sample maxim, he quotes a verse of Euripides, "No man is in all things prosperous, nor wholly free," and adds the clause, "since all are slaves of money or chance." But all such maxims must be proven by experience, so they carry more weight in the mouths of mature and experienced people than they do in the "silly or ill bred."[43]

Elsewhere, in his treatise *Topics*, Aristotle draws attention to the part played by particular "topics" in the arguments of different disciplines. Each discipline has its special field of debate, within which people of experience share *koinoi topoi* ("commonplaces")—that is, bodies of experience that underlie the forms of argument that guide deliberation and discussion in the particular field.[44] In book III of the *Topics*, for instance, he offers an example particularly relevant to ethics: how topical considerations are used to adjudicate the choices among different desirable goods. In terms that anticipate the felicific calculus of Jeremy Bentham (who probably knew the passage well), he argues that we weigh different "goods" by asking, for example, how lasting, secure, productive, or near each of these is in comparison with the others. Both *Topics* and *Rhetoric* thus make it clear how strongly Aristotle understood the presumptive (or "probable") character of rhetorical, moral, and other practical arguments: this set ethics off from all exact science and separated his maxim-governed view of practical reasoning about "particulars" from the Platonic vision of a "universal," axiomatic ethics based on intuitions of the Absolute.

During the centuries after Aristotle, all of these varied topical and rhetorical subjects were taken further by classical rhetoricians, notably the use of examples, maxims, and enthymemes as forms of proof in "probable" and "practical" reasoning. In due course, as we shall be seeing, they were put to extensive use by moral theologians in the era of High Casuistry. For the moment we may complete our examination of the classical roots of casuistry, with a brief look at the Roman philosopher, jurist, and orator, Cicero.

3

Cicero: Philosopher, Orator, Legislator

Marcus Tullius Cicero (106–43 B.C.) bequeathed to history the first set of clearly formulated moral "cases." In book III of his essay, *On Duties* (*De Officiis*), he described a number of examples in which individuals are perplexed by a conflict of moral duty.[1] Some of these are invented cases that became staples of moral debate: for example, the shipwrecked companions who cling to a plank that is buoyant enough to support only one; the merchant who brings grain to a drought-stricken city, knowing that a plethora of grain will arrive in a following fleet; the real estate agent who advertises houses that are termite-ridden; and the starving man who can sustain himself only by taking food from another's table. He also relates many episodes from history, including the story of the noble Regulus, who had to decide whether he would keep a promise to return to his captors, knowing that this return would mean his death.

Similar moral dilemmas, of course, abound in ancient literature. Socrates under death sentence is offered a chance to escape; Antigone must choose between loyalty to family and allegiance to ruler. Many cases were made up to illustrate a particular point: for example, the madman who leaves his sword in the care of a friend and then, bent on murder, demands it back reappears often.[2] But Cicero's *On Duties* was the first "case book" that related a number of these episodes in order to analyze their moral logic.

Apart from examples drawn from myth and history, Cicero borrowed his cases from other authors, particularly from the literature of Stoicism and of its critics. It has been said that Stoicism invented casuistry,[3] but it was Cicero who made that invention public, especially for readers in the Middle Ages. An avowed eclectic in philosophy, he was impressed by Aristotelianism but inclined toward the moral teachings of the Middle Stoa. His boyhood tutor, Diodotus, was a Stoic, and in early manhood he traveled to Greece to study with Posidonius, who had himself been a pupil of the founder of the Middle Stoa, Panaetius. In his moral writings Cicero combined Platonic, Aristotelian, and Stoic elements in a way that avoided both the abstractness of the Academy and the absolutism of the Old Stoa while emulating the practicality and realism of the Peripatetics. But he was a practicing advocate and politician as much as a philosopher and writer, and his speculative tastes were whetted by the demands of practical life. He had a deep appreciation of civic achievement and abhorred opportunism and unprincipled pragmatism. He had, then, intellectual viewpoints and personal inclinations that led him to become the first casuist.[4]

In order to understand Cicero's contribution, it is helpful to examine the reasons that led the Stoics to invent casuistry. From the fragments left by the founders of Stoicism, Zeno and Chrysippus, the moral doctrine of the Old Stoa proposed one and only one principle, "Live according to nature." The virtuous life consisted in a conformity between the rational nature of human beings and the rational nature of the universe. This conformity was attained by a single virtue, *apatheia*—literally, "absence of passion." The choices of a wise agent were determined not by irrational impulse but by reason alone. Such *apatheia* was the sole human good: all other realities, such as illness and health, wealth and poverty, praise and ignominy, beauty and ugliness, strength and weakness, were considered external to rational nature and so were labeled "indifferent." Their value lay not in themselves but only in their use by the wise person; and the task of the wise person was not to change the world but to become a harmonious part of the cosmos.[5]

The wise agent, whose reason and emotions were thoroughly attuned to the Reason of the Universe, was the Stoic ideal. His wisdom was the source of morally good actions, called *kathormata*. All other people were fools, unconformed to universal reason and hence morally defective; all their acts, regardless of how good they appeared, were morally wicked, *hamartema*. With this sharp, unshaded differentiation between good and evil, the original Stoic ideal soared far beyond ordinary human attainment. It inevitably raised questions about the practical values of daily life and the insistent demands of personal and social activity; in particular, it raised questions about the value and meaning of the actions of those who were not wise. Hence its paradoxes and puzzles: "The wise," said the old Stoics, "will not know they are wise: indeed, there may not actually be any wise men." Some Stoic teachers were even reported to have said that, for the wise, acts execrable to common sensibilities, such as incest or cannibalism, might be morally right.

The Skeptic Carneades, one of the most outspoken critics of the Old Stoics, challenged the Stoic doctrine by posing cases which he claimed would expose its inner contradictions. These cases were intended to show both the unattainable nature of the morality of the Old Stoa and the paradoxical nature of all moral ideals. They demonstrated that whatever choice was made, the wise person could not help being either a fool or unjust. These cases were commonly debated in the philosophical schools of Greece and Rome. Cicero became familiar with them in that context, and when he turned to a discussion of the apparent conflict between utility and virtue in book III of *On Duties*, he put them to good use: not to reveal the unattainable or paradoxical nature of all morality but to suggest how a reasonable resolution could be proposed. In this he followed the lead of the second generation of Stoic teachers, the most renowned of whom were Panaetius and Posidonius.[6]

These philosophers recognized that the idealistic rigorism of the Old Stoa was intellectually paradoxical and practically inapplicable. While retaining the general outlines of the earlier doctrine they introduced further distinctions, hoping to render it more reasonable and practical. Beside *kathormata*, the perfect morality of the wise, was set *kathekonta*, the imperfect duty incumbent upon all persons. Within the category of action called "indifferent," *oudetera*, they introduced levels distinguishing the preferable, the rejectable, and the neutral. Preferables were those things that contributed to harmonious living and inspired desire; rejectables tended to disrupt harmonious life and inspired aversion; neutrals neither added to nor subtracted from a harmonious life. The preferables and rejectables

were not, strictly speaking, "good" or "bad"; that appellation belonged only to perfect virtue. But they were advantageous or
disadvantageous—that is, they had a "utility."

The task of moral deliberation was, then, to identify what was the
appropriate or fitting action in any particular situation. This was
identified as an action that could be supported by "reasonable justification."[7] Thus the major problem was introduced of possible conflicts between the "good" and the "useful"; moral philosophers
turned to the justification of decisions by "probable argument." By
posing the issues in this way, the Stoics of the Middle Period
"invented casuistry" and anticipated the casuistical enterprise of the
Middle Ages.

Cicero modeled his essay *On Duty* on the reformed Stoicism of
Panaetius, but he revised this master's teaching in some significant
ways. For instance, he wove it together with the Aristotelian doctrine of virtue, stressed the problem of conflict of duties, and added
some distinctively Roman examples. He agreed with the Stoics that
there were three kinds of moral actions: virtuous, vicious, and intermediate (*officia media*). Virtue, in its fullest sense, could be found
only among those hypothetical persons who were endowed with
ideal Wisdom—persons rarely or never seen in this world. So it was
his intention to write about the intermediate duties, "whose observance is incumbent upon everyone in the world . . . among whom
many, by natural decency and education, can live up to them."[8]

These intermediate duties were rooted in the four cardinal
virtues: wisdom, courage, temperance, and justice, which, in turn,
were rooted in that most fundamental aspect of human nature—the
instinct for preservation of the individual and the community. In the
first book of his essay, Cicero combined the Peripatetic doctrine of
the virtues with the Stoic doctrine of the natural law. The abstract
and absolute "natural law" of the Stoics was given a human face and
Roman dress, as *humanitas*, the profound fellow-feeling that binds
human communities together. The terse motto of the classical Stoics,
"live according to nature," was elaborated into a majestic definition
of the natural law: "Right reason in conformity with nature, present
in all men, unchanging, eternal, commanding all to the performance
of duty, prohibiting evil."[9] But in Cicero's view, this noble law of
nature was not by itself a sufficient guide to moral decision and
action. He wrote,

in the performance of all these duties, we shall have to consider what is most needful in each individual case. In this way, we shall find that the fundamental moral claim of social relationship (*humanitas*) is not identical in every circumstance. . . . . These different circumstances should be carefully scrutinized in every instance of duty, so that we may become skilled evaluators of duty and by calculation perceive where the weight of duty lies, so that we may understand how much is due to each person.[10]

Duties can conflict with one another; and duties can apparently conflict with advantage. Even actions that at first appear wrong turn out, on reflection, to be right: "There are occasions when even promise keeping or returning something left in your charge would not be right: when, for example, it would be harmful to the one to whom the promise was made, or would do more harm to you than good to him."[11] Cicero notes that general moral duties must be interpreted by considering "what is needful in each case." Thus the claims of social relationship vary with time and importance: one should, for example, help a neighbor whose harvest is threatened, rather than a brother or friend who is in better circumstances. We must become, he advises, "good calculators of duty in the circumstances, so that by adding and subtracting, we may see, by the sum, where our duty lies."[12] This calculation is performed by seeking to justify the decision by "probable reasons." In some cases the adding and subtracting will not total a definitive result and genuine doubt will remain where duty lies. When this is so, Cicero advises, "Consult persons who are wise and experienced."[13]

After discussing the nature of advantage and utility in book II, Cicero approaches the problem that he considers central to the moral life: the apparent conflict between moral goodness (*honestas*) and advantage (*utilitas*). The problem of this apparent conflict had, of course, been raised by the Stoics. Panaetius had promised to devote a chapter to it in his own treatise, *On Duties*, but had not delivered the chapter. Cicero expressed astonishment at the omission, for "there is no more vital theme in the whole range of philosophy."[14] Although a few Stoics, he remarks, had written about this theme, they had done so inadequately. He now undertook to remedy the omission, and in book III of *De Officiis*, he offered posterity the first example of casuistry. His central thesis is plainly stated:

When we encounter advantage in some plausible form we cannot help being impressed. But close examination may reveal something morally wrong with this apparently advantageous action. In such a case the question of abandoning advantage does not arise, since it is axiomatic that, where there is wrong, there can be no true advantage: for Nature demands that all things be right and harmonious, consistent with Nature and therefore with each other.[15]

Cicero did not attempt to prove this axiom but set out to reveal its truth by presenting and discussing classic cases of the apparent conflict between duty and advantage both fictitious and real. After reviewing the position of the various philosophical schools on this problem, he concludes that "it is sinful to compare [morality and utility]—even to hesitate between them": the moral action must always be preferred. However, "certain sorts of contingencies admit doubts and special consideration, for certain situations are difficult to assess." Cicero offers as an example "a particular instance that admits of wider application": it is a terrible wrong to kill one's close friend, but if that friend happens to be a tyrant, it is no crime but "the most splendid of noble actions."[16]

Cicero then states his thesis that according to the law of nature that binds all humans into a community, the morally right action is also the truly advantageous one. He tests this thesis by posing a number of cases, some from history and myth, some created for pedagogy. These cases are "efforts to define our obligations in particular circumstances." Plato's myth of the Ring of Gyges[17] sets the scene. When he has reason to suppose that he will never be detected, may a person act in a way that is advantageous to himself but harmful to others? Cicero offers a number of historical instances in which an apparent advantage, gained in contravention of the morally right, turned to serious disadvantage, and then reviews the pedagogical cases proposed by the Stoic teachers. One of these, Hecato of Rhodes, Cicero dismisses curtly as a philosopher who surrendered to the attraction of advantage, and he recites the Carneadean cases that Hecato claimed to have resolved: "If a fool snatches a plank from a shipwreck, should a wise man wrench it away if he can, since the wise man is more worthy?" "If two wise men are clinging to a plank that can support only one, should one give way to the other?" "Should a son publicly reveal the secret wrongdoing of his father if it was contrary to the good of the Republic?" "Should a man who has received a counterfeit coin pass it on?" Hecato answers each of these questions by reference to the consequences, except that he requires the two equally wise men to cast lots for the plank; to Cicero's taste this kind of casuistry smacks too much of utilitarianism.[18]

In the early pages of book III Cicero had posed and resolved other cases in a manner he considered more faithful to his axiom that the good and the useful can only be in seeming conflict. May a person of quality who is starving to death take food from a person who is of no account? May an honest man, freezing to death, steal the clothes of an evil tyrant? These cases, says Cicero, are easy ones: in principle it is immoral to rob even a completely useless person merely for one's personal advantage. But if the starving man's qualities are such that, should he survive, he will render great service to humankind, "there is nothing blameworthy in taking the food for that reason." This resolution of the problem, Cicero warns, is not mere utilitarianism but rests on what is natural and unnatural. Neglect of the common good of humankind is "unnatural" because Nature's law coincides with the interests of the community of humankind. "Therefore, this law must ordain that sustenance be transferred, in case of necessity, from the feeble, useless person to one whose death would be a grave loss to society."[19]

Cicero also rehearses a debate between two Stoics, Diogenes of Babylon and Antipater of Tarsus. These teachers discuss two cases. In the first a merchant brings grain to Rhodes during a famine. Having seen other grain dealers setting sail for the island, he wonders whether he should sell his cargo at the highest price he can obtain or whether he should reveal to the Rhodians that more grain is on the way. Diogenes declares that while the seller is under an obligation not to defraud customers, it is morally permissible for him to sell his goods as profitably as possible. Antipater responds that this conclusion ignores the further obligation to protect the interests of others and of society. That obligation flows from the natural principle that one's own advantage should benefit the public as well. Thus concealment of the following grain fleet is immoral. Diogenes counters Antipater's point by arguing that downright concealment and merely keeping silence are not the same. The dealer is merely keeping silent; no one is under an obligation to tell others everything they might like to know. Antipater, in turn, objects that there is indeed such an obligation, because the brotherhood of all humans is cemented by Nature. Diogenes acknowledges this general truth, but he doubts that society is so constituted that nothing belongs to any private person: if this were so, no one should ever sell anything. Cicero concludes this mock debate by noting that the argument is not about whether one should do something advantageous that is, at the same time, immoral; rather, it is about whether or not the actual advantage of acting in this way or that is real or only apparent.

The two Stoic teachers are shown in a second debate: should an honest man, when selling a house, reveal to the buyer that the house is not really as good as it looks? Antipater contends that he should; Diogenes argues that so long as the owner does not claim that the house is perfect, he has no obligation to reveal its specific faults. In resolving this case also Cicero sides with Antipater. He supports his position by stating that concealment depends not merely on keeping silence but also on the desire to keep interested parties ignorant, so as to profit by their ignorance. As he had previously shown, taking advantage of others in this way is clearly contrary to Nature's law, which dictates that the society of humans remain undisturbed and that cooperation be fostered and protected. This "probable reason" demonstrates in both cases that revealing the truth is not only virtuous but also advantageous, since it supports the social cooperation required by the Law of Nature.[20]

Cicero concludes book III of the *De Officiis* with an extended discussion of oaths and promises. After several preliminary cases, including the venerable sophistic case of breaking a promise to return a sword to a madman, Cicero turns to his leading case, the story of Regulus. He argues that the duty to keep oaths is an absolute duty from which one cannot be excused by any apparent advantage. Moving through this story with casuistic finesse, he considers a series of objections to Regulus returning to Carthage, as he has sworn to his captors he will even though return means death. The first objection is a theological one: "What is there to an oath, since the Gods to whom we swear do not experience anger, nor do they punish the deeds of men?" Cicero responds that the objection is irrelevant. Oaths bind not because of fear of divine punishment but because they engage the trust necessary to society. Second, it is objected, Regulus should choose the lesser of the two evils: namely, to violate his oath rather than to die. Cicero responds by asking, "Is there any greater evil than immorality? Swearing to do what you do not intend to do is perjury and, so, is immoral." Finally, it is said one need not honor an oath that is extracted under duress. Cicero exclaims, "Could duress ever be effective in the case of a brave man such as Regulus?" Cicero concludes the case by affirming, "There is nothing advantageous that is not also right; nothing is right because it is advantageous; it is only because something is morally right that it is advantageous."[21]

The third book of the *De Officiis* is the cradle of casuistry. In its pages Cicero showed the teachers of the Stoa debating the nature of morality not with theoretical arguments alone but in terms of specific cases. Cicero himself took up this method, using both the traditional cases and stories from myth and history, to make his own theoretical point that true morality will always coincide with true advantage. Many of the cases related in this book have passed into the common stock of later moral philosophy and theology; subsequent thinkers have merely refined or repudiated the ancient resolutions of these problems. In almost every case Cicero's own solutions or suggestions seem less than satisfactory. His arguments are often sketchy and his personal and philosophical prejudices show through. Yet through Cicero's writings, the casuistry born in the Stoa was nurtured and was given a sturdy send-off into the moral traditions of Greco-Roman and Christian culture.

CICERO AS ORATOR AND LEGISLATOR

In 161 B.C., a decree of the Roman Senate banished all "rhetoricians" from the city. The sober Fathers of the Republic had presumably become anxious about the craft (or craftiness) of these teachers, who were mostly Greeks and, as Plato had said long before, were notorious for "making the worse the better case." Still, they soon returned, and their instruction became popular among young men who were ambitious to rise to prominence in the affairs of the Republic. The rhetoricians brought with them a long tradition, compiled into manuals that classified the branches of oratory, and laid out rules for the construction of speeches.

The most famous of these manuals had been composed by Hermagoras of Temnos in the mid-second century B.C. Hermagoras contributed to rhetoric the theory of *stasis*, which outlined the rules for clarifying the central issue in any speech and organizing the standard arguments for accusation or defense. Establishing facts, defining issues, justifying or excusing particular actions constituted the essential features of the oration. Emphasis was not merely on polished literary style: at this stage rhetoric was still conceived as the preparation of a substantive argument, rather than as dressing it up in a decorative package.[22]

Cicero absorbed the lessons of Greek rhetoric, and in his youth he composed his own manual, *De Inventione*, which he later criticized for its immaturity and incompleteness. Still, it was the *De Inventione*, rather than his more mature *De Oratore*, that exerted a powerful influence upon the conception and teaching of rhetoric throughout antiquity and until the Renaissance.[23] In this book Cicero combined, somewhat indiscriminately, the rhetorical systems of Aristotle and of Hermagoras of Temnos, describing practical argumentation in ways that became deeply embedded in the Western mind and were to reappear in the structure of later casuistical argument. Quite unlike modern rhetoric, which stresses style of composition and elocution, the classical rhetoric found in these books was concerned primarily with how one constructs an argument in order to make a case "by marshalling arguments that lend credibility, authority and strong foundation."[24]

Cicero began his treatise by agreeing with Aristotle that the art of the orator covers three classes of subjects: the "epideictic," devoted to the praise and blame of individuals; the "deliberative," proper to political debate; and the "judicial," which concerns accusation and defense in a court of law. Judicial oratory concerns what is just, epideictic what is honorable, and deliberative what is honorable and also expedient. Cicero then proposed some basic concepts about the construction of speeches, in which he followed the system of Hermagoras, though with some demurrers. The Greek rhetoricians had invented the concept of *stasis* which Cicero translated as *constitutio*, i.e., "the issue." Noting that an oration might discuss either a general question such as "Is marriage good for men?" or a particular question such as "Should Alexander marry?" Hermagoras divided orations into those that treat the first kind of questions, called *theses* (or, by the Latins, *questiones*), and those that treat particular cases, called *hypotheses* (or, by the Latins, *causae*). The first are more properly the subject matter of philosophy; the latter pertain properly to rhetoric.

In dealing with *hypotheses* or *causae*, the essential thing is to define correctly the *stasis* or *constitutio*, that is, the "issue" in the case. For various kinds of issues different kinds of arguments are used to define and make the case. For example, suppose that the question is raised, "Should Orestes be condemned for killing his mother, given that she killed his father?" On being charged, Orestes might answer,

"I was justified in so doing." Asked why, he may answer, "Because she killed my father." The accuser might then respond, "That is not a sufficient reason for matricide"; and with this the argument has reached the *issue,* which must now be argued by accuser and defendant. The relevant arguments will be those that treat such subjects as honor to parents, the duty of revenge, and so forth. So the initial question about a particular person and particular circumstances is universalized: "Should anyone who slays his own mother be condemned?" While the rhetoricians recognized this close relationship between the philosophical *thesis* and the particular *hypothesis,* Cicero emphasized its importance: the orator must be able to show that the case under current discussion involves a matter of general principle.[25]

As the title of Cicero's essay indicates, the major activity of the discipline of rhetoric is "invention, that is, the discovery of true or apparently true arguments that will render one's case plausible (*causam probabilem reddant*)."[26] Cicero sets out the general direction of this activity, stressing the part of discourse called "confirmation," in which the orator lays out the justification for the case he is attempting to make. The confirmation rests heavily on "the attributes of persons and actions": namely, for persons, their name, nature, manner of life, fortune, character, feeling, interests, purposes, achievements, accidents, speeches; and for an action, its nature and purpose, place, time, occasion, manner, and consequences. In these attributes lie the essence of the resulting argument: "Nothing need be considered in these quests for argument except the attributes of persons and actions."[27]

From these attributes one can construct arguments that are either necessary or probable. The former are irrefutable, demonstrated by rigorous proof; the latter are "what usually comes to pass or are part of the ordinary beliefs of mankind."[28] All argument is carried on by what Cicero called "induction" and "deduction"; but as he described them, these were forms of reasoning by analogy, using the kind of rhetorical argument that Aristotle had called the "enthymeme." Cicero describes both forms as "reasoning which draws a probable conclusion from the fact under consideration; when this probable conclusion is set forth and recognized by itself, it proves itself by its own import and justification." (*Ratiocinatio est oratio ex ipsa re probabile aliquid eliciens quod expositum et per se cognitum sua se et vi sua confirmet.*)[29] He expounded at length, and with many examples, the construction of various kinds of argument. The form of reasoning by analogy is particularly important in dealing with cases in which there is no clear principle of law. In such cases, he suggested, one refers to a similar case in which the principle is clear and then compares the circumstances of each; on showing similarities, the application of the clear principle to the new case can be justified.[30]

Each aspect of an oration has its proper *topics*—that is, standard forms of argument appropriate to the subject. Some topics are peculiar to the particular case being argued, but many topics are "common"—that is, adaptable to many types of cases. The common topics are amplifications, either of propositions that all the hearers will accept as undisputed fact or of doubtful propositions for which the speaker must construct a plausible argument. For example, in discussing the topic, "the cause of an action," the speaker must discuss whether the act was performed out of impulse or premeditation and, if because of the latter, in order to attain what advantage or avoid what disadvantage. Cicero defines each of these points and describes the steps by which they can be developed. For any question a stock of arguments can be proposed pro and con, "all ready to be hurled like a spear equipped with its thong."[31]

The part of the oration called the *indignatio* illustrates in small compass how the arguments are proposed. The *indignatio* comes at the end of the speech and serves to arouse hatred of the accused persons or disgust at their action. It repeats briefly and forcibly the arguments of the *confirmatio,* as based upon the attributes of persons and actions. Cicero describes the steps to be covered in the *indignatio* in terms very like the structure of the "case" that the later casuists will construct. First, the authority of those who have previously discussed such cases is to be assessed. Then those affected by the action are to be described. The voluntary and intentional nature of the act is to be examined. The circumstances of the action are to be recounted. Comparison is to be made with other acts commonly regarded as dishonorable or unjust. Then it is asked what would happen if everyone did such things, and what should be thought of similar cases. Finally, the audience is invited to consider how they would judge if they themselves were the injured party.[32] This set of "topics" or common arguments contains many of the important elements of the *casus* that we shall find in the later casuists: indeed, it contains the elements needed in almost any discussion of a practical ethical problem.

Cicero acknowledges that skilled use of the commonplaces and stock arguments can easily become facile, and so debase rhetoric into rabble rousing. The sound rhetorician must also be a student of moral philosophy and be able to employ the soundest arguments in favor of virtue and against vice.[33] In discussing the topics proper to epideictic and deliberative oratory (both of which are concerned with "the honorable"), Cicero, like Aristotle in the first book of the *Rhetoric*, reviews the principal notions of what constitutes the "honorable"—namely, the virtues. In this section of the *De Inventione* he crafts precise definitions of the four cardinal virtues (wisdom, justice, courage, and temperance) and their subvirtues; and he appends to each definition a miniature treatise about each. For example, after defining justice he grounds this virtue in the law of nature, which he also defines and relates to customary law and statute. These definitions were so succinctly stated that they became classics for subsequent writers on morality, right up until modern times: "Justice is a habit of mind which gives to each his due, while preserving the common good"; "Temperance is the firm and well considered mastery of reason over desire," and so on. The miniature moral treatises contain statements of principle, for example, "The greatest necessity is that of doing what is honorable; next, of preserving safety, and third is the necessity of convenience." These principles are then applied. In a case in which honor and security appear to conflict, for instance, it is permissible to be concerned about safety, but only if honor may be recovered in the future.[34]

Another crucial feature of the training in rhetoric was familiarity with the use of *sententiae* or maxims. These were short sayings drawn from folk wisdom, literature, or the epithets of the wise. For example, "Money is the root of all evil," and "Rumor is an evil more swift than any other." The maxim, commonly recognized as true or partly true, was used as the starting place for an argument. Students of rhetoric were required to develop short presentations in which they explain, expand, and contrast maxims.[35]

Cicero's *De Inventione* and the *Rhetorica ad Herrenium*, which was widely attributed to him, were powerful influences upon the culture and scholarly tradition of the Middle Ages, along with the *Institutio Oratorica* of Quintillian (A.D. 40–95), and a third book, the *De Rhetorica quae supersunt*, which was incorrectly attributed to St. Augustine. Through these works the rhetorical theories of other

ancient authors, particularly Hermagoras of Temnos, became familiar to the Christian culture of the West. The discipline of rhetoric
became an essential part of education, educational theory, preaching, and, through its influence on letter writing, even diplomacy.[36]
Rhetoric likewise provided the forms and concepts that shaped the
discussion of moral issues since, as both Aristotle and Cicero had
emphasized, rhetoric was persuasion about the honorable, the virtuous, and the right and about particular cases in which the honorable,
the virtuous, and the right were at issue.

So it was that classical rhetoric provided the elements out of which
later casuistry developed: the concentration on an *issue* about which
there was an unresolved controversy, the introduction of *maxims*
which were relevant to the issue, the presentation of *set arguments*
that were appropriate to either side of the issue, the emphasis on the
attributes of persons and actions, and the move to *closure* in arriving
at a verdict or judgment. Rhetoric and casuistry were mutual allies.
It is not surprising to find the Jesuits, who were dedicated to teaching classical rhetoric in their colleges, become the leading proponents of casuistry.

PART II

The Precursors

In the next four sections of this book we will relate the birth, maturity, and decline of the casuistical tradition in the Christian Church. We have chosen this particular history not because parallel casuistic traditions, such as those of Judaism and Islam, are unimportant, but because Christian casuistry has had a significant influence on the moral thinking of our culture, both in substance and in style. Also, we are more familiar with the authors ideas, and background of this tradition. A review of this history will allow us to illustrate the principal features of casuistic thinking: notably, the ways in which moral argument is marked by its presumptive character and depends for its force on maxims interpreted in the light of circumstances.

This long story begins in the early decades of the Christian era and reaches its peak in the century between 1550 and 1650, followed by a slow decline. The first chapter will relate the beginnings of the tradition, from the era of the primitive Christian community to the heights of scholastic theology in the thirteenth century. During this time casuistry as a full-scale enterprise did not yet exist; rather, the varied elements of casuistry were brought into existence, in the counsel of Church Fathers, the practices of penance, the formulations of the canon lawyers, and the speculations of the theologians. The next section will review the period we shall call "high casuistry," beginning in the early fourteenth century and peaking between the mid-sixteenth and seventeenth centuries. It was during these centuries, filled with extraordinary religious, political, and economic changes, that "casuistry," properly speaking, flourished. There was a well-recognized casuistic enterprise, with its own authors and public debate. During this period the casuists found their method and presented it with a clarity and vigor that made them the advisors of popes and princes. But that method had its frailties also. We shall give an account of the two main blows that shattered the public reputation of casuistry. One of these shattering blows, the dispute over "probabilism," came from within the casuistic enterprise itself: the other, which is more familiar to modern readers of intellectual history, came from outside, in the form of the satirical attack on the Jesuit casuists in Blaise Pascal's *Provincial Letters*.

We add to this historical section a review of three cases that are illustrative of this crucial debate. These cases discuss the morality of usury, truth telling, and self-defense. The casuists wrote on these issues repeatedly, at length, over a long span of time, and their opinions were of considerable social, cultural, and religious moment. A review of the casuists' discussion not only provides a concrete example of casuistry at its most vigorous but also serves to illustrate the general features of this style of practical moral thinking. In these three exemplary cases we see the casuists at work.

Our account of this long history is unavoidably sketchy and fragmentary. Much of the relevant material lies unstudied in libraries and archives; many of the important authors have slipped from scholarly view; their works are scarcely known, and their cultural situation is only dimly understood. Even the major texts from the era of high casuistry remain almost inaccessible: not a single one of the leading Catholic casuists of that era has been published in a modern critical edition. Further, the volume of casuistical literature is enormous: even the single works of individual casuists are massive books and discuss hundreds of cases. Given the amount of material involved, it would be a daunting task to produce a comprehensive scholarly account of this subject; but despite these limitations, it is possible to offer a general account of the casuistical tradition that reveals many of the features that make this tradition interesting for the analysis of practical moral thinking.

4

Christian Origins

The Christian faith came into being within the bosom of Rabbinic Judaism which already had a flourishing casuistry. Rabbinic casuistry grew out of the extensive case law of the canonical books of Exodus, Leviticus, and Deuteronomy, in which Jahweh revealed to the People the "commandments, statutes and ordinances." Not surprisingly, we find echoes of that casuistry in the New Testament. Jesus is acknowledged as a rabbi—indeed, as a great rabbi—but he chooses to teach in controversial and contentious ways. He asserts that the Law of Judaism in its highest form, the Decalogue, is incumbent upon his followers, but he ranks discipleship to himself as even more imperative. "Observe all these Commandments, but if you would be perfect, go sell all you possess and follow me."[1] Duties to family, even the sacred duty to bury the dead, are abrogated in order to follow him.[2] He antagonizes the rabbis by annulling the Jewish law of divorce, violating the sabbath, and tolerating laxity about ceremonial precepts among his disciples.[3] He answers their objections using forms of arguments that are already familiar to them: appealing to a text of canonical scripture, drawing distinctions, and offering contrasts and comparisons. Over and over he adds the unconventional and shocking reference to himself: "You were taught. . . but I tell you," and even more outrageous, "Whoever would save his life will lose it, and he who loses his life for my sake will find it."[4] Moral challenges, moral paradoxes, hard sayings, and abrupt revisions of familiar rules constitute the ethical teaching of Jesus. This sort of teaching was an invitation to casuistry.[5]

In the decades after Jesus' death, his followers repeatedly encountered the kind of problem that generates casuistical thinking: a conflict of basic obligations. The original converts to the new faith came from within Judaism, but they soon found themselves joined by gentiles and pagans. Were all of the moral and ritual obligations of Judaism to be imposed upon these new converts? Should they even be observed by Christians of Jewish origin? In the year 44, a gathering of leading Christians at Jerusalem wrestled with the problem and decided that the gentile converts need observe only those moral precepts that God had imposed upon Adam and which, according to the rabbis, were binding not only on Israel but on all humankind.[6] This so-called Noachic law required abstinence "from the pollution of idols, from unchastity, from what is strangled and from blood." The Council justified this resolution by stating, "There is no distinction between us and them . . . God who knows the heart has made no distinction between us . . . for all are saved by the grace of the Lord Jesus."[7]

Sent to preach the faith to the gentiles, the Apostle Paul faced similar cases. In Corinth, which was a center of pagan cults, Christian converts were troubled in conscience. Could they eat the meat sacrificed to idols, which was commonly sold in the market? Should they do so if invited to dine with pagans? Paul analyzed the case in rabbinic fashion. He cites Psalm 24, "The earth is the Lord's and everything in it": this means, he reasons, that nothing is unclean and that ritual meats may be eaten. Christians might refrain from eating it, however, if they saw that eating would lead their pagan hosts to believe that Christians did not distinguish between their own God and the idols to whom the meat had been sacrificed. Paul adds that if an individual Christian did believe that the idol meats were unclean, then for that person they were so. "Nothing is unclean in itself, but it is unclean for him who thinks it so."[8] Paul's letters dealt with many other cases of conscience: for instance, conduct toward an unfaithful Christian, marriage between Christians and unbelievers, and the behavior of women in liturgical services.[9]

The literature of the early Church exhorted Christians to follow the way of Christ rather than the way of the world: they must avoid violence, anger, and adultery and live in peace, patience, and fidelity. But as the young Church encountered the exigencies of the world within which it had to live, it became increasingly necessary to decide how one might actually fulfill those imperatives in real situations. Service in the military, cooperation with pagans, observance of vows, questions about marriage, behavior during persecution, all became the subjects for casuistical consideration. So we find early ecclesiastical councils rendering decisions about particular cases. These cases were often of major import. The Council of Elvira (A.D. 300) decreed that a married Christian who leaves her adulterous husband and remarries must refrain from the eucharist until her deathbed. Other cases may appear to us as trivial: the Council of Ancyra (A.D. 314), for example, required Christians who favored vegetarianism to dip vegetables occasionally into meat gravy, so as to show that their dietary practice was based on personal preference, not on any Christian principle.

The three centuries after the founding of the Church are commonly referred to as the Patristic era, after the eminent writers on Christian belief and practice, known as the *Patres Ecclesiae*, or Church Fathers. Although these authors concentrated on scriptural exegesis, theology, controversy, and exhortation, they included in their pages many cases dealing with the confrontation between Christians and the pagan world and secular life. Two examples of this patristic case morality are St. Cyprian's "On the Treatment of Lapsed Christians," and St. Clement of Alexandria's "Can a Rich Man Be Saved?" St. Cyprian discussed the case of Christians who had apostacized during the Dacian persecution (A.D. 250), some of whom excused themselves by claiming they renounced their faith out of fear of torture. The bishop argues that this is not an excuse, since the apostates had the opportunity to flee persecution rather than renounce their faith. Although flight might be considered cowardly under ordinary circumstances, it was obligatory if they anticipated that their weakness might betray them into apostasy.

Clement of Alexandria responded to the problems of conscience that were experienced by wealthy Christians who were troubled by Jesus' words, "It is harder for a rich man to be saved than for a camel to pass through the eye of a needle."[10] Clement's case study, "Can a Rich Man Be Saved?" distinguishes between spiritual poverty—that is, a personal detachment from one's possessions demonstrated by the willingness to give generously from them—and actual poverty—that is, a sheer lack of material possessions. He concludes that it is the "poor in spirit" who will be saved. The same author composed a lengthy treatise, *The Teacher*, which has been described as "a book of casuistry in which stoic and Christian inspiration are blended." Many other Church Fathers left their own samples of casuistry. Still, although the concern to give moral advice is everywhere apparent, the patristic literature does not provide a developed casuistry, either in content or in method.[11]

Several of the Church Fathers made a concerted effort to apply the principles of Stoicism to the Christian ethos. Clement of Alexandria did so in the fashion of the popular Stoic teacher, Musonius Rufus, offering sage advice, many examples, and much exhortation. Others followed closely in the footsteps of Cicero: for example, Lactantius and Ambrose of Milan, both of whom commented on the moral quandaries cited in book III of Cicero's *De Officiis*, turning Cicero's casuistry to Christian purpose by introducing the example of Christ and Gospel texts as "maxims." Lactantius (240–320) agreed with the skeptic Carneades, who had originally proposed the cases, that no one can completely escape the moral paradoxes they present. He then suggested that persons illuminated by God's grace and by the example of Christ would willingly sacrifice life rather than allow another to die.[12] Ambrose, Bishop of Milan (339–397) patterned his own *De Officiis Ministrorum* on the Roman's treatise, and also revised Cicero's resolution of the cases. In discussing the case of the shipwreck survivors, he noted that a Christian would never be justified in saving his own life at the cost of another's.

> Although it might be advantageous for the common good that the wise man rather than the simple man should live, the Christian does not have the right to save his life by the death of another; just as when he meets an armed robber, he cannot return his blows lest by defending himself, he should stain his love toward his neighbor. The Gospel is plain, "Put up thy sword."[13]

Ambrose revised the fundamental distinction of Stoic moral theory: *kathormata* or *officia perfecta* are equated with the Gospel imperatives of sacrifice, forgiveness, concern for the poor; whereas *kathekonta* or *officia imperfecta* are equated with observance of the commandments. He based this revision on the Gospel story of the young man whom Jesus first exhorted to "keep the commandments" and, when pressed, then added, "If you wish to be perfect, go sell all and follow me."[14] So Ambrose introduced into Christian moral thought the hierarchical distinction between "commandments" and "counsels of perfection," a distinction that was to become one of the major interpretative principles of subsequent casuistry.[15]

In the vast corpus of his writings, Augustine of Hippo, too, proposed a multitude of cases. His two treatises on lying will be discussed later; but over innumerable other moral issues, such as questions about sexuality, war, commerce, and political authority, Augustine's opinions came to be accepted as magisterial, and his dicta became standard maxims for later casuistry. Yet even in the work of this great spiritual genius it is once again not possible to discern a systematic moral theory.[16]

One curious patristic text deserves notice. Pope Gregory I (540–604) composed an allegorical interpretation of the Book of Job. At the text, "the sinews of Behemoth's testicles are tightly entwined,"[17] the pope takes a verbal cue from the Latin word for "tightly entwined": namely, *perplexi*. He remarks that the temptations of the Devil (Behemoth) are such as to cause "perplexity" to good people, since the devil can make it appear that whatever a person does to resolve a moral difficulty will itself be immoral. Gregory offers three cases. In the first case, two men promise to observe total honesty with each other, on condition that all shared information is kept between them alone. One partner then learns that the other is involved in adultery and plans to murder his mistress's husband: should he now break his promise, or must he become an accessory to murder? In the second case, a man takes a vow of obedience to a religious superior as a means of avoiding the temptations of secular life, and that same superior then orders him to engage in worldly business: should he disobey or, by obeying, place himself in danger of sin? The third case concerns a priest who has obtained a pastorate by bribery and now, having repented, wonders whether he should give up his office and so leave his parishioners without spiritual care. The pope proposes these three cases as genuine moral paradoxes. In all such cases (he advises), the lesser evil must be chosen. This advice is, in itself, less interesting than the appearance in these cases of the "perplexed person," who cannot help doing wrong whatever course is followed: the subject of the *perplexed conscience* was to become a common topic in later casuistry.[18]

In a primitive way, the patristic literature hints at several features of more mature casuistry. First, although this literature is in great part theological and exegetical, it contains moral teachings that are not only general and exhortative but practical and advisory. It initiates the genre of moral writing called "pastoral." Certain of these authors also make important moves toward casuistry. Ambrose introduces a hierarchy of principles of different stringency; Augustine, as we shall see later, develops his argument by testing apparent exceptions to a strong rule; Gregory concedes the possibility of a genuine conflict of principles that allows no "faultless" resolution of a moral dilemma. All these ideas were to flow into the stream of thought that became the Christian casuistry of late medieval times.

PENITENTIAL BOOKS

Christian concern with the state of each individual's life and soul introduced a crucial new element into the moral discussion. The Christian message was one of salvation offered to the individual; the individual alone, regardless of social status or tribal identity, was responsible for grasping the Divine offer of Grace. As St. Paul declared,

> There is neither Jew nor Gentile, there is neither slave nor free, there is neither male nor female; for you are all one in Jesus Christ. . . . Let each one test his own work, and then his reason to boast will be in himself and not in his neighbor.[19]

Controversies during the early centuries of the Church, particularly over the Pelagian and Manichean heresies in the fifth century, sharpened the appreciation of the individual's uniqueness and personal responsibility.

In particular, theological disputes over the nature of Jesus as God and Man introduced the notion of "person" to describe the rational individual. In Roman law the word "person" had referred not to the unique self as such but to the legal status of the individual. The jurist Gaius had written, "The main distinction in the law of persons is this, that all men are either free or slaves."[20] By the sixth century of the Christian era, it was agreed that the term "person" referred to an individual, called by God to accept grace, fully and freely responsible for acts that welcomed or rejected this divine call.[21]

This theological stance was translated into ecclesiastical practice. Initially life in segregated Christian communities (e.g., monasteries) had encouraged the practices of spiritual guidance and self-examination that developed into confession and the performance of penances. From the sixth century the state of every Christian's soul became a matter of intense concern. The individual stood accountable before God and God's Church for his or her deeds, and individual confession and penance became customary in the Church. The books written to guide clergy and faithful in that practice—called *Penitentials*—became the earliest examples of casuistry. Because the individual person was the penitent sinner, the nature and seriousness of any sin, and the corresponding penalty imposed by the priest, could be highly individualized. In the preface to a *Penitential* attributed to the Venerable Bede, who died in the year 735, we find a taxonomic concern with "the circumstances of the case" clearly manifested:

> Not all persons are to be weighed in one and the same balance, although they be associated in one fault, but there shall be discrimination for each of these, rich or poor; freeman or slave; small child, boy, youth, young man or old man; stupid or intelligent; layman, cleric or monk; bishop, presbyter, deacon, subdeacon or reader, ordained or unordained; married or unmarried; pilgrim, virgin, canoness, or nuns; the weak, the sick or the well.
>
> The priest shall make a distinction for the character of the sins or of the men—a continent person or one who is incontinent; [for acts performed] wilfully or by accident; in public or in secret; with what compunction [a penitent] makes amends; under compulsion or voluntarily; the time and place [of the fault], and so on.[22]

This appreciation of individual distinctiveness and of the diversity of situations in which persons find themselves is essential to casuistry. The *Penitential Books* are the first manifestation of this appreciation working itself out in a primitive casuistry. These books are rich but tantalizingly terse sources of information about the Christian understanding of morality at a time when Christian culture was emerging from its pre-Christian antecedents.

During the early centuries of Christianity, theologians hammered out a doctrine of sin and repentance. Sin, in one important sense, is defined as an act contrary to the law of God, done knowingly and freely. The sinner could, with God's grace, repent; and after confession before the Church and its ministers could be absolved and restored to communion, on condition that certain humbling acts, imposed by the Church's ministers, were performed as an outward sign of repentance and submission. The severity of penance was measured by the seriousness of the offense. Three offenses (apostasy, murder, and adultery) demanded a lifetime of public humiliation and exclusion from communion, until the imminence of death. For these sinners only one repentance and absolution was available. The early book, *Pastor of Hermes* (c. 120 A.D.), advised that an adulterous woman should be taken back by her husband, "but only once, because, to the servants of God, there is but one penance."[23] Other sinful acts were considered less serious and deserved less severe and extended penances.

In its earliest form the penitential rite consisted of public confession before the bishop and the assembled community. In the sixth century the older rite began to be replaced by the practice of private confession to a priest followed by public penance. This new format was particularly popular in the British Isles; and in the churches of Ireland, England, and Scotland lists of sinful acts and appropriate penances were drawn up. These lists, compiled by local church councils and by "most learned persons," were intended to aid the confessor in selecting a penance proportionate to the seriousness of the sin. These lists composed the substance of the *Penitential Books* and retained their popularity until the tenth or eleventh century, although in later years they were often criticized by Church authorities as "filled with clear errors by unclear authors."[24]

The typical list consisted of very short statements in which a sinful act is named and an appropriate penance assigned. The sins are generally the familiar repertoire: homicide, battery, adultery, fornication, theft, and so on: homosexuality and bestiality are frequently mentioned. Mixed in with these are ritual offenses that arise in the performance of religious duties. The penances include exile from one's home, suspension from clerical office or duties, fasts of varying lengths from particular foods or wine, restitution or donation to the poor, abstention from marital relations, recitation of certain prayers. In many but not in all cases, some aggravating or mitigating circumstances are noted that increase or diminish the necessary penance. Thus the *Penitential of Cummean* (c. 650) describes the sin of perjury, subdividing it according to various additional features:

8. He who makes a false oath shall do penance for four years.
9. He who leads another in ignorance to commit perjury shall do penance for seven years.

10. He who is led in ignorance to commit perjury and afterward finds it out, one year.
11. He who suspects that he is being led into perjury and nevertheless swears, shall do penance for two years on account of his consent.[25]

Though sometimes prefaced with a short essay on the nature of sin, repentance, and grace, usually excerpted from the Scripture and the writings of the Fathers, the early *Penitentials* contain little more than these bare lists. However, the confessor is instructed "to note how long the sinner persisted in the sin, what understanding he has, by what passions he was assailed, how great was his strength and by what oppressions he was driven to his sin."[26] The role, rank, and station in life of the penitent is important: priest or monk or bishop, married or widowed, mature or youthful, relation by blood or marriage, neighbor or stranger. Differences in accountability are recognized: "he who slays his brother, not from malice aforethought, but from sudden anger," receives a lesser penance than the severe seven-year exile prescribed for an unqualified homicide.[27] Later penitentials become quite explicit about conditions and motives. The *Penitential of Burchard* (c. 1010), for example, writes,

> Robbery deserves a heavier penance than burglary, for it is worse to seize something by force in the owner's sight than to take it while he sleeps or is away from home. If theft is committed because of penury so great that one has no means of sustenance and is pinched by hunger . . . and the thief does not have the habit of stealing, what has been stolen shall be restored and penance of three Fridays on bread and water shall be done. If it cannot be restored because it has been devoured, a heavier penance should be imposed.[28]

The idea of differences in the seriousness of sin, with some proportionate severity of penance, dominates these books. They are concerned with "weighing the seriousness of acts" in a way unknown in earlier moral writing. Money, then as now, serves as a convenient metric or measure of value, and (though it is rare to find a specific monetary penance stated in the books) it became common practice to permit the penitent to donate specific amounts of money to the Church or to the poor as a substitute for the difficult physical penances. In this way the seriousness of acts was given some quantitative reference. The penitentials hardly ever set forth any rationale for the various distinctions; but a primitive thesis about the evaluation of moral action does appear in some of these books. The *Bigotan Penitential* (c. late seventh century) compares the task of the confessor to that of the physician:

> Let the power of the physician become greater to the degree the illness of the patient increases. He who would heal spiritual wounds should carefully consider the age and sex of the sinner, his social condition and so forth . . . the cure should be contrary to the sin.[29]

This comparison derives from a contemporary medical doctrine, Methodism, which proposed that "contraries be cured by contraries." This medical maxim had been popularized as a spiritual metaphor by Abbot Cassian (360–35) and was applied in a rough-and-ready way to penances: exile for homicide, seclusion in a monastery for adultery, fasting for various sorts of self-indulgence. This thesis became a common theme in the Penitentials and was invoked later by the Lateran Council (1215) in a decree that was to stimulate the growth of casuistry.

The penitential literature, then, was a seedbed for later casuistry. It emphasized acts and decisions as central elements in the moral life. It defined the basic structure of any moral situation: an individual, characterized in a certain way, performs an act of a certain kind, with a specific intention, and in a particular state of mind. It stressed discrimination between acts and their evaluation in the light of the stated circumstances. But in this literature all these things still remained inchoate and unorganized: little theory elucidated practice. Yet the seeds of casuistry had been planted, and the outlines for a taxonomy of moral action had been sketched, broadly but in a more detailed way than in earlier moral philosophy. The descriptions, distinctions, justifications, and evaluations of actions that made up this primitive taxonomy are the starting points from which the moral discourse of our own time has evolved.

5

The Canonists and Confessors

As an explicit procedure for resolving moral problems, casuistry did not originate until after A.D. 1000, and one can learn something by asking why this was so. Certainly the central issues for moral analysis were recognized much earlier. As *questions* they were discussed more or less unsystematically in classical times by Sophists and philosophers from Gorgias to Aristotle, by legislators and rhetoricians from Solon to Cicero, and by pastors and theologians from St. Paul to St. Augustine. Yet only from around A.D. 1050 did there exist groups of practitioners—confessors and canon lawyers—whose professional tasks demanded more explicit and systematic *answers* to those questions. In this respect, the emergence of casuistry was a direct response to the specific needs of professional practice.

Behind the new method lay a particular historical occasion. What was it, then, about the years between A.D. 1000 and 1200 that made those professional needs urgent at this particular stage? Casuistry is only one of a group of novel intellectual achievements of this period; and we shall understand its origins only by seeing them all in their historical setting and relating them in turn to other broader changes—social and economic, political and institutional—that were under way during the eleventh and twelfth centuries. A European Rip van Winkle who fell asleep in the late tenth century and awoke two hundred years later would have found it hard to recognize the culture and society he had left behind. In city and country, urban life and social organization, and above all in literacy and learning, the years from 1050 to 1200 saw the true beginnings of that new age which comes into our minds when we hear the phrase "medieval Europe."

After the decline of Rome and the Germanic invasions, population in Western Europe became highly dispersed and largely rural. As late as A.D. 1050 none of the great cities of medieval Europe, with their splendid cathedrals and busy mercantile centers, yet existed. At this time Constantinople, heir to the Byzantine or Eastern Roman Empire and focus of Orthodox Christianity, had hundreds of thousands of inhabitants: in Western Europe, perhaps two dozen towns had more than 2,000, and only two (Venice and London) had as many as 10,000. From 1050 to 1200 there was an urban explosion much like that which has taken place in tropical Africa and other underdeveloped areas during the last half of the twentieth century. By A.D. 1250 dozens of European cities had populations larger than 30,000, and the largest trading and manufacturing centers had more than 100,000 inhabitants each.[1]

So dramatic a demographic transformation did not leave the social or political character of national life untouched. Before A.D. 1000 political authority was as dispersed as the human beings who were subject to it. Even the Merovingian monarch Charlemagne, who was crowned Emperor of the Franks at Aachen in A.D. 800 and ruled a wide area from France to Northern Italy and as far east as Hungary, never had anything resembling a capital city of the kind that Rome had previously been and Constantinople still was. His court was continually on the move, traveling around his territories on circuit, dispensing royal justice, patronage, and clemency. Nor before A.D. 1000 were mercantile activities any more extensive or centralized: the economic life of Western Europe was as dispersed and localized as its population and political power. The world of masters and apprentices, guilds and moneylenders that is familiar to us today from *Die Meistersinger von Nürnberg* came into being only as part of the "new creation" of medieval urban Europe.

With the rise of commerce and urban life there grew up also a newly self-confident class of literate persons, or *clerici*, who could read, write, and figure. They included not just "clergy" or "clerics" in the modern sense of those terms, but also lawyers, bankers, scholars, teachers, and physicians, and their knowledge gave them power. Earlier the tasks of the Christian priesthood in Western Europe were as local and limited as all other social functions. Now the Church was in a position to mobilize its capacities as a universal community of literate scholars and administrators who could assert their claim to operate in a strictly professional way independent of the rough, uneducated, and often illiterate kings, dukes, barons, or other magnates who exercised local power over provinces and nations.

The initiative in pressing these claims was taken by Hildebrand, who was elected pope in A.D. 1073 as Gregory VII. Gregory made it his task to transform the Church of Rome from the loose spiritual association of local priests and bishops that it had been in the West for hundreds of years into a centralized ecclesiastical organization with its own political and judicial power. Perpetuated and reinforced by the work of his successors, his work enabled the Church to take over prime responsibility for defining, discussing, and pronouncing on all kinds of higher intellectual questions—questions of collective jurisprudence, mercantile propriety, and political sovereignty, quite as much as personal ethics. And the kings and barons, whose social control was localized and fragmented, could not ignore the well-argued decrees of this literate and opinionated new transnational institution. Now and then secular rulers might be tempted to resist it, but the papacy very soon got the bit between its teeth, recruited military help from more cooperative sovereigns, and used it to bring recalcitrant sovereigns (quite literally, in some cases) to their knees. At the close of this consolidation, in the year 1302, Pope Boniface VIII could declare with impunity that all temporal and spiritual power resided, by Divine decree, in the Roman Pontiff.[2]

A key part in the consolidation of ecclesiastical power was played by the new communities of scholars and teachers that grew up at Bologna, Paris, Oxford, and elsewhere. For lack of specialized functions, the social institutions of Western Europe before the year A.D. 1000 were largely undifferentiated. Gregory VII's reforms claimed for the Roman Church "universal" and transnational authority and functions, as a basis for declaring the Church an institution with corporate power: so it became the first corporation or, in legal Latin, *universitas*. This same name and status (of corporations, or "universities") attached to the new academic collectives as well. These soon became magnets for able young men from all over Europe who, in joining a pan-European élite of administrators and ecclesiastics, teachers and scholars, looked for a more rewarding career than they could ever have as liege subjects and soldiers to an illiterate Frankish count or petty English earl.

A major attraction of Bologna lay in the legal curriculum developed there by "Irnerius" (Guarneri) and his colleagues. Beginning about 1087, this teaching was copied in universities across Europe, from Salamanca in Spain to Cracow in Poland. Before A.D. 1000, matters of law and ethics were settled in accord with customary beliefs and traditional procedures, which were as local and diverse as most things in Europe at that time. From the late eleventh century the "universal" community of churchmen and scholars began to ask searching questions about ethics, politics, and law, seeking a basis for their arguments that would be less dependent than hitherto on the oddities and vagaries of local custom and belief. In short, twelfth-century Europe saw a new class of literate scholars and lawyers setting out to "rationalize" the confused bodies of customary law and morality by which life and society had hitherto been governed.

A prime instrument for this rationalization was Roman law, which came to Bologna by way of a compilation originating at the court of the Emperor Justinian in the sixth century A.D. This compilation is sometimes referred to as "the Code of Justinian"; but if the word *code* is understood in its modern sense, it is a misnomer. Just as Roman lawyers were slow to develop generalized rules of law (*regulae*), they never did much to "codify" or "systematize" their legal doctrines. In legal affairs as in other matters, the Roman taste for practicality expressed itself through an emphasis on the concrete, with minimum attention to theories or concepts. Most Roman lawyers were content to work with unsystematic collections of earlier holdings about actual cases, together with edicts from praetors about other hypothetical cases, and the compilation of Justinian was little more systematic than this.[3]

The notion that Roman law formed a complete and systematic "body" or corpus (the *Corpus Juris Romani*) was an invention of medieval scholars of jurisprudence at Bologna in the twelfth century. This very use of the term *corpus* is, in fact, a twelfth-century coinage that was not shared by the classical Romans themselves:

> Law students in Europe today, who study Roman law as it has been systematized by university professors in the West since the twelfth century, find it hard to believe that the original texts were so intensely casuistic and untheoretical. They are taught to show that

implicit in the myriad of narrow rules and undefined general terms
was a complex system of abstract concepts . . . [in] contrast to the
alleged particularism and pragmatism of English and American law.

But that is to view the Roman law of Justinian through the eyes of
later European jurists; it was they who . . . made a theory of contract
law out of particular types of Roman contracts [and] systematized the
older texts on the basis of broad principles and concepts.[4]

The medieval belief in the systematic character of Roman law was
thus a fiction. Yet this fiction had great value for the "clerics" of the
new age. To begin with, it gave them a template to use in the critical
analysis of the new legal and moral issues that needed resolving in
their own times. This is not to say that the doctrines that scholars
inferred from the Roman *corpus* were taken as generally binding in
the world of practical affairs: kings and dukes did not overturn
immemorial customs in response to an academic whim. Still, Roman
law did provide medieval scholars with a "model code," which lent
color to the view that better could be done in a newly literate period
than simply accept, in all their variety, local doctrines and procedures inherited from an earlier oral age without criticizing them
against "rational" standards.

Two examples will illustrate the spirit in which that criticism was
conducted. First, in matters of procedure, judicial practice over
much of Western Europe still required accused persons to bring into
court friendly witnesses who were prepared to swear to their innocence ("oath-helpers"). Both the accused and their witnesses were
subject to physical tests of veracity ("ordeals")—procedures that are
typical of preliterate cultures. By contrast, the new ecclesiastical
courts were run by literate clerks and judges who introduced many
procedures that are regarded today as indispensable for the administration of true justice: written accusations, representation by counsel, and sworn answers to questions. Indeed, in the year A.D. 1215 a
decree of the Fourth Lateran Council prohibited priests from taking
part in ordeals, so "forcing the secular authorities to adopt new trial
procedures in criminal cases."[5] Second, in matters of substance,
many Germanic tribes still encouraged parents, for example, to
marry off children at an early age. The Church and its lawyers,
however, regarded matrimony as a matter for consenting adults; and
by taking over matrimonial law, the ecclesiastical courts imposed
more modern and "rational" practices on the preliterate society of
northern and Western Europe. Thus the Church courts came to play

many of the same exemplary roles in the judicial practice of medieval Europe that the federal courts are supposed to play in the judicial practice of the contemporary United States: as a forum that insists on stringent procedural standards or safeguards and presents more enlightened legal interpretation than is always practicable within the courts of the individual states.

The assumption that Roman law had always been systematic was of value also for purposes of legal instruction. At Bologna the law curriculum was initially built around the systematic exposition and discussion of Roman texts. Soon summaries and glosses by medieval commentators displaced those texts: these served (in a modern sense) as "restatements" of the different branches of the law. So historical developments that had begun in Rome were finally worked out in medieval Europe.[6] It was there that in response to critical appeals by scholars to "the demands of rationality," the traditional multiplicity of oral laws, procedures, and jurisdictions gave way to a uniform literate code of concepts and practices. And it was the resulting standardized code that the universities transmitted under the title of "Roman law," as providing an ideal standard for assessing and reforming actual bodies of local substantive law.

The fundamental motives for the medieval codification of Roman law were accordingly practical and concrete, not theoretical or abstract. The need to consider the whole corpus of law as a "system" sprang not from any theoretical taste for the abstract rigor and necessity of mathematics but from the practical needs of men who sought to teach effective ways of dealing with concrete problems of law and justice. The general concepts and principles in terms of which medieval scholars restated the implicit content of Roman law were thus taxonomic rather than geometrical. They organized the detailed holdings and edicts embodied in the classical texts *substantively*—in terms appropriate to any particular subject matter—not *formally*, as "theorems" deduced from universal and invariable "axioms." Then as now, a law professor's tasks were to expound the basic doctrines covering issues of each kind, to present cases that illustrated those issues, and to discuss particular examples designed to elucidate and resolve any apparent ambiguities and inconsistencies in the doctrines.[7]

Against this historical background we may look at three final topics before turning to the evolution of Catholic casuistry between the eleventh and seventeenth centuries: (1) the relations of casuistry to the case law and politics of the time; (2) the presumptive character of judicial and moral proof, based on paradigmatic cases and analogies; and (3) the adaptability of the medieval *corpus juris*, and related moral ideas, to changes in the social, economic, and political conditions. As we shall see, casuistical methods for resolving moral issues developed in ways that paralleled and were strongly influenced by the emergence of the professional class of churchmen and lawyers, the establishment of the ecclesiastical courts, and the associated innovations in legal methods and procedures.

Hitherto the distinction among law, ethics, and politics had been ill-marked. The turbulence of participatory democracy in Athens provided little occasion for insisting on these distinctions, and the customary basis of Roman life turned *mores* into a broader category than our own morality.[8] Meanwhile in Judaism, the contrast between the legal and the moral was (and still is) little more than a subdivision within the broader sphere of "the Law." By Pope Gregory VII's time a distinction was recognized between, on the one hand, questions about sin, grace, and actions for which a Christian agent ought to experience private shame or satisfaction, and, on the other hand, questions about crime, innocence, and actions for which public praise or punishment were appropriate. The division between the "ethical" and the "legal" thus became clearer; but although the realms were more clearly *distinct*, they were not kept *separate*.

After Gregory VII's centralization of Church authority, the informal rulings of the bishops and abbots, rendered often in penitential contexts, were absorbed into the Church's canon law and became the concern of the ecclesiastical courts. Thereafter differences among moral, legal, and political issues were acknowledged without insulating politics and law from moral criticism. Findings of individual fault could be an occasion either for private penance or public punishment, or both. So, after the assassination of Thomas à Becket, King Henry II of England was required, in 1172, to do penance by walking barefoot to the Cathedral at Canterbury, making public submission to the papal legate in Normandy and renouncing the offensive parts of the "Constitutions of Clarendon" in which he had reasserted royal power over the English Church. In this way the judicial action of the Church publicly exposed him to both political and moral humiliation at the same time.[9]

In its judicial capacity the Church reserved jurisdiction over certain classes of persons—clergy, students, and crusaders; the poor, widows, and orphans; Jews in dealings with Christians; sailors, merchants, and other travelers. All these persons fell outside the local network of citizens with whom the secular courts might be relied on to deal fairly, so they stood in need of the Church's protection. (It was, in any case, objectionable for literate professionals to be exposed to the rough justice of an oral folk law.) The Church reserved jurisdiction over some kinds of subject matter, too: for example, matrimony and the sacraments, benefices and testaments, oaths and pledges of faith, and other matters of Church concern. All these issues had strong moral components and demanded subtler and more reflective consideration than the secular folk courts could provide.[10] In this way the Church's stake in ethics projected its concerns beyond the realm of the personal and required it to act in the judicial and political realms also.

The methods of medieval law, politics, and ethics were also interconnected. If over the next centuries the standard pattern of moral analysis was casuistical, that was an inheritance from Roman practical law, which had been equally casuistic. And just as Roman law was taught as a taxonomic (not a geometrical) "system," so too the ethical doctrines of medieval theologians and philosophers were taxonomic and practical, not geometrical and theoretical. Sound judgment in resolving problems of moral practice depended on recognizing crucial resemblances and differences between new and problematic cases and available paradigmatic cases. Ethics was not a "moral geometry" in which one could "prove" that any new case fell unambiguously under some strict universal and invariable definition of, for example, courage or temperance, treachery or murder. Nor were the merits of a case formally entailed by any such definition. Rather, arriving at sound resolutions required one to see how far and in what respects the parallels between problematic cases and more familiar paradigmatic cases could justify *counting them as* cases of "courage" or "treachery."

Nor were the resulting judgments beyond question. Questions of practical morals might always be reopened in the light of fresh considerations. The interim conclusions reached were, at best, presumptive and provisional: deeper understanding of the character of an agent and the circumstances of an act might oblige one to reconsider the conclusions and perhaps qualify them. In practical morals as in case law, the need was not to come up with only *one* label (or "paradigm") that settled a matter beyond all possible doubt: rather, it was to be open to all relevant objects of comparison and weigh the question, just *which* of the alternative models best matched the detailed "fact situation" in the current case.[11]

The difference between an axiomatic and a taxonomic approach to ethics becomes clearer if we contrast the way in which Thomas Aquinas and other medieval writers used the Latin terms *absolutus, absolutê* and their cognates with the ways in which the corresponding English words—"absolute," "absolutely," and the like—are understood today. Writing in the rhetorical tradition of Aristotelian ethics, Aquinas describes an action as wrong *absolutê*, or *malum in se*; but in doing so he is not declaring that it is wrong necessarily and universally, invariably and without exception. Quite the reverse:

> A thing taken in its primary consideration, *absolutê*, may be good or bad; yet when additional considerations are taken into account may be changed into the contrary.[12]

The wrong of homicide or theft, for example, is a point of principle in one sense: it is a type of action whose presumable wrongness is not *generally* in doubt—*malum abstracte accipiendo, in se malum, simpliciter malum*. But it is not a universal and invariable axiom: because of their special circumstances, a few particular acts of homicide or theft became pardonable, justifiable, or (at the very least) excusable. Medieval scholars, in fact, used the Latin words *absolutus* and *absolutê* much as we use the phrases, "all other things being equal," "in itself," or even (in our modern "dog" Latin) *prima facie*. To say that theft (say) is wrong *absolutê* thus meant to them, "In the absence of exceptional extenuating circumstances, theft is wrong." In other words, "You should *presume* that any act of theft is wrong, unless and until those exceptional extenuating considerations come to your attention."

But such abstract consideration was a luxury. Medieval theologians and philosophers well understood what limits the needs of their time placed on the scope of their speculations. General discussions of theological doctrine, and particular reflections on concrete moral issues, were alike pursued under the pressure of practical demands, legal and political on the one hand, pastoral or personal on the other:

Realism in the Platonic sense, however convincing it might be as metaphysics, was wholly alien to the effort of twelfth century jurists to classify, divide, distinguish, interpret, generalize, synthesize, and harmonize the great mass of decisions, customs, canons, decrees, writs, laws, and other legal materials that constituted the legal order of the time.

To have postulated, in Platonic style, the external reality of justice, equality, consistency, procedural regularity, and the other universal principles, and to have attempted to deduce from them specific legal rules and institutions, would have been a futile academic exercise. Such an abstract system would have been no use to the emerging polities, ecclesiastical or secular.[13]

An unlegalistic, unlitigious attitude toward law and ethics had deep roots in Western Europe. The *Laws of Henry the First*, promulgated between 1110 and 1120, presented a traditional view:

> [It] repeatedly emphasized that English law preferred friendly settlement to litigation, *amor* or *amicitia* to *judicium*. "All causes are . . . preferably to be settled by friendly concord [*pax*]. . . .
> "Where any of them has the choice . . . of amicable agreement . . . this shall be as binding as a legal decision [*judicium*] itself."[14]

In the Anglo-Saxon jurisdiction, in fact, a preference for mediation was well established a century earlier. So the question to be asked is not "How was the idea of justice as equity *won*?": rather, it is "How was it *lost*?" As we shall see, the seventeenth-century intellectual revolution concealed the basic reasonableness of the casuists' approach to moral practice and ethical theory. And when we turn to consider seventeenth-century developments, we must ask why equity—like casuistry and rhetoric—was condemned to disrepute, and how the renewed demand for "geometrical" certainty by Descartes, Pascal, and their colleagues so completely overpowered the Aristotelian practicality of the medieval *clerici*.

Finally, we may note that the assumption that a religious system of ethics is always more *rigorous* than a secular system is one of two related misconceptions: its twin is the assumption that a religious system of ethics will always be more *inflexible* than a secular one. Here again our perception of the Aristotelian "practical philosophy" that evolved in Western Europe from A.D. 1100 on is clouded by the aftermath of the Reformation. There is in fact a striking contrast between the relative adaptability of the accepted corpus of legal and moral ideas in the period of the Church's greatest self-confidence, from 1150 to 1550, and the conservatism that set in as part of the Counter-Reformation, and particularly after the French Revolution. The scholars of twelfth-century Europe had a great advantage: they were an international body of learned professionals, and their problems were formulated in terms that did not depend on the special self-esteem or concerns of any particular nation or community:

> For three hundred years, from 1050 to 1350 . . . the whole of educated Europe formed a single and undifferentiated cultural unit. In the lands between Edinburgh and Palermo, Mainz or Lund and Toledo, a man of any city or village might go for education to any school, and become a prelate or official in any church, court, or university (when these existed) from north to south, from east to west. . . .
>
> The world of Church and State was often rent by schisms and wars, while the bulk of the population, fast rooted in the soil, knew nothing beyond the fields and woods of their small corner. But on the level of literature and thought there was one stock of words, forms, and thoughts from which all drew and in which all shared on an equality.[15]

So when it came to discussing the central issues of ethical theory, Christian scholars were in a different position from, for example, the rabbis of Judaism. The Judaic Law comprises 613 divine ordinances, addressed to the Jewish people as such: in the rabbinical tradition moral or legal obligations rested on one foundation for Jews, and on quite another for Gentiles. For twelfth-century Christians, by contrast, the further question opened: "Are not the fundamental insights of ethics a possession of all human beings equally?" No doubt believing Christians were subject to certain special obligations, which did not affect everyone else; but these special obligations could themselves be seen as falling under more general headings—as resting on the claims of loyalty, fidelity, or as duties that arose in consequence of a vow.

It was not courtesy alone, therefore, that led Christian scholars in medieval Europe to accept Cicero as an equal. Jewish and Muslim teachers have always found it hard to admit nonbelievers to discussions of moral issues on fully equal terms, even when they, too, are "People of the Book";[16] but this was not a problem for medieval scholars, who came from such varied backgrounds. Nor was there any insuperable difficulty when, following up Cicero's view of human nature, Thomas Aquinas pursued the same idea further, that the "common morality" shared by Christians and non-Christians alike rests on a *ratio naturalis* (a natural reasonableness or rationality) that is shared by human beings of all kinds equally.[17]

Then as now, the actual diversity to be found in moral beliefs and practices was of two kinds, "synchronic" and "diachronic." At any given time different peoples live rather differently; and any given people changes its ways of living from one time to another. Even today rabbinical scholars are locked in vehement disagreement about the historical status of the Jewish Law. Can social or historical circumstances change so radically as time goes on that one may need to revise traditional interpretations of the Law? Or do its terms speak to Jews in all lands and at every period so unambiguously that it is blasphemous to speak of it as having to be "interpreted" at all? Modernist rabbis contemplate an *evolving* Torah whose meaning to Jews in each historical period must be restated in terms appropriate to the current conditions of life. Orthodox rabbis resist this suggestion, arguing that the Law has an immutable and uninterpreted meaning for devout Jews in all places and at all times.[18]

Islamic theologians have similar disagreements about the meaning and relevance of the Qur'an for believers at different times and in different lands. They ask, "Is the Qur'an 'created' or 'uncreated'?" If it is created, then its present form presumably reflects the historical circumstances of that original creation; but if it is uncreated, then its current form is not conditioned by place or time, and can speak directly to the Faithful in all places and times. For a long time orthodox Islam has paralleled orthodox Jewish teaching: Muslim fundamentalists today reject any hints that the Qur'an's "meaning" is a cultural or historical variable. Given the rapidity of technological and social change in the Islamic world, however, from Iran to Indonesia and from Muscat to Morocco, other more "progressive minded" Muslims cannot help asking how far traditional readings of the Qur'an are relevant to their present situation, and looking for a view closer to that of Reform Judaism.[19]

To the literate and transnational élite who, from the year 1150 on, were responsible for the intellectual construction of European thought and practice, fundamentalism was uncongenial. In particular, when they described law or morality as a *corpus*, the implicit metaphor of an organism was meant seriously. A "body" of legal or moral practice might not, as it stood, consist of so many universal and eternal rules, all of them in strict conformity with Divine Command; but the notion that one could simply dismantle all of the inherited "positive" laws and customs and replace them at a stroke by the "immutable" Law of God was unrealistic to say the least. All of these positive practices were, evidently enough, the current outcomes of historical development in multiple localities over a thousand years; and there was no reason to suppose that this process was at an end. So theological appeals to "natural law" or "natural morality" were not arguments for imposing a single fixed system of moral rules on all nations at all times. Like the legal scholars' idealized system of Roman law, the moral theologians' idea of natural law served as a criterion for criticizing actual beliefs and practices at different times and among different peoples. Particular practices that met the rational demands of the natural law were, for the time being, free of criticism; those that could be modified so as to bring them more in line with those demands were, to that extent, improved; and so on. That is the only standardization that the general situation in twelfth-century Europe admitted, and it is all that the medieval "clerics" were really concerned to insist on.

When the creation of Europe began around 1150, no one could foresee what social and moral problems would become urgent during the next few centuries, either through the rise of the new cities, or with the European settlement of other continents, or as a result of the development of banking and mercantilism. The literate and transnational professional *cadre* of moral theologians, canon lawyers, legal scholars, and casuists, however, were confident of their capacity—using the demands of the natural law as a criterion—to discuss and resolve whatever problems of moral judgment or taxonomy the future might bring, and to do so in whatever detail the situation and circumstances of the problems required. This was the mission of "casuistry"; and we shall now look more closely at its historical evolution.

CANONISTS

The discipline of the Catholic Church, that is, the practical implications of its beliefs and theology for the form of society and the conduct of believers, took shape gradually over a millennium of missionary expansion and consolidation in Europe, the Near East, and North Africa. That shape was as vast, complex, and diverse as the various cultures in which it had grown. As the first millennium grew to a close, however, many forces combined to press that diversity into uniformity, the variety into order. The law of the church, together with its liturgy, stood at the center of its discipline. The end of the eleventh century saw an emerging interest in collating, formalizing, and interpreting the heterogeneous body of ecclesiastical law. The rediscovery around A.D. 1070 of the great text of Roman civil law, the *Digest* of Justinian, stimulated this effort and provided it with a model. So the classical age of canon law opened in 1140 with the appearance of the greatest and most enduring of the canonical collections, the *Decretum* of Gratian.

The importance of canon law for casuistry is fourfold. First, canon law consisted primarily of the responses of ecclesiastical authorities to particular cases. Its corpus was built out of innumerable decrees of ecumenical and local councils, letters of popes and bishops, statutes of dioceses and religious orders, and dicta of reputable ecclesiastical writers. Many of these sources were highly particular in content; yet for a variety of reasons they had taken on wider significance. Second, the diversity of sources demanded an overall interpretation whereby the diversity could be reconciled and the obscure rendered clear. The evolution of a theory of legal interpretation, carried out by jurisprudents of civil and canon law, was the great achievement of the era. Third, the confluence of ideas from Christian belief, Roman jurisprudence, and Greek philosophy created a unique concept—*aequitas canonica,* or canonical equity—which was to have major implications for casuistry. Finally, the teaching of canon law employed the case method, giving a name and suggesting a technique to moral casuistry.

The infant Church, which had been inspired by little more than a common acceptance of the Gospel message, evolved formulas of belief, together with liturgical and moral practices, to meet the particular needs and problems of successive generations. Law arose within the Church, as it did in civil life, not as a rational system but as the accretion of many particular solutions. This multiplicity of laws was gathered into "Collections" with little attention to their origins in particular problems. Law came not from some single juridical or legislative system but from many persons and institutions endowed with authority and significance of very different value. This diversity of sources was not the result of temporal and cultural diversity alone: it was also theological and doctrinal. Through painful crises, as well as through peaceful cultural adaptation, the Catholic Church had come to recognize the claims of the secular

world on the lives of the faithful. The wisdom of the pagan philosophers found a place, subordinate but significant, beside the wisdom
of the saints. So from the fourth century on, the Church existed side
by side with the empire, accepting its legitimacy and its law.
Ecclesiastical legislation coexisted with the law of the state. The law
of nature, expressed by pagan scholars of philosophy and jurisprudence, was a revelation, diminished but still compelling, of the will
of God, more clearly expressed in the Gospels. Thus the opening
words of Gratian's *Decretum*:

> The human race is governed in two ways, by natural right and by cus-
> tom. Natural right, found in the Law and the Gospel, commands that
> each do to the other what he would wish done to him. Thus, Christ
> said, "Whatever you wish men to do to you, do also unto them. This
> is the Law and the Prophets." Thus, Isadore says, "Divine law is by
> nature; human law by custom."[20]

The canonists, accepting divine law and human law, super-
natural and natural revelation, each according to its different authority, saw as their work "the integration of human jurisprudence
in the divine order of salvation."[21] This integration required a theory of interpretation whereby order and consistency could be instilled
into heterogeneous sources. The earliest interpretative rule, that of
Isadore of Seville (560–636), was obviously insufficient: "When
canons are discordant, the more ancient and authoritative (*antiquior
et potentior*) prevails."[22]

The *Panormia* of Ivo of Chartres (1092) sets out a more refined
method. After determining the authenticity of a text, locating it in a
hierarchy of sources, and examining the sense of its words, the inter-
preter should attempt to discover the local and temporal circumstances that prompted the legislation. Ivo distinguishes immutable
laws, which originate from divine revelation, from mutable laws,
which are made by men for their utility (*ratione utilitatis*). The observance of these mutable laws is not necessary for salvation; they simply serve to safeguard the path to salvation and "like excess cargo in
a storm, can be jettisoned as the church sails through the seas of
time."[23] From mutable laws dispensation can be granted when
authorities suspend the obligation to observe them; but dispensation
must be based on a just cause that will be determined by "the need
of the church and the necessities and moral welfare of individuals,
viewed according to the quality of persons and the opportunity of

place and of time."[24] Ivo states that the law must be interpreted and modulated so that it refers all that is taught therein to the reign of charity. This is his primary rule of interpretation.[25]

This rule, simply formulated, grows into the concept of "canonical equity" (*aequitas canonica*). Canonists fashioned this concept by amalgamating three distinct traditions. One of these was the tradition of Roman jurisprudence, in which *aequitas* was almost a synonym for *justitia*. (In Cicero's words, "equity is the suitability whereby similar law is applied in similar cases."[26]) A second heritage was Aristotelian *epieikeia*, the interpretation of a law in a case that the legislator did not foresee.[27] The law, being stated in general terms, requires correction when faced with the particularity of situations. Finally, the canonists, impressed that the Gospel required mercy and compassion, glimpsed a similarity between Aristotelian *epieikeia* and Christian charity. They forged a new definition of *aequitas*, "justice tempered by the gentleness of mercy." In this sense the mildness of equity came to be contrasted with the severity and rigor of the law. As one eminent modern canonist writes,

> In the mind of the classical canonists, justice and mercy did meet on the plane of law . . . the ideal of *aequitas canonica* permeates their analytical thought and their solution of cases. All tension and dissonance, all the apparent incompatibilities of the spiritual and the temporal, the supernatural and the natural, could be brought into harmony.[28]

Canon law was preeminently a practical discipline. Its study called for attention to actual rulings and their interpretation. The material was presented to students through the didactic device of the "gloss": that is, brief comments in which the teacher would explain, compare, distinguish, and reconcile texts from the classical sources such as the *Digests* or the *Decretum*. Frequently the gloss would include examples introduced by the words, "take the case" or "imagine the case." After a theoretical exposition of the text, the teacher would propose these cases to the students. They also formed the agenda for the weekly or biweekly academic disputations. By the thirteenth century these canonical "cases" had taken on a life of their own and were published in separate collections for the convenience of academic exercises.

The word *casus*, which we now simply translate "case," derives from the Latin verb *cadere*; that is, "to happen, to take place." In its early technical use it indicated the factual reference of a legal decree.

For instance, it might be stated, "the case of this decree concerns a certain bishop, Eleutherius . . ." meaning that this is the way it happened—these were the circumstances that gave rise to this ruling. A thirteenth-century definition of *casus* is "a specification of the understanding of a decree," that is, the particular instance issuing in the legislation.[29]

Canon law spanned the intermediate domain between morality and civil law, attending to the spiritual life of the church as well as to its external forms and practices. The law developed distinctions to suit this double purpose. The "internal forum" designated the power of the Church over the conscience of believers; the "external forum," its authority over public and social behavior. Sins were punished by divine sanctions, which the Church was divinely authorized to impose or to lift; violations in the external forum could be punished by censures and impediments which were manifest in the public realm. (Our later discussion of self-defense will show, for example, that a person who has shed another's blood by accident might incur an impediment to priestly ordination even though not guilty of the sin of homicide.) These intricate associations between the external and internal forums provided later casuists with ample material for refined distinctions, though this distinction also presaged the modern debate about whether morality lies in the agent's intention or in the consequences of the action. This was not an issue that initially troubled the canonists and the casuists, for whom the external and internal forums hung together as integral parts of the moral or Christian life.

The rich heritage of canon law contributed several important elements to later casuistry: a strong appreciation of diversity and practicality, awareness of the necessity for interpretation, understanding of the need to correct and mitigate the generality and rigor of law in the uniqueness of situations, and, finally, the pedagogical technique of cases illustrating how all this is to be accomplished.

THE CONFESSIONAL BOOKS

The endeavors of the canonists were quickly put to practical use. By the twelfth century the sacrament of penance was beginning to be commonly administered in private confession by a penitent to a priest. As the result of this practice, clergy needed to be instructed how to match the complexities of the new canon law to the cases their penitents presented to them. A new genre of literature supplied this need. We designate this genre *confessional books*, in order to distinguish them from the earlier and cruder *Penitentials* and from the later *Summas*, which were influenced by the speculative theology of the thirteenth century. One of the first of these confessional books was written by Peter, who was Cantor of the Cathedral of Paris (d. 1197). A recognized scholar in many fields, he was deeply involved in civil, ecclesiastic, and academic circles. His *Summa de Sacramentis et Animae Conciliis* reflects his combined concern for canon law and pastoral care, and brings this combination to bear on practical issues of morality for "masters, princes and merchants."

The volume opens with several discursive treatises on the theology of penance and on the nature of sin and repentance. Peter then offers a vast number of cases, often beginning with the formula, "take the case" (*si sit casus*). The legal and moral questions that might be presented to a medieval confessor are proposed: theft, simony, incest, usury, vows and oaths, discipline of unruly clerics, and so forth. These cases appear as short questions with brief answers. There is little attempt to organize the many questions into a systematic presentation: Peter's modern editor describes them as a "mosaic of cases." The cases are resolved by reference to common maxims from Scripture, canon law, and the Fathers and by pointing to relevant circumstances. Asking whether a prince may employ tasters to test his dinner wine for poison, for example, Peter answers that exposing another person to danger in this way is complicity in homicide. He cites as a maxim a phrase taken from an exegete's gloss on the words of Matthew 12:35: "The good man out of his good treasure brings forth good, and the evil man evil." The gloss on this text reads, "Your deed extends as far as your intentions." Peter, however, allows the suspected poisoner to be forced to drink the possibly toxic potion himself. He then poses the question of whether the potion can be given to the suspected poisoner secretly, but he leaves this final case unresolved, either because he is unsure how to answer it or as an open question to students. Peter's modern editor calls his work the "first important book of medieval casuistry." This first casuist shows himself to be a person of good sense, moral seriousness, and judiciousness; but he does not reveal any consistent method or theory to justify his handling of cases.[30]

Several years after the appearance of Peter Cantor's work, another master of the University of Paris, Alain of Lille (1128–1203) produced

his *Liber Penitentialis*. This book introduced more order in the treatment of cases. Aiming to elucidate the principle enunciated in
Gratian's *Decretum, poenitentiae sunt arbitrariae*—that is, "penances
are a matter of judgment"—Alain reviews questions the confessor
should ask the penitent. These questions will reveal the circumstances that allow judicious determination of the seriousness of sin,
and suitability for absolution and penance. These questions bear on
motive, responsibility, condition of life, time and place of action: On
what occasion was the act committed? What age was the penitent?
Is the penitent rich or poor, of high or low station? What is the penitent's emotional complexion, choleric or phlegmatic? Was the act
done out of desire, hatred, drunkenness, deception?

Following this interrogatory, Alain treats certain acts, such as perjury, killing, fornication, and theft. He sets out the relevant canons
in orderly fashion and notes the relevance of various circumstances
for the application of the canons. Although, like Peter Cantor, he
proposes no general theory, many of his distinctions appear quite
relevant to the contemporary reader. For example, murder committed while insane deserves a lighter penance, "because his infirmity
can be judged the cause of his sin . . . between sanity and insanity,
rationality and irrationality, there is a clear distinction." Other distinctions appear less plausible: "it is a lesser sin if a man seduces a
beautiful woman than an ugly one, for he is compelled by beauty,
and, where there is greater compulsion, there is less sin."[31]

In the early decades of the thirteenth century many confessional
books appeared, some of them remarkable for their extensive scope
and vivacious style. Several came from the hands of the pupils of
Peter Cantor. Thomas of Chobham's *Summa Confessorum* (c. 1216)
was, says the modern editor, a "medieval best seller." It is a vast collection of cases arranged under the headings of the Seven Sacraments and the Seven Deadly Sins. It is prefaced by a remarkable
essay on the importance of circumstances that, after discussing a
pseudo-Augustinian text, *de Vera et Falsa Poenitentia*, comments that
the "nature of circumstances is better explained in the secular writers such as Cicero."[32] Robert of Courson produced a "perfected version of the *quaestiones* of Peter Cantor."[33] Several authors who were
canons of the Church of St. Victor were vigorous advocates of sacramental confession; two of their number, Robert of Flambrough and
Peter of Poitier, wrote guides for penitents and confessors. Robert's
Liber Poenitentialis presents a dialogue between a confessor and a

penitent who, in the course of the dialogue, admits to every sin in the book. While still emphasizing the canonical aspects of the problems proposed, both authors show great sensitivity to the morally relevant features of motive, responsibility, and circumstances.[34]

The most esteemed and influential of all authors in this genre was Raymond of Pennafort (1175–1275), a Dominican scholar who was actively engaged in civil and ecclesiastical administration. His *Summa de Poenitentia* (1221) represented "an astonishing change of perspective and balance over the previous literature";[35] and despite the putative claim of Peter Cantor to be the first casuist, it can be claimed that "casuistry, properly speaking, begins to appear in his [Pennafort's] pages."[36] This novel "casuistry, properly speaking" consists not merely in the presentation of cases or in the appreciation of circumstances but in the orderly arrangement of those cases and circumstances. Raymond divided his work into sins against God, such as blasphemy and heresy, and sins against the neighbor, such as killing, violence, and adultery. He adds special sections on the duties of various states of life. Each section of Pennafort's *Summa* begins with a proposal about how the matter will be presented, followed by definitions of the principal terms, such as lying or simony. He then relates the "true and certain opinions" on the question under discussion, drawn from earlier writers, followed by those questions and cases about which the received answers are more doubtful. In the treatise on perjury and lying, for example, the general doctrine of Augustine that all lies are sinful in varying degrees is set as "true and certain"; but, confronting Augustine's case, which we will consider at length later, about concealing an innocent person from seizure by an unjust authority, Raymond notes that there are diverse opinions, none of which is conclusive.[37] As we shall see, this way of ordering the case material becomes one of the basic techniques of "casuistry, properly speaking."

The real charter of the new casuistry was, however, not the literature of these incipient casuists but a decree by a universal council of the Church, the Fourth Council of the Lateran, held in 1215. The Albigensians, whose heresy was currently troubling the Church, had preached that confession to a priest was unnecessary and even idolatrous. To counter that teaching, the council required all of the faithful who reached the age of discretion to confess to a priest at least once a year. Canon 21 of the council admonished the priest

to be discreet and careful in the manner of experienced physicians . . .
diligently inquiring about the circumstances of the sin and the sinner,
whereby he can learn what sort of advice to offer and what remedies
to employ, making diverse attempts to heal the ailing person.[38]

This canon reflected a development of the doctrine and practice
found in the penitential and confessional books, which had contained a clear (if still crude) understanding of the role of circumstances, a sensitivity to the particularity of cases, and an appreciation
of the diversity of opinion about the evaluation of specific instances.
This Lateran decree gave impetus to the development of case morality by issuing the imperative of annual confession, thereby heighten-
ing these ideas in the minds of all clergy and laity. From then on
casuistry was to have a distinctive place in the teaching and practice
of the Catholic Church. "Casuistry properly speaking" awaited one
further embellishment: the contribution of speculative theology.

6

The Theologians

During the early Middle Ages the moral life formed a common topic for reflection; but because these reflections were typically written by monks for monks, they tended to be theological rather than philosophical, spiritual rather than secular. Their themes were the attainment of salvation, the avoidance of sin and worldly temptation, and above all the appreciation in one's life of the Love of God. Much of this instruction was by way of *exempla*, stories of the activities and virtues of the saints. Although patristic writings, pastoral exhortation, and fragments of the Latin classics were widely used and imitated, there were no systematic treatises on ethics. Collections of quotations from all these varied sources were particularly popular. Short and edifying passages as well as moral maxims ("Impose on another nothing you are unwilling to bear") and classical quasi-definitions ("Justice is the queen of all virtues") were cited from Cicero, Seneca, Plutarch, Virgil, and Ovid. Occasionally these quotations would be prefaced with brief essays on moral topics, such as the nature of good and evil, virtue and vice, wisdom and folly.[1]

One of the first approaches to a systematic treatise, Abelard's *Ethica seu Scire Teipsum* scarcely went beyond these themes, except to propose the controversial doctrine that good is differentiated from evil by intention alone. Meanwhile Roger Bacon's *Philosophia Moralis* (c. 1250) grafted the Aristotelian scheme of virtues on to Seneca's Stoic admonitions.[2] Because Ethics was not recognized as a distinct academic subject, moral questions were customarily discussed in the *trivium*, the first segment of the liberal arts education, which comprised grammar, dialectic, and rhetoric. Quintillian's *Institutiones*, one of the few classic works known to the Middle Ages in its entirety, was a book on rhetoric, but it contained ample matter for moral commentary and was held to be "a moral classic."[3] Thus on the threshold of high scholasticism, Ethics remained associated with rhetoric, and we shall see the importance of this association for subsequent casuistry. In the course of the thirteenth century, however, the study of morality was promoted out of the *trivium* into the prestigious discipline of theology. So it moved from the meditations of monks to the lectures of the masters of the universities.

Just as the twelfth century had seen an effort to draw legal norms into systematic synthesis, the thirteenth saw an attempt to impose order and method on moral doctrine. Many streams flowed into this endeavor: the writings of the Church Fathers, the Latin and Greek philosophers, the scholars of civil and canonical jurisprudence. Treatises began to appear on particular subjects, such as the nature of sin, of human liberty, of conscience, and of virtue. These treatises were usually in the format of the *quaestio*: a short essay in which definitions were proposed, a thesis and arguments in its support was stated, and alternative theses criticized. Attention was paid to the logic of discourse and to the precision of terms. In addition to these *quaestiones*, commentaries were written on the recently recovered *Nicomachean Ethics* and on other major works of antiquity. By the end of the thirteenth century, with such treatises as the *Prima Secundae* of Aquinas' *Summa Theologiae*, which set forth "the movement of the rational creature toward God" in exquisite detail and coherent argument, a full-scale doctrine of morality was devised for the first time in Western Christendom.[4]

For the history and theory of casuistry, several elements of Aquinas' doctrine are especially relevant: notably "natural law" and "natural reason," "conscience," "prudence," and "circumstance." Although the great scholastic theologians devoted little attention to casuistry as such, their analysis of these crucial concepts flowed into the independent stream of casuistry, which developed in the confessional literature of their own and subsequent centuries.[5] Beginning in the late twelfth century theologians took these previously vague ideas, which had been inherited in a fragmentary way from Scripture, patristic writings, and classical philosophy, and began to

shape them into more coherent concepts. By the end of the thirteenth century the theological and moral meanings of these concepts
had, in essence, reached the form they retained until the Enlightenment of the eighteenth century. So the high casuistry of the sixteenth and seventeenth centuries grew up within intellectual bounds
set by the medieval understanding of all these ideas.

The casuists, who were educated either as theologians or as
canonists, did not actually elaborate a formal theory of casuistry on
the basis of these concepts; but their appreciation of them did leave
their minds free to "think casuistically." The basic moral notions
with which they were familiar, and which were totally accepted in
the Church and in their culture, not only put no obstacles in the way
of casuistry but encouraged it—indeed, made it possible. High
casuistry can only be understood, then, if we take care to understand
how the casuists thought about these ideas and how different their
views were from the conceptions associated with modern colloquial
use of the same terms. Such words as *prudence, conscience* and *natural law* have vastly different connotations for the modern mind than
they had for those nourished in medieval tradition. In the following
sections we hope to clarify why these medieval notions were so congenial to casuistry and why, when Enlightenment ideas appeared to
undercut and discredit them, later casuistry faltered and even deteri-
orated into mere "situationism."

NATURAL LAW AND NATURAL REASON

The notion that the moral life is governed by a natural law was
familiar to the Church Fathers in its Ciceronian and Stoic form. St.
Paul gave license to use the notion in a Christian sense:

> When Gentiles who do not have the [Mosaic] Law do by nature what
> the Law requires, they are a law unto themselves . . . they show that
> what the law requires is written in their hearts.[6]

The Church Fathers often equated the "law written in the heart" with
the "natural law" of Greco-Roman philosophy. Despite Pauline
endorsement and common acceptance of the notion, the Fathers did
little to explicate it or employ it systematically. Jurisconsults drew
attention to the notion in the twelfth century by commenting on
Ulpian's definition, which opens the *Digest* of Justinian, "Natural
law is what nature teaches all animals." Gratian opens his *Decretum*

with an equally succinct but contrasting and perplexing definition: "The law of nature is that which is found in the Mosaic Law and the Gospels."[7]

Theologians found these disparate fragments at hand as they considered a problem of central concern to the Christian faith: "What was the precise nature of man's Fall from Grace, as related in the opening chapters of *Genesis*?"—a story the literal truth of which they accepted and took as a basic datum of Christian faith. More exactly, what was the moral and spiritual status of the human race before Original Sin; after Original Sin until the revelation of Christ; and, after that revelation, for those who did not know of it? These questions had been debated vigorously in the fourth century, when the Pelagians had proposed, and orthodox writers opposed, certain views of nature in relation to grace. When twelfth-century theologians attempted to respond to these ancient questions in a more systematic way, they wove together the various ideas about natural law that they found in pagan and Christian authors.

For almost a century theologians offered various suggestions. Some claimed that natural law was the primitive moral law of humanity, which survived the Fall from Grace. It consisted only in the dictate of natural reason, obliging all human beings not to harm and to do good to others: onto this minimal concept of moral obligation was grafted the Pauline identification of the natural law with the Mosaic law, as expressed in the Decalogue. Going further, some theologians and jurisconsults suggested that the natural law comprised not only the strict precepts of the Decalogue but also certain "recommendations about what is suitable to human nature, such as the possession in common of the goods of the earth and the liberty of all individuals." William of Auxerre (d. 1231) proposed that natural law be distinguished into "primary precepts," observance of which was necessary for salvation, and "secondary precepts" which, though not indispensable, are useful and helpful to salvation. Distinctions such as these aided theologians in explaining how behavior of the "saints" of the Old Testament (e.g., Abraham, David, Solomon, and Samson) could be squared with the morality that seemed necessary for salvation, in light of Christian revelation and of "natural law." The Old Testament's tolerance toward frequent cases of polygamy and lying particularly exercised the Fathers of the Church; and the medieval theologians offered a resolution of these moral puzzles by distinguishing between various levels of natural moral precepts, with different implications for stringency and "knowability."[8]

Aquinas wove the rather loose considerations of his predecessors into a tidier pattern. He opens his *Questiones* on natural law—which are only a part and, indeed, not the central part of his moral doctrine—by linking the Augustinian notion of "eternal law," which had strong Platonic antecedents, with the Aristotelian and Ciceronian notions of natural reason. The natural law is "participation of the rational creature in the eternal law." That participation is spelled out in terms of Aristotelian reasoning: "just as the speculative reason grasps certain self evident principles, from which all true propositions are derived, so practical reason grasps as its first self evident principle, that good is to be done and evil avoided."[9] This first principle of practical reason is analogous to the principle of noncontradiction in the order of speculative reason.

Aquinas goes on to propose that every principle of natural law and all right moral reasoning is based (*fundatur*) on this first principle. Other principles arise because practical reason apprehends natural inclinations—that is, the essential tendencies of any natural being to move toward its own proper end. Being part of universal nature, the rational creature shares an inclination with all other substances to preserve itself in existence; shares an inclination with all animal beings toward sexual congress and the rearing of offspring, and, in addition, being specifically rational, is inclined to seek the truth and to live in society. These inclinations, apprehended by practical reason, issue in the first precepts of the natural law, which are known to all rational creatures and are binding upon all.[10]

Aquinas then argues that there are other principles, "rather like conclusions from the first, which are known generally but not universally or inevitably." These may fail to oblige in unusual situations because of "hindrances" (*impedimenta*), or they may fail to be recognized owing to "reason deformed by passion or by poor education and bad habits." To these secondary precepts Aquinas applies the term *jus gentium*, derived from Roman law. From the primary precepts concerning the sustenance of society, it follows that justice must be observed in the arrangements of social life, such as respect for contracts and for political authority, but the forms that these social arrangements take may differ greatly.[11] Thus private property or communism, monarchy or democracy may be suitable at different times or in different places. The natural law, says the theologian, is unchangeable in the primary precepts but may be changeable in the secondary, "in some particular way and on rare occasions." Thus in one respect, moral law admits of no exception: one should always act in accord with natural reason as it reflects the primary precepts. But in other respects, the moral law admits of exceptions owing to "accidental causes." Aquinas borrows Plato's and Cicero's venerable example: it is according to natural law to return a deposit to its owner, yet it would be contrary to reason to return a sword to its owner if he were bent on murder and suicide. He also concludes that while the polygamy of the biblical patriarchs may be contrary to those secondary precepts that promote the mutuality of spouses, it does not violate primary precepts, as procreation and education of offspring are still possible.[12]

The casuists inherited this Thomistic concept of natural law. The natural law grounded moral reasoning in what all persons would presumably acknowledge as the most radical of human needs: self-preservation, the preservation of the species, the search for understanding, and the pursuit of social coherence. As it moves beyond these basic assertions, moral reasoning encounters the myriad circumstances of the human situation, where generalities must be particularized and generic terms tailored to allow for exceptions. So, as the casuists knew it, natural law doctrine provided room for, and even demanded, a casuistry for its completion. The great sixteenth-century Thomistic commentator, Francisco Suarez, whose work was well known to the casuists of the high era, elaborated and refined Aquinas' doctrine. While he created a highly structured theory of moral reasoning, he affirmed the place of casuistry: "Not all natural precepts are equally well known or equally easy to understand; they require interpretation in order that their true sense may be understood without diminution or addition."[13] This interpretation was the mission of the casuists, and their conception of conscience guided them in carrying it out.

CONSCIENCE AND PRUDENCE

The medieval term for what we call casuistry was "cases of conscience" (*casus conscientiae*). It is important to recognize how the medieval theologians understood the idea of conscience, for this idea helped to shape the activity of casuistry. Yet as one present-day author notes, "The scheme within which medieval thought treated conscience is so different from that of recent philosophy as to make it difficult to appreciate the questions posed by medieval authors."[14] As with the closely related doctrine of natural law, the question that stimulated the theologians was an ancient one: "How do human beings, whose reason is dimmed and whose will is weakened by sin, perceive the way to salvation amid the welter of conflicting desires?" The early scholastic theologians pulled together the extensive patristic reflection on this problem into systematic *quaestiones*. Their attention was captured by the same Pauline text that spoke of natural law: it contains the phrase, "their conscience also bears witness (to the law) and their conflicting thoughts accuse or excuse them."[15] They also were intrigued by a curious text of St. Jerome (342–420), who interpreted as an allegory a vision of the Prophet Ezekiel in which creatures with four faces appear.   Three faces, said Jerome, represent Plato's tripartite division of the soul into rational, emotional, and appetitive parts: this division of the soul explains the conflict of desires among themselves, and their opposition to reason.   The fourth face is a fourth part of the soul, over and above these three, the spark of conscience called by the Greeks *synderesis*:   this spark was not extinguished when Adam and Eve were expelled from Paradise, and by it humans discern that they sin, when they are overcome by lust or frenzy, or are misled by false reason.[16]

The first great master of medieval theology, Peter Lombard (1100–1160), cited Jerome's text in a *quaestio* about conflict of motivation.   Philip the Chancellor (d. 1236), who wrote the first complete treatise on conscience, made much of Jerome's comments.   He exploits the presence of two different words in Jerome's text—one Latin, *conscientia*; the other Greek, *synderesis* —to make an important distinction.   There is a power in human beings that does not err, which can be named *synderesis*:   this power "murmurs against sin, and correctly contemplates and wants that which is good without qualifications."   The phrase "without qualifications" means that this power lifts the mind to the highest good but does not examine the detailed features of particular deeds.   The other power, named *conscientia*, exists at the conjunction of *synderesis* and free choice: because of its association with free choice, it can be in error.[17]   This distinction provides the foundations of the medieval doctrine of conscience.   It also raises difficult speculative problems about the relationship between knowledge and will and between universals and particulars, which questions were a challenge to the theologians.

Once again it was Aquinas who devised the synthesis that dominated the theological concept of conscience during subsequent centuries. Aquinas links natural law and conscience by identifying the intellect's grasp of the first principles of practical reason as *synderesis*, "a natural disposition concerned with the basic principles of behavior, which are the general principles of natural law."[18] He takes up a suggestion of his teacher, Albert the Great, that conscience names the *conclusion* of the practical syllogism as described by Aristotle; namely, that "so-and-so is to be done." *Synderesis* provides the major *premise* of that syllogism—namely, that "such-and-such things are, in general, to be done or avoided." Thus *synderesis* can no more err than can the intellectual power by which first principles of theoretical reason are apprehended. Aquinas, then, reserves the word *conscientia* for "the application of general judgments of *synderesis* to particulars." This application can be either prospective, in discovering what is to be done in a particular situation, or retrospective, in testing what was done in order to discern whether one acted rightly. In this sense, although *synderesis* cannot err, *conscientia* can; for the application of general moral insights requires a particular premise, and one can be mistaken about such particulars or fail to use a valid argument in reasoning from the general to the particular.

If conscience, as a source of judgments about particular actions, can be in error, is a person morally obliged to act in accord with conscience, even when it is erroneous? The medieval theologians repeatedly struggled with this issue. Aquinas finally proposed that if the error arose from an ignorance of some circumstance, and if that ignorance was not itself a result of negligence, then an erroneous conscience was excused from sin. But a mistaken conscience binds in a different way from a correct one. A correct conscience binds "without qualification"—for example, in every circumstance covered by the judgment—but an erroneous conscience binds only conditionally, for if the error is detected, it must be set aside. A correct conscience binds *per se*, an erroneous one *per accidens*, for one who acts in accord with an erroneous conscience does so not because it is erroneous but because in his eyes it is correct. The arguments Aquinas sets out to support these theses are solid and subtle, if not entirely satisfactory to the modern critic.[19] This theory of conscience, which left wide room for error and uncertainty, arising both from the difficulty of perceiving particulars and of reasoning correctly, evidently helps to open the way for casuistry.

The medieval theory of conscience was closely linked to the doctrine of prudence. The theologians who pondered the relative ranking of the different virtues required for the Christian life found various lists and priorities in the Scripture and in patristic writings. Seeking to impose some order on this diversity, they followed Cicero's choice of the Latin word *prudentia* to translate the Greek word *phronesis* as used by Plato and the Stoics in the broad sense of "moral wisdom." Cicero classed *prudentia/phronesis* as one of the four cardinal virtues, defined as "knowledge of what should be done and what avoided."[20] Philip the Chancellor further proposed that because the various virtues looked to particular goods, they must be linked to some more general virtue that sought the good itself. Recalling the image in Plato's *Phaedrus*, he asserts that "prudence, being the unity between all virtues, is 'the charioteer of virtues.'"[21]

The rediscovery of Aristotle's *Nicomachean Ethics*, about 1245, opened up new vistas for the theological discussion of prudence. Albert the Great recognized the usefulness of Aristotle's discussion of *phronesis* in books VI and VII of the *Ethics*, where that word refers not to moral wisdom in general but to the choice of particular acts: "prudence," while a virtue or state of soul, also issues in particular choices. As Aristotle had intimated, choice can be viewed as the outcome of a practical syllogism; so Albert suggested the possibility of integrating the ideas of natural law, conscience, and prudence. His disciple, Aquinas, took up this suggestion and defined prudence as "correct reasoning about what ought to be done" (*recta ratio agibilium*). In order to choose prudently, one must deliberate about the various means to a given end, judge soundly about the best means, and firmly undertake the steps indicated by this judgment.[22]

From Aquinas' detailed discussion of prudence we can draw a picture of "the prudent person." Such a person possesses knowledge both of universal principle and of particular situations; is capable of drawing together memory of past experiences and foresight into future possibilities; and is able to recognize what is at issue in new and hitherto untried situations. The prudent person is aware that although the final end of human life is fixed by divine providence, the means to achieving that end are "of manifold variety according to the variety of persons and situations." Thus one feature of prudent action is *circumspectio*, literally, "looking around." This is required because prudence bears on the choice of particulars, and this judgment may involve many combinations of *circumstantiae*, literally, "what is standing around." The circumstances of any action, notes Aquinas, are potentially infinite; but out of this infinity, only a few are significant enough to modify judgment about what ought to be done or avoided in any particular situation. Prudence, he says, selects those that are relevant. Carefulness (*cautio*) is also required because human action is so varied (*multiforma*) that evil and good are mixed together. The prudent man cannot avoid evil altogether because it is sometimes disguised as good, but he should be careful to avoid, by foresight, the common pitfalls so that as little harm as possible is done.[23]

CIRCUMSTANCES

The "prudent" person, as described by medieval theologians, must exercise circumspection—that is, the awareness of circumstances. The medieval doctrine of circumstances was highly nuanced, and it had a much more central significance for morality than is suggested by modern usage, in which the word "circumstantial" means merely "incidental." The theologians wove this doctrine out of strands they found in several places: in the discipline of rhetoric, in the *Ethics* of Aristotle, in the penitential literature, and in canon law; and each strand contributed its own subtle coloration to the doctrine. In the form finally given to it by Aquinas, the importance of circumstances in moral evaluation is nicely balanced against the significance of principles.

Rhetoric was one of the few Greco-Roman academic disciplines to survive during the intellectual impoverishment of the early Middle Ages. The rhetorical works of Cicero, Quintillian, and Boethius, as well as a work attributed to Augustine, were known and studied as an integral part of liberal arts education; and the doctrine of circumstances had its roots in rhetoric. As the rhetorical texts frequently stressed, an oration must describe persons and situations in detail, and the effect of the oration on the audience depends on this description. This was particularly important in forensic orations, when the actions of persons were being blamed or defended for the purpose of adjudication. For the rhetoricians the *questio* ("question") addresses general issues, such as "Is there any good other than honor?"

These kinds of questions, which often approached the subject matter of philosophy, required certain forms of evidence and argument. The *causa* ("cause") was much different. It addressed a controversy involving specified persons. Questions, says Boethius, are "naked of circumstances, while a cause is surrounded by a multitude of them." According to Cicero, a cause is "constructed out of statements about certain persons, places, times, actions and affairs," while Quintillian defined a cause entirely in terms of the circumstances, using the words of his predecessor, Apollodorus: "the collection of persons, places, times, causes, manners, events, deeds, instruments and words."[24] In causes, as the rhetoricians emphasized, detailed description can be most influential in "making a case." Without such details, they said, a "probable argument" cannot be constructed; and they devoted lengthy sections of their treatises to the selection and mode of presentation of these details. Cicero divided circumstances into attributes of persons (name, nature, manner of life, fortune, skills, feelings, interests, purposes, achievements, expression) and attributes of action (place, time, occasion, manner). He did not himself employ the word *circumstantiae* for these attributes, but he reported that the Hellenistic rhetorician, Hermagoras, had used the Greek equivalent, *peristasis*: "it is the circumstances, as Hermagoras says, which make the cause: without them no controversy can proceed."[25] In the early Middle Ages an unknown rhetorician composed the resulting elements into the hexameter used as a mnemonic by students: *quis, quid, ubi, quibus auxilis, cur, quomodo, quando* (who, what, where, by what means, why, how, when?). This hexameter became the standard enumeration of circumstances in subsequent medieval discussions.

In discussing the subject of voluntary action in book III of the *Nicomachean Ethics*, Aristotle noted that "ignorance of the particulars, that is, of the circumstances of an action and the objects with which it is concerned, can render an action involuntary." He enumerates these particulars: a man may be ignorant of who he is, what he is doing, what or whom he is acting on, and sometimes also what instrument he is doing it with, and to what end and in what manner he is doing it. Aristotle offers several illustrations. For example, a man shoots a slingshot and injures a bystander: he excuses himself, saying, "I only wanted to see how it worked." Of the various sorts of ignorance that exculpate, Aristotle concludes, "the most important are thought to be the circumstances of the action and the end."[26]

Just as Cicero did not use the term *circumstantia*, Aristotle did not use the Greek *peristasis* but preferred certain idiomatic circumlocutions. The earliest medieval translation of the *Nicomachean Ethics* into Latin, however, introduced the word *circumstantiae* into the text and enumerated them as of eight kinds. Thus the medieval theologians found a congruity between the familiar Ciceronian list of circumstances and the newly discovered Aristotelian one. Aquinas wondered whether the eighth Aristotelian circumstance, "about which or on whom," should be added to Cicero's seven, and argued in favor of doing so.[27] Thus two strands of thought about circumstances reached the theologians. The rhetorical tradition stressed the importance of detail for the description of a forensic issue; the Aristotelian focused on the moral problem of imputability of actions to agents.

Another strand of thought came through the penitential books and canon law. In the early penitentials penances were proportioned to the wickedness of the deed. The wickedness of the deed was related to such features as the rank, age, and experience of the person who performed it and the time and place it was done; but only rarely was any explanation of this relationship offered. By the tenth century the principle "the penance should be measured by the manner of the sin" was firmly established in penitential practice. The concomitant principle of differentiation of degrees of sinfulness was elaborated in canon law. The *Decretum* comments on a text of St. John Chrysostom, "The Christian falls gravely into sin, both because of the seriousness of the sin and because of the height from which he falls." To this quotation Gratian appended a text incorrectly attributed to Augustine, which was to have great influence in determining canonical and penitential practice. The pseudo-Augustine states that such features as rank, wisdom, and age, as well as time and place of action, are crucial to judgments of the seriousness of sin. The canonical doctrine was summed up, again with the use of the word *circumstantiae*, by Huguccio of Pisa (d. 1210): "Circumstances of time and place, rank, dignity and knowledge aggravate the sin: thus, in the same sort of sin, a cleric may sin more gravely than a lay person, an educated person more seriously than an uneducated one."[28]

These canonical teachings led to a problem that was properly theological. The brilliant nonconformist Abelard (1079–1142) denied that clerics sinned more seriously than laity simply because they happened to be clerics: motive alone, he claimed, determined the seriousness of the sin. Circumstances are, after all, the creatures of a good God and cannot aggravate or mitigate the evil choices of humans. This contention opened the question of the metaphysical and psychological nature of human action and its place in the order of creation. This meant, as Aquinas noted, that the role of circumstances involved properly theological questions and is not merely a matter for rhetoric. The theological question was addressed first by Albert the Great, who linked the Aristotelian and Ciceronian analyses. Circumstances, he said, are "the unique conditions which surround some activity in an unsystematic fashion and from which the orator can draw arguments to aggravate or excuse an accusation or to amplify or attenuate praise." As Cicero says, "circumstance is the proof whereby an argument is given credibility and authority."[29]

Aquinas drew these threads together and provided an analysis that weaves them into an Aristotelian metaphysics. In the *Summa Theologica* he discusses circumstances in two places: first in I–II, quaestio 7, as an element in the psychology of human action, and then in I–II, quaestio 18, in relation to the moral evaluation of actions. Circumstances, as enumerated in the Ciceronian hexameter, stand as accidents do to the form or essence of an act. That form or essence is determined by the relation of the act to the general end of human life. Just as any material being is completed not only by its substantial form but also by its proper accidents, so circumstances perfect an action and are integral to its description. Circumstances, though extrinsic to the substance of an act, touch it (*attingit*) in important ways. From this metaphysical starting point Aquinas proceeds to design an elaborate scheme showing how the seven Ciceronian or eight Aristotelian circumstances "touch" the substance of acts. Circumstances enter into the evaluation of an act in two ways. Usually they affect the degree of seriousness attributed to the action and attenuate or augment the blame attached to it. The circumstances may also, however, change the very nature of the moral act: because reason determines the particular time and place of action, it may happen that these particular circumstances involve something so contrary to reason that they become an essential feature of the act.

Aquinas cites an example that is commonly found in medieval discussions of the subject. As such, "theft" is constituted by its object (i.e., the taking of another's property); but the theft of a sacred vessel from a church is "sacrilege" and so falls under a different "species" of moral act. So, Aquinas taught, circumstances can not only modify the goodness and badness of an act of a certain kind; they can also "establish an act as a particular species of good or bad." In light of this teaching, Aquinas concluded,

> Speaking in a formal sense alone, the just and the good are always and everywhere the same, since principles of natural reason are immutable. But, in the material sense, justice and goodness are not the same everywhere and always . . . this is so, because of the muta-bility of human nature, the diverse conditions of persons and their affairs and the differences of time and place.

In sum, "the human act ought to vary according to diverse condi-tions of persons, time and other circumstances: this is the entire matter of morality."[30]

That last text from Thomas Aquinas could almost serve as the motto for the whole enterprise of casuistry. The theological doctrines of circumstance and conscience, prudence and natural law provided the casuists of the high era with an understanding of morality that made casuistry a feasible, respectable, and even necessary activity. The doctrine of natural law gave them a strong but limited system of principles: strong because the principles, though few, were definitely stated and rooted in a generally accepted moral psychology and meta-physics; limited because the principles were of the most general purview. Principles were related to particular cases, not because any particular conclusion could be deduced from them but because they provided a context for all deliberation about the case. The doctrines of conscience and prudence showed that although the completely gener-al first principles of morality might be universally and ineradicably known, deliberation about the merits of particular actions moved in the more obscure realm of individual facts.

The ultimate act of "conscience" was a judgment in which the universal and the particular were known together (con-scire): this specific behavior, arising from a specific motive and performed in a context of detailed circumstances, was the right act for one to per-form. Finally, the doctrine of circumstances incorporated the setting of an action into the moral meaning of the action itself, not as its essence but as its accidents. Circumstances, in this Aristotelian view, are integers to be added up in the description of an action: add or subtract one relevant circumstance, and the act may have to be described, named, and evaluated in a quite different way from before. The casuists of the high era were surrounded by these doctrines, took them seriously, and used them as the background of their work. That work was to set out descriptions of moral behavior in which moral precepts and the details of actions were looked at together. How should a person, concerned to act rightly, make a judgment of conscience in any specific kind of situation? This was the "case of conscience."

Part III

High Casuistry

THE BACKGROUND TO HIGH CASUISTRY

By the close of the thirteenth century, the raw materials for casuistry "properly speaking" had been collected and assembled into rough shape. Theologians had fashioned refined treatises on natural law, conscience, and circumstances. Canonists had collated decrees and dicta arising from past cases and meant to be applied to similar cases. Private confession, in which priests adjudicated particular cases presented by penitents, had become relatively common practice. The education of those priests in the relevant theological and canonical doctrines had inspired the composition of confessional books, which greatly augmented the earlier penitential books. Against this background casuistry proper came into being. This part of our history describes the growth of casuistry from the early fourteenth century to its most mature expression during the century 1556–1656, which we shall call "high casuistry."

We begin with an account of the first forms that casuistry took, after being touched by the contributions of the theologians. These works, which we call *Summas*, continued the tradition of the penitentials and confessionals but incorporated the theological doctrines formulated by the scholastic theologians. Next, we review the social and political background that helped bring casuistry to its maturity, with particular attention to the role played by Ignatius Loyola's newly established Society of Jesus, the Jesuits. Finally, we shall relate the course of the most vigorous intellectual debate that took place within the intellectual world of the casuists, the dispute over the doctrine of probabilism.

7

Summists and Jesuits

The theological accomplishments of the thirteenth century could not fail to influence the authors of the more practical confessional books. Before the century was over, John of Fribourg had composed *Summa Confessorum* (c. 1280), in which the opinions of Albert the Great, Thomas Aquinas, and other major theologians of the previous half-century were integrated into the canonical and moral discussions. Most of the major theologians of the century were members of the two mendicant orders founded in the early years of the century, the Order of Friars Minor, or Franciscans, and the Order of Preachers, or Dominicans. These friars responded generously to the mandate of the Fourth Lateran Council requiring annual confession of the faithful. They promoted and engaged seriously in the ministry of the confessional. To aid their confrères and other priests, members of both orders produced manuals modeled on the earlier confessionals but enriched from the modern theological doctrines. As early as 1259, the Dominicans prescribed regular study of cases of conscience in the convents of the order; another order of great influence, the Hermits of St. Augustine, appointed a reader in cases of "practical theology" in their monasteries.[1]

The *Summa de Poenitentia* of Raymond of Pennafort and the *Summa Theologica* of Thomas Aquinas, written about the same time, influenced the order and content of a vast number of such manuals during the next three centuries. Chief among these were the *Summa*

Astesana by an anonymous Franciscan of Asti in Italy, written about 1317; the *Summa Pisana* by the Dominican Bartolomeo de Santoconcordio (d. 1347), and the *Pupilla Oculi* by John de Burgo, chancellor of Cambridge University (d. 1386). About 1480 the Franciscan friar Angelo Carletti wrote a *summa* that came to be called *Summa Angelica*. (Martin Luther dubbed it *Summa Diabolica* when, in 1520, he cast it into the bonfire of books he judged to be detrimental to Christian faith.) In 1516 the Dominican Sylvester Mazzolini of Priero (1456–1523) published a work he entitled *Summa Summarum*, in which he professed to surpass and render useless all previous books of this sort: in fact, he did little more than repeat the cases, analyses, and solutions of his predecessors. Another Dominican, John Cagnazzo of Thabia, produced a work with the same title and the same purpose. The two books were distinguished by being called *Summa Sylvestrina* and *Summa Tabiena*.

While not novel in content or method, both books were encyclopedic in the number of authors cited and the range of topics covered. Like many of their predecessors, these authors arranged the subject matter in alphabetical order, starting with Abbot and Absolution and ending with Usury and Uxoricide. Each short article contained definitions of terms that had become classical, references to relevant sections of canon law, and brief statements justifying conclusions, often abbreviated from such authors as Aquinas and Pennafort. Among the myriad cases found in their pages it is rare to encounter a case of conscience, in the sense in which that term was later used: namely, a conflict of moral principle. Most cases simply show how some maxim is applied when certain particular circumstances obtain. Often a question is answered merely by citing some canon from the Church law. Frequently the opinions of other summists are repeated verbatim: agreement or disagreement is usually noted, and on occasion there is an extended (but not always illuminating) debate on the various positions taken by the authors cited. Nowhere in this literature does one find a serious discussion of method or theory.

A few years later, in 1523, one of the leading theologians of the age, the Dominican Thomas de Vio Cajetan, contributed his *Summula Peccatorum*. In the preface he complains that other works of this genre "multiply opinions and, thus, confuse and perplex the reader." He will avoid speculation and contentious questions and merely present what is, in his view, the best-reasoned and most authoritative position. His Dominican colleague, Bartolomeo Fumus (d. 1545), followed the same program in his *Summa Armilla*. He states that he will avoid "multiple distinctions, infinite citations of doctors, prolix series of debates that provoke the reader's soul *ad nauseam*." Rabelais' hilarious description of the civil jurisprudence of the era, in book III of *Gargantua and Pantagruel*, would have fitted these summists equally well. Many of their works were written as ready reference books for a relatively uneducated clergy. One unknown author quite frankly entitled his book *Summa Rudium*—that is, the Summa for the Uneducated (c. 1534). It even became common to render the more popular works into crude verse as an aide-memoire; one of these was called the *Summa Metrica*. Despite their defects, these works enjoyed wide popularity and, as the age of printing opened, were reissued in many (not always accurate) editions.[2]

The authors of the summas made much of certain distinctions that had matured at the hands of the scholastic theologians. The theologians had sharpened the distinction between mortal and venial sin, which had been unclear and confused in earlier periods of Church history. Under theological scrutiny the distinction came to be explained in terms of the analogous meaning of the word "sin": mortal sin was a human act performed with full knowledge and full consent and bearing on a matter that is essential to one's relation to one's last end, the vision of God. A sin was venial when it lacked one or all of these characteristics. The theologians proposed that gravity of sin could be judged in view of the object of the act, as well as by the intent of the agent. They adapted from Aristotelian metaphysics the complex notion that an act might be distinguished as good or bad *by genus*: that is, in and of itself, regardless of motive or circumstance. They also refined the Stoic distinctions, among good, evil, and indifferent acts, explaining how actions can be distinguished into different species and conceptually separated into discrete, enumerable actions. They justified the moral distinction between precept and counsel, as originated by Clement of Alexandria and Ambrose. They noted the greater stringency of negative precepts as compared with positive ones. They formulated the relevance for moral accountability of the distinction between sins of commission and sins of omission. They explored the implications of dividing sins into those of thought and those of deed. The scholastic theologians had brought order and clarity to these distinctions, which the earlier confessional books had mentioned in a confused and unclear way. The authors of the summas put them to use as practical tools for the more precise analysis of actions, particularly as instruments to weigh the burden of human accountability.[3]

These distinctions did more. They suggested, for the first time in Western culture, a systematic taxonomy of human behavior. This taxonomy was developed in the service of a practical pastoral goal. In the hands of the summists, distinctions and classifications that had been scattered and inchoate in the classical and patristic authors were shaped into standard ways of describing moral behavior. This taxonomy provided a more detailed set of concepts and a more artic-ulate form of communication about practical morality than any that had previously existed. It replaced the eloquent generalities of the classical authors with an exactness of expression that reflected the nuances of moral deliberation, choice, and action. So it provided for morality the same precision that canonical and civil jurisprudence gave to the law during the same period.

The summists' incorporation of these concepts into their books of practical advice made it possible for confessors to learn and to teach ordinary people how to examine their own moral lives and how to communicate about them with another person—namely, their con-fessor or spiritual director. These distinctions introduced into the appreciation of common people a refinement about the morally rele-vant features of actions and about imputability that had hitherto been appreciated only by scholars. The common people could now be shown the relative importance of intentions, dispositions, conse-quences, and circumstances to the moral evaluation of their acts. In so doing the summists, in the words of a modern author, were able to "make a great contribution to the affirmation of the personhood of each Christian, manifested in personal responsibility for one's own conduct."[4] These distinctions have endured into our own cul-ture and still constitute the vocabulary of psychological and moral discourse, even for many moral philosophers who have not the slightest acquaintance with these forgotten predecessors.

THE CENTURY OF MATURITY: 1556–1656

Casuistry's century of maturity opens with the publication of a vol-ume that marked a new beginning in casuistic method: the *Enchiridion* of Martin Azpilcueta, who was usually referred to as the

Doctor of Navarre, or Navarrus. The century ends with the publication of a series of essays that dealt casuistry a blow from which its reputation never recovered, *The Provincial Letters* of Blaise Pascal. Between these two events an immense outpouring of casuistical literature flowed from the presses of Europe, and even of America. This literature constitutes the classical form of casuistry. At its best it learns and benefits from the heritage of theology, canon law, and penitential discipline, as developed over the previous centuries, and draws from those sources reasonable and convincing moral discriminations. At its worst it remains mired in the confusion of distinctions without differences, and overwhelmed by the diversity of available opinions.

Major social events precipitated this flourishing endeavor. One of the most dramatic and traumatic was the Reformation, which began exactly fifty years before our opening date. When Martin Luther cast the *Summa Diabolica* into the flames, he did not destroy casuistry, although he dampened his own followers' enthusiasm for it.[5] In fact the Reformation gave a new impetus to Catholic casuistry. In 1545 the Council of Trent was convened to effect reforms within the Roman Catholic Church. During its twenty-five sessions it reviewed the theological doctrines of the Catholic faith and reaffirmed its liturgical and disciplinary practices, though with many modifications. In the face of Protestant denial, the council reiterated the canons of the Fourth Lateran Council about personal and private confession. In addition, it incorporated into the laws of the Church a requirement, on which theologians had long agreed, that the penitent should confess sins according to species, number, and circumstances. This decree countered the contention of some reformers that confession to a priest was not necessary, and that repentance was for sinfulness in general rather than for particular acts of sin. The Council also legislated the establishment of seminaries for the orderly education of clergy. These decrees stimulated the activity of casuistry in several ways. The decree requiring confession of sins by species, number, and circumstance called for a clarification of how these terms were to be applied in the examination of the penitent's conscience and to the judgment of the confessor. The second decree ensured that educational institutions would be created in which theology would be taught not only as a speculative science but as a practical art, applied to the direction and care of souls.[6]

In addition, the Reformation posed certain moral problems that required casuistical resolution. For the first time, Europeans found themselves faced with allegiance to diverse Christian faiths, which split realms, villages, families, and religious orders. How, then, was the daily business of life to be carried on, as between Catholics and Protestants? Did a Catholic owe obedience to a Protestant ruler? Could a Catholic serve as a judge or an officer in a Protestant realm? Could one marry between faiths? Did differences of religion affect commercial contracts? Could a Catholic carry on ordinary dealings with heretics? Were they obliged to seek their conversion? How could loyal Catholics dwell alongside persons who were committed to different beliefs and practices? The presumptions of a common morality were cast into doubt and turmoil.[7]

Political and economic life was also changing. During the century of casuistry's maturity Europe was torn by devastating wars. Far from confining itself to the pulpit, religious militancy instigated street battles, massacres, and warfare. Many of the multiple tiny princedoms of Europe were coalescing into nation-states while other previously great realms were fragmenting. Monarchs were consolidating strong centralized power over previously independent dukes and barons. Old political forms were cracking under the strain of emerging nationhood and novel ideas about national government. Meanwhile commerce was profiting from improved transport, more efficient manufacture, and the expansion of exchange and banking. New forms of financing were rapidly utilized to underwrite international trade, and lands beyond the seas, previously unknown and undreamed of, were opened up to exploration and exploitation. These changes provided ample material for casuistry: new "cases of conscience" were constantly being posed by new conditions. To people of the sixteenth century, activities we now distinguish into different kinds—as political or economic, religious or social—were all "moral" activities. All of them were matters of conscience; and "cases of conscience" were not confined to the private matters of personal conduct that so many moderns regard as the realm of conscience.[8]

Nor were these cases limited to the secrecy of the confessional. There were "Great Cases" of major public moment. In 1539 at the request of Emperor Charles V, Francisco Vitoria, Professor of Theology at Salamanca, wrote *Relectio de Indis et de Jure Belli*, a case study on the government of the indigenous people of the newly discovered Americas. In 1613 Francisco Suarez wrote the *Defensio Fidei Catholicae adversus Anglicanae Sectae Errores*, a case study on the obligation of subjects to a heretical ruler, occasioned by the claims of

King James I over the religious conscience of his Catholic subjects. Casuists became counselors to kings and popes. It was not uncommon for rulers to summon a commission of casuists to render expert advice on a political case. In 1530 Charles V assembled a junta of theologians at Barcelona to debate Spanish colonial policy. Several times during the sixteenth century popes created committees to advise on the usury question. Major questions about the resolution of the Thirty Years' War were put to a commission of theologians by Emperor Ferdinand II in 1634. Position papers by casuists influenced policy. Casuists wrote the *Pacis Compositio* (1628), interpreting the obligations arising from the Peace of Augsburg of 1555, and the *Justa Defensio* (1631), which unraveled the complex issue of property rights relative to restitution of monastic properties in formerly Protestant domains. The hundred years beginning around 1550 were made for the casuists, and the casuists made the most of them.[9]

Finally, casuistry flourished in the era known as the Baroque period. Its products—immense, elaborate volumes filled with minute distinctions and detailed, sometimes contorted, arguments—are reminiscent of the art and architecture of the Baroque era: in fact, the epithet *Barockmorale* has been seriously applied to the style of moral reasoning associated with casuistry.[10] A modern philosopher has recently (and perhaps inadvertently) noted this similarity in speaking of

> the aesthetic preference most of us [moderns] have for the economy of principles, the preference for ethical systems in the style of the Bauhaus rather than the Baroque.[11]

The analogy reflects more than a difference in style. The Baroque era was marked by a massive presence of the temporality, agony, and conflicts of the world and the flesh in the sanctuary of the Church. The Baroque era signals the definitive irruption into Christian culture of the secular as reality, and as value. The dominance of the spiritual and the superiority of the religious over the lay state were no longer seen as obvious. Serious consideration of the moral import of secular activities of all kinds, from studying to soldiering, was incumbent on the moralists of the time.

This irruption of the secular had already begun in the fifteenth century: it had created great disturbance and incongruity in the church. The dominant moral theologian of the Renaissance, St. Antoninus, Archbishop of Florence (1389–1459), was a rigorous moralist, but he was also a man of the world, of politics, and of finance, and he recognized the change of values: "It is not a precept, but only a counsel to follow the more sure way to salvation; otherwise most persons would be obliged to become monks and nuns . . . just as many roads lead to a city, although one is the safest, so some will travel toward the heavenly city more securely, others less so."[12] By the Baroque period the initial paradox of whether life in the world could be as "good" as life in monastic isolation had been resolved. Life in the world of public activity had won its place in the moral view of Christians; so Christian moralists were called to scrutinize the activities of the world and to advise Christians how best to travel along "the less secure way" to salvation. The *Summae Sylvestrina et Angelica,* almost a century old, were obviously outmoded. They looked back to a medieval world that no longer existed: the simple lines of moral rule and precept they provided were no longer adequate. In a complex baroque world, casuistry created its "baroque" response of correspondingly complex arguments.

THE JESUITS

The burgeoning of casuistry was nourished by a new religious order, the Society of Jesus, or Jesuits. This name almost came to be equated with "casuistry," particularly (though unfairly) in the sinister sense of the word.[13] The circumstances of their establishment and work, as well as their peculiar notoriety, linked the Jesuits with both the growth and the decline of casuistry. Founded in 1534 by a Spanish nobleman, Ignatius of Loyola, they received papal approval and established their headquarters in Rome in 1540. The small band quickly won a reputation as men dedicated to reform within the Church and as formidable opponents to those other reformers who had repudiated Rome. They served as competent theological consultants at the Council of Trent, and accepted special papal missions throughout Europe and the Far East. They established outposts at the frontiers of Catholic and Protestant Europe and in the New World. Sixty years after its founding, the Society of Jesus counted 13,000 members, distributed throughout thirty-two provinces around the world.

Loyola and his colleagues recognized that one essential thing for the reform of the Church was improved education for clergy and laity alike. They dedicated the energies of the society predominantly, though not exclusively, to that work; so by 1600 the Jesuits were conducting 372 colleges in the major cities and towns of Europe, South America, and India. By 1640 the number had grown to 520 schools with 150,000 pupils. Some of the pupils came from noble families, but at least half were sons of artisans and peasants, who were taught without any charge for tuition. In its size, uniformity, and orderly plan of studies the Jesuit educational system was unique. The education provided in these colleges was a synthesis of scholasticism and humanism, and it was widely acknowledged to be the best available. Descartes was a pupil at the Jesuit College of La Flèche; Molière, a student at the College of Clermont; Calderón studied at the Colegio Imperial in Madrid; and, to the Fathers' chagrin, Voltaire was a prizewinner at the College Louis le Grand in Paris.

The Jesuits were not confined within their college walls. They entered with vigor into the religious and political affairs of the era. They represented the pope in mission to bishops and rulers; became confessors to reigning princes, princely counselors, and ambassadors, and favored scholars at the courts of rajahs and khans; and even won acceptance in the Mandarin bureaucracy of the Empire of China.[14] During the incessant strife of the post-Reformation years, they were deeply involved in policy decisions: at a time when the criterion of policy was the "conscience" of a ruler and of his or her advisors, the sovereign's confessor gave advice not only about what was morally right but also about what was politically wise or admirable. An official instruction, *On the Confession of Princes*, was issued by the Jesuit General Acquaviva in 1602 and confirmed by the General Congregation in 1608. When confessors and counselors to the courts of monarchs were trained in cases of conscience, casuistry was sure "to catch the conscience of the king."

The Jesuit commitment to casuistry was a natural consequence of their organization. The ancient monastic restrictions of cloister and choir were not imposed upon them: their constitutions required individual Jesuits to travel wherever they were sent on missions for the Church. They were the first fully "worldly" religious community, bound by the traditional vows, but mandated to work among secular persons in secular institutions. This novel form of religious life aroused hostility and skepticism among the older orders; yet it was approved by Rome and provided a model for later congregations. Given their secular vocation, the Jesuits stressed the role of activity rather than contemplation, involvement rather than withdrawal, in the religious and ethical duties of the Christian. Thus they were forced to acknowledge the genuine problems of practical decision faced by agents in complex circumstances involving conflicts of principle. Their members, vowed to strict obedience to their superiors, found themselves worlds away from the control of authority: bound to fulfill diplomatic missions, they were distant from the voices of those who sent them and were instructed to rely upon their discretion, interpreting their orders according to the actual situation. So they approached moral questions in the spirit of Aristotle and Aquinas rather than of Plato and Augustine: the problem that occupied them was how to choose a course of action prudently and virtuously, rather than how to ascend to a vision of eternal truth. The principal document of Jesuit spirituality, the *Spiritual Exercises* of Ignatius of Loyola, thus centered on the problem of personal choice and provided practical rules for "discernment of spirits": that is, awareness of one's preferences and their causes. Casuistry was a natural consequence of this practical approach to the problems of the moral life.[15]

Another reason for the importance of the Jesuits as casuists was more paradoxical. The late sixteenth century saw a revival of philosophical skepticism, and this in turn encouraged suspicions of the moral license traditionally associated with skepticism. The protests of the Reformation had shattered confidence in all claims that there was a single source of undivided truth. Montaigne's heartfelt and eloquently expressed doubts became fashionable; and both Descartes and Pascal set out to refute his skepticism. In quite different ways both men claimed to have found certitude. The Jesuits, likewise, repudiated the spirit of skepticism in religious and philosophical thought. Their founder's *Spiritual Exercises* proposed a method for arriving at spiritual assurance about one's own form and state of life. In an era of fashionable agnosticism, their casuistry sought to bolster confidence about certain values and principles; although, as we shall see, it was the assurance of moral probability rather than certitude.

Pascal upbraided the Jesuits for catering to the intellectual and moral weakness of their powerful and wealthy clients. By making distinctions and allowing excuses and exceptions in moral matters, they were, he claimed, only fostering skepticism further. His own solution was to cling to the certitudes of faith and adhere rigorously to moral principle; the solution of his Jesuit opponents was probabilism and reasonable, argued moral counsel. Both Pascal and the Jesuits were confronting the same intellectual milieu. Yet paradoxical though it may seem, casuistry was intended to be an anchor in the seas of uncertainty roiled by the controversies of the time.[16] As educators, confessors, and disputants in theological controversy, the Jesuits gained powerful influence and inspired powerful enmity both within and outside the Church. Their energy and influence promoted the rise of casuistry: the enmity they inspired contributed to its decline.

The predominance of the Jesuits in civil and religious affairs explains why they were able to propagate casuistry; it does not explain why they were casuists in the first place. For this we must look to the program of education instituted for their own members. The Constitutions of the Society of Jesus required a lengthy and demanding sequence of studies for all aspirants to the priesthood. It divided these aspirants into two classes: those being prepared for an academic career (the Professed) and those training for the pastoral ministry (the Spiritual Coadjutors). The Spiritual Coadjutors followed an abbreviated course designed for pastoral rather than scholarly activities. While students in the "long course" studied moral theology in the *Summa Theologica* of Aquinas, those in the "short course" studied cases of conscience. A Professor of Cases of Conscience was designated to instruct these students and was specifically directed to be "practical rather than speculative." All students, whether in the long or the short course, as well as most of the members of the community, were required to attend a weekly case conference, at which the Professor of Cases presented and resolved several difficult cases of conscience; participants were admonished to come prepared "to ask and be asked questions." On occasion the students themselves, described in the text of the document as *casistae*, were given the task of resolving the case in the presence of their critical brethren.[17]

In 1581 Father General Claudius Aquaviva initiated the preparation of the *Ratio Studiorum*, a detailed plan of education for the Society. All provinces of the Society were consulted; draft plans were circulated and criticized extensively before the third draft was adopted in 1593 and implemented in 1599. During the decade of discussion considerable attention was given to the place of "cases of conscience" in the educational program. Some commentators felt that the rigid separation of practical casuistry from speculative moral theology, as taught from the *Summa Theologica*, was to the detriment of both. The final *Ratio* struck a balance, requiring both an explanation of principles and a study of casuistry for students in the long and the short course alike.

The *Ratio* stated Rules for the Professors of Cases, directing them to explain briefly the principles relevant to any case, "without knowledge of which the case analysis would be quite shaky (*non parum vacillat*)"; but they were to refrain from detailed exposition of more speculative and theoretical questions. Some three cases should suffice to illustrate each principle; all "probable" opinions about the resolution of the cases should be noted, except those that were obsolete or patently false. The professor should point out various problems about each opinion and propose his own conclusion, confirmed "by at least two or three excellent reasons."[18]

Thus casuistry came to occupy a central place in the education of the Jesuits. This pedagogy definitively shaped the manner in which casuistry was practiced. The rules of the professor of cases established the format: avoidance of speculative questions, succinct presentation of principles, acceptance of probable opinions, and resolution by solid argument. Every member of the Society became familiar with this technique; practiced it in case conferences as a student; heard it weekly for his entire career in the Society; and made use of it in his ministry. Lay students, secular priests, and, on occasion, members of the public were permitted to attend these conferences. Professors of cases were appointed even in colleges for the lay students, thus familiarizing their pupils, who were destined for leadership in many walks of life, with casuistical reasoning.[19]

This extensive teaching bred a need for textbooks. The *Enchiridion* of Navarrus was regularly used in the early years. In 1554 the secretary of the Society, Juan Polanco, published his *Breve Directorium*, a "short guide" to the study of cases. One of the first distinguished theologians of the Society, Francesco Toletus, published *Summa Casuum Conscientiae* in 1569. By the last decade of the sixteenth century the lecture notes and case analyses of Jesuit professors were redacted into books, initiating a flood of literature that amounted to some six hundred volumes by 1669.[20]

In addition to casuistical works, Jesuit theologians also contributed to the nascent discipline of moral theology, in which the treatises on human acts, conscience, and natural law that had been created by the scholastic theologians were elaborated as foundations for casuistry. They also wrote major treatises on government, warfare, economics, and international law, which frequently appeared under the title *De Jure et Justitia*. These works, most of them by Jesuits, who were primarily speculative theologians but occasionally also casuists, such as Molina, Toletus, Lessius, de Lugo and Suarez, were in some ways precursors of modern treatises on economics, political science, and sociology. But above all, they were studies of the moral principles that were to be applied to the practices of ruling and judging, trading and banking, fighting and making treaties.[21]

While they were not the only authors of casuistical books, the Jesuits became its major and most prolific proponents. Casuistry was integral to their education; and they realized that it was integral to their ministry. As confessors to the nobility and to an emerging mercantile class, in a time of rapid social, economic, and religious change they encountered many perplexing moral cases. As educators of pupils destined to be (as their teachers said) *insigni*, or outstanding, they prepared their charges to meet problems of conscience with "discernment"—a favorite Jesuit word. As leaders in the Counter-Reformation, they would particularly face the problems posed by interactions between Catholics and Protestants. In all this a knowledge of principles needed to be supplemented by a sharp perception of the novel and unprecedented nature of these problems, and by a refined capacity to discern the morally relevant similarities and differences between cases. The education they prescribed for their members and their students thus encompassed not only the theology and philosophy which would teach principles, but the humanities, which taught discrimination and discernment. They were particularly insistent on the mastery of rhetoric, an art that, as we have seen, provides a structure of argument suitable for casuistry.[22] Thus the Jesuits were trained to be not only humanists and theologians but also casuists, and the words "casuistry" and "Jesuitry" were fated, for better or worse, to become near synonyms.

8

Texts, Authors, and Methods

The century of casuistry's maturity begins in 1556. In that year Martin Azpilcueta, an Augustinian cleric and Professor of Canon Law at the Universities of Coimbra and Salamanca, published the Spanish edition of his *Enchiridion Confessariorum et Poenitentium* (Handbook for Confessors and Penitents).[1] Commonly called the Doctor of Navarre (or "Navarrus") he was universally respected for learning and prudence, and his advice was sought by the kings of Spain and Portugal. He concluded his career in the important position of consultor to the Sacred Penitentiary, where his duties were to provide expert advice on the moral and legal cases referred to Rome for resolution. Trusted by three successive popes—Pius V, Gregory XIII, and Sixtus V—he was also esteemed by the Jesuits. He was, it is said, a kinsman to one of the best known of Loyola's original companions, Francisco Xavier, and the Jesuits made wide use of the *Enchiridion*, modeling their style of case analysis on it.

The *Enchiridion* first appeared in Portuguese at Coimbra in 1549. In its original form it was in fact an edited version of a manual for confessors written by an Augustinian colleague, Rodrigo da Porto, which had been accused of doctrinal inaccuracy. Navarrus had undertaken to correct and issue the work under his own respected name: the Spanish version of 1556, and the subsequent Latin editions, were fully the work of Navarrus himself. The Latin edition appeared in Rome in 1573 and went through some fifty reprintings and revisions. Though heavily influenced by such earlier confessional books and summas as the *Sylvestrina* and *Angelica*, it introduced a significant change of style. Instead of the alphabetical order typical of earlier books, Navarrus adopted a scheme in which his cases were discussed under headings taken from the commandments of the Decalogue. This plan had occasionally appeared before, as in the *Expositio Praeceptorum Decalogi* of Jean Nyder (d. 1438), but Navarrus gave it currency and established it as the standard method of exposition. This style of ordering cases introduced "a strength of reasoning and logical sequence" that the alphabetical works lacked.[2] Navarrus' innovation was of great importance to the maturation of casuistry.

The contents of the *Enchiridion* were not as original as its method. In general, Navarrus followed the solution of cases favored by the summists. When he disagreed, he set out his arguments concisely. New types of cases occasionally appear and call for new solutions. For instance, he respectfully dissents from an opinion of the eminent Cardinal Cajetan, that pretending to be a heretic out of fear of one's life is itself a mortal sin against faith. He so dissents in resolving a case presented "by a certain Jesuit working among the Saracens" who requested advice about the conduct of newly converted Christians who pretended to be pagans in order to avoid capture. He contributed some significant ideas to the evolution of the doctrine about usury, revealing his appreciation of contemporary economic conditions. In a case we shall examine later, he argued at length against Soto's subtle distinctions, which seemed to allow someone defending his own life to intend the death of the aggressor.[3] In general, Navarrus' book of casuistry was a balanced work. A modern commentator says that it gave confessor and penitent alike a "perfect confessional guide in which the author has stabilized, for many serious moral problems, an opinion that is prudent, shrewd and sound."[4] But what was to have the greatest influence on the methods of casuistry was the propagation of Navarrus' new manner of ordering cases.

The premier Jesuit casuist was Juan Azor (1535–1603), professor of moral theology first at Alcala and then, for the last twenty years of his life, at the Jesuit College at Rome. Azor's *Institutionum Moralium*, published in Rome from 1600 to 1611, is an immense volume of 3,800 folio pages. It bears the subtitle, "in which all questions of conscience are briefly treated."[5] Azor followed Navarrus' order but prefaced his cases with six books containing detailed essays on such topics as the nature and imputability of human acts, the definition and conditions of sin, and the nature of conscience. He also prefaced the sections on certain commandments with similar treatises: book III, for example, which discussed the commandments regarding killing, adultery, and theft, is prefaced by a treatise on justice. This manner of introducing the actual treatment of cases became standard in subsequent works of casuistry: the discussion of cases followed a theological exposition that drew heavily on Aquinas and the later scholastics. In doing this Azor responded to the advice of the *Ratio Studiorum* of 1599, to combine theoretical with practical materials.

In his treatise on circumstances, Azor showed his appreciation of the importance of understanding circumstances in the resolution of cases. He defined circumstances as those common and external attributes of persons and things from which law and morality determine the appropriate forms of contracts, as well as the suitable penalties for fault and crime. According to circumstances, it will or will not be correct to assert that this or that action is right. Circumstances are of great importance in understanding human acts; they can and often do change the very nature of an action; they allow diverse judgments about their imputability. Circumstances are particularly significant in evaluating the validity of business contracts. "In law," he says, "circumstances change everything so that from circumstances the equity of the case can be grasped"—*circumstantiae in jure variant omnia ut inde aequitas colligatur.*[6]

When Azor turned to the substance of his work, explaining the obligations of the Decalogue, he followed an equally orderly pattern. The meaning of each Commandment was first explained in a general way. He explained, for example, that the Fifth Commandment, "Thou shalt not kill," prohibits the taking of a human life, the physical mutilation of the body of oneself or of another, and acts of physical violence, as well as acts that lead to violence, such as expressions of anger. Then, particular cases were taken up: What about homicide in the course of defense against an unjust aggressor? What conditions must be present if a defense is to be judged just? What if the aggressor has certain features—for example, is one's relative, one's ruler, a religious, and so forth? What about circumstances of time and place? In a church? In the dark of night? What about killing an adversary in a war one considers unjust? What about killing in pursuit of a fleeing attacker, in defense of one's property, in defense of one's honor or of one's virtue, in defense of another's life, or another's property?[7] Chapters follow that are devoted to specific types of killing: judicial execution, suicide, abortion, dueling, and warfare, among others; subsequent chapters deal with related issues such as collusion in or encouragement of murder, and with the moral affections suggested by the Commandment such as anger, hatred, and cruelty.

In each chapter the same pattern is repeated: a general statement about principles, followed by particular cases that exemplify the principles in particular circumstances. Azor's systematic analysis established an important feature of casuistical methodology: the general principle is first exhibited in an obvious case and only then in other cases in which circumstances make its application increasingly less clear. The initial cases are those in which common agreement of all theologians and moralists supports the conclusion: there is no room for serious diversity of opinion about what is the right course of action. As the subsequent cases become more complex, the resolution becomes more uncertain, and the discussion expounds the debates that commentators have carried on about them. In some cases a preponderance of opinion is noted; in others, the lack of any general consensus is admitted. This technique of marshaling, comparing, and contrasting "probable opinions" became a central feature of casuistry and was itself to become the subject for vigorous debate in the dispute over probabilism.

Azor's *Institutionum* enjoyed vast popularity, and its author was quickly accepted as "classical"—that is, as belonging to the class of authors whose opinions could be taken most seriously. The leading Jesuit casuist of the nineteenth century, Jean Gury, said of Azor, "He is, among authors, the most commendable for his wisdom, learning and the weight of his reasoning."[8] In the half-century after Azor similar works appeared in great number from many pens. In most of these works the sequence and pattern of Azor's work was followed. Even before the publication of the *Institutionum*, professors of cases had presumably begun to employ this pattern as their usual classroom approach in academic courses. Among the many other Jesuits who produced books of casuistry, several achieved considerable fame or notoriety. One of these was Antonio Escobar y Mendoza (1589–1669), whose *Liber Theologiae Moralis Vigintiquatuor Societatis Jesu Doctoribus Resertus*, published in Lyons in 1644, was the unfortunate target of Pascal's brilliant sarcasm.[9] (We shall see more of this "good father.") Another was Herman Busenbaum

(1600–1668), whose *Medulla Theologiae Moralis*, published in Münster in 1645, ran to two hundred printings by 1776[10] and became the basis for the magisterial treatise of the greatest of moral theologians, Alphonsus Ligouri (1696–1787).[11] Busenbaum was a judicious, cautious moralist who, interestingly, is never mentioned by Pascal among his casuistical villains.

Not all of the best-known casuists were Jesuits. Ironically, the two casuists who most merited Pascal's scorn were not themselves Jesuits. Antonius Diana (1585–1663), a Theatine cleric, was known as the "Prince of Casuists" and the "Atlas of the Casuistical World." His immense *Resolutiones Morales*, published in Palermo in ten volumes (1629 to 1659) deals with some twenty thousand cases.[12] He was, says a modern commentator, "the pure casuist."[13] Since he cited a crowd of authorities for alternative positions on many cases, and found most of their opinions "probable," he left those issues open so that the consciences of the penitent and confessor were free to choose among them. His general authority was great: *Diana dixit* ("Diana says so") was a term of high approbation. His work also had a great vogue: compendia and resumes, such as the *Diana Coordinatus* of Martin de Acolea (Lyon, 1667) and the *Summa Diana* of Antonio Cotonio (Anvers, 1656) made his vast work widely accessible.[14] Yet despite his popularity, Diana represented an aberration. A modern scholar writes of him:

> Diana had a passion for cases the way other men have a passion for gambling. The more bizarre and unreal the case, the happier he is, for it calls for an even more ingenious exercise of his wit . . . He represents not so much an example of noble human reasoning about moral matters as an itch for subtlety and complexity which is to reason what illness is to health.[15]

Another prominent casuist, Jean Caramuel-Lebkowitz (1606–1682), was a Cistertian monk, abbot, and bishop and a man of prominence in political and even military affairs: he is said to have led his troops in defense of his episcopal see against Swiss troops. Caramuel was acknowledged in his time as a genius in many fields. Like Diana, with whom he shared a mutual admiration, he had an exaggerated confidence in the authority of authors of note. His *Theologia Moralis ad Prima Eaque Clarissima Principia Reducta* (Louvain, 1645) earned him the epithets of "the prince of laxists" and "the Carneades of casuists." Once having found any opinion favoring liberty over law, he allowed it to be embraced and so stimulated doubt about the validity of all law.[16]

These two authors, who were extremely popular in their own time, represented casuistry at its laxist extreme. They were willing to take on, or create, any kind of moral case; they were amenable to opinions from every side, delighting in the most subtle and specious distinctions; and they made of moral reasoning "a sort of marvelous computer programmed for any complexity."[17] In their enthusiasm about the case at hand they lost all sense of moral seriousness; and in their love of subtlety they lacked a sense of moral balance and perceptiveness. Given the association between "Jesuitry" and casuistry, it is ironic that the genuine shortcomings of casuistry were most evident in two authors who were not Jesuits. It is also perhaps revealing that Pascal, whose antagonism was aimed more against the Jesuits than casuistry itself, refers to these two notorious authors less than a dozen times.

THE ENGLISH CASUISTS

The Reformation rent the "seamless garment" of Catholicism. Startling new institutions replaced ancient practices; new allegiances shifted the focus and form of religious belief. However, many of the old ideas and ways remained under various guises. The intellectual approach that fostered casuistry antedated the Reformation and, despite differences, continued afterward. Even where freedom of conscience and faith were preached the need for spiritual and moral guidance persisted, and the need for agreement about moral practices and the extent to which one could tolerate departures from them survived even after the sacrament of confession and the judicial authority of the ministry withered. Luther despised the casuistry of the summists and cast the *Summa Diabolica* into the bonfire as a sign of his disdain. But his disdain was fostered less by an outright rejection of the casuistical problem and method than by his perception that this elaborate distinction of sins and determination of penances was one of the more unsalutary outgrowths of a theology of "works" that he repudiated.[18]

In general the theological ideas and ecclesiastical institutions fostered by the Reformation were not particularly fertile ground for casuistry. This approach gradually ceded to a different form of presenting Christian ethics, which emphasized inner disposition and freedom of choice rather than principles, consequences, and circumstances. Still, in some of the major Protestant denominations, moral theologians continued to produce casuistical works that differed hardly at all from those of the Roman casuists.

In this, as in many things, the English Reformation differs from the Continental Reformation. It had indigenous roots of reform in Lollardry and the preaching of Wycliff. It flirted for several decades with Lutheran and Calvinist theology but gradually evolved a theology and ecclesiastical forms more suited to the English situation. In thought and institutions alike, the Anglican tradition fostered a *via media*, which preserved much of the ancient way and blended in much of the new. Even the Puritans, who were Calvinist sympathizers, chose a "godly way," which, while certainly not compromise, was peculiarly English. In this ecclesiastical atmosphere a vigorous casuistry flourished in parallel with the casuistry of Catholicism, from the last decades of the sixteenth century through to the late seventeenth century. This literature is interesting not only in itself but in its literary successor: a moral philosophy written in a peculiarly British fashion and in the characteristic moral style of eighteenth-century English prose and poetry.

The most vigorous casuistry is typically generated by a confrontation between values that are thought of as long settled and emerging conditions that apparently challenge those values. This is certainly true of Anglican casuistry. During the first half-century after the break with Rome, the English Church maintained, though with the greatest difficulty, a structure and ecclesiastical policy not radically different from the policy it had for many centuries. Gradually that ancient tradition was eroded by those who favored a Calvinist theology and policy. In 1643 the episcopate was abolished; and three years later a congregational or presbyterian form of church order was established. Three years later the influence of religious disputes on political life played a part in the attacks on and eventual execution of King Charles I. As the Calvinist or Puritan party gained ascendancy in the country, they proposed "cases of conscience" about the use and misuse of power; while the routed traditionalists raised, and faced, questions much like those that the persecuted Catholics had encountered a generation earlier. Thus in this turmoil, case divinity was produced by both Puritans and Anglicans.[19]

It was a public "great case"—that of King Henry VIII's divorce —that had precipitated the original split between England and Rome in 1532. The initial debate about that case, and others generated by the resulting religious upheavals, took polemical rather than casuistical forms. During this period the Catholics looked to their own books; the Anglicans used Catholic books when it suited them or made do without a fresh, homegrown casuistry. Little original casuistical literature was produced in England in the second half of the sixteenth century. But the absence of spiritual and moral direction was soon noted: Francis Bacon was embroiled in a difficult case of conscience regarding bribery and complained that the English theologians of his day provided no assistance. He wrote, "they draw not their directions down *ad casus conscientiae* that a man may be warranted in his particular actions whether they be lawful or not."[20] The lack of a casuistry to suit the new conditions was also noted by many ecclesiastical writers. Thomas Pickering, who edited the first posthumous contribution to this original English casuistry, William Perkins's *Whole Treatise of Cases of Conscience* (1606), complained that

> the want of this doctrine (of releeving and rectifying the Conscience) together with the true manner of applying the same, is, and hath beene the cause of many and great inconveniences . . . for there be many, who in the time of their distresses, when they have considered the waight and desert of their sinnes, and withall apprehended the wrath of God, due unto them; have been brought unto hard exigents, mourning and wayling . . . They have either growne to phrensie and madness or els sorted unto themselves fearfull ends, some by hanging, some by drowning . . . or have abused, or els quite relinquished and forsaken their callings, and thereby become scandalous and offensive to others.[21]

William Perkins, Reader in Divinity at Christ's College, Cambridge, undertook to remedy this distressing lack of direction of consciences. His *Discourse of Conscience* appeared in 1596, and his Holyday lectures were published as *The Whole Treatise of Cases of Conscience* four years after his death in 1602. Perkins shared with many of his Cambridge colleagues a sympathy with Calvinist theology, and thus belonged to the Puritan wing of the English Church. His Puritan sympathies show in frequent references to Scripture for the resolution of cases, and in the almost total absence of reference either to ecclesiastical authority or to his theological predecessors. In this respect a comparison with Azor's *Institutionum*, which appeared at almost the same time, is striking. Perkins uses the Virtues as a basis for the organization of cases, dividing them into Prudence, Clemency, Temperance, Liberality, and Justice. In substance, however, many of his resolutions, such as those concerning use of force in self-defense, are similar to Azor's.

Perkins's work was emulated by other Cambridge Puritans, such as William Ames, who produced *De Conscientia, ejus jure et casibus* in 1630, and Richard Baxter, whose *Christian Directory or Summ of Practical Theology and Cases of Conscience* appeared in 1673. The latter author was particularly concerned to differentiate his casuistry from that of the Jesuits, having published a *Key for Catholicks To Open the Juggling of the Jesuits* in 1659. The prominence of these Puritan casuists at Cambridge prompted Dr. John Knightbridge to found the Knightbridge Chair of Casuistical Divinity at Cambridge University in 1677. (Its first occupant, a certain Dr. Smoult, would undoubtedly be astonished at the teachings that, as we shall see, eventually issued from that chair.)

The first Anglican writer to produce an original work of casuistry was Robert Sanderson, who held the Regius Professorship of Case Divinity at Oxford. His *De Obligatione Conscientiae* was composed in 1649, the year in which Charles I was beheaded by order of the Puritan Parliament. Sanderson himself had been deprived of his chair in the previous year by Puritan Visitors because he had written, at the request of the university, its official argument against the Solemn League and Covenant. After the Restoration he was consecrated Bishop of Lincoln, where he died in 1662. The Anglicans greatly revered Sanderson for his prudence and sage resolution of cases of conscience; we shall see an example of his work in our later discussion of equivocation. According to Izaak Walton, Charles II declared, "I take my ears to other preachers, but my conscience to Dr. Sanderson."[22]

In the very year that King Charles returned from exile, one of the leading figures of Anglican theology, Jeremy Taylor, Bishop of Down and Connor in Ireland, published his enormous work of casuistry, *Ductor Dubitantium*. He too complained of the paucity of sound literature for the guidance of conscience and regretted that it was still necessary, even at that late date, to have recourse to Jesuitical and Papist casuists: "Like the Children of Israel, we are forced to go down to the Philistines to have our shares and coulters sharpened."[23] Earlier distaste for Jesuit casuistry rested on the general reputation of Jesuits as Papal agents and enemies of the English realm: by

Taylor's day, that distaste was fed by a familiarity with Pascal's critique of Jesuit casuistry, which had been translated into English in the very year of its publication.

Despite the repudiation of what Sanderson called "the Jesuitical shell game" (*Jesuitarum argutiola*),[24] the case resolutions of Anglican and Puritan casuists do not differ greatly from their Roman counterparts. Yet the style is quite different. Among the English, resort to Scripture for proofs and maxims is more frequent, reference to canon law is almost absent. Theological differences produce some difference in conclusions: for example, the English writers followed the Continental reformers in repudiating the distinction between "mortal" and "venial" sin. Sanderson called it "that rotton distinction, a leven with which the Roman casuists have foully corrupted the whole lump of moral theology."[25] This distinction, which had become settled in the late Middle Ages, served as a fulcrum for many case resolutions by the Roman casuists; and in its absence the resolutions of the English casuists are often more rigoristic.

At the same time, most of the English casuists repudiated the legalistic tenor of Roman casuistry. They were hardly concerned at all about the appropriate application of Church law to cases. They praised Christian liberty and wrote in a more hortatory, idealistic tone than the Roman casuists. They proclaimed as their purpose the formation of the conscience of the Christian. As Taylor wrote, "Men that are wise may guide themselves by this book in all their proportions of conscience, but if the case be indeed involved, they need the conduct of a spiritual guide to untie the intrigue and state the question and apply the respective rules to the several parts of it."[26] The study of casuistry can benefit parish priests, "who," as George Herbert wrote, "may guide their people exactly in the ways of truth so they decline neither to the right or to the left."[27] Thus English casuistry had as its explicit aim "intensive and extensive moral education," an aim that was especially necessary in the English Church, given the absence of strong hierarchical authority and penitential confession.[28]

The English casuists also repudiated "probabilism," as they knew it from the Jesuit writers and from Pascal's parody. This doctrine they considered to be laxist. At the same time, they recognized that moral teaching drew on probable opinions. Taylor's position rejects the ideas that "any probable opinion" might be used as the justification for moral choice, but in probabilities, I prefer that which is the more reasonable, never allowing to anyone a leave of choosing that which is confessedly the less reasonable in the whole conjunction of circumstances and relative considerations.[29]

He described the function of probable opinions in a way that presaged Cardinal Newman's description two centuries later of the formation of moral certitude:

> Probable arguments are like little stars, every one of which will be useless to our enlightening . . . but when tied together by order and vicinity make a constellation . . . to guide and enlighten our way . . . This heap of probable inducements is not of a power as a mathematical and physical demonstration which is in discourse as is the sun in heaven, but it makes a milky and white path visible enough to walk securely.[30]

A modern historian of Anglican case divinity notes that "the seventeenth century is the only century in our history when casuistical divinity would be truly described as a subject of popular interest."[31] Then, as Bishop Kirk wrote, "at the end of the seventeenth century, this reformed casuistry died as sudden a death as any in history. No single cause can be assigned to this."[32] Still, some causes can be surmised.

The ecclesiastical life of Great Britain had been tumultuous. Anglicans and Catholics struggled for ascendancy; Puritans, Presbyterians and Dissenters struggled for recognition. Religious leaders fought to control, or to be free from, political authority. Finally, in 1689 Parliament passed the Toleration Act, which "finally killed the old idea of a single state church in which all Englishmen were members. . . . The attempt to punish 'sin' by judicial process was virtually abandoned. The laity had won its centuries-long struggle against church courts. In this respect the Middle Ages were over."[33] Casuistry, too, was over. The religious and political conflict that engenders conflict of conscience was muted. The questions of moral failure were privitized. Issues of ethics were transmuted into matters of politics. The seedbed for casuistical thinking was no longer fertile.

During the decades that produced Anglican casuistry, Thomas Hobbes was writing. He posed a problem for moral reflection that absorbed the attention of English academic moralists for a century: what is the basis in human nature and psychology for the laws that bind human relationships? At Cambridge, Cudworth and More gave a Platonic answer that was an "almost geometrical exposition" of ethics.[34] Other scholars, such as Cumberland, Locke, Shaftsbury, and Butler, devised other theories of moral psychology. The attention of scholars turned away from resolving particular questions of moral choice to the construction of general theories of morality. By the time William Whewell was elected to the Knightbridge Chair of Casuistic Divinity in 1839, he found it necessary to change his title to Professor of Moral Philosophy.

Although he affirmed that the work of casuists, particularly of the Anglican tradition, did provide "guidance . . . whereby men may strengthen themselves against the temptations that cloud judgment when it is brought into contact with special cases," still it was the principles and foundations of moral reasoning rather than the particular application that deserved study and exposition. Indeed, Whewell believed that the English casuists were themselves much more concerned to set out the foundations and principles of morality than to resolve particular cases. Taylor, for example, "introduced cases with wonderful fertility of invention, but only as illustrations of the principles he is employed in expounding."[35] So Whewell encouraged ways of studying morality that became, in the hands of Henry Sidgwick, his successor in the Knightbridge Chair, the elaboration of moral theory and the analysis of methods of moral reasoning.[36]

Even so, English casuistical divinity did not entirely disappear after 1700. Notable scholars, such as R. C. Mortimer and Kenneth Kirk, have continued the tradition right into the twentieth century. Still, at the end of the seventeenth century English casuistry went, as it were, underground. It left the mainstreams of academic reflection and flowed into popular literature and even journalism. In 1690 a periodical appeared in London named *The Athenian Mercury*, a forerunner of the more famed *Tatler* and *Spectator*. The subtitle of the *Mercury* was *The Athenian Gazette: or, Casuisticall Mercury*, "resolving all the most nice and curious questions proposed by the ingenious of either sex." This popular journal invited readers to send queries about their perplexities of conscience in every area of life, although these queries tended to concentrate on "cases matrimonial." The queries are answered by sage advice, often drawn from the great works of case divinity, sometimes with explicit reference to "a famous case in Bishop Sanderson," or "Mr. Perkins's Case." Thus the elevated endeavor of academic casuistry found its way into the agony column.[37]

Casuistry affected other literary forms as well. At the beginning of the century John Donne had been deeply affected by casuistical argument; Milton's mind moved in casuistical ways; actual casuistical argument can be found here and there in the speeches of Shakespeare's plays (e.g., Cardinal Pandulph's speech on keeping oaths, in *King John*, Act III, Scene 1). But the writer who incorporated casuistry most wholeheartedly into his fiction was Daniel Defoe. Defoe's stories, notably *Robinson Crusoe*, *Moll Flanders*, and *Roxana*, are filled with "cases of conscience," fleshed out in the characters and plots of eighteenth-century English life. For a while the conception of the novel as a case, or series of cases, dominated English literature.[38] Thus in its short life, English casuistical divinity engendered a vigorous and unusual progeny. In the academic world of moral reflection, it led to the growth of its opposite—moral philosophy—while in the literary field it encouraged a style and content that are today scarcely thought of as "moral" reflection at all.

PROBABILISM

As we have defined them, the temporal boundaries to the era of high casuistry (1556–1656) nearly coincide with the period during which the doctrine of "moral probabilism" was accepted without serious challenge. That doctrine was stated explicitly for the first time in 1577 by the Dominican Professor of Theology at Salamanca, Bartolomeo Medina. In his commentary on the *Summa Theologiae* of St. Thomas, Medina wrote,

> It seems to me that, if an opinion is probable, it is licit to follow it, even though the opposite opinion is more probable.[39]

Medina admitted that this position departed from the teaching of his esteemed Dominican predecessors, Soto and Cajetan: it was also a definite departure from the teachings of the medieval theologians. Yet despite its novelty, Medina's thesis was readily accepted and was elaborated by theologians and casuists for almost a century. Casuistry in the proper sense cannot be understood apart from the doctrine of probabilism.

The year 1656 saw the first explicit challenge to the authority of Medina's thesis. In the *Lettres Provinciales*, which appeared in that

year, Pascal rightly recognized that the "doctrine of probable opinions . . . is the foundation and ABC of all (the casuists') moral
teaching,"[40] so he attacked that doctrine with vigor. But meanwhile
a more serious challenge was coming from another source; for in the
same year the General Chapter of the Dominican Order issued a
warning against "lax, novel and less certain opinions" in moral matters.[41] So there opened a debate that was to shake moral theology
and casuistry to their foundations.

Novel though it was, Medina's thesis flowed out of broad
medieval traditions about the kinds of knowledge required for
moral judgment. The theologians and jurisconsults had devised theories about the impact of ignorance on imputability, while the theologians had settled notions about the erroneous conscience. They
also recognized the reality of moral doubt, which they defined as the
inability of the mind to give assent to either of two contradictory
propositions: in such doubt judgment was suspended. They unanimously taught that it was sinful to act while in doubt: to do so was
to hold the law in contempt, and one's moral obligation was to
resolve the doubt by investigation, prayerful reflection, and recourse
to wise and prudent advisors. Should doubt persist, medieval
authors unanimously recommended that the decision favor the
safest course—that is, the action most likely to avoid sin and to safeguard one's salvation. For example, the medieval theologian,
Alexander of Hales, posed the case of a priest who wondered
whether a particular contract involving receipt of money for some
spiritual benefit constituted the sin of simony, recognizing that some
canonists considered it so and that others did not. Alexander
answered, "Being in doubt, he should avoid such a contract, for it is
less evil to suffer a temporal loss than a spiritual one."[42] The moral
stance common to medieval theologians seems to have been advoca-
cy of the *via tutior*, the safer way.

At the same time, the medieval authors also regularly distinguished between doubt and opinion. From both the Ciceronian
tradition of "probable reasons" and the Aristotelian teaching about
the nonscientific nature of moral reasoning, they inferred that the
certitude of moral judgment was a "probable certitude which, for the
most part, attains the truth, even though in some instances it fails to
do so."[43] Probable certitude was opinion, an assent to one proposition, coupled with the acknowledgment that its opposite might be
true. This probability was the quality of a proposition—its

"verisimilitude"—which made it worthy of assent. In this sense only one of two contrary propositions could be probable; this one determined assent and commanded moral action. For the medievals, then, opinion was the field of moral knowledge and decision, and they found nothing strange in asserting that a judgment enjoyed "probable certitude."

By the time Medina proposed his thesis, the accepted theological interpretation had drifted almost imperceptibly away from the medieval position. The ideas of "opinion" and of "doubt" had become confused: several propositions could be designated as probable in cases in which none of them could command unquestioning assent. The comparison of "more and less probable" opinions that would have been inconceivable to medieval authors had become legitimate because "probable" had come to mean "plausible" or "possibly true." As a result, many opinions about a subject could be called "probable"—that is, capable of eliciting assent, albeit hesitant. Medina's own definition of probability reveals this minimalist position, "an opinion is probable if it can be followed without reprehension or vituperation." He hastens to add, "Of course it is not probable, merely because it has proponents who state apparent reasons, but because wise men propose it and confirm it by excellent arguments."[44]

Divested of its antique terminology, the thesis of probabilism simply asserts that a person who is deliberating about whether or not he is obliged by some moral, civil, or ecclesiastical law may take advantage of any reasonable doubt whether or not the law obliges him. To anyone used to the workings of the United States income tax code, this point is not unfamiliar. Given a ruling or professional advice favoring your right to a "deduction" or "exemption," you may take advantage of it even when it does not strike you as particularly sensible or reasonable. The advice or ruling can give your claim an "extrinsic probability" even in the absence of any obvious "intrinsic" merits.

Medina's formulation of this principle may strike modern readers as odd. We may follow the less probable opinion even though its opposite may appear to us more probable. In that person's mind the argument favoring freedom is weaker than the argument favoring obligation, so what justification can there be for accepting the argument favoring freedom? Medina evidently believed that because both arguments—stronger and weaker—were still open to doubt, either might be chosen. However, he did not spell out the relationship between the strength or weakness of opinions (or rather their justifications) and the assent of the mind. Throughout the subsequent dispute, this lacuna remained a weakness of probabilism.

Another important aspect of Medina's thesis is not immediately apparent to the modern reader, who reads it as if it concerned the deliberation of a single person about the moral rightness of an action that he is contemplating as an individual. In fact, Medina envisaged a person deliberating about the advice he should give to another, or about a judgment he should render about another's action. He was writing at a time when theologians addressed moral questions not only in speculative and abstract terms but also in the context of the ecclesiastical practices common to Catholic Europe. Penitents approached confessors for advice and for absolution. The moral life was a tissue of laws, from the eternal laws of God to the canon law of the Church. The confessor often had to face the problem whether to place an obligation on a penitent, when one or another of those laws seemed less than absolutely binding to him, to other confessors, or to the penitent. Suppose, for example, that the confessor believed a certain law to be binding under particular circumstances. The penitent states in response that he, perhaps with the approval of another confessor, believes in good faith and with good reasons that the law does not oblige under the given circumstances. Is the confessor morally bound to judge the penitent by his own opinion, which in his view is more sound? Or may he accept the less sound, though still reasonable, opinion of the penitent or other confessor? In the cultural context of confessional practice, this problem is not outlandish, and Medina's thesis is quite comprehensible.[45]

Although first stated by the Dominican Medina, the thesis of probabilism was adopted by leading theologians of the Society of Jesus. And in the theological debates that followed, the Jesuits became its most fervent advocates. As we have seen, Medina suggested that the authority of "wise men with excellent arguments" could make an opinion worthy of being called "probable." The first Jesuit to espouse probabilism, Gabriel Vasquez (1551–1604), immediately separated the two components of this view: an opinion could be *intrinsically* probable—that is, founded on "excellent arguments"—or *extrinsically* probable—founded on the authority of "wise men."[46] This logical distinction, inspired perhaps by the theologians' need to have a proper word for every notion, subsequently led to a conceptual split that badly damaged the thesis. In understanding the notion of extrinsic probability, the "authority of wise men" gradually became the "preponderance of experts"; and the weight of scholarly opinion, in the modern sense of "heads counted," replaced the weight of reason and argument.

Certainly in moral counsel the authority of wise persons often carries greater weight than mere good arguments. Aristotle recommended having recourse to the wise, as did Cicero; the medieval authors offer it as conventional advice to those in doubt. Thus Peter Cantor frequently concludes a perplexing case by suggesting a visit to "wise and prudent persons." In the baroque age of high casuistry, however, this sensible advice underwent a bizarre distortion. Aware of the diversity of arguments that might be offered for and against many opinions, authors began to suspect that the reputation or rank of the proponents of an opinion counted heavily in favor of its "probability." Numbers, too, were important. The Jesuit Sanchez proposed that "the authority of a single doctor, if he is wise and prudent, renders probable any opinion he maintains." Caramuel even quantified the authority of the experts: one professor holding a distinguished chair prevailed over four lesser professors, and so on. Quickly the books of casuistry filled up with lists of authors who could be cited in favor of or against various opinions. In the shadow of these lists "intrinsic" probability began to wither.[47]

In this lush efflorescence of authorities every opinion became "probable," and it was difficult, if not impossible, to rule out even the most extravagant opinions. Caramuel rejoiced at this result, declaring

> these multiple opinions are a sign of salvation . . . many who might be damned are saved by a probable opinion [*damnaretur plurimi quos sententiae probabilitas salvat*].

Even the more cautious Escobar was satisfied that "diversity of opinions in moral matters renders the yoke of the Lord more sweet and His burden more light." Such remarks reveal one of the underlying motivations for the doctrine of probabilism: to lighten the burden of conscience on the scrupulous and troubled. At the same time, excessive reliance upon probabilism inevitably led some casuists to an evisceration of morality and to the toleration of excessive laxism.[48]

The marshaling of partisans for and against various opinions did have some positive effect. It revealed how arguments could be constructed with considerable subtlety, and how the justification and rebuttal of moral arguments can be carried out. The more judicious moralists and casuists used the multiplicity of authors not as direct evidence of the quality of arguments but as evidence that certain lines of argument had a plausibility that attracted authors to them. By looking to extrinsic probabilities they were led to inspect intrinsic probabilities. Nevertheless the vogue of "extrinsic probability" was a fatal flaw in high casuistry, and the strength of Pascal's criticism of casuistry lay in his quick recognition of this flaw. He worried it unmercifully:

> I see, [he says] the benefit you [casuists] derive from the contrary opinion held by your doctors on every subject. For one of them is always helpful and the other never harmful. If you do not find what you want on the one side, you jump over to the other and never a risk.[49]

The second Jesuit to elaborate Medina's thesis was the Society's most eminent theologian, Francisco Suarez (1548–1617). In his hands Medina's thesis was built into the full doctrine of probabilism, which aroused violent attack and spirited defense before the century was out. Though a theologian of great breadth, Suarez was at heart a student of jurisprudence and is sometimes honored as the "father of international law." His juristic propensities are obvious in his major contribution to the doctrine of probabilism—namely, the introduction of "practical, reflex principles" to moral deliberation. A person, Suarez recognized, might have "speculative doubt" about several opinions, each of which had good reason and solid authority behind it. Yet as all theologians taught, if his action were not to be sinful, this same person must form a certain conscience about the rightness of one of those opinions. This move from "speculative doubt" to "practical certitude" might be accomplished by the use of what he called "practical principles"—a phrase he seems to have coined. Suarez suggested that these practical principles should be drawn from the realm of law. In resolving doubtful issues, jurisconsults had commonly referred to a number of maxims. Since the time of Pope Boniface XII, the canonists had cited a list of eighty-eight maxims, most of them drawn from Roman legal practice.[50] Among these Suarez found two that seemed particularly relevant to the problem of moral deliberation—namely, the principle of possession and the principle of promulgation. As Suarez phrased these principles, "in doubtful matters, presumption is in favor of the possessor, and a law does not bind unless adequately promulgated."[51]

Suarez extended these general principles of jurisprudence into the realm of morality. This was not, of course, a shocking or surprising move. Canon and civil law were never neatly distinguished from morality; theologians had consistently used principles drawn from jurisprudence to resolve certain types of cases, particularly in matters of justice. Suarez, however, applied these principles in a wholly novel way. They were to be employed in all situations of doubt about the morality of an act. He also interpreted them in a novel way. The principle of possession designated the claim of personal liberty which was "in possession of the human will prior to any law," and the principle of promulgation referred to a person's awareness of the existence of a moral rule. Thus in cases of genuine doubt about whether there was an obligation to act or refrain, a person could, by referring to these practical principles, arrive at a certain judgment of conscience about whether he was or was not obliged.

These practical principles, it should be noted, do not bear directly on the moral matter under deliberation in the way that the rules "Do not steal" or "Give to each what is due," for example, bear directly on a matter of justice. They are general principles to guide deliberation, which are imported into an issue, and they are valid in any moral matter. The Jesuit moralist Paul Laymann later named these practical principles "reflex principles," given that by reference to them speculative doubt was resolved into practical certainty, and this subsequently became their standard designation.[52] A modern moral theologian describes these reflex principles in this fashion:

> Direct principles immediately and of themselves produce intrinsic evidence or evidence of credibility for a conclusion; reflex principles are general norms that are not probative of themselves, but serve to remove practical doubt and to attain moral certainty in a particular case of action.[53]

So together Medina's thesis about the acceptability of the less probable opinion, Vasquez's distinction between intrinsic and extrinsic probability, and Suarez's introduction of practical reflex principles filled out the doctrine of probabilism.

For almost half a century this doctrine was unchallenged. Authors sharpened definitions, refined distinctions, and strengthened arguments. Rules were devised to guide practical application of the doctrine. Reliance on a less probable opinion was prohibited in matters of justice; when the certain rights of another party would be damaged; when a grave spiritual or temporal harm to another or to oneself would result. According to the latter rule, for example, physicians were always obliged to take the more probable opinion in prescribing for their patients, as were lawyers in advising their clients.[54] The casuists of the period made use of the doctrine and rules of probabilism to resolve innumerable cases, and in so doing, they created innumerable new probable opinions. One modern author has described probabilism as a sort of "wonderful moral computer" capable of calculating all sorts of new combinations.[55] Another explains why probabilism went unchallenged for almost a century:

> There is an apparent good sense in the system. Is it not obvious that one cannot easily or immediately attain certitude about matters of moral choice? If a probable opinion does suffice, is it not obvious that a less probable one also suffices, so long as it is still probable? Further, is not the correspondence between speculative and practical knowledge so imperfect that, while speculation remains hesitant, action must have certainty? Probabilism presents itself as a system, which takes account of the proper order of action, which has a sense of the difficulties and complications of practical life, and which sincerely proposes that apart from it, there will only be rigorism or the tormented conscience.[56]

During these years there was almost no serious theological or pastoral challenge to the doctrine of probabilism. Ironically the few protests that were heard came from Jesuit theologians, and even from Jesuit authorities; yet the Jesuits were soon to appear as the stoutest defenders of the doctrine. After 1656, the year in which the General Chapter of the Dominican Order expressed concern, criticism of the doctrine and its consequences for moral life began to grow. Pascal's attack was published in the same year. Although certainly the most famous and the most damaging criticism of probabilism, Pascal's complaint was not theologically incisive. He saw and struck at the fatal flaw of extreme probabilism. He rightly recognized the inherent tendency of probabilism to slide toward moral skepticism, where every opinion is as good as any other, and into moral laxism, where all law falls before liberty. In Letters V and VI he set up these consequences as the target of his attack. Yet he missed the main point. His own words reveal this: "I am not satisfied with probability. I want certainty."[57]

The probabilists themselves made the same demand: they insisted that one must have "practical certitude of conscience" in order to act morally. They also recognized, however, that in moral matters, certitude is somehow a certitude about opinion or, in the words of St. Thomas, a "probable certitude." Pascal himself was a moral rigorist who could not tolerate ambiguity in his personal moral life; in addition, he was a mathematician who hoped to find the certainty of that discipline in the moral life. Temperamentally and intellectually he was not equipped to appreciate the probabilists' problem: once diversity of opinion about moral matters is recognized, how can practical certainty be achieved? Pascal and his Jansenist colleagues aimed to destroy probabilism and casuistry entirely, but in so doing they hit too widely. Deman writes:

> In condemning a bad casuistry, they did not appreciate the necessity of a good one. In denouncing the follies of probabilism, they showed no care for the proper role of a sound and properly understood probabilism.[58]

The theological critics were more precise in their aim than was Pascal; although as the debate heated up, polemical zeal often obscured their sights. The most penetrating critiques came from a Roman canonist of great repute, Prosper Fagnanus (d. 1678); an indignant Irish Jansenist, John Sinnigh (d. 1666); and strangely enough, a Jesuit who became General of the Society, Thyrsus Gonzalez de Santilla (1624–1705). These men, and many others, marshaled arguments against probabilism which did not at the same time ignore the basic problem of "probable certitude" in moral matters. The probabilists answered these criticisms with equal vigor.[59]

The matters under debate merit attention. How is one to define certitude, opinion, doubt, probability? How can we attain assurance that we are acting rightly? Are rules of jurisprudence properly employed in moral matters? If so, how are they to be defined, defended, limited? Is there a real difference between the "speculative" and the "practical" in moral matters? If so, how are these realms to be described? How can an appreciation for the diversity of opinion be prevented from slipping toward moral laxity and skepticism? These questions still lie at the heart of the debates among moral philosophers, and the answers are still far from clear.

However, the manner of the debate over probabilism, as distinct from the matter, is disappointing to the modern reader. Much of it is sheer polemic; many of the arguments rest on theological presuppositions about moral psychology that the modern reader rarely shares. The style of many of the authors is excessively subtle and contorted; their volubility is almost interminable. The manner of the debaters makes it difficult to appreciate the matter of the debate. Leibniz, who followed the debate with interest, admitted his dismay that a Jesuit friend whom he esteemed as a scientist

> should defend the ridiculous ethic of probability with its frivolous subtleties, unknown to the primitive church and even repudiated by pagans.[60]

Yet out of this debate came several significant points. First, it established definitively that casuistry must rely on a theory about moral deliberation that leaves room for a variety of opinions and appreciates the possibility of diversity. Second, the debate made it patently clear that up to that time the procedures of casuistry left open the road leading toward laxism and skepticism as it did the alternative road leading to rigorism and dogmatism; and that the casuists of the high era had not found a theoretically satisfactory way to restrain casuistical reasoning from sliding down either slope.

Over one central point the debate was particularly disappointing. It failed to make clear the logical relationship between moral opinions and their justification—a point that seems crucial to the modern reader. In the early phase of the doctrine's popularity, the reliance on extrinsic probability diverted attention from the problem of intrinsic probability; in the later phase, emphasis on defense of reflex practical principles diverted attention from direct principles and their function in practical reasoning. This is not to say that the problem of practical knowledge was unexplored. The leading theologians of the era—for example, Cajetan, John of St. Thomas, and Suarez—wrote exquisitely detailed treatises on what in modern parlance would be called "moral psychology"; and much of this literature is reflected in the probabilism debate. Nevertheless when reading this literature, or even the literature of a twentieth-century reprise of the probabilism debate written in an idiom more congenial to the modern reader,[61] one is left with the feeling that certain crucial questions about the logic of moral reasoning have not been addressed—questions that, had they occurred to the debaters of the seventeenth century, could have resolved many an inconclusive argument. We shall return to these questions in the later chapters of this book.

Some helpful sparks of illumination do flash from the debate. One of these comes from a most judicious (if rigorist) critic of probabilism, Prosper Fagnanus. He distinguished between "probable certitude" and "certitude arising from probabilities." The former expression, despite its use by St. Thomas, he considers a contradiction in terms, and he faults his opponents for causing confusion by its use. The latter expression, however, can be properly applied to a certitude, an "assent of the mind," engendered by the convergence of many probable arguments toward the same conclusion. This, says Fagnanus, is a genuine certitude, even though of a different kind from the certitude reached by formal demonstrative reasoning; and such a convergence of probabilities toward a certain conclusion can be a rule for action.[62] In a remarkable way Fagnanus anticipated the theory of moral certitude that John Henry Newman put forward in his *Grammar of Assent*.[63]

A second spark of illumination comes from Suarez's major contribution to the doctrine of probabilism: the notion of reflex practical principles. The illumination we receive, however, is not exactly what the Jesuit theologian intended to shed. He suggested that certain principles of jurisprudence, such as presumption in favor of the possessor, could be imported into moral deliberation in order to transform speculative doubt into practical certainty. However, it may be that Suarez was the first to suggest that moral deliberation functions not only with the principles proper to the subject matter under consideration but also with other more general principles that operate alongside these—principles that keep the properly moral line of thought on the track, as it were. There Suarez's reflex practical principles may be the unsuspecting ancestors of, say, Kant's categorical imperative, Mill's utility principle, or R. M. Hare's theories of prescriptivity and universalizability.[64]

The theological debate was not, however, in vain. By intellectual push and shove the probabilist doctrine was cleansed of its excesses, such as its practitioners' intemperate reliance on extrinsic probability. A balanced view gradually emerged that tolerated a range of opinions on moral matters and favored freedom of choice within stated limits when genuine doubt prevailed. Despite considerable pressure from national governments, particularly of France and Spain, the ecclesiastical authorities acted diplomatically, issuing condemnations of particular casuistical opinions that manifested excessive laxity or rigor but never condemning "probabilism" as such. Decrees of the Holy Office issued under Pope Alexander VII in 1665 and 1666 and under Pope Innocent XI in 1679 comprised long lists of propositions drawn from casuists who manifested extreme laxity in resolution of certain cases. Among these condemned opinions can be found the case of the insulted nobleman, which we shall examine shortly. Another decree, issued under Pope Alexander VIII in 1690, struck at the rigorist casuists, though with a much shorter list of condemned opinions! A historian of the controversy writes,

> Rather than touching probabilism in its essence, these decrees touch the extenuation of the idea of probability, permitting a solid probability to be employed, except in certain sorts of cases . . . henceforth, authors are distinguished not as zealots of probable opinion pure and simple, but by carefulness and moderation in their practical judgment.[65]

Out of the debates a clear and sound presentation of the problems finally issued. Alphonsus Ligouri (1696–1787), who is now ranked as the premier moral theologian of the Catholic Church, created a balanced approach to the problem of choice in face of diverse opinions. Called "equiprobabilism," it is similar to probabilism in substance. It permits choice of any solidly probable opinion in matters of doubt, but it rejects the thesis with which Medina initiated the debate—namely, the acceptability of a less probable opinion in face of a more probable one. Nowadays, therefore, it is permissible for a Catholic moral theologian to follow either equiprobabilism or probabilism in the resolution of cases of conscience.[66]

PART IV

Three Samples of Casuistry

The casuists of the high era produced myriad cases drawn from the actual and possible occasions of familial, religious, civil, and commercial life. As the work of the casuists came into disrepute in the late seventh century, their critics found it easy to select out of these myriad cases certain ones that were particularly susceptible to criticism or ridicule. Pascal employed this technique skillfully. Yet to be fair to the casuists, it is important to view even those maligned cases in their context to see how they emerged as moral problems, how the casuists debated them over time, and how the "opinions of approved authors" settled on "greater or lesser probability." The next three chapters will follow in this way the case of charging interest on loans, the case of equivocation under oath, and the case of defense of one's honor.

In these next chapters we begin to open the tomes of the "approved authors." The modern reader is likely to find in those pages ideas and arguments that are quite foreign to twentieth-century minds. A remark of philosopher Bernard Williams comes to mind:

> The trouble with casuistry, if it is seen as the basic process of ethical thought, is not so much its misuse as the obvious fact that the repertory of substantive ethical concepts differs between cultures, changes over time and is open to criticism.[1]

In these next pages we shall encounter that "obvious fact." Substantive concepts that are unfamiliar to us will be taken for granted
by the classical casuists; concepts once quite congenial appear to us
absurd. Yet as we shall see in the three cases, the casuists themselves
were "open to criticism" and, indeed, employed a method that was
itself self-critical.

Before opening the casuists' pages to the three cases we have chosen, we must acknowledge that these pages also contain opinions
that are not only unfamiliar to the modern reader but are morally
repugnant. The modern reader is not so much outraged by their laxity, as Pascal might have been, but by the moral obtuseness they represent. It is difficult for the modern to imagine how a "moralist"
could tolerate such an opinion. Brief mention of three such opinions
will suffice: their attitude toward "infidels," their acceptance of
judicial torture, and their teachings on sexuality. We offer no excuses for the casuists' opinions; we merely display them as illustrations
of the truth of Williams's comment that ethical concepts differ
among cultures. At the same time, we are confident that the casuists' self-critical methods could also be used to dissolve these opinions, as indeed they have been used in more recent years.

The casuists generally maintain positions about relations between
Christians and "non-believers," particularly Jews, that we would
find abhorrent. A Christian should not marry a Jew, should not eat
with Jews, should avoid common baths used by them; a Christian
should not accept medicine from a Jewish physician (but can buy
those he prescribes).[2]

Similarly, the position of the casuists on the use of judicial torture
strikes the modern reader as morally repugnant. If anything might
be considered "absolutely and totally immoral" by the modern it
would be torture. The casuists did not find it so. They wrote of it
within the general framework of the rules of law: torture might be
applied only if there is "quite, but not entirely convincing" evidence
of guilt from other sources; torture should never be used against
nobles, professors, the elderly, the mentally disturbed or pregnant
women; torture should not be applied a second time for the same
accusation, etc. Torture might be inefficient and open to abuse, but it
is not condemned as cruel and inhumane.[3]

The casuists also maintained doctrines about relations between
men and women and about sexual practices that are a world away

from modern thinking in Western culture. Until the mid-seventeenth century they debate whether or not an offended husband might kill his adulterous wife without sin. The permissive opinion was condemned by Pope Alexander VII in 1665.[4] The teaching on sexual activities was almost uniformly rigid: no act that afforded sexual pleasure, either physical or mental, was free of suspicion of sin. Even intercourse between spouses had to be directed by the intention to procreate and not by desire, lest it be an occasion of sin. In sexual matters no sin was venial; all illicit acts were "mortal by their entire nature." To the modern mind it seems morally perverse to rank masturbation, rather than torture, as a wholly evil act, never mitigated by circumstances.[5] The casuists were obviously men of their time. Their values were, naturally, conditioned by their culture, as are ours. But does not this cast in doubt their legitimacy as moralists? Should not the moralist be the ideal observer, "knowing all the relevant facts, visualizing them perfectly and loving all sentient beings strongly and equally?"[6] Should not their methodology enable them to transcend the values and rules of their culture and grasp normative principles of universal validity? Why did they not recognize that torture was intrinsically evil, and that discrimination on the basis of race or religion or sex was morally reprehensible? Is not Bernard Williams's critique of casuistry quite accurate?

Our purpose in the next three chapters is only to reveal that although opinions considered at any one point in time can appear to later critics as reprehensible, the casuistic method—rhetorical and responsive to historical change—also suffices to lay bare the weakness of just these outdated positions.

9

Profit: The Case of Usury

The history of the Catholic Church's teaching on usury during the Middle Ages and the Renaissance offers a striking example of the development, clarification, and refinement of a moral problem by casuistry. From the eleventh to the eighteenth century, the problem of usury exercised the finest theological and canonical minds. The history of this problem is perhaps the best documented of all of the moral problems treated by the casuists. It reveals a complex of moral considerations based on scripture, theology, and philosophy, mixed with factual developments in the economic and social life of Western civilization.

Those who know that history only superficially sometimes say that the doctrine of the Church on usury, which moved from uncompromising condemnation to toleration over the course of ten centuries, reveals that the Church's teaching on moral matters is not, as it often claims, immutable. Others comment that the history of usury shows that any moral doctrine, no matter how intransigently preached, can be compromised to meet the opportunities of economic life. From the viewpoint of the present study, however, the history of usury shows how successive developments in economic and social life gradually suggested that the original paradigm on which the formal moral views about moneylending had been based was too limited. The casuists perceived a need for a new paradigm, and in the course of vigorous debates, particularly in the sixteenth and seventeenth centuries, they provided one.[1]

The history of the long debate over usury opens with a text from the Book of Deuteronomy:

> You shall not lend upon interest to your brother, interest on money, interest on victuals, interest on anything that is lent for interest. To a foreigner you may lend for interest, but to your brother you may not lend upon interest.[2]

Although this text recognizes a distinction between taking interest from brothers and taking it from strangers, the early Christian Church rejected the distinction. St. Jerome argued that the prohibition of usury was universalized by the universality of salvation: under the salvific will of God all humans were now brothers.[3] Another Old Testament text became the favored reference of the Church Fathers: Psalm 15 describes the just man as "one who does not put out his money at interest" (Ps 15, 5).

With few exceptions, the Church Fathers condemned charging any interest at all from any borrower. The first Ecumenical Council of the Christian Church, held at Nicea in 325, dealt with the serious doctrinal aberration of the heretic Arius but also issued a severe condemnation of clerical usurers, citing the words of Psalm 15:

> Many clerics, motivated by greed and a desire for gain, have forgotten the scriptural injunction, "He does not put out his money at interest," and instead demand a monthly rate of one percent on loans they make. . . . they shall be deposed from their clerical status.[4]

It appears that the condemnation was aimed at clerics who were responsible for the care of the poor but who made a profit out of their misery. A papal decree of Pope Leo the Great (440–461) forbade clerics to lend at interest, and declared that even laymen who did so earned "shameful gain."[5] The second Lateran Council (1139) declared that "the detestable, shameful and insatiable rapacity" of usurers stood condemned by both Old and New Testaments, and excommunicated them. The same condemnation was repeated forty years later at the next Lateran Council. Pope Urban III, in 1187, cited for the first time a text from the New Testament (Luke 6:35), "Lend freely, hoping nothing therefrom" and declared an absolute divinely sanctioned prohibition of gain from a loan. From that time on this text stood beside Psalm 15 as a divine prohibition of usury.

Modern readers should note that for the medieval authors, usury did not consist in reaping excessive interest but in charging any interest at all. A canonical document of A.D. 806 gives the first medieval definition of usury as "when more is asked than is given." This definition becomes definitive in Gratian's *Decretum*.[6] Until very late in the history of this debate, usury is understood as any return to the lender over the principal lent. "Loan," though never clearly defined in that era, appears to mean the giving of money or some other substance to persons in need and in an emergency. St. Albert the Great, in his commentary on the text from Luke, states,

> Usury is a sin of avarice; it is against charity because the usurer without labor, suffering or fear gathers riches from the labor, suffering and vicissitudes of his neighbor.[7]

This understanding of a loan implies that the usury prohibition was directed principally against professional moneylenders or pawnbrokers, the "notorious [i.e., public] usurers" cited by Lateran Council III.

It can plausibly be supposed that in general, a "loan" was understood as assistance to someone in need or distress. In the subsistence economies that existed from the time of the writing of Deuteronomy up through the early Middle Ages, the failure of a crop or the loss of a flock could threaten the life of a poor man and his family; and the loan of seed, of an ewe for breeding, or of food might be lifesaving. In such circumstances, to demand "more than was given" would clearly be exploitation of one's "brother" or neighbor. While loans were certainly given in other circumstances, the paradigm for the moral analysis of usury appears to have been aid in time of distress.

During the twelfth and thirteenth centuries, the theologians shaped a treatise on usury out of these diverse texts. In attempting to construct rational arguments against the taking of interest, they moved beyond scriptural citations and fulminating condemnations. The first major contribution to the casuistry about usury came when the theologians began to classify it under the general heading of theft. Peter Lombard (d. 1160), the first major systematizer of theology, accepted this designation: so began the construction of a paradigm for the moral analysis of usury.[8]

The next step in the development of this paradigm was the introduction of a definition that served as a maxim: *mutuum est quasi de meo tuum* (a loan is, as it were, my property made yours). The Latin word for loan, *mutuum*, was defined by an etymological pun, *meum* (mine) becomes *tuum* (yours). This definition, framed by a canonical commentator on Gratian, recalled the treatment of loans in Roman law: a *mutuum* was a form of loan in which ownership was freely and temporarily transferred to the borrower. The one who has loaned has no right to charge for its use while it does not strictly belong to him. This suggested to the medieval authors a "natural law" argument against interest: once one has loaned something to another, it becomes the property of the other. To deprive the one who now owns it of any portion of its increase would, these authors reasoned, be theft. Thus the maxim *mutuum est quasi de meo tuum* provided a powerful warrant to support the condemnation of usury.[9]

The argument that could be drawn from this definition of "loan" was at best a tenuous one and required some bolstering. St. Bonaventure, treating usury under the heading of the Seventh Commandment, "Thou shalt not steal," offered three reasons to prove his point. First, in a loan, mine becomes yours. Second, the industry of a borrower is his own. Third, time cannot be sold. Thus, he concluded, usury is "a perversion of order" and so contrary to the natural law.[10] Aquinas introduced a new element, an argument based on Aristotle's discussion of the nature of money. The Philosopher had noted that money, by convention, represented demand for goods and that "it exists not by nature but by law, so that it is in our power to change it or make it useless." Elsewhere he remarks that money does not have value in itself but only as a measure of the value of other things.

Around these ideas Aquinas built an argument against usury that in due course became classical. It is contrary to the nature of money, he said, to be vendible; money by nature is a consumptible, for which ownership and use are identical. Usury consists in selling separately the use of money and its substance. "Thus," concluded Aquinas, "he sells the same thing twice, which is clearly against natural justice."[11]

Despite variations on the natural law argument, the theologians and canonists were at one in supporting the absolute prohibition on profit from a loan. This intransigent stand seemingly marks all commerce as intrinsically immoral. Yet public and private economic life went on, and the Church itself was deeply involved in it. The Jews, who fell outside the ecclesiastical prohibitions (though they had their own rabbinical ones to deal with), became the major moneylenders; but others, such as the Lombards, also engaged in the business. The teaching of the Church, then, might be viewed as gross hypocrisy, yet it made sense in the history of the times. The usury prohibition made its appearance in an era when the economy of Europe was largely composed of subsistence farming. Demand for credit was low; most loans were made only for consumption; and they were made out of "idle" money or goods.

At the same time, productive commercial activity was recognized as a legitimate activity. From the beginning, the canonists, civil lawyers, and theologians had admitted as perfectly legal and moral the *societas*, or partnership, a form of commercial financing that might today be regarded as involving a loan. This was a financial arrangement in which two or more persons pooled their money or skill for some common purpose, usually profit. Canonists distinguished between a *societas* and a usurious loan. Aquinas developed the argument: one who commits his money to a joint enterprise does not give up its ownership; he takes the risk of its loss should the enterprise fail. He can take part of the profit that comes from the enterprise because it comes from his own property. Both partners are joint owners; both bear any losses and enjoy any profits.

The *societas* had been a recognized business arrangement in Roman law; but it was not widely used in medieval Europe until the growth of trade at Venice and Genoa in the eleventh and twelfth centuries. The most frequent joint venture was that between a merchant and a sea captain, and indeed the chief canonical document on the legitimacy of the *societas* was entitled *Naviganti*: that is, "to one setting out to sea." The joint enterprise was at risk both of loss at sea and from variable market conditions on return. Under these conditions the provision of money by one partner was not defined as a loan and did not fall under the prohibition of usury. The crucial moral difference between loan and *societas* rested on the sharing of risk. By introducing the concept of risk as a modality in the argument, the first step toward a revision of the paradigm was taken.[12]

Once this modality was admitted, innumerable forms of partnership could be devised, and as fast as ingenious parties devised them, theologians and canonists scrutinized them. John Noonan, the leading modern historian of the usury doctrine summarizes the basic position that served as a touchstone for the various cases:

> The early scholastics were working with two different theories of money, one of which applied to loans, the other to partnerships.

According to one theory, money was sterile, risk was no title to profit, ownership was the same as use in consumptible goods. In the other theory money produced a surplus value, risk became the ground for reward, and ownership was determined not by the identity of use and possession but by the assumption of risk.[13]

Aside from the distinction between loans and partnerships, theologians and canonists also allowed specific exceptions to the usury prohibition itself. It was a basic tenet of their legal theories and ethical doctrines that all laws admitted of exceptions, except those explicitly identified as primary precepts of the natural law. In the matter of usury, the canonist Hostiensis listed thirteen exceptions. Each of these was characterized either by some special relationship between creditor and debtor, such as that between vassal and lord, enemies in war, or between father-in-law and son-in-law in matters of dowry, or else by some special condition, such as doubt about the future value of the loan. The presence of one or another of these special circumstances might justify some repayment over and above the principal itself.[14]

The most important of these recognized exceptions concerned a situation in which the creditor suffered some damage from the failure of the debtor to fulfill contractual agreements. For example, the lender might be prevented from purchasing a needed item because his debtor failed to repay him on time. Roman law had allowed the payment of this difference—"what stands between," or, in Latin, *quod interest*—between the injured party's present position and the position he would be in had he not been injured. In the primitive sense of compensation for damages, this "interest" constituted a moral and legal title to payment beyond the principal; but the right to interest obtained only when damage could be demonstrated at the end of a loan.[15]

The basic structure of the medieval theses on usury, as constructed during the thirteenth and fourteenth centuries, stood firm until the middle of the fifteenth. The chief monument to that traditional structure was the work of the first of the moral theologians, St. Antoninus, Archbishop of Florence (1389–1459). As spiritual leader of the city that was the banking capital of Europe, Antoninus wrote about usury in terms that revealed a clear and unbending allegiance to the medieval theses. His *Summa Moralis* (1449) and *Summa Confessionalis* (1440) strongly defended the general prohibition of profit from a loan and carefully restricted the specific exceptions. He proposed many cases, tested them against the basic doctrine, and found wanting the justification of many of the most frequently claimed exceptions. By his standards (remarks Noonan) most of the population of capitalist Florence were committing mortal sin. In stating the legitimate exceptions, however, Antoninus objected to calling them "permissible usury." That term was applied improperly, he said, because of a misleading resemblance between the permitted cases and the forbidden ones; if gain were morally permissible, then in his view there was no usury. Yet Antoninus developed his analysis on the basis of the first paradigm; it was badly cracked, but it still functioned as the basis of moral analysis.[16]

Antoninus' work marked the end of the medieval synthesis. From the fifteenth century vast new mercantile opportunities were opened up, following the European discovery and exploitation of the American and Oriental markets. Transport and communication greatly improved, and the demand for credit greatly increased. In addition, the growth of nation-states, which for much of the sixteenth century were engaged in almost incessant and costly warfare, created a need for state financing on a large scale. These innovations prompted new perceptions of the meaning of money and credit, and theologians, canonists, and civil lawyers began to examine with great care the novel financial arrangements these developments encouraged. Contracts of insurance, credit transactions, and exchange banking all came under scrutiny. Limits and conditions of permissibility for profit were laid out. In particular, the effects of supply and demand on money began to be more clearly seen: the phenomenon of inflation was noted, particularly in Spain, and the casuist Navarrus was the first author to relate this to the influx of gold and silver from the New World.[17]

In this new economic and cultural setting the medieval theses were bound to come under pressure. In addition to pressures generated by the practical needs of rulers, bankers, and merchants, theologians and canonists felt the intellectual need to understand the new developments in light of the old theses. As a result they began to recognize certain implications latent in the earlier doctrines. The interest doctrine, which had been limited to compensation for damages actually suffered, had particularly important implications. Money invested for a commercial enterprise ceased to be available for other, more immediate purposes; and its unavailability put the investor at some disadvantage during the period of the loan. Thus two new entitlements to interest were devised: *lucrum cessans* ("profit ceasing") and *damnum emergens* ("loss occurring") during the term of the investment. These justified interest not at the end of a loan but from its very inception. The concept of risk, always recognized in the *societas*, and the concept of the utility of money were integrated, given the unique cultural and economic circumstances of the age. As Noonan writes, "from the recognition of individual exceptions, there arose a theory of interest."[18] A new paradigm was emerging: the casuists of the high era established it with clarity.

The casuists inherited the medieval synthesis but were vividly aware of the new social and economic realities that called it into question. They gradually realized that the old paradigm had become so surrounded by exceptions that it no longer provided a sound basis for analysis. The first move toward a new paradigm was the introduction of a theory of interest popularly referred to as the "triple contract," the "German contract," or the "5% contract." It marked a notable departure from the medieval thesis and opened the way for a modern theory of profit from loans. The summist Angelus de Clavasio had given tentative approval to a form of insured investment; a lender might charge a fair price in view of sustaining potential losses. This position apparently eliminated the requirement that the risk be shared, as in the partnership. In 1515 John Eck, Dominican theologian of the University of Ingolstadt, who became famous five years later as Luther's debating opponent, defended de Clavasio's thesis in public. His defense won wide acclaim and, it is said, earned him a financial subsidy from the Fuggers, the international banking house in Augsburg.[19]

The name "triple contract" expressed the essence of the arrangement that Eck popularized. Partners entered into three distinct contracts with each other. First there was a contract of partnership, which was considered legitimate by all commentators. Second, a contract of insurance was signed; under this the investor was insured against loss of his capital and, instead of paying a premium, agreed to accept a lesser percentage of the total profits than would otherwise come to him. Third, a contract was signed that guaranteed the investor a return at a set rate of interest, usually 5 percent. Thus the investor was a "sort of debenture holder without industry or danger of losing his capital."[20] This was an attractive form of investment, which provided the active partner with considerable working capital. Commentators conceded that, if made with different parties, each of these three contracts would be legitimate, but most of them doubted the morality of the triple contract between two parties. They suspected "usury" in the strict medieval sense: drawing profit without labor, loss, or risk. However, Eck replied that this form of investment entailed a loss by virtue of the title *lucrum cessans* since the investor could certainly have put his money to other, more profitable but less risky use.

When the Jesuits arrived in Augsburg in 1555, they were dismayed to find the German contract in common use among the bankers and merchants of that great commercial city. Adhering to the more conservative view, they denounced the contract as usury, and withheld absolution from those who were engaged in it: notably, members of the Fugger family, who were bankers to the Holy Roman Empire and one of whose scions was studying to be a Jesuit. This stance stirred up a furor in the capital of European banking, and before long there was an excited exchange of letters between Augsburg and Rome. The Fuggers and the local bishop sought advice from Rome, while the German Jesuits sought advice from their headquarters. A special commission of Jesuits, including the distinguished theologian and casuist Cardinal Toletus, was instructed to present a report on the morality of the German contract to the Fourth General Congregation of the Society of Jesus (1580). The Pope himself submitted to the commission a *casus* given him by the Duke of Bavaria at the urging of Father Jasper Haywood, an exiled English Jesuit who was strongly opposed to the contract.

This *casus* and the response to it represent a classical example of casuistical argument:

> Titius, a German, loans Sympronius a sum of money. Sympronius is a person of means, and the money is lent to him for no specific purpose. The conditions are that Titius is to receive annually five florins for every hundred lent, and afterwards have the whole capital back. There is no danger to the capital, and Titius must get his 5%, whether or not Sympronius makes a profit.

The response of the commission first noted that this case could not be resolved until all of the actual circumstances had been carefully specified and examined. In response to the question whether knowledge of the general form of the contract was sufficient to warrant approval or disapproval, the commission answered in the negative.

All the circumstances must be carefully specified: in particular, it must be ascertained whether the money was going to someone who could make it "fructify." In general, stated the commission, it would be prudent to advise someone considering such a contract to look for a morally less suspect investment. Next, Titius' profit would be legitimate only if it rested on one of the certainly moral entitlements such as *damnum emergens* or *lucrum cessans*. Finally, the profit would be clearly immoral if it were acquired merely in virtue of the loan. This response showed that the commission considered de Clavasio and Eck to have proposed a "less probable opinion": this was not to be considered certainly immoral but at best suspect.[21]

On the basis of the commission's report, the General Congregation reaffirmed the decision of the Third Congregation, held seven years earlier, that the German contract was morally licit, and confessors could so advise their penitents. This decision, which may appear odd to the modern reader, rested on the thesis, accepted by the Jesuits, that a probable opinion was sufficient to establish moral licitness. Subsequently three leading Jesuit theologian-casuists, Louis Molina, Leonard Lessius, and John De Lugo, wrote exacting analyses of this form of investment, offering both practical and theoretical arguments to distinguish it from usury. The central theoretical argument was that the contract necessarily involved *lucrum cessans* and that this remained a legitimate title to interest, even when risk was eliminated. In retrospect the German contract appears almost absurdly complex; yet some seventy-five years of debate about it led to radical change in the usury doctrine. By concentrating on this particular *casus*, moral theologians had recognized the dynamics of modern investment and the nature of economics in a world of production, banking, and trade. Addressing the Council of Trent on the issue of usury in 1554, Father Juan Polanco, the secretary of the Society of Jesus, spoke words that presaged this evolution—or revolution—in an ancient doctrine:

> As it is supremely necessary to avoid cheating one's neighbor in business or acting toward him unjustly, so it is extremely difficult to detect when such deception or injustice takes place in commercial dealings. On the one hand, neither Scripture nor the ancient Fathers and philosophers deal with the matter in detail, and, on the other, the astuteness of merchants, fostered by their lust for gain, has discovered so many tricks and dodges that it is hardly possible to see the plain facts, much less to pronounce judgement on them. This is the reason

why modern writers, whether theologians or jurists, are so confused and at variance with one another. Finally, the matter, being a question of morals, only admits of probability, because its nature is such that the least change of circumstances renders it necessary to revise one's judgement of the whole affair. Consequently, to decide such variable questions exactly one must be an Argus with a hundred eyes. As St. Basil well says, "to understand justice calls for a great intellect and a perfect heart."[22]

The morally relevant differences among various forms of economic activity thus became apparent only as the result of case analysis. As each new case appeared, representing some new form of transaction devised by merchants, traders, or landlords, it was measured against the relevant paradigmatic case: a loan made to someone in distress. In the eyes of all the moralists, the taking of profit on a loan to one in distress was clear immorality. It was simply theft and so contrary to the virtue of justice. How did each of the new cases differ from this paradigm? Did the structure, function, and purpose of the new arrangements include morally relevant circumstances? If so, did they justify or excuse the activity? Did they aggravate or alleviate guilt? Did the new circumstances radically change the nature of the case? These questions were insistently asked and answered as the debate over usury moved through the sixteenth century. The movement of question and answer can now be summarized.

To the original paradigm of the distress loan was added an arrangement in which money was given to share in a venture that entailed risk. The fact of sharing risk, referred to as *jus fraternitatis*, was considered morally relevant. Profiting from a shared risk was not the same as theft: the additional money returned was, in an important sense, one's own. It was then recognized that even apart from risk, damages suffered by the lender justified the payment of the difference between what was in fact returned and what would have been returned had the damage not occurred: that difference was called "interest." Next, it was noted that for the duration of a loan the lender does (or may) experience loss because he loses the use of his money for alternative purposes. This conception gave rise to the *damnum emergens* and *lucrum cessans* titles. Insurance contracts, first introduced in the maritime trade of the fourteenth century, were also considered different from usurious loans because the burden of risk was exchanged between the insurer and the insured.

Compensation was justly allowed to the insurer in return for his assuming the burden. Finally, a guaranteed investment was allowed because although the element of risk was eliminated, partnership itself was recognized to consist not so much in a common assumption of risk as in the common sharing of talents and resources.

Commercial loans, then, were distinguished more sharply from gratuitous distress loans when it became clearer that by choosing to invest his money rather than engaging in manufacture or farming himself, the lender lost the direct benefit of the money for the duration of the loan. What he earned in interest was considered to be no more than he could have earned in trade. So an awareness of the moral relevance of loss or gain led to a further awareness that the value of money is affected by supply and demand. Putting money out at loan at one point in time and under particular circumstances—such as war or peace, famine or prosperity—may affect the value of the money in an uncertain future. Money is not stable at its face value, as the medieval scholastics had assumed, but has a value that fluctuates in the market. Given this perception, a lender's claim to interest can be based on an additional morally relevant feature: namely, that the future value of his money depends on the knowledge and ability of its users. Interest may thus be justified not merely, as earlier moralists had conceded, by the specific risks or losses of profit of the particular lender but by the collective risks of the business community that raises its money in the market.

Other historical innovations presented other cases. Loans made in fifteenth-century Italy to the poor by the *montes pietatis*, or public pawnshops, were allowed to incur a charge to pay for the administration of the operation. This was considered a just title to compensation on the part of its operators. Also, the poor themselves were considered the real owners of these facilities: they benefited from the cheap loans, and thus they should bear the cost of their maintenance. Again, some cities issued bonds to finance public works and had laws requiring persons of means to purchase them. This entitled the purchaser to interest because he could have earned more by voluntary investments in business. Meanwhile exchange banking, made necessary by the voracious demands of the new nation-states, justified interest on the credit extended under the title of "virtual transportation": that is, they made the money effectively present, through credit, in a place where it was not physically located. In modern terms this interest was a "service charge" and so a just title to compensation.

By the middle of the seventeenth century, then, the theory of usury had been turned on its head. Many different cases representing many different forms of financial transaction in different social and cultural circumstances had been debated and analyzed. The maxims from Old and New Testaments had lost their force because the general terms in which they were expressed could hardly cover the multiple kinds of transactions that passed for "loans." And a more subtle appreciation of the nature and functions of money, investment, and credit weakened the natural law arguments that had convinced the medieval scholastics. In light of these conceptual and factual developments, the definitions of usury changed from those that prevailed in the Middle Ages (e.g., "where more is asked than is given" and "whatever is demanded beyond the principal") to the definition offered at the close of the debate by St. Alphonsus Ligouri: "Usury is interest taken where there is no just title to profit."[23] At this point "usury" has taken on the modern sense of "excessive interest." No longer does the paradigm of the distress loan preside, even remotely, over the analysis; no longer does interest fall under the prohibition of theft. The new paradigm, reflecting the emerging science of economics, viewed money as a commodity, and the moral question asked how one could determine a "just price" for its use.

This long debate shows casuistry at work. Over five centuries there emerges a moral doctrine of precise definitions and distinctions, of narrowly limited solutions and well-reasoned arguments. This doctrine was developed in a context marked by the pressure of powerful social, economic, and cultural changes. New circumstances pressed the casuists into new doctrines. From the thirteenth to the eighteenth century, the economy of Europe moved from subsistence farming to an extensive mercantile and commercial market. The thin lines of trade between Europe and the Near East expanded into wide streams of commerce between Europe, Asia, Africa, and America. Population increased; towns grew into cities; improved transportation facilitated travel and trade. The jigsaw puzzle of feudal principalities merged into powerful nation-states. Doctrinal dissonance and political incursions fractured the religious hegemony of the Roman Church. Finally, from the nascent power of nation-states and the impassioned belligerence of religion there arose continual and devastating international strife, with its voracious appetite for money. So new circumstances pressed the casuists, as the economists of their time, to set new doctrines.[24]

Although fostered by social circumstances, these new doctrines about the morality of economics were not merely a passive reflection of those circumstances. The casuists did not concede their novel points merely at the insistence of imperious rulers, avaricious prelates, or greedy bankers: they sought, in the midst of the economic pressures, to bring to light the morally relevant circumstances that would permit meaningful moral discriminations. The cases they considered were genuine manifestations of new social, cultural, and economic conditions; the moral arguments they worked out to deal with these cases were honest efforts to direct the consciences of rulers, prelates, and bankers.

Doctrinal modifications did not come easily. Each new formulation was the product of extended, detailed debate among highly capable moralists and jurists often involving lengthy exchanges of petitions and decrees among rulers, prelates, and businessmen. Even those moralists who felt the pressure for change most acutely maintained conservative positions and countered vigorous demands with careful responses, yielding only when they found a morally relevant circumstance or a conceptual clarification that justified a step away from the firm base of the ancient paradigm, with its revered maxims and arguments.

This history of doctrinal change reveals not an evasion of morality but its progressive refinement, marking more precisely the grounds and limits of moral judgments about economic life. This refinement necessarily called for many distinctions and qualifications; some of these might be specious, but many of them were fair and reasonable interpretations of the moral principles of justice and charity in the new circumstances. Certainly the casuists' discussions of usury were more substantial than is allowed by Pascal's caustic description as "magic words . . . which have occult virtue to dispel usury."[25]

10

Perjury: The Case of Equivocation

The casuists' teaching on truth-telling particularly was held up to criticism. Pascal puts their teaching into the mouth of the Good Father:

> One of the most embarrassing problems is how to avoid lying, especially when one would like people to believe something untrue. This is where our doctrine of equivocation is marvelously helpful, for it allows one "to use ambiguous terms, conveying a different meaning to the hearer from that in which one understands them himself," as Sanchez says, *Moral Works*, II, 3, vi, n. 13.

The Good Father explains that when one cannot find equivocal words, the "new doctrine" of mental restriction can be employed.[1]

This "new doctrine" must be viewed against the background of the ancient Catholic doctrine about truth-telling. The moralists of antiquity had praised truth and condemned falsehood. Aristotle wrote, "Falsehood is in itself mean and culpable, and truth noble and full of praise." Yet the ancients had tolerated and even recommended certain kinds of deception: for the rulers of the Republic, Plato's "noble lie" was an actual obligation.[2] The Scriptures, both Old and New Testaments, condemned the liar in strong terms: "Jahweh hates all workers of iniquity; He will destroy all that speak a lie" (Ps 5:7). Yet early Christian moralists could not help but be perplexed by certain episodes related in the Scriptures, such as the Israelite women lying to Pharaoh and the supposedly omniscient

Jesus declaring that he "knew not the day nor the hour" of the Last Judgment. Indeed, although the wrongness of deception was widely recognized, the practice of deception was not uniformly condemned in the early Christian community.[3]

Any hesitation about the immorality of lying came to an end with the overpowering arguments of St. Augustine, whose two treatises, *On Lying* (*De Mendacio*) and *Against Lying* (*Contra Medacium*), established the standard doctrine during the Middle Ages and until the era of high casuistry. Even when some casuists, with their "new doctrine," strayed some way from Augustine's absolute prohibition of lying, his rigorous argument loomed always in the background. Augustine had been troubled by the teaching of the Priscillian heretics that it was permissible to lie in order to preserve the mysteries of the faith from prying pagan curiosity. In response, Augustine questioned whether it could ever be morally permissible to tell a lie. The argument of *De Mendacio* begins with a definition of lying as uttering one thing by words or signs while having another thing in one's mind, with the intention to deceive. He then cited pertinent scriptural texts, such as "Thou shalt not bear false witness" (Dt 5:20), "Let your communication be yes, yes and no, no; anything more comes from the devil" (Mt 5:27) and "Throw off falsehood; speak the truth to one another" (Eph 4:25). The scriptural texts that dominated Augustine's analysis are selected from the Psalms, "The mouth that lies shall kill the soul," and "Thou shalt destroy the man who speaks loosely; the Lord abhors the bloody and deceitful man" (Ps 1:11, 5:6).

Augustine examined, in the light of these texts, the problematic cases from the Scriptures, such as the deception of Pharaoh by the Hebrew midwives in Exodus 1:20. He also posed several hypothetical cases, one of which was to remain the classical case about the immorality of lying up to the time of Kant: An innocent man, who has been unjustly condemned, is hidden in your house. May you lie to the authorities who come to arrest him? Augustine considered various arguments that might justify answering that question deceptively, and concluded that possible good consequences could never justify a deliberate lie: "Since by lying eternal life is lost, never for any man's temporal life must a lie be told."[4]

Augustine allowed little latitude into this absolute prohibition. He did, however, distinguish eight species of lying as varying in gravity. The degree of sinfulness depended on the seriousness of the harm done by the deception and on whether the resulting benefits from the lie accrued to the deceiver himself or to some other party. The malice ranged from the most serious—namely, a lie that leads another to deny religious belief—to the least sinful—a lie that actually helps another without harming anyone but the teller.[5]

The Augustinian teaching stood throughout the Middle Ages. In due course St. Thomas Aquinas repeated it with only minor modifications in definition. However, he added one seemingly simple comment that was to play a large part in casuistic discussions and lead eventually to the formulation of "the new doctrine": "It is licit to hide the truth prudently by some sort of dissimulation (*licet tamen veritatem occultare prudenter sub aliqua dissimulatione*)."[6]

Aquinas' contemporary, the canonist Raymond of Pennafort, repeated the Augustinian position almost verbatim, but he classified Augustine's eight species of lie into three types. The "pernicious" lie harms someone without even bringing any benefit to the liar; the "officious," or dutiful lie benefits someone other than the liar; the "jocose" lie does no harm to anyone. Each of these kinds of lies, regardless of harm done, remained sinful because the malice of a lie depended not on its consequences but on the very discrepancy between what is in the mind and what is uttered. However, because by the thirteenth century theologians had come to distinguish more clearly between mortal and venial sin, Raymond noted that even if the pernicious lie would always be mortal, dutiful and jocose lies might be venial, depending upon the circumstances. Even then he admits that there is some dispute whether the jocose lie might even be a venial sin.

Raymond then addressed Augustine's famous case of the person who harbors an innocent fugitive. He acknowledged the perplexity of someone facing this situation: he fears sinning by betrayal of the innocent man and by complicity in his death or, conversely, he fears sinning by lying. Augustine had spoken unambiguously: "One must not do evil, even to prevent greater evil." Others, admits Raymond, consider that in this case a lie might be permitted. His own judgment in the case is threefold. First, as Augustine himself had recommended, one should simply remain silent before the question; if silence would be dangerous, one can attempt to distract the questioner. Finally, if compelled to answer, one many respond "in equivocal words." An ingenious Latin equivocation is suggested: "*non est hic*," which can mean either "he is not here" or "he does not eat here" (the same equivocation is possible in German: "*er ist/isst*"

nicht hier"). Raymond then offers some biblical examples that illustrate and justify the use of equivocation, and then moves even far-
ther from the strict Augustinian position. He says, "Alternatively,
one can simply deny that the person is present. If one does so conscientiously, one is not speaking contrary to one's conscience. Thus,
one does not lie even in Augustine's sense." Raymond concludes his
discussion by asking whether the speaker of such a dutiful lie
should be subject to blame or praise; he is unsure, closing with the
words, "this I leave to further debate."[7]

The summists dutifully repeated the Augustinian doctrine but
showed some readiness to relax its vigor. The *Summa Sylvestrina*
asked "whether it is permitted to hide the truth (*celare veritatem*)"
and answered that it is permitted "in many ways, if one is not
obliged to answer in accord with the questioner's intent." For example, if several answers were available, it is legitimate to offer one of
them and remain silent about the other; or one may use an expression that has a double meaning without clarifying which of the
proper senses is meant. Each of these was illustrated by a story from
the Old Testament (Gn 7, I Kgs 15, Tb 5). An example of the second
way was offered: "If someone seeking to kill another person asks
you, 'did he go this way?' you may answer, 'no, not this way,' meaning 'his feet did not tread the very ground you are pointing at.' If
asked about something you are obliged to keep secret, you may say,
'I do not know,' understanding in your mind (*subintelligendo*) 'so that
it may be revealed to you.'" This was what Christ did when he said
he did not know the day nor the hour of the Judgment. Sylvester
then added,

> about this manner of concealing, caution should be exercised: scandal
> should not be given; it cannot be used in a law court before an autho-
> rized judge nor when the questioned person is bound to answer truth-
> fully to a lawful superior.

In the article on Oaths Sylvester repeated the oft-cited case of a
traveler arriving from a city where plague was suspected. Knowing
for a fact that there is no plague in his city of origin, he answers "no"
to the guards' question whether he comes from that city. For
Sylvester this answer is not a lie, for it fulfills the ultimate purpose
of the question—to keep out plague.[8]

The summists' discussion of truth-telling is not entirely lucid;
many different elements of the problem were mixed together. Yet it

represented the state of the question from the thirteenth to the fifteenth century. The Augustinian paradigm of speaking before God
as well as man was retained; the classical warrants, in the form of
scriptural maxims, were repeated; certain modalities that were only
tenuously compatible with the paradigm, such as the use of ambiguous answers, were admitted. But in general, no clear and consistent
view had emerged. In 1552, however, the professor of theology at
Salamanca, Dominico Soto, gave a course of magisterial lectures on
the subject, and these were later published as *Reasoning about
Revealing and Concealing Secrets*. Strikingly, this treatise was written
during the height of the Spanish Inquisition, when many of the
accused were sorely pressed to reveal secrets under duress. Soto,
Dominican though he was, provided an ethical justification that
must have comforted such unfortunate persons.

Soto presented a carefully argued case analysis, posing first, as
paradigm, the clearest case: "Is a witness under oath bound to
reveal a committed secret when questioned by an authorized judge
in the prescribed manner?" In general he would be bound; the rare
exception to this general obligation would be the case in which revelation threatens great public harm. Soto then moved confidently
through a series of more complex cases. An interrogator questioning
unjustly or illegally need not be answered: one can answer deceptively but not lie. Where the justice of the inquisition is in real
doubt, there is no obligation to answer unless failure might cause
great public harm: for example, if the secret concerns treasonable
acts or a plot to assassinate the ruler.

Finally, Soto reached the crucial question: "When questioned outside the law, may a person employ obscure and ambiguous expression in order to delude the questioner?" He remarked in passing,
"On this matter, I would prefer to listen to others' opinions rather
than offer my own, but I must attempt a response." After careful
reflection he allowed that equivocation may be permissible, as any
genuine equivocation does have the sense intended by the speaker
as one of the proper meanings of the word used. He also conceded
one type of "mental restriction"—the answer, "I do not know," spoken with the unexpressed qualification, "in a way I can state publicly." He argued for this position very cautiously. He was quite
certain that it held good in one type of case: that of a priest asked
for information that he knows only from sacramental confession,
"for the whole Christian world knows that such information is spo-

ken to the priest as to God." He is less certain but still confident that the same denial may be morally justifiable in some secular situations; but after careful examination, he repudiated more extended and elaborate forms of restriction. These, he wrote, do "violence to common sense." To his final case, that of a person whom an unjust questioner threatens with death unless he reveal a secret, Soto answered (switching to the first person), "If I had no legitimate equivocation available, I ought to accept death rather than lie."[9]

Soto's reference to the priest questioned about knowledge gained in confession is important. The problem must have arisen frequently during the Inquisition, as this institution sought out religious aberrations that might often have been discussed in confession. The insistence on the inviolability of the seal of confession had grown during the tenth and eleventh centuries. In 1215 the Fourth Lateran Council imposed a severe penance upon the priest who violated the seal: he was to be deposed from priestly office and confined for life to a strict monastery. Thus a priest called to testify before the Inquisition or before any court about matters imparted under the seal was in a moral quandary. The interrogated priest—who as confessor heard sins only as God's representative easily recalled the Augustinian view that human speech was always to be understood as spoken before God. In this way a new paradigm for truth-telling appeared.[10]

Lecturing several years later in the same university, the influential canonist Navarrus exploited the new paradigm and in so doing becomes less scrupulous about mental restriction. He suggested that it was legitimate to withhold "in tacit thought" a phrase that, if uttered openly, would manifest that the spoken statement was incomplete and thus, on its face, false. This was Navarrus' novel interpretation of the text from Gratian's *Decretum* on which he was commenting:

> "human ears judge words as they sound externally; divine judgment, however, takes the external sounds in accord with internal intent." Intention should not be made to serve the words, but the words the intention.[11]

This text, the initial words of which are excerpted from the *Moralia* of Gregory the Great, was originally meant to affirm that untrue words spoken without intention to deceive were not culpable. Navarrus finds in them grounds to separate spoken word and intention. God hears the inner words and judges them true; even though man may not know that inner and outer words differ. This interpretation, recalling in a perverse way the Augustinian belief that humans are bound to truth because they speak in the presence of the God of Truth, was plausible in the case of the priest interrogated about committed confessional secrets. It was hardly plausible as a thesis about truth-telling in general. Yet the "mental restriction," interpreted in this broad way, came into the casuists' analysis of truth-telling.

Navarrus' opinion did not remain unchallenged for long. The Jesuit Azor cited it and noted the apparent concurrence of Sylvester and Angelicus. He then commented, "from this rule much can be inferred: some of it true and some of it false." He illustrated the correct use of the rule by recalling the case of the man coming from the city incorrectly suspected of plague. But he advised that the use of *tacita cogitatio* is permissible only in particular kinds of cases: for instance, the priest asked about confessional matters and the person questioned by an unjust judge acting illegally. In such cases the *injuria* (literally, injustice, not injury) done to the person questioned allows him to evade a direct answer in this way. But if there was no *injuria*, "we must answer frankly using words according to their usual and ordinary meaning." Aside from these special cases,

> it is not licit to use prevarication, because by such prevarication, all lies would be excused and human intercourse as well as charity among neighbors would be abolished.[12]

Over the following fifty years a few authors recognized Navarrus' singular doctrine on the validity of restriction as "probable"; but more of them adopted the skepticism of Azor and emphatically rejected the thesis.[13]

During this period the casuists refined and elaborated the concepts relevant to judgments about telling or concealing the truth; sorting out interpretations they could morally tolerate from those they found unacceptable. They finally formulated a distinction that drew a sharp line between equivocation and mental restriction. The former takes advantage of the fact that linguistic usage permits a word or phrase to have several legitimate meanings: the speaker merely avoids making it clear which meaning he intends his utterance to have, hoping that his questioner will interpret it in some sense other than he intends. For example, someone might ask a physician, "do you care for this person?" hoping to discover whether the person was the physician's patient. The physician, observing the confidentiality of the relationship, might answer, "No," meaning "I don't care for him in the sense of being fond of him."

The extent of the casuists' tolerance for such equivocation depends on the circumstances. Does the questioner have some authority entitling him to the truth? If so, the majority of casuists did not permit even this equivocation. Does the person questioned have some duty to conceal the truth? If so, as in the case of a priest questioned about confessional secrets or the physician questioned about his patient, equivocation is certainly permissible.

The notion, then, that a "mental restriction"—an unexpressed condition that would save a statement known by the speaker to be contrary to fact from being a "lie"—appeared for the first time in several sixteenth-century authors. Cajetan simply rejected the idea out of hand; as we have seen, Soto treated it with great caution. It gained some currency from the weight of Navarrus' approval, but it quickly came under criticism from his contemporaries. That criticism, however, led to further refinement in the concept. The notion of mental restriction depended not so much on linguistic usage, as did the equivocation, but upon more complex features of communication. One speaks a sentence that literally does not express the state of affairs, but by adding a qualification in his mind, the speaker rendered the spoken statement true "as far as he and God were concerned." If the questioner could have heard both the expressed and the unexpressed parts of the speaker's idea, he would have realized the true state of affairs.

In its simplest form, this kind of dissimulation reflects certain conventions of common speech. "Is your husband at home?" asks the unwelcome caller; "Do you have any money?" asks the insistent sponger. The answer, "no (not for you)" was, suggested the casuists, understood by people at large. Soto's approval of mental restriction had been limited to this sort of convention. Everyone should realize, he says, that a priest answering "no" to a question involving confessional secrecy meant "I don't know with a knowledge communicable to anyone but God." The casuists came to call this kind of restriction "broad" and treated it in much the same way as they did equivocation: it was acceptable in circumstances when it was the only way to preserve a legitimately committed secret or to avoid serious harm, primarily to others but occasionally to oneself. This simple form of broad mental restriction, however, is often quite transparent: it fools no one. Was it also morally legitimate to go further, "reserving in the mind" some phrase expressing conditions that the questioner might never suspect or imagine? Could such an inner qualification ever preserve an apparently untrue spoken expression from being a lie?

For many English Roman Catholics in the last decades of the sixteenth-century, that question was translated from academic exercise to terrifying reality. In the great houses of the Catholic gentry who sheltered Roman priests from the Queen's pursuivants, concealing an innocent person in one's home was no longer a hypothetical case but an actual drama. The story begins in 1559, when Queen Elizabeth signed the Act of Supremacy, which separated the English Church from Rome and made the English ruler Supreme Governor of the Church in England. This act required an Oath of Supremacy from all officeholders, clergy, and candidates for office or degrees. In the same year Parliament passed the Act of Uniformity, instituting the English Prayer Book as the sole ritual, outlawing the saying or hearing of the Roman Mass, and penalizing by fines all who failed to attend Anglican church services every Sunday and Holy Day. In 1570 Pope Pius V, having abandoned hope of reconciling Elizabeth to Rome, issued the Bull, *Regnans in Excelsis*, in which he excommunicated her, declared her no longer queen, and absolved her subjects from obedience to her.

Four years later English Catholics who had gone abroad to be educated at the newly founded seminary at Douai (later moved to Rheims) began arriving as missionaries in their homeland. The first Jesuit priests, Robert Persons and Edmund Campion, arrived in 1580. The seminary priests and the Jesuits on the English Mission were dedicated to serving their fellow countrymen who had remained faithful to Rome and to converting the realm to the Roman faith. In 1585 Parliament passed an act banishing all Jesuits and seminary priests, declaring it treason for any Englishman ordained overseas to enter England. (Treason was a capital offense: the traitor was hanged and drawn and quartered.) The first seminary priest had, in fact, been hanged five years earlier under an act of 1571; the Jesuit Campion was caught, tried under the ancient Act of Treason of 1352, and executed in 1581. Eventually, 183 Catholics, of whom 123 were priests, were executed during the reign of Elizabeth.

English Catholics were now in a difficult moral situation. Obliged by law to attend religious services they considered heretical and forbidden to attend those they held necessary for their salvation, required under certain circumstances to swear allegiance to a ruler whose claim to be Supreme Governor of the Church they repudiated and from whose civil authority the pope had released them, and threatened on occasion with the dangers of harboring the outlawed priests whose sacramental offices they desired, English Catholics faced a serious crisis of conscience. As persecution intensified, fueled by the pro-Catholic Northern Rebellion (1569), by the Spanish Armada (1588), and by the Gunpowder Plot (1605), Catholics felt the crisis more acutely.

In the last three decades of the sixteenth century, English Catholics increasingly turned from an attitude of respectful dissent to a posture of adamant refusal to accept the religious settlement of 1559 (whence they earned the title "recusants"). Penalties for recusancy were stiffened; efforts at detection and prosecution were intensified. Conscientious Catholics were plagued with many questions: "Should I outwardly attend Anglican services while refusing inwardly, all the while secretly hearing Mass?" "As a judge, may I swear the Oath of Supremacy while withholding true allegiance in my heart?" "As a Jesuit, may I deny my name, my true reason for traveling hither, my religious profession, my faith?" "What should I, a Catholic gentleman, say to the pursuivants at my door, when they inquire about the priest hidden in a secret closet of my house?" So Augustine's case became a real-life drama on many a night in many a manor house in England.[14]

In this situation the moral problem whether to tell the truth became excruciating. Although the moral issues raised by Catholic recusancy ranged from the very basic one of *communicatio in sacris* (that is, participation in heretical religious rites) to the extreme problem of tyrannicide, truth-telling was the most prominent one that everyone with Catholic sympathies must have faced almost daily. The problem became most acute for those Catholics who were haled before a magistrate and interrogated about their beliefs or behavior. Some of them, usually the priests, had to decide how they should answer the judge's "bloody question": "If England were attacked, which would you support—the queen or an army blessed by the Pope?" As one historian comments, "to Elizabeth this was a political question; to the priests, a complicated problem of conscience with no simple answer."[15]

It was widely believed in England that Catholics would unblushingly perjure themselves in such situations. The leading Anglican casuist, William Perkins, wrote,

> In their doctrine they (Catholic casuists) maintain perjury: because they teach with one consent that a papist examined may answer doubtfully against the direct intent of the examiner: framing another meaning unto himself in the ambiguity of his words.[16]

It was, in fact, not quite fair for Perkins to say of his Roman counterparts, "they teach with one consent." Not only was there no general agreement in favor of the opinion Perkins quotes; there was, in fact, general agreement against it. However, reading the still current thesis of Navarrus could give the impression that the "mental restriction" was an accepted Roman doctrine. This was far from the case: the anonymous English Catholic author of a pamphlet entitled *A Lawful Manner of Answering to Questions of Going to Church* stated,

> In my judgment, the answer given must be such as is lawful in a religious sense. For otherwise, the answerer giveth just cause that the demander conceive a sense dishonorable to God. So, it is not lawful to say he goeth to church, meaning a profane going to St. Paul's; nor that he hath received (i.e., the Eucharist) because he has received his rents or a piece of bread at home.[17]

Yet the suspicion of sanctioned perjury was borne out in many a case. An astonishing example is found in the State Papers of 5 February, 1606. The Dean of Durham was writing to Lord Salisbury about the testimony of a certain Father Ward:

> First, he swore he was no priest, that is, saith he (in a subsequent explanation), not Apollo's priest at Delphi. Second, he swore he was never across the sea, it's true he saith, for he was never across the Indian Seas. Third, he was never at or of the Seminaries. *Duplex est Seminarium, materiale et spirituale*, he was never of the spiritual seminary. Forthly, he never knew Mr. Hawksworth; it is true, saith he, *scientia scientifica*. Fifthly, he never saw Mr. Hawksworth, true, he saith, *visione beatifica*.[18]

These equivocations were, of course, outrageous and Father Ward was accused of "childish shifts and impostures." Certainly such answers merited the derision of contemporaries and defamed the casuistry that justified them. Even Shakespeare took notice: in *Macbeth*, written shortly after the trial of the Jesuit Garnet for com plicity in the Gunpowder Plot (1605), the drunken porter declared an equivocator to be "one who could swear in both scales against either scale, who committed treason enough for God's sake, yet could not equivocate to heaven." When the young Macduff asks his mother "what is a traitor," she replies, "why one that swears and lies. Everyone that does so is a traitor and must be hanged."[19] Some modern commentators have described the equivocation as "repulsive" and "self-exculpatory near lies."[20]

Yet these "repulsive, near liars" would bravely go to their deaths for their faith. How, then, did they justify their equivocations? We are fortunate to have copies of the *casus conscientiae*, dictated to the English seminarians at Rheims and Rome in the late decades of the sixteenth century. These cases dealt with the many moral problems that these men would encounter once they returned as missionaries in their homeland. Numerous cases discussed the problem of truthtelling. One case put the question, "How may Catholics brought before heretics answer without sin, either sworn or unsworn?" The casuist answered, "He may refuse the oath, which is more prudent, or may swear and answer sophistically." This may sound sinister but, when an example of a sophistical answer was provided, can be seen to be quite innocent. When asked "Is the Queen a heretic?" one can answer, "Who gave you the right to judge her?"[21]

Indeed, the Rheims casuist's teaching was quite strict, yet at the same time commonsensical. He asked, "May priests or Catholics, being asked if they are such, hold their peace or delude the questioners with their answer?" He responded, "When interrogated by the highest royal officials, they sin mortally if they are silent or equivocate, for so doing would deny their faith before those who hate it." If, however, they are questioned out of curiosity, as by fellow travelers, or out of cupidity, as by customs officers, who do so only to line their own pockets, they may be silent or equivocate. The duty to confess the faith was a positive command that obliged only at certain times, not everywhere and always.[22]

The permission to equivocate in response to casual unofficial inquiry was argued more fully in other cases. One of these asked, "Can a priest deny his name?" If asked in a judicial inquiry, he may not; if others will be scandalized by hearing his denial, that is, induced to sin themselves, he may not. If he has changed his name from Peter to another, he may deny that his name is Peter, for it no

longer is. If asked by someone in authority, he may deny straight-
forwardly, since denial is equivalent to saying "I deny that I am
Peter (who is bound to respond to you by the authority you claim.)"
Finally, if asked whether such a place is his home, he may answer
"no," meaning that he no longer recognizes it as his home. The
casuist commented on this case,

> changing one's name or adopting a disguise is not a lie, but pretence.
> Pretence is lawful Christ pretended to go further on the road to
> Emmaus (Lk 24.13), ambush of enemies is permitted in the Old
> Testament (Josh 8) and Pope Adrian has proven that pretence is lawful
> (Comm. in. Sent. IV, q. 1).[23]

These references make it clear that the casuist's source was
Navarrus, whose *Enchiridion* was the textbook of casuistry studied at
the English Seminary of Douai-Rheims. So the consciences of the
English seminarians were formed in this matter by a teaching that
was still immature. Azor's criticism had not yet succeeded in bringing it to greater maturity. The casuist discusses two final cases.
First, a priest, if questioned outside a juridical inquiry, may avoid
answering "by trickery or ambiguous reply. . . using equivocation,
silence, returning the question or any method he likes, so long as he
neither denies his faith or lies." Even in a judicial inquiry the obligation to be truthful is attenuated, since "I claim that these interroga-
tions are never lawful, since the queen is a heretic and acts not as
queen, but as tyrant."[24]

In 1595 an anonymous pamphlet appeared which confirmed the
suspicion of many Englishmen that the Jesuits were unscrupulous
equivocators. Composed by a Jesuit of the English Mission, who has
now been identified as the Jesuit Provincial Henry Garnet, *A Treatise
of Equivocation or Against Lying and Fraudulent Dissimulation* was written soon after the trial of Father Robert Southwell. Southwell had
been charged with treason; in the arraignment it was stated that he
had instructed a gentlewoman that, if asked under oath whether he
was hidden at her father's house, she might "swear no, with the
intention to herself that he was not there so she was bound to tell
them." Garnet's treatise defended this teaching. He opened with
the question,

> whether a Catholic or any other person before a magistrate being
> demanded upon his oath whether a priest were in such a place may,
> notwithstanding his perfect knowledge to the contrary, without per-

jury and securely in his conscience, answer no, with this secret meaning reserved in his mind, "that he was not there so that any man is
bound to reveal it." . . . We will endeavor to prove that whosoever
frameth a true proposition in his mind and uttereth some part thereof
in words, which of themselves being taken several from the other part
reserved were false, doth not so speak false or lie before God, howso-
ever he may be thought to lie before men.[25]

This astonishing thesis was justified by appealing to the warrant,
"The proposition is in the mind and God seeth the mind"; and this,
of course, was the thesis of Navarrus. Garnet marshaled support for
his thesis by the exegesis of a number of scriptural texts that had
long exercised the ingenuity of theologians. Each text related an
apparent falsehood uttered by a patriarch, prophet, or apostle. How
could these holy persons lie and yet be approved by God? Indeed,
Jesus himself at times seems to have spoken falsehood (Jn 7, Mk 13).
Garnet's exegesis of these texts endeavored to show that in all these
cases, the actual statement uttered, if taken with a hypothetical
reserved phrase, made up a true proposition known to God. For one
reason or another, the questioners in these scriptural incidents had
no claim on the truth in the particular situation in which the question was asked. A lie, said Garnet,

> consists in this, that a man intends to deny with words the very truth
> he conceives in his mind. But this is not so in these cases, for he con-
> traryth not the truth which to himself he conceiveth, but rather signi-
> fyeth another diverse truth . . . it mattereth not whether those which I
> speak to understand it amiss or no so long as unjustly, rashly or
> wickedly I am asked by them.[26]

Garnet noted that accepted authors had distinguished two types
of equivocation. In one a word or expression had several ways of
being understood in ordinary language; the speaker simply did not
specify which of these proper meanings he intended. This was, literally, "equivocation"—that is, words with the same or similar sound
or spelling. In the other type, "besides the word uttered, we understand some thing which according to usual speech cannot be understood. For example, 'I did not do this (so that you should know)' or
'I will give you one hundred pounds (if I find it at Cheapside).' This
second sort of equivocation, which nowadays we would call deceptive prevarication, was rejected, Garnet pointed out, by many early
doctors who did not allow that it excused from a lie. "Soto was first

to scruple on this point, but his opinion seems to other divines and to almost all of our age too severe and scrupulous."

In defense of the second type of equivocation, Garnet offered the familiar problem of the confessor asked a confessional secret. However, Soto had recognized that the confessor's problem was quite special. It was therefore morally perilous to extend this kind of restriction to other cases or to confuse it with the literal equivocation of the first sort. Within a decade other casuists of great repute, such as Laymann and De Lugo, were to label it a simple lie. But armed with Navarrus' prestige that had not, at that date, been challenged, Garnet espoused the more lax opinion and approved of the second type of equivocation.

Strangely enough, Garnet neither used nor needed to use the more lax opinion to make his own case. He could defend Southwell's equivocation as a straightforward illustration of what was later called "broad mental restriction" in which the responder simply said, "no (he is not here for you, who have no right to know)." The real fulcrum of Garnet's argument is the claim that the questions that were put to recusants were unjust and wicked questions. He warned the reader that his thesis about equivocation required "certain fit limits and convenient moderation without which neither God would be pleased nor the link and conjunction of human society newly preserved."[27] That convenient moderation was in accord with Aristotle's mean of virtue: one observed this mean in truthfulness "by neither deceitfully concealing that which should be uttered nor rashly babbling out whatever they knew."[28] What should be uttered was determined by the obligations of faith, charity, and justice. In particular it was a mortal sin to equivocate when answering upon oath "before a competent judge lawfully examining."[29] The conditions for competency and lawfulness were set out in terms congenial to the common law. Then, Garnet asserts,

> the oath propounded to a Catholic and taken by him with equivocation wants not the first condition of an oath, namely verity. Any oath is taken with the understanding, even if not expressed, that one will utter only what one lawfully can utter. No one, even under oath, need answer an unlawful question. In this matter of one's religion, we are by God's law exempt from all civil magistrates . . . for the law which persecutes Christ's priests persecutes Christ himself. . . . If we doubted the injustice of this law we would live like atheists and heathens in this world.[30]

He concludes that there is no moral obligation "to deal plainly and lay open our secrets to our own prejudice."

Garnet went on to teach that if they took the oath, Catholic respondents might answer in three ways. To answer yes would be an injustice, for it would acknowledge the rightness of the law. To hold one's peace is itself a manner of confession: "Why will not these scrupulous casistes as well condemn of perjury for not answering as for not answering directly and trewly?"[31] There was, concluded Garnet, no other answer but denial. Garnet then offered some practical advice: anyone in such a situation should by preference refuse to swear at all, "if not urged by the necessity of the cause." If he must swear, he should do so in formal terms, such as "I will answer all I can lawfully tell." If he swore without this limitation, "let him persuade himself he is not bound by his oath to do anything which becometh not an honest man."[32]

Father Robert Persons, Garnet's partner in the English Mission, agreed with his colleague. In *A Treatise Tending toward Mitigation* (1607), he taught that equivocation was licit. Surprisingly, he asserted that although licit in general, equivocation was not permissible in the matter of the Oath of Allegiance, which was devised to test the allegiance of Catholics in the aftermath of the Gunpowder Plot. Parliament, too, had read Garnet's pamphlet, and in this new oath inserted the clause, "I do plainly and sincerely acknowledge and swear, according to these express words by me spoken and according to the plain and common sense and understanding of the same words, without any equivocation or secret reservation whatsoever." Although Persons, like most English Catholics, rejected the Oath because it declared the doctrine of papal authority to be heretical, he admitted that Catholics could not equivocate about this Oath; since the oath contained an express denial of the practice of equivocation, to equivocate with respect to it was "to equivocate upon equivocation *procedendo in infinitum*: so these men will like eels slip out how fast so ever you think you hold them," wrote Persons in another treatise, *A Discourse against Taking the Oath* (1606).[33]

Persons adopted a strict position. The judges in the Gunpowder Plot were competent and observed the form of law required. In addition, it was not right to equivocate in matters of faith, "since it is all one in effect to equivocate and to deny the faith." He concluded,

in religion, in ordinary traffic, negotiation, and conversation, if equivocation caused injury to a neighbor in soul, body or goods, it is not justifiable. It is not permissible to read the oath and only pretend to swear it, inwardly refusing, for in man's court, we must follow the outward and apparent proofs, tokens and presumptions to judge of men's actions and not the intents inwardly reserved and known only to God which no way are known to us but by external means.[34]

For a period of thirty years Navarrus' interpretation had the effect of relaxing the strict Catholic teaching on truth-telling, particularly as it applied to truthful witness under judicial oath. The notion that one could use a word that does, in fact, have several legitimate meanings without specifying which meaning one intended—a notion quite unobjectionable in certain circumstances—was expanded into the idea that one might utter a phrase that was susceptible of diverse interpretations, depending on the reservation of some crucial additional phrase "in the mind." The reservation of one recognized meaning of a single word thus becomes the reservation of an alternative and unrecognizable meaning of an entire statement.

As broadcast by Garnet's pamphlet, Navarrus' thesis gave rise to the accusation that, encouraged by casuistry, Catholics were unscrupulous equivocators who could never be trusted. Even Garnet's Jesuit colleagues quickly repudiated his interpretation in favor of a return to the earlier stricter doctrine. They rested their case not on the notion of mental restriction but on the claim that the questioner was an "unjust judge" without authority. In so doing they anticipated a doctrine that was to be formally enunciated by Hugo Grotius a century later, that the obligation to tell the truth was correlative to the right of the questioner to know the truth. (This doctrine, though congenial to twentieth-century ears, was to be damned by Immanuel Kant, not surprisingly, as "primordial falsehood.")[35]

This is not the end of the story. Fifty years after English Catholics had been obliged to examine their consciences about oaths of loyalty, their fellow countrymen of the Established Church faced the same problem. After the execution of Charles I and the establishment of the Commonwealth, Parliament imposed a new oath of allegiance, known as the Engagement Oath:

> I do declare and promise that I will be true and faithful to the Commonwealth of England as it is now established without King and House of Lords.

It was now the turn of persons of Royalist and Anglican persuasion to be troubled in conscience. Could they, in good conscience, take the oath, whereby they repudiated their dedication to the restoration of the monarchy, or were they obliged to refuse it and pay the penalty? Robert Sanderson, Professor of Case Divinity at Oxford, responded to this question in an elegant casus, carefully reasoned and balanced. Though explicitly repudiating the device of mental restriction employed by "those who play fast and loose with Oaths and swear to one thing on Monday and another on Tuesday," he came to a conclusion not unlike that of the Jesuit casuists. Royalists may take the oath and at the same time retain allegiance to the Royalist cause, even continuing to work for its restoration. Sanderson stated the moral dilemma. On the one hand, a person sinned by taking an oath contrary to allegiance to the lawful sovereign; on the other, refusal of the oath exposed one to great dangers. After a lengthy analysis of the nature of oaths, vows, and promises, he concluded that anyone who believed that the king and his heirs do constitute the rightful sovereign power and who believed that the Engagement Oath repudiated the allegiance may not take the oath without sinning.

Oaths, however, must be interpreted in accord with the common use of language. This normal use binds the swearer even if the one imposing the oath has some ulterior purpose. Sanderson then argued that the language of the Oath could be interpreted as compatible with allegiance to the king. The Oath contained key words that were in themselves ambiguous. "Commonwealth" might mean either the party currently in power or the English nation as a whole. If taken in the second sense, the Oath obliged one only to live peaceably under the *de facto* rulers and did not imply an acknowledgment of their *de jure* right to hold power. The final phrase, "without King or House of Lords" might either signify approval of this form of government or merely describe it. Finally, "true and faithful" might refer either to the fidelity that everyone owed to his country or the faith promised by prisoners of war to their captors. In light of these ambiguities, Sanderson concluded that a Royalist may take the Oath understanding it to be a promise "to do what every good member of a Commonwealth ought to do for the safety of my country and the preservation of civil society," in this sense compatible with continued allegiance to the king. The Oxford casuist had employed the long-honored casuistic technique of equivocation that had prevailed before Navarrus' time and was to return to its place of honor.[36]

The problem of truth-telling reveals the essential features of casuistical argument. Initially the Catholic tradition bequeathed to the casuists a rigorous, absolutist doctrine inherited from the most prestigious of Church Fathers, Augustine. The definitions and analytic categories expressed in the *De Mendacio* were respected throughout the Middle Ages. During the late Middle Ages a circumstance then appeared which posed a serious paradox: namely, the evolution of a strict duty to maintain absolute confidentiality about information learned by a priest in sacramental confession. Thus the paradigmatic case for casuistical analysis became that of the priest questioned by lawful authority. The priest actually possessed the information sought by authorities, but he had it only in strict confidentiality. In this situation dissimulation through the use of an equivocal term or expression was admitted on the grounds that, given the actual double meaning of the words used, the questioner could take either of the meanings. But the ingenuousness of this solution was its own downfall: it was too transparent to be effective in protecting the secret. Add the circumstance that a full and truthful answer might bring great danger to some party, either the confessor or the penitent or some third person, and it becomes clear that a more effective means was needed to preserve one's conscientious obligation to the truth and, at the same time, to preserve the obligation of confidentiality generated by the seal of the sacrament.

Under this pressure casuists began to show toleration for the extended form of equivocation that came to be known as restriction. Instead of relying on the ambiguity of words, it exploited the conventions of common language. The argument for restriction still reflected the theology of the confessional: just as the penitent spoke to God through the priest, so the priest's knowledge of the truth was known to God alone. The priest remained truthful before God if he "reserved" some words from the verbal communication with his interrogators. Even when equivocation and restriction were justified by forms of language, however, the more important circumstance was that the question or the questioner was "unjust." Either the questioner does not have the authority to ask the question, or the forum in which it is asked is extralegal, or the question is an unfair one, seeking information that would put someone in undeserved jeopardy. Faced with legally authorized judges in legally correct forums, the casuists of all eras required the truth and the whole truth.

Thus the casuistry of truth-telling was on its most solid ground when it dealt with its paradigmatic case, the confessor questioned about sacramental matters. As it moved away from this case to cases of persons questioned under oath in legally dubious situations, it still marched on reasonably firm ground. Once into the general area of private parties interrogated by other private parties for their own purposes, the devices of equivocation and restriction became somewhat shaky expedients. The laxist opinion that tolerated their general use was quickly repudiated by most casuists and finally condemned officially by the Roman authorities in 1679. The Holy Office condemned three theses, expressed in sentences excerpted from the Jesuit casuists Sanchez and Lessius.

> If someone alone or before others, either under question or spontaneously or merely for amusement or any other reason, answers an oath that he truly did not do something that he in fact has done, understanding in himself that he did not do it, in that way or on that day or something of that sort, he does not lie or commit perjury.
>
> There is just reason to use equivocation as often as is necessary or useful for the protection of one's physical wellbeing, one's honor or one's possessions, so the hiding of the truth can be considered expedient or desirable.
>
> Anyone who, by way of gift or favor to an official, has been promoted to public office, may take an oath with mental restriction that is customarily given to all such officials by the king without respect to the intentions of the king; this is so because one is not required to confess an occult crime.[37]

After the condemnation of 1679, the casuists' doctrine on truth-telling reverted to the state of the question before Navarrus. Concealing the truth was considered permissible when questioned unjustly or when revealing it could cause great harm to another. Truth could be concealed simply by not answering, or else by answering in an equivocal way. It was also permissible to use the "broad mental restriction," based upon conventional uses of language. The appearance of a probable opinion that had approved the "pure mental restriction" was brief and was quickly battered down by critics. However, during the brief popularity of that doctrine, it compromised the moral probity of conscientious Catholics and contributed to the bad name of casuistry. As one of the most esteemed modern casuists of the Catholic Church wrote, is there any way to reconcile the prohibition of lying with the obligation of keeping a secret? The doctrine of mental restriction was a particularly unhappy way to do so.[38]

11

Pride: The Case of the Insulted Gentleman

One day Pascal has his fictional good Jesuit Father say, "According to the common consensus of all casuists, it is morally licit to kill someone who intends to slap or hit you, when this cannot be avoided in any other way." This "damnable doctrine" so horrified Pascal that he could hardly contain himself. In his eyes no case can be made for such a teaching: he exclaims to his unflustered mentor, "The law of God forbids us to kill!" As a devout Christian, he recalls the Lord's more stringent command, "if anyone strike you on the right cheek, turn to him also the other" (Mt 5:39). One need not be a believer, much less devout, to find the good Father's doctrine reprehensible, even outrageous. How, then, could the casuists ever have taught it? How could it ever have commanded "the common consensus of casuists"?[1]

The casus of "killing for a slap" appeared in the history of casuistry for a brief moment, was entertained as a probable opinion, and quickly vanished. Like the teaching on equivocation, its fleeting popularity illustrates the dynamic development of casuistry as well as the pitfalls into which it can fall. It illustrates, in particular, the way in which the doctrine of probabilism affected the formulation of a moral opinion. This particular moral opinion, grotesque as it appears in retrospect, is somewhat more comprehensible and its rise and downfall are more explicable if it is viewed within the whole history of Christian teaching about the taking of life in self-defense.

Killing for a slap achieved a transient status as a probable opinion simply because a number of reputable casuists thought the defense of one's honor was a reasonable extension of the defense of one's property. But it was an opinion located at the farthest extreme of the various cases of justifiable killing considered in the casuistical literature. Its very remoteness from the primary analogue of killing in self-defense assured that its "probability" would be exposed to severe criticism. Such criticism was quick to come and, given the changing cultural values of the time, soon demolished the offensive teaching. But this did not happen until after casuistry's most severe critic had his chance to flaunt it as another instance of the outrageous moral affrontery of his Jesuit antagonists.

The Christian Church inherited from the Hebrew scriptures a strong prohibition against the willful taking of human life. The command of the Decalogue was absolute: "You shall not kill" (Ex 20:13). Other texts reinforced this prohibition. Yet at the same time, there were injunctions to kill the evildoer, the blasphemer, the murderer, the adulterer; "do not allow evildoers to live" (Ex 22:13). But in all these cases, God, who is the Lord of life, decrees the killing. Throughout ancient Judaism the rabbis were all but uncompromising in their view of the sanctity of life. Jesus reinforced this position, and makes it even more stringent:

> You have heard it was said to the men of old, 'you shall not kill.' . . . I say to you that everyone who is angry with his brother shall be liable to the judgment. . . . You have heard it said, 'an eye for an eye, a tooth for a tooth.' I say to you, do not resist one who is evil. If anyone strikes you on the right cheek, turn to him the other also. (Mt 5:21, 5:38)

This teaching was illustrated when Jesus reprimanded Peter for attempting to defend him: "Put your sword back in its scabbard, for all who take the sword will perish by the sword" (Mt 26:52). Recalling this incident Peter later wrote, "When he was reviled, he did not revile in turn, but trusted to Him who judges justly" (1 Pt 2:23).

The tenor of Jesus' words was grasped by the primitive Church. At the Council of Jerusalem (A.D. 44), a debate over the conditions for the conversion of the Gentiles was resolved by dispensing converts from the observance of Jewish ritual law but requiring them "to refrain from idolatry, unchastity and . . . from blood" (Acts

15:20). The Early Fathers interpreted these words as referring to three major sins and took the word "blood" as meaning the shedding of blood. It seems clear that for the first three centuries, a stringent doctrine prevailed: even shedding blood in self-defense was repudiated. Justin Martyr (c. 200) cited the text from Matthew 5 and concluded, "the Christian must not resist attack"; while the great apologist, Origen, wrote, "The Christian lawgiver . . . did not deem it becoming to allow the killing of any man whatever."[2]

In his discussion of the cases of moral perplexity posed by Cicero, St. Ambrose affirmed this doctrine: "Some ask whether a wise man ought to take a plank from an ignorant sailor when both are shipwrecked. Although it seems better for the common good that the wise man rather than the ignorant one survive, a Christian ought not save his life by the death of another." Ambrose then commented on the case of self-defense: "Similarly, when a Christian meets an armed robber, he cannot return his blows, lest in defending his life, he should stain his love toward his neighbor. The Gospel is plain: put up thy sword."[3]

Ambrose's convert, Augustine, was somewhat less absolute. He wrote to a Christian lawyer who sought his counsel,

> with regard to killing men so as not to be killed by them, this view does not please me unless perhaps it be a soldier or a public official who is permitted to kill in the course of his duties. . . . We are not to resist evil lest we take pleasure in vengeance.[4]

The word "unless" introduced several exceptions into the previously rigorous prohibition of killing. This slackening of the earlier Christian rigor occurs at a time when the Church and the Empire had begun to find common interests. Since the Edict of Milan in A.D. 313, Christians had been more involved in the affairs of civil society; the earlier prohibition against military service by Christians had been relaxed; Christian judges and prefects were appointed; and on occasion, they were required to try criminals under laws of capital punishment. In Augustine's qualification we find a hint that he would tolerate killing carried out by those who have public responsibilities; and this became the accepted doctrine throughout the Middle Ages.

Augustine's words contain another idea that will have great influence on future teaching. He repudiated killing in self-defense because the killer might be tempted to take pleasure in vengeance.

Augustine also made other distinctions that would serve well the later casuists:

> When one man is killed by another, it makes a great difference whether it happens through a desire of injuring him or a desire of carrying off something of his or in obeying an order, as a judge, or through self-defense or the rescue of another, as a thief killed by a traveller or an enemy by a soldier.[5]

Augustine has now made room for legitimate self-defense, although the suspicion of bad motive clouded even this act. However, this move—from actual physical killing to the motives behind the killing—was itself a significant shift in moral focus. In addition, the various reasons that could legitimate taking a life provided the material for a casuistry about justified killing.

Augustine shored up the uncertainty of his position, which departed notably from the tradition, by appealing to Christian clemency and the moderation of Christian forbearance. The ruler had a right to impose the death penalty, but he should not forget that a sinner's repentance is a great good. So if possible, punishments, such as whipping, which allowed the criminal to live and repent, were preferable to execution. Augustine thus left to the later Church an ambivalent tradition. Killing another human being was morally wrong and forbidden by God's law, yet those who administered the law of the state might take life, even though for reasons of clemency they should seek the repentance of the sinner rather than his death. Self-defense by individuals who were not public officials was tolerated but is tainted with guilt. Augustine also incorporated his reluctant acceptance of self-defense into the concept of "just war" which he fathered.[6]

Both Ambrose and Augustine probably knew by heart the classic justification of self-defense in Cicero's speech for Milo:

> If ever there is a time when one might rightly kill another, certainly that time, not only just but necessary, is when aggression is met by force. . . . This is reasonable for the wise, necessary for the barbarians and a custom for all people. Nature itself has prescribed it even to animals so that they might by any means repel from themselves any attack upon body, head or life.[7]

Cicero's words echoed a famous text of Roman law. The jurisprudent Paulus had framed the classical phrases: "One who would otherwise be killed will be held harmless for harm he causes . . . for a

forceful defense against force is permitted by all law and all right."
The forceful defense against forceful aggression against one's body, a
standing principle of Roman law, begins now to spread to Christian
teaching and to erode the hitherto absolute prohibition against
killing of all kinds.

The sin of murder was severely sanctioned in the Penitential
Books of all eras. This sin brought upon its perpetrator the terrible
punishment of exile for many years, sometimes for life. In some lists
of penances exclusion from sacramental communion and intercourse
with Christians must last until the deathbed. At the same time,
some exceptions and qualifications were noted. The Synod of the
Grove of Victory decreed a canon that has the ring of the Old
Testament: "He who slays his brother, not with malice aforethought
but from sudden anger, shall do penance for three years."[8]
The Penitentials frequently mentioned such mitigating features as
passion and such aggravating features as premeditation. Moreover,
the canons frequently distinguished between the sin of murder committed by a layman and by a cleric. Clerics were not excused by mitigating circumstances, and suffered heavier penances. The *Corrector
of Burchard*, a late Penitential, set out a full canon on murder:

> Hast thou committed murder willfully, without necessity, not in war-
> fare, but because of a desire to steal? . . . . If by accident, not inten-
> tionally, and if thou didst not in thine anger intend to strike but did so
> incidentally, thou must do penance for an ordinary homicide inten-
> tionally committed . . . if by design and in anger a more severe
> penance is given.[9]

This complex and confused canon marks off willfulness and intention as necessary elements of true murder; it makes exceptions for
"necessity" and warfare; it allows accident as mitigation; and it presents anger either as a mitigation or an aggravation. Thus in adjudi-
cating the seriousness of the sin of taking another's life, the confessor
is allowed to employ many distinctions.

Church law contained several canons of importance, which
placed the doctrine of legitimate killing, and killing in self-defense,
squarely within Christian morality. The *Decretum*, which collected
only canons prior to the twelfth century, stayed close to the rigorist
tradition of the Early Church: killing was legitimate only when

done according to the just judgments of the law and by public authorities. Individuals were conceded no right to kill in self-defense; indeed, this was specifically forbidden in the case of clerics, who were visited with serious penalties for doing so. In the century following the *Decretum*, however, several canons allowed a right of self-defense. The decretal "Significasti" of Pope Gregory IX (1227–1241) incorporated a phrase from Roman law permitting the use of "force to repel force, always requiring due moderation in the defense." The decretal of Pope Clement V, "Si furiosus," issued in 1317, removed the censure of irregularity (i.e., a prohibition on exercising ministerial duties) from clerics who killed in self-defense. The decretal "Interfecisti" permitted killing in defense of "one's self and one's own" (*te tuaque liberando*) but imposed severe penalties for unjust killing; though it suggested that a penalty should be imposed, even if there is no fault, "just to be sure" in the ambiguity of the situation. So, by the thirteenth century, most of the elements of the Roman Law of self-defense had been incorporated into Christian morality.[10]

These Roman Law distinctions created a tension with the strong repudiation of self-defense found in the Gospels, and that tension intrigued the theologians. During the late twelfth and early thirteenth century they compare, contrast, and distinguish the words of the Gospel, of the civil law, and of the canon law. Typically Aquinas drew these considerations into a comprehensive doctrine. In the initial articles of Aquinas' *quaestio* on killing, he proposed the traditional doctrine that killing was permitted only to public authorities acting within the law. Clerics may not be the agents of killing; and only evil persons, not the innocent, could be put to death. In the seventh article he asked, "is it legitimate to kill in self-defense?" His response immediately broached a distinction that was later to become celebrated in casuistry: the doctrine of the "double effect." This was its first appearance in moral literature.

A single act, says Aquinas, may have two effects, one of them intentional and the other going beyond intention. The moral quality of the act depends on the nature of the effect that was intended. Thus the two "effects" of an act of killing in self-defense are the saving of one's own life and the death of the attacker. Self-defense is legitimate because the defender seeks to save his own life. This is in accord with natural law, in that each thing seeks to preserve itself in being. Yet even with proper intention, an act is vitiated if it is not proportioned to the intended end. Thus the use of more force than necessary to save one's life renders self-defense immoral. Also, there is no obligation to refrain from self-defense because a person is under greater obligation to care for his own good than for the good of another. Aquinas concludes that self-defense is legitimate. He interprets Augustine's position against killing in self-defense as excluding only the direct intention to kill, and construes the words of St. Paul, "Beloved, never avenge yourselves" (Ro 12:19), as referring only to self-defense inspired by vengeance.[11]

As was his custom, Aquinas prefaced his analytic argument with a quotation that intimated the direction in which his analysis would move. He prefaced article seven with a text from Exodus 22:2: "If a thief is found breaking in and is struck so that he dies, there shall be no murder; if the sun has risen on him, there will be murder." Aquinas used this text as the premise for an *a fortiori* argument: "but it is more justifiable to defend one's life than one's property." This text, and similar ones had had an honored place in legal history. The rabbinic interpretation of Exodus allowed the householder to kill a nighttime intruder because in the darkness of night there was doubt about the intruder's intentions and about his possible reaction to being opposed. Killing was here justified not because it was a defense of one's goods but because it could be considered, under the circumstances, as equivalent to defense of one's life. Roman law also allowed the killing of a thief in the night but not a daytime thief. Again, the justification was the threat to the householder's life, as well as the difficulty of flight or pursuit. The canon "Si perfodiens" also permitted the killing of a nighttime burglar, based on a comment of St. Augustine on the Exodus text, that it cannot be known whether the intruder comes to kill or to steal. In this classical legal interpretation killing the burglar was viewed not so much as defense of property as a defense of life; yet St. Thomas seems to take the text as justifying the defense of one's property by killing.[12]

After Aquinas, most of the elements were in place for a full-scale casuistry of self-defense. Killing another human being was evil. It could be justified in the name of public order and the common good. Killing in self-defense or in defense of one's own was also justifiable under certain conditions: the killing must be an unavoidable necessity, without malice or vengeance, and it must be done with "due moderation"—that is, the result of only such force as is necessary to repel the attack. Subsequent debates among the theologians focused on more exact specification of each of these points. During the next two centuries discussions of two of these points—"What constitutes unavoidable necessity?" and "What is due moderation?"—led to the cause célèbre, killing for a slap.

In discussing "unavoidable necessity," Raymond of Pennafort added a consideration that influences the subsequent debate. He suggested that "avoidability" may refer not only to the immediate danger from which the person attacked could escape if he wished and tried, but also to the case in which a person, by his own fault, turns an avoidable situation into an unavoidable one. He gives the example of a general who, seeing an army coming to besiege his camp, closes himself up inside even though he has no obligation to defend it. Raymond infers that it was the general's moral duty to flee rather than defend by killing the assailants. Thus avoidability was more a moral than a physical feature of the case.[13]

In the fourteenth century matters of social status entered the debate. The question was raised whether "less noble persons" had the right to defend themselves against their "betters." The question suited the times for, as one author writes,

> The fourteenth and fifteenth centuries were times of great civil and regional strife in Western Europe. Private vendetta, casual violence over almost any disagreement, the warfare of petty and powerful princes, contributed to an atmosphere of constantly threatening violence. Within this situation, a particularly widespread circumstance was the discrimination between "gentlemen" and the rest of the people in bearing arms; gentlemen could bear them; others could not.[14]

Eminent moralists such as Gerson and Antoninus considered social status irrelevant to self-defense. The distinguished canonist, Panormitanus, however, took up the question in terms of the avoidability of flight. He reviewed the opinions of the authors: some held there was no shame if an equal fled from an equal or a subordinate from a superior; others held that there was always shame in flight. Panormitanus concluded that only an inferior had the obligation to flee in order to avoid killing; a superior could stand his ground. Killing the aggressive inferior was unavoidable. *Summa Sylvestrina* accepted this position and extended it: "No one is bound to flee from an attacker if flight would bring shame."[15] This puts us at the threshold of the case that so outraged Pascal.

Azor, the premier casuist of the age, posed the question about the defense of honor in the terms he found in *Sylvestrina*: "Is one obliged to flee from an attacker if flight would be shameful?" He reviewed two current opinions. The first was that of Malderus, who argued that one is obliged to flee and even take shameful flight because "by right and by order of charity, the life of the neighbor must be preferred to one's own honor . . . it is inhumane and barbarous and unsuited for Christians not to do so." Azor cited Navarrus, Soto, and Sylvestrina to the contrary. These authors responded to Malderus's point by making a distinction: one is indeed obliged by charity to prefer the life of the neighbor to one's honor, but not when the choice is coerced by some evil act of the neighbor. This latter opinion was, in Azor's judgment, the more probable one. Still, he noted that all authors who held it had qualified it by pointing out that standing and fighting was not permitted to any for whom flight would not be shameful. Thus the religious, who were vowed to humility and the perfection of the Gospel, were always obliged to flee.[16]

Azor then became more specific: "Might one morally kill another who insults one by beating or slapping him?" Again, there were two significant opinions. Major had said that it was not licit because the life of one's neighbor must be held more precious than one's honor. Soto and Navarrus said that it was licit; otherwise the honor of innocent persons everywhere could be defamed by evil men with impunity. This latter opinion seemed probable to Azor. Obviously, he commented, there must be no alternative means of redressing the insult.

Several years later the Jesuit Lessius took up the argument. He expressed his agreement with Azor and then added a new point: the insult steals honor, which is more valuable than money. If defense of one's money was permitted, so was defense of one's honor. So an honorable man who has been dishonored may immediately strike back, or may follow his insulter and inflict those beatings and wounds necessary to redress honor. Some might deny, Lessius remarked, that there was an analogy between the defense of property and the defense of honor. The stolen goods still existed, these critics object, and might be recaptured by pursuit, whereas honor is gone for good. Lessius defended the analogy: honor, like goods, can be recovered, for honor consisted in signs of excellence and the estimation of men. Finally, as Azor had said, if pursuit and punishment for insults were not permitted, license would be given to wicked persons to pour all sorts of contumely on anyone and then run away. Of course, if the insulter asked pardon, the insulted must grant it, as this would constitute a restoration of honor.

All of these reasons, considered Lessius, seem to make this a "speculatively probable opinion." All the same, it should not be permitted in practice because of the "danger of hatred, vengeance and excess . . . the danger of altercation and pitched battles." The moral argument might, in Lessius' eyes, be reasonable, but it was so only in theory; in practice confessors should not tolerate it because of the consequences. Pascal was outraged by this distinction, which he condemned as merely pragmatic, not moral.

Lessius qualified his position on killing in self-defense for defense of honor by noting that although it is permissible to kill for these reasons, it is a moral counsel of perfection to allow oneself to be killed rather than to kill. This was more in conformity with the example of Christ and the martyrs. Charity, though it does not oblige, favors the salvation of the neighbor. For these reasons, said the Jesuit, the counsel should be taken seriously by Christians, particularly by clerics and religious. If, however, one is in mortal sin, one must defend oneself rather than die in that state: one is obliged to prefer one's own eternal salvation to that of the neighbor.[17]

Escobar, Pascal's whipping boy, formulated the issue succinctly. He cited Lessius as favoring the opinion that a nobleman may kill someone who approaches to slap or strike him. The Jesuit Laymann had pointed out that for a soldier or courtier, honor was a precious asset, the coin of his livelihood and advancement. Escobar then added to his predecessors' arguments the comment, "in some regions, it is particularly dishonorable to allow slaps or beatings to go unrequited. The opinion allowing requital applies only to gentlemen, since it is hardly shameful for a common person to be slapped or beaten." Escobar also favored the opinion of those authors who allowed a gentleman to pursue and kill an insulter; though this opinion can be considered "probable and safe" only by abstracting from the public disadvantages. Defense was permissible so long as injury remained.[18]

Another Jesuit, Cardinal De Lugo, dealt with the problem much more judiciously than did his predecessors. The gentleman who defended his honor by killing rather than by taking shameful flight, he opined, was justified only to the extent that the killing was a necessary defense of life. Like Pascal, De Lugo was critical of Lessius' note that permissible pursuit of the insulter was an opinion "speculatively probable, but not to be admitted in practice." His criticism, however, was more to the point than Pascal's outraged cry, "This is a political, not a religious prohibition."[19] If such public inconveniences did really follow from allowing pursuit, then the doctrine could not even be speculatively probable. Moral probability, declared the cardinal, includes any consideration that in the actual circumstances would render the act illicit. So if evil results would follow from permitting pursuit, pursuit itself would be evil, even speculatively considered. De Lugo concluded that the pursuit and killing of the insulter "smacks more of worldly manners than of Christian morals." Rather than defending one's honor, this was "to seek another vain honor, the approbation of worldly persons." The Austrian Jesuit Adam Tanner was said to have commented that this opinion was probable "only in Spain"![20]

In 1654 the theology faculty of Louvain, which was inclined toward Jansenism, condemned a number of propositions found in the works of casuists. Among them was the proposition we have been discussing, as framed in the words of the non-Jesuit casuist Martin Becanus: "It is permitted for a gentleman to kill an aggressor who attempts to calumniate him, if the shame cannot otherwise be avoided; similarly, he may kill one who slaps or beats him, then flees." In 1679 Pope Innocent XI approved the Louvain document as a censure of laxist morality.[21] This papal condemnation might have been expected to be the last word in the history of this bizarre doctrine, but it was not quite. In 1763 the magisterial casuist Alphonsus Ligouri commented, "this opinion is most rarely to be employed in practice, for as Silvius rightly says, 'although honor is more valuable than riches, we judge that there is never or hardly ever a case in which it would be permitted to kill an aggressor for honor's sake alone.'" These words reflected the casuists' Gilbertian unwillingness to say "never" without adding a cautionary "well, hardly ever."[22]

In 1772 the Dominican Concina, a fierce opponent of the probabilists, reviewed the arguments. He took a firmer stand than Ligouri, describing the doctrine as "bloody." He argued against it by recalling the example of Christ and by condemning the "honor" at stake as "vain, fleeting, fictitious, to be despised by every Christian." He also argued that responding to an insult by killing the insulter cannot be "within the bounds of a blameless defense," which was one of the standard conditions for self-defense. The "blameless defense" was one that could be avoided by flight. It was irrelevant that flight might be shameful, given that the shame arose only from worldly opinion: shame of this sort, exclaimed Concina, "is the glory of Christians." He concluded,

> if one can avoid the death of an aggressor by flight, whether the aggression is by words of defamation or slaps and thrashings, you are bound to flee, be you commoner or gentleman, knight or monk: for there is one Law of the Gospel and one spirit of Christianity for all. The mincing distinctions of probabilists in this matter are vain![23]

The offensive doctrine, then, had a short life. Its fleeting vitality sprung from the fact that a number of reputable casuists had considered the argument as a reasonable extension of the doctrine of defense of life and property. Insofar as honor was a "property"—and this seemed plausible for those who "lived by honor" in an era when personal honor was culturally valued—the extension seemed to make some sense. But it was troublesome even then, and although it made sense, it had some obviously undesirable consequences, which forced the level-headed casuist Lessius to draw his peculiar distinction between "the speculative probable but practically dangerous."

Like a modern utilitarian, De Lugo quickly demolished the doctrine by showing that the consequences of the act could not be divorced from the assessment of the act itself. Thus from its early appearance as a "probable" doctrine, around the time of Navarrus to De Lugo's criticism, published some four years after the *Provincial Letters*, the doctrine won a temporary toehold of qualified respectability, from which it was soon to be dislodged, but not before it had given the scandal that Pascal publicized.

PART V

The Crisis

12

Casuistry Confounded: Pascal's Critique

Blaise Pascal has been mentioned frequently in these pages. No history of casuistry can ignore him. He was born in 1623; and, by the mid-1650s he had already made the pivotal contributions to mathematics and physics that earned him his reputation as a scientific genius. But he was yet to write the *Pensées* that would win him fame as a religious genius. It was in 1656 that he took up his pen to write the tracts that would mark him also as a genius of satire, *Les Lettres Provinciales*. He wrote these tracts not so much on his own account (indeed, the *Lettres* were published anonymously) but as the spokesman of the Jansenist party.[1]

The Jansenists were a small group of pious French Catholics made up of priests, nuns, and laypersons who espoused the theological doctrines of a certain Bishop Cornelius Jansen. Jansenism, with its abstruse and gloomy theology, might have been confined, like probabilism, to an academic debate. The Jansenists themselves, with their rigorous piety, might have lived, as they avowed they wished to, a cloistered life of prayer. Yet both the personalities of the leading Jansenists and the political implications of Jansenism impelled them out of convent and library into a violent public controversy, which troubled church and state in France from the mid-1640s until the early years of the next century. In bitter exchanges that ranged from subtle theology to vituperation and, finally provoked royal decrees and Papal Bulls, reputations were ruined and institutions destroyed. Among the victims of the controversy was casuistry.[2]

The beginnings of the controversy were innocent, even laudable. After the wrenching years of the Religious Wars and harsh religious disputes within the Church, many Frenchmen and women of spiritual quality and social prestige were moved by a genuine desire to reform religious life in France. Known as the *parti devot*, this group included clerics, influential nobility, and courtiers who were committed to purifying and strengthening the Catholic faith in its doctrine and to promoting charitable works. Jean Duvergier de Hauranne (1581–1643), called Abbé de Saint-Cyran, played a particularly important role in these circles. Brilliant and pious to the point of austerity, yet ambitious and elitist, he won a reputation as an extraordinary director of souls. Around him gathered a band of disciples who became known as Jansenists, after Cornelius Jansen (1585-1638), a close friend of Saint-Cyran during their student days at the University of Louvain, who subsequently became professor of theology at Louvain and then Bishop of Ypres.

Jansen had written a massive theological treatise, *Augustinus*, that was published in 1640, two years after his death. This treatise proposed a doctrine of divine grace based, Jansen claimed, on the teaching of St. Augustine: This doctrine contradicted some of the crucial points in the theology of grace that had been espoused by the Jesuits—the version usually called Molinism after their principal theological spokesman, Luis Molina. Certain of the central theses of Jansen's treatise, particularly his discussion of original sin, human freedom, and predestination, looked to the Jesuits suspiciously like the theology of John Calvin. Rancorous and bloody political struggles between Catholics and Calvinists had racked France for almost a century. Catholic victory had at last been achieved in 1629. The apparent resurgence of anything resembling Calvinist doctrine, particularly from within the Catholic Church, was not welcomed by Cardinal Richelieu or by King Louis XIV. Yet now the Abbé Saint-Cyran espoused his departed friend's suspiciously Calvinist theology as a guide in his spiritual direction of his followers.

Among Saint-Cyran's disciples were the Abbess of the Convent of Port-Royal, Mère Angélique Arnauld (1591–1661), and her brother, Antoine (1612–1694), a lawyer-turned-theologian, who became Saint-Cyran's successor as leader of the Jansenist party. Their father was a leading lawyer who, in 1594, had represented the Sorbonne in its lawsuit to exclude the Jesuits from participation in the education activity of the University of Paris. Six women of the Arnauld family entered the Cistercian Convent of Port-Royal as nuns, and that Convent, in the fields outside Paris, became the spiritual home of Jansenism. Thus by coincidence, the theological antagonism between Jesuits and Jansenists was fueled by both disagreement about the interpretation of the doctrine of grace and by the animosity of a prominent family against the Jesuits. Initially this antagonism prompted a severe criticism of the Jesuit casuists; but in the long run it led to the defeat of the Jansenists and the effective disappearance of Jansenism.[3]

Blaise Pascal was attracted to the spiritual atmosphere of the Convent of Port-Royal, where his sister Jacqueline had become a nun. By the mid-1650s the fortunes of the Jansenists had changed: where before they had met with general approbation at the Royal Court, in the universities and among the clergy (except, of course, the Jesuits) they were now losing favor in many quarters. At this point the Theological Faculty of the Sorbonne threatened to censure Antoine Arnauld, now the theological spokesman of the Jansenists. He summoned to his side the brilliant but reticent Pierre Nicole and the new convert, Blaise Pascal, who had, until a few months before, admired the "Gentlemen of Port-Royal" from a distance. Nicole and Arnauld persuaded Pascal to employ his talents in writing a defense of the Jansenist positions that would have wider public appeal than the turgid, abstruse theological writings that had hitherto dominated the debate. Pascal consented. On 23 January, 1656 the first of his polemical tracts appeared: *Letters Written to a Provincial Gentleman by One of His Friends on the Subject of the Present Debates in the Sorbonne.* Over the next fourteen months eighteen letters appeared, and they were met with instant and avid public response. Pascal's authorship of the anonymous tracts was not suspected for several years after the last letter was published, and even then the attribution was contested.

Like some others of the *parti devot*, Pascal was offended by what they considered the Jesuits' lax treatment of penitents. Even the most notorious public sinners, it seemed, were readily absolved by Jesuit confessors. King Louis XIV, it was said, would abjure his mistress on Holy Thursday, confess to his Jesuit confessor on Good Friday, take Communion on Easter Sunday, and bring back his mistress on Easter Monday. Modern readers who tend to see such acts as confession and Communion as matters of private religious devotion may miss the full significance of this issue. In the mid-seventeenth century those acts were public signs of one's adherence to the Catholic faith and so matters of great importance in a Europe divided politically into Protestant and Catholic nations.

Particularly in France, where the Protestants were still tolerated under the terms of the Edict of Nantes (1598, amended 1629), the distinction remained crucial, since this toleration was hardly unlimited: non-Catholics were still subject to definite civil, religious, and economic liabilities. In some other countries, such as England, civil law required regular attendance at religious service, and even the taking of Communion, in the Established Church. Everywhere certain legal acts, such as marriage and the validity of inheritance, required "good standing" in the Church. Thus for Catholics, being admitted to Communion—which presupposed absolution in confession—was not merely an act of private devotion; it was a public expression of one's civil state and political sympathies. Being recognized as a "good" Catholic was thus important for social and political as well as religious reasons. In these circumstances an argument over the moral conditions for absolution was more than a theological quibble.[4]

Any charge of laxity, of course, assumes certain standards of moral probity. Those standards may be either personal ones or the standards realistically expected in the society concerned. Pascal and his Jesuit antagonists both had very high personal standards; but, unlike Pascal, the Jesuits were appointed to teach, preach, and act as confessors to people whose moral lives were much less admirable. St. Vincent de Paul, an outside observer of the Jansenist-Jesuit controversy who was himself a most virtuous man, "was no doubt drawing his own intimate experience of the popular mind when he said that, if the clergy applied Jansenist discipline, people would simply refuse to come to confession or communion at all."[5]

Pascal was not a trained theologian so much as a literary genius with a lucid, urbane style. Arnauld and Nicole supplied him with ample material, and this he turned into a powerful polemic that even Voltaire was to praise as satire at its best. His tracts were not academic theology, but they represent skilled theological amateurism brilliantly expressed. In the best style of debating rhetoric his arguments incessantly concentrated on the weakest points of the adversary. The first three letters, dated 23 and 29 January and 2 February, 1656, argued one of the central theses of the Jansenist position on grace: the question of "sufficient" and "efficacious" grace, for which Arnauld was in danger of censure. After Arnauld was ac- tually censured on 15 February, Pascal launched a sustained attack on the Jesuits who had been partially responsible for his colleague's humiliation. Now the prime target was not the complex Molinist doctrine of grace but a far more diverting topic: the moral teaching of the Jesuit casuists. The next eleven letters pilloried casuistry, exposing it in turn to witty sarcasm, shrewd rhetoric, and sincere outrage.

The issue of laxist moral teaching had been on the periphery of the Jansenist-Jesuit debate for some years. A decade earlier, during bitter disputes between the Jesuits and the Sorbonne, an anonymous booklet had appeared entitled *The Moral Theology of the Jesuits Faithfully Extracted from Their Books*. This booklet collected more than one hundred citations that the authors branded as scandalous and offensive to Christian morals, many of which had already been cen- sured either by the Sorbonne, or by Roman authorities. The anony- mous authors of this booklet were François Hallier, Professor of the Sorbonne, and the young Antoine Arnauld, but it had little impact at the time. Arnauld and Nicole now placed the volume into the hands of Pascal, who "brought to life its abstract formulas and delivered the casuists to the immortality of ridicule."[6]

Pascal also had at hand a second source book of casuistical teach- ings, *The Book of Moral Theology Woven out of Twenty-Four Doctors of the Society of Jesus*, which gave Pascal access to the opinions of many of the principal Jesuit casuists. This volume was the Latin version of a Spanish handbook for confessors written some years earlier by Father Antonio Escobar, a Jesuit from Valladolid who was active in pastoral ministry. He presented the teachings of the "Twenty-Four Jesuit Doctors" on a variety of moral problems in extremely abbreviated form, without providing any theoretical basis or any extended argumenta- tion. A modern historian writes, "As an anthologist of Jesuit opinions, Escobar could not be bettered, and his compendium conveniently saved Pascal (as well as Arnauld and Nicole who kept him supplied with texts) from having to check a multiplicity of references."[7]

Four years before Pascal began to write, however, Escobar had started work on a more copious treatise, *Accepted and Problematic Opinions in Moral Theology (Universae Theologiae Moralis Receptiores Absque Lite Sententiae Nec Non Problematicae Disquisitiones*, Lyons, 1652–1663); and by 1656 the first two volumes of this six-volume work had appeared. Pascal referred to its existence in Letter XII, but only to remark, "on the first of these volumes I may one day have something to say to you."[8] The *Universae Theologiae Moralis* provides quite a different picture of Escobar than does Pascal's caricature: now the author sets out the theoretical basis for the opinions he proposes, states with some precision the points at which the cited casuists disagree, and attempts to reach a reasoned resolution of these "problematic cases." Though not the most accomplished of moral theologians, Escobar was more judicious than Pascal allowed him to appear. Nevertheless this pious Spanish Jesuit is the figure of whom it has been said, "he succumbed under the terrible blows of his adversary . . . he lacked nothing but talent in the face of genius."[9]

Pascal used an inspired rhetorical device. He put the offending opinions of the Jesuit casuists in the mouth of one of their own enthusiastic adherents, a fictitious "good Jesuit Father," who, with (almost) unfailing geniality, produces for Pascal from the texts of the casuists case after outrageous case "in the spirit of a collector of rare and choice specimens"[10] The good Father cites Escobar, Bauny, and others with uncritical, almost religious awe. The rhetorical effect is devastating; this spokesman for casuistry, "a marionette on whom Pascal has with puckish delight fixed an ass's head," is not vicious, just hopelessly naive.[11] In his naiveté he is entranced by the inexhaustible ingenuity of his casuist doctors. So, Pascal implied, casuistry could be only for the simple-minded. Only after Letter XI, written in the wake of the first of the Jesuits' replies, does the benign but simple good Father disappear, and the delightful satire gives way to harsher controversy.

Armed with weapons plundered from the enemy, Pascal wades into the conflict. He justifies the shift of focus from the complexities of the theology of grace to the more intriguing moral questions by asserting of the Jesuits that "in their moral laxism you will easily recognize the cause of their doctrine regarding grace."[12] He explains the Jesuits' penchant for laxism, not as the result of their personal lives, which were notably austere, but as being an unhappy effect of a goal they prided themselves on: "to be all things to all men."

> They believe it is useful and virtually essential for the good of religion that they should enjoy universal credit and govern the conscience of all. . . . this is why they find it necessary, having to deal with people from every walk of life and such different nationalities, to have casuists to match such great variety. . . . They keep their friends and

defend themselves against all their enemies. For if they are criticized for extreme laxity, they at once publicly produce their austere directors . . . whereas the multitude of lax casuists is available for those who want laxism.[13]

No one goes away dissatisfied . . . Lessius will speak like a pagan on homicide and a christian on almsgiving; Vasquez like a pagan on almsgiving and a christian on homicide.[14]

Pascal rightly recognizes the doctrine of "probable" opinions (or "probabilism") as the root cause of this multiplicity of opinions. In Letters V and VI he presents the common understanding of that doctrine in honest but shallow terms, easily open to satire. He does not go deeply into the merits and demerits of probabilism. Rather than analyzing the theoretical arguments, he merely catalogues the decisions that those casuists who had adopted probabilism rendered in particular cases. As these decisions are cited one after the other by the enthusiastic good Father, Pascal's disbelief and outrage manifestly increase. They are indeed outrageous and unbelievable. Calumniators may be murdered if there is no other way to stop their calumny; a judge may accept a bribe in an inconclusive case; a monk may doff his religious garb in order to visit a brothel incognito; a nobleman may kill someone who offends his honor by merely slapping him; a vengeful man who burns down the wrong barn is not bound to make restitution; dueling is of course forbidden, but one who is challenged may simply stroll about the dueling field until he finds himself under attack; and so the appalling catalogue goes on. This, concludes Pascal, is the kind of "morality" to which probabilistic casuistry inevitably leads. How can such a doctrine be true? It is to be hoped, he prays, "that God will make those whom you (casuists) have deceived realize that your false rules will not protect them from his wrath."[15]

Pascal's caricature of casuistry has survived the centuries. His casuists take moral prohibitions that are at first sight unqualified and find them full of exceptions and excuses. They reconcile moral prohibitions that are apparently incompatible. They keep adding definitions and distinctions until the seriousness and force of moral law are thoroughly dissipated. Before their sophistry all moral scruples evaporate "except sinning just for the sake of sinning." Pascal recalls the words of one of the Fathers of the Church, Tertullian:

"Shall I laugh at their folly or deplore their blindness?"[16] He laughs
and has made his readers laugh at the casuists' evasions of serious
morality. But in the end his laughter faded before his indignation:

> Let the casuists consider before God how shameful and pernicious for
> the Church is the moral teaching they spread far and wide; how scan-
> dalous and excessive the moral license they have introduced.[17]

Pascal's attack demolished the reputation of casuistry for all
subsequent generations. In most Western languages, the term "casuistry" came to mean "a quibbling, evasive way of dealing with difficult cases of duty; sophistry."[18] Yet although his critique discredited
casuistry rather than demolishing its actual substance, it did reveal
vividly the most serious theoretical fault of high casuistry. The casuists were professed and dedicated Christians, quite as much as was
Pascal. Both acknowledged the moral dimensions of Christian faith:
the sovereignty of God over the actions of men, the love and mercy
of God drawing humans toward Him and forgiving their sins, the
example of Jesus Christ, and the imperatives of Gospel and Law, as
well as the authority of the Church. All these things both the Jesuit
casuists and their Jansenist critics accepted despite nuances in interpretation.

Still, as the casuists pursued their analysis of the moral life into
more and more detailed cases, they seemed to move further and further away from the clear light of those beliefs. Each series of cases
began with a strong affirmation of Christian ideals; but as the cases
became more complex, the loftiness and rigor of those ideals faded
into the background. Pascal accuses:

> You casuists break the great commandment on which hang all the law
> and the prophets; you attack piety in its heart; you take away the spir-
> it that gives it life; you say that the love of God is not necessary to sal-
> vation.[19]

Many subsequent critics of casuistry, such as the Dominican Concina
(1687–1756), would repeat this criticism.[20] Casuistry, they said, dis-
penses "cheap grace" by showing Christians how to evade the
imperative call of their Lord "to sell all and come follow Him."

This weakness of casuistry was not a result of the intemperate
zeal of Jesuits for winning the hearts and minds of the worldly and
powerful. It has been, and still is, a general theoretical problem for
Christian ethics. Even today Christian moral theologians are trou-

bled by the problems of linking a faith that includes moral imperatives of paradoxical sublimity with the incessant demands of a
rough and mean world. Some resolve the problem by dwelling in a
realm of ideal generalizations and exhortations; others plunge into
the welter of practical life attempting to cut and shape their ideals to
fit its fragmented demands. The casuists of the high era took the latter course. Lacking a clear and precise theoretical way of ar-
ticulating the moral ideals of Christian faith with the moral reasoning open to practical persons, they created a body of opinion that, at
certain crucial points, seemed oblivious of the overarching divine
commands and the pervasive example of Jesus Christ, in which they
sincerely believed.[21]

Pascal found all looseness in morality repugnant. Convinced that
casuistry inevitably bred laxity, he repudiated it root and branch.
This repudiation of laxism is often attributed to his Jansenist sympathies, but the moral teachings of the Jansenists in fact differed hardly
at all from those accepted by all devout Catholics of the time, and
Protestants too. The observance of the commandments of the Old and
New Law, fidelity to religious observance, scrupulous sexual purity,
generous charity to the needy, forgiveness of enemies: all of these ideals were preached by Jansenists and Jesuits, Pietists and Puritans
alike. The writings of François de Sales or Vincent de Paul, like the
sermons of Berulle, Bossuet, and Bourdalue, inculcate these ideals as
the way of Christian morality. The Jansenists differed only in their
insistence upon the exact and unrelaxed observance of these ideals in
practice—an insistence that, as the movement grew older, became an
unbending rigor. Like many other Christians of the time, they were
attracted to the austere self-discipline of the Stoics, in which they saw
an unbaptized version of the Gospel's "hard commands."[22]

Yet the Jansenists proposed no unique moral doctrine. Pascal's
own profession of his personal moral ideals is beautiful but hardly
novel, presenting the ideal common to all devout Christians.

> I love all men as my brothers because all are redeemed. I love poverty
> because Christ loved it. I love goods because they provide the means
> to assist the poor. I keep fidelity with all the world, not doing evil to
> those who do me evil. . . . I try to be just, truthful, sincere and faith-
> ful to all men and have a deep affection for those with whom God has
> linked me closely. Whether alone or in the company of others, I
> believe all my actions are done in the presence of God Who judges
> them and to Whom I consecrate them.[23]

This lovely but unremarkable profession does not differ in any detail from one that the Jesuit casuists might have made. Their books of spiritual direction were filled with similar sentiments; and Father Escobar himself was noted for his personal austerity and his untiring generosity to the poor. What separated the Jansenist Pascal and the Jesuit Escobar was not a difference over moral laxity as such. The root of their difference went much deeper into the ground of theology and philosophy.

Pascal was a vigorous critic of Montaigne but as often happens with antagonists, he wholly shared Montaigne's central belief—that is, his radical skepticism, or Pyrrhonism, with regard to the nature and destiny of man. *"Le pyrrhonisme est le vrai,"* Pascal wrote. "Before Jesus Christ, men knew not whence they were or whether they were of value or of no account: they knew nothing and guessed irrationally and at random."[24] Only the revelation of God in Jesus Christ brings truth and illumination to men's minds and strength to their wills. The splendid passages in the *Pensées* that describe the human paradox end, "Humiliate yourself, impotent reason! Be silent, feeble nature. . . . Listen to God."[25] Caught in the paradox of his nature, man is thoroughly infected by the twin vices of pride and apathy: "these vices are cured by one remedy alone: the simplicity of the Gospel."[26] Behind these sentiments lie the rudiments of Jansenist and Augustinian theology. Man's nature is totally corrupted by sin, his reason blind, and his will to do good impotent. At the same time, man is redeemed by God's grace in Jesus Christ and his reason and will restored by the truth of the Gospel. "All faith consists in Jesus Christ or in Adam; all morality in self love or in grace."[27] "Man without faith knows neither true good nor justice."[28] All human effort at constructing a morality "builds on self love, admirable rules of civil order, morality and justice; but these are, at bottom . . . only a disguise for the evil heart of man."[29]

In Pascal's eyes the casuists were just such "builders on self love." They employed impotent reason, arising from the evil heart of man, to erect "admirable rules." Their fundamental fault was not that they were laxists but that they were rationalists who sought truth outside the "simplicity of Gospel." Pascal never confronted the practical problem of how to deal with the conflicts and complexities of actual moral decisions, beyond exhorting the perplexed "to listen to God." Had he done so, he would no doubt have argued that casuistry, though indispensable, would always manifest "the evil

heart of Man," self-love, and impotent reason. With their rationalism the casuists led men into the same moral skepticism that
Montaigne had espoused, but they did so with the dishonest
promise that in this way there lay salvation and certitude: "We seek
the truth (outside the Gospel) and discover only incertitude."[30]

With his passion for certitude, however, Pascal could never be a
thoroughgoing Pyrrhonist. He was a mathematician and physicist
of genius who prided himself on solving "insoluble" problems. (He
even awarded himself the prize in an international competition that
he himself had sponsored, to solve the problem of constructing the
cycloid.) The mathematician can reason soundly, he believed,
because he knows the first principles of his science and can draw
logical conclusions. But the "first principles" of practical life are
simply unknown to a human reason that is corrupted by sin. Here
reason and sensibility cede to the intuitions of the heart: these intuitions offer an immediate knowledge, inspired by God's grace alone,
that reveals at once the depravity, the dignity, and the destiny of
human life:

> Principles are felt (by the heart), propositions are proved (by the
> mind); both have their certainty but by different means.[31]

In a sense Pascal did introduce the methods of mathematics into
spiritual and moral matters: not the logic of mathematical reasoning
but the rules of probability on which his famous wager about the
existence of God relied.[32] Just as it was rational to bet in favor of the
existence of God, where one had everything to win and comparatively little to lose, so it was with the choices of the moral life. A
modern scholar summarizes Pascal's position: "What is, in any case
of doubt, the absolutely certain choice to procure peace of soul, salvation and the truth that guarantees these? The response to this
question never varies: opt for the unconditioned obligation of the
revealed law of God."[33] This was what the casuists would have
called moral tutiorism. But unlike their form of tutiorism, it was
based neither on the extrinsic authority of the doctors nor on the
intrinsic evidence of the rational arguments: it rested only upon
intuition into the absolute primacy of the "simplicity of the Gospel."

So in Pascal's view, casuistry was the denial of true morality. It
held out no vision of the ideals to which humans should aspire. It
commanded no sacrifice, insisted on no heroic dedication. Not only
did it trivialize the lofty precepts of the Gospel; it did not even hint

at the "natural life of virtue" that had been espoused by Aristotle and Cicero. It was a mere farrago of excuses, loopholes, and evasions. After Pascal's denunciation many other critics of casuistry, even some who acknowledged its theoretical legitimacy, found similar faults in its practice. Yet casuistry had never been intended as a substitute for ethical theory or moral theology. It was not, in itself, a doctrine about what is the best life for man, what virtues characterize the good person, or what ideals humans should strive for. It did not even offer a general or fully elaborated doctrine about what sorts of acts are right, or about how principles and rules are to be justified. It was a simple practical exercise directed at attempting a satisfactory resolution of particular moral problems. In this respect it resembled philosophy or theology less than it did present-day "counseling" or, as it would earlier have been called, "the cure of souls."[34]

True, at all the stages in the history of casuistry certain doctrines about the good, the right, and the ideal were presupposed. Behind the Penitential Books stood the idealism of the Church Fathers whose exhortations appear occasionally among the sentences about stealing, mutilating, and violating. Behind the Confessional Books soared the medieval monastic aspirations for holiness and asceticism the lofty goals of which were sometimes described as being too high for secular persons. Behind the Summas loomed the great achievements of scholastic theology: creating a strong structure of ideas for reflection and discussion of the moral life and giving shape to the manifold opinions about money lending, self-defense, and the swearing of oaths that we examined earlier. The casuists of the high era were familiar with these ideals, aspirations, and refinements; and from time to time they wrote in similar vein. Those who were Jesuits taught the noble spirituality of their founder's *Spiritual Exercises*, which called for deep self-knowledge and generous self-sacrifice. Most of the Anglican casuists wrote pious books of devotion, such as Jeremy Taylor's *Holy Living*. But as casuists, they were not the designers of the moral life; they were its mechanics. They knew how easily in real life ideals can fail us; how often we are caught in perplexing traps of ambiguity or conflicting principles; and they were aware that even good persons have their private weaknesses, social life its public dilemmas.

Casuists dedicated themselves to examining just such situations. In general their work served well the needs of confessors and counselors who were themselves conscientious; though it could mislead those who were not. Its virtue lay in its nearness to experience; its shortcoming was its neglect of the larger realms of moral ideals. As Bishop Kirk has written,

> The casuist, like his critics, is of the earthly, and though he attempts to show men the best way of discharging their obligations in the complications of life, the earth still clings to his decisions. They may help save from the absolutely wrong, but, for sheer frailty of vision, they cannot envision the absolutely right.[35]

The Jesuits at once replied to *The Provincial Letters*. Père Annat, the king's confessor, and Père Nouet, a celebrated preacher of Paris, wrote a refutation that appeared after the publication of the seventh letter. Their rebuttal was competent but uninspired; but it stung Pascal, who "abandoned his exquisite ridicule for a tone of aggrieved personal apology."[36] Another Parisian Jesuit, Père Georges Pirot, published, contrary to his superior's wishes, *Apology for the Casuists Against the Calumnies of the Jansenists* (Paris, 1657). This defense only added fuel to the flame. One by one Pirot tried to justify the extreme cases cited by the author of the *Lettres*. This collection of borderline cases could only give the impression that the author, and his casuist friends, supported the most indulgent and liberal views. As the General of the Jesuits, Father Nickel, wrote to the French Jesuit Provincial, Father Renault, the *Apology* "aroused a tempest of spite and ill will."[37] The ironic result was that the Holy Office of the Inquisition placed the books of both Pascal and Pirot on the Index of Forbidden Books. Several of these other refutations were quite competent and some were quite eloquent; but even the best of them, such as Père Gabriel Daniel's *Conversations Between Cleander and Eudoxius* (1694), did not "prevent Pascal's literary masterpiece from winning an audience, and being taken for the truth by superficial readers."[38]

Was Pascal's critique of casuistry fair? That is a hard question. Fairness is not, of course, the prime virtue demanded of satire. Yet this particular satire had a serious purpose: namely, the intellectual demolition of an entire body of theological and moral doctrine. So its avowed appeal to the broad public did not absolve it from the demands of intellectual honesty—for, as Pascal himself would have agreed, the ends do not justify the means. On several points Pascal's criticism was certainly fair. He did not misquote his adversaries.

Readers of *The Provincial Letters* may often wonder whether the casuists could have really said the things attributed to them; but on
checking the original passages, they will find that, aside from a few
verbal changes to make a rhetorical point, Pascal quoted them accurately. He was also fair in that he selected for his most urbane sarcasm opinions that had already been—or were soon to be—censured
by the academic and ecclesiastical authorities.

In some other important respects, however, Pascal was decidedly
unfair. He relied for his sources on mere compendia, one of which
had been compiled by admitted enemies of the Jesuits; so he did not
present either the methods of casuistry or the particular casuistical
opinions in their proper context. When placed back in the context of
the original discussion, indeed, some of the moral opinions that
Pascal castigated are entirely reasonable. Casuistry, as an exercise in
practical reasoning, involved a tissue of distinctions, qualifications,
and exceptions; and when the resolution of a moral problem was
torn away from this fabric of reasoning, it could easily be made to
look ridiculous. Considered within that fabric, which was intended
as a representation of the complexities of real life, it will appear
much more plausible. Having compared several of Pascal's criticisms of Escobar against Escobar's own discussion, the eminent
Jesuit historian Father Broderick concludes that "most of the cases
pilloried by the elegant sarcasm of Pascal could be justified by reference to Escobar's own plain spoken text."[39]

One example will suffice to make the point. In the eighth letter
Pascal criticizes the casuists for their approach to matters of money,
citing Lessius' opinion, which Escobar had quoted with approval:

> May a declared bankrupt retain as much of his assets as is necessary
> to support his family suitably lest he live less decently (*ne indecore
> vivat*)? With Lessius I maintain he may; and this is so, even if he has
> acquired his assets illegally and by crimes known to all, although in
> that case he may not retain as much as otherwise.[40]

Pascal comments, "By what sort of strange charity do you prefer to
let these assets stay with those who stole them . . . rather than allot
them to his creditors to whom they rightly belong!" and then has the
good Father lamely reply, "You can't please everybody."[41] If we
look up the original passage in Lessius' *De Justitice et Jure*, however,
we discover the full range and subtlety of the casuists' position.
First, Lessius stated, a man who was reduced to extreme need and

was unable to pay his creditors without sacrificing his own and his children's lives was not obliged to pay, provided that he had no other legitimate way to support his family. Second, a person who had sustained a major loss and was in great need might defer payment until his fortunes improved, provided that his creditor was not in the same straits. Third, a person who had lost his fortune through extravagance or vice must repay his debts without delay, even if this resulted in a loss of social standing. But if he had lost his fortune honestly, and not through extravagance or vice, he need not reduce himself to beggary simply in order to repay in full: even someone who had acquired his fortune by fraud might retain enough means to support life. Similarly, he might retain enough to keep himself from sinking in his social scale, by holding back as much as was necessary *ut tenuiter vivat* (i.e., "to live sparingly and modestly according to his station").[42]

These opinions, said Lessius, were held by Sylvester and Navarrus. Furthermore they conformed to the civil law of the Low Countries (Lessius was a Belgian), which conceded to a debtor the right to retain after bankruptcy sufficient of the goods acquired to live without dishonor. To this we might add that many of these distinctions are preserved to this day in most countries in the accepted laws of personal bankruptcy. In a heated retort to his Jesuit critics, Pascal asserted in Letter XII that he had read the full passage in Lessius; but that it was not Lessius' opinion but Escobar's "brief articles independent of what precedes or follows" that must be defended.[43]

In this way Pascal hit home against his immediate foes. By his abbreviated style Escobar had opened himself to the blow, and he was much more cautious in his more extended discussion of the topic in his *Universae Theologiae Moralis*. But Pascal did not score against *casuistry as such*, for effective casuistry depends precisely on "what precedes and follows." Casuistical arguments comprise chains of cases arranged in order of increasing complexity. If a particular opinion is broken out of these original chains, it can be exposed to criticism or ridicule; but its full moral relevance is apparent only when it is replaced and viewed within those chains of cases.

Like many other critics of casuistry, Pascal also missed an essential point about the doctrine of probabilism. The "probable opinions" of the classical casuists—and every opinion cited by Pascal fell under this heading—were not recommended actions, let alone obligatory ones. They were actions that the casuist judged to be morally permissible in certain special circumstances. Bishop Kirk has expressed this distinction clearly:

> Probable opinions . . . are no more than determinations of deviation from the normal which might sometimes be allowable within the general limits of Christian morality. No "probable opinion" was always allowable. There must always be some doubt as to the application of the normal rule in the particular case in question, some valid ground of urgency, necessity or justice to suggest the legitimacy of the divergence.[44]

Pascal deliberately chose to give the impression that an odd collection of out-of-context opinions that were at best occasionally permissible deviations from a quite different norm represented a coherent morality.

Pascal's treatment of the underlying theoretical questions was also unfair to the casuists. He identified these concisely—"Interpreting terms, observing favorable circumstances, and using the double probability of *pro* and *con*"[45]—yet his treatment of these three issues was superficial. It certainly did not reflect the serious theological discussion that we have reviewed here: instead, he aimed at eliciting laughter and incredulity. A modern historian of the Jansenist controversy comments:

> All knowledge of the principles of casuistry and moral theology, which alone could have qualified him to judge the value of the casuist's propositions, was sedulously withheld from Pascal [by Arnauld and Nicole]. He approached the most complex problems of moral direction with no more effective instruments of criticism than a sensitive conscience and a lucid prose style, and continued to discredit the Jesuits, as he had vindicated the innocence of Arnauld for the cultured public at large.[46]

It can, of course, be argued that it was not Pascal's business to provide a fair hearing for the casuistical ideas of interpretation, circumstances, and probabilism. He was not a moral theologian seeking to clarify these issues; he was a zealous and angry apologist for a definite point of view, namely, Jansenism. Still, his dedication to Jansenism introduced a fundamental confusion into his argument, one that he either did not notice or chose to ignore. His critique was not directed against casuistry as such but against one particular corruption of casuistry: extreme laxism. Pascal was deeply affected by the spirit of Jansen and Saint-Cyran, who believed in the theological doctrine of the special election by God of a few chosen souls; while in morals they demanded of the elect an adherence to the highest and most austere ideals—ideals that were, even in the words of a modern scholar sympathetic to Pascal, "counter to the most innocent instincts of humanity."[47] The Jesuit, Father Broderick—who is hardly a scholar sympathetic to Pascal but an honest one—describes the Jansenist view of morality:

> Confounding precepts with counsels, they preached an ideal perfection, a *morale géometrique*, impossible to nine-tenths of mankind, and so circumscribed the pale of Christianity that, in Saint-Beuve's words, to find inclusion in it one must be an *individu paradoxe de l'espèce humaine*."[48]

Whatever its merits, such an extreme view of the moral life held no place for "interpretations, circumstances and probabilities." All the same, the situations under which actual moral problems have to be decided must still be defined in terms of their "circumstances"; similarly, moral imperatives always stand in need of interpretation, and moral conclusions are rarely more than probable. This practical view of the moral life inspired the casuists; it repelled the Jansenists. In their rigorous, scrupulous view of morality, any departure from an absolute ideal was a lapse into laxism; and even the admirably holy nuns of Port-Royal regularly abstained from the Sacrament of the Eucharist because of their supposed "imperfections."

No doubt the viewpoint and methodology of casuistry open it to the possibility of laxism. As a matter of history too, no doubt, a few casuists—ironically, not Jesuits—were thoroughly laxist; and a few of the opinions presented by almost all casuists of the high period may be branded by some as laxist. Yet equally, the ecclesiastical authorities frequently condemned laxism and laxist opinions; and from the late seventeenth century on especially, moral theologians were careful to avoid any excess of this kind. To the extent that Pascal's critique encouraged this more cautious approach it may be praised; but the critique of laxism is a very different thing from a critique of casuistry as such. To the extent that Pascal also encouraged that confusion, his critique must be viewed with skepticism. Perhaps the most judicious appraisal of Pascal's and Nicole's critique is that given by the Dominican theologian Père Deman, who was himself a critic of the Jesuits' reliance on probabilism:

> In condemning a bad casuistry they did not appreciate the necessity of having a good one; in denouncing frivolous probabilism, they made no place for a sound and balanced one.[49]

Finally, Pascal's book was less a criticism of casuistry than a broadside against the Jesuits: "There is nothing quite like these Jesuits," began the fourth letter.[50] Jansenists and Jesuits were theological and political enemies for a decade before he wrote, and the leading Jansenists, notably the Arnauld family, for whom Pascal had such respect, hated the Jesuits with a passion. Casuistry was merely a breach in the Jesuit defenses through which a bold Jansenist assailant could hope to sally.

Pascal may have been outraged by the laxism to which casuistry can lead; but he mentioned the best known of the laxist casuists, Diana, only seven times—usually to show Diana's agreement with some Jesuit—and he referred only four times to Caramuel, who was called the "Prince of Laxists." (Neither of these men was a Jesuit.) As for the leading Jesuit casuist, Busenbaum, who was a man of notably balanced judgment, Pascal never cited him. Yet Busenbaum's *Medulla Theologiae Moralis* had appeared in 1645, and it was well on its way to a total of two hundred editions. Nor does Pascal ever acknowledge that probabilism was initiated by the Dominican Medina—the Dominicans felt kindly toward the Jansenists—or that the first critics of probabilism were themselves Jesuits.

One of the towering religious figures of the time, the Jesuit Louis Bourdalue, launched the most stinging criticism of Pascal. In a sermon that never mentioned him by name but undoubtedly referred to Pascal, he spoke about the vice of "slander, so widespread in our days . . . they invent, they exaggerate, they poison, they tell only half the story, they confound the general with the particular." This was not merely the view of a partisan critic. Indeed, the astute St. Beuve considered the words of Bourdalue to be a more effective criticism of Pascal's book than those of all its critics. It was not theology, it was not ethics, it was not satire; it was simply slander.[51]

Our comments here are not prompted by any scorn for the merits of Pascal's book but are only meant to indicate that its reputation as the hammer of casuistry—crushing it once and for all under irresistible blows—has been greatly exaggerated. The theological critics of casuistry were far more acute in their analyses; and their criticism, hardy though it was, ended not by destroying the activity but by refining and purifying it. Though *The Provincial Letters* gave casuistry an evil reputation that it has yet to live down, they could not destroy the plausibility of "case analysis" as an approach to the resolution of moral problems. There was room (as we shall see) for casuistry to have a continued life, even after *The Provincial Letters*.

13

The Achievement of
Casuistry

High casuistry flourished for little more than a century. It continued
to be practiced actively, but with less originality, for a further two
hundred years. During this period no formal "theory of casuistry"
existed. For a theoretical justification of their activity, casuists
looked to theologians and jurisprudents: indeed, they themselves
often assumed these professional roles, much as a practicing physician might also be a medical scientist. From theology and jurisprudence casuistry took a strong but limited doctrine of natural law,
which proposed primary, secondary, and, in the Renaissance, ter-
tiary moral principles that were general in scope and expression. A
doctrine of "conscience" required that these general principles be
matched to particular instances of moral choice. A doctrine of "circumstances" characterized the particular instances and, in conjunction with the doctrine of conscience, showed how exceptions and
excuses qualified the apparent stringency of the obligations imposed
by general principles.

Still, although expressed in exquisite detail by the theologians,
these theoretical presuppositions were never gathered into a theory
that explained how the various components were related or how
they could be brought to bear on actual decisions and actions. Like
modern physicians who rely unreflectingly on the science of
medicine, the casuists took this theoretical background for granted
and worked as practitioners of "moral" medicine: diagnosing, pre-

scribing, advising "as good physicians of the soul" (Lateran IV). If casuistry developed any formal theory at all, this was the doctrine of "probabilism," and the rules for weighing rival opinions about moral matters stirred intense debate. This debate revealed that further "reflex practical principles" were needed, in addition to direct moral principles, if one was to reach a morally certain judgment about any action. This debate also called attention to the problems involved in describing the formal structure of a moral argument and indicated that, like medical practice without medical science, casuistry was in danger of degenerating into moral quackery.

Leaving theory aside, the casuists' method can be inferred only from their practice. Neither they nor their theological and jurisprudential colleagues formulated an explicit methodology. Their general essays, such as *On the Origins, Sources and Excellence of Casuistic Theology* by Francis Zaccaria, S.J., assessed the relative importance of scriptural, patristic, and ecclesiastical teaching on the formation of opinion but did not set out the intellectual steps required in analyzing a case. So only a study of the casuists' actual practice reveals the steps they consistently took but seldom reflected on. As we read the casuists' cases arranged in rank and file, six of those steps are noteworthy for an understanding of the casuistic method: the reliance on paradigms and analogies, the appeal to maxims, the analysis of circumstances, degrees of probability, the use of cumulative arguments, and the presentation of a final resolution. We shall discuss these six steps in turn.

PARADIGM AND ANALOGY

Casuists of the high era organized their cases into an orderly taxonomy. From the mid-sixteenth century on, they abandoned the alphabetical arrangement of the confessional books and Summas and adopted broader classifications, such as the Ten Commandments or the Seven Deadly Sins. In this way they were able to set out their cases in a way that showed the connection between a specific kind of case and a given principle. In treating killing under the fifth commandment, for example, or false witness under the eighth, the casuist first offered a definition of key terms, such as "killing" or "lying," usually drawn from some renowned author such as Cicero, St. Augustine, or St. Thomas. He then proposed sample cases in which the question can be raised whether an action described in a certain way might fall under the moral offense so defined. The cases are arranged so that the most obvious deviation opens the series. Under the Fifth Commandment, against killing, this might be a direct unprovoked attack resulting in the death of another; under the eighth commandment, against false witness, a deliberate deception intended to harm another.

These extreme examples served as "paradigm cases" illustrating the most manifest breaches of the general principle, taken in its most obvious meaning. The paradigm cases enjoyed both "intrinsic and extrinsic certitude": all authors would concur that there is no reason *not* to consider the act an offense. Then, in succession, cases were proposed that moved away from the paradigm by introducing various combinations of circumstances and motives that made the offense in question less apparent. Under the Fifth Commandment, it might be asked whether a judge was morally permitted to impose the death penalty; whether subjects may kill a tyrant; or whether self-defense extends to killing in defense of one's family, one's property, or one's honor. Under the Eighth Commandment, it might be asked whether deception is justified by great benefit to the deceiver, or if it can prevent a great harm, whether harmless deception is permissible, whether mere concealment by itself constitutes deception. This gradual movement from clear and simple cases to the more complex and obscure ones was standard procedure for the casuist; indeed, it might be said to be the essence of the casuistic mode of thinking. In his defense of casuistry against Pascal, Father Gabriel Daniel, S.J., remarks that the resolution of a difficult case—for example, whether one can kill another in anticipation of deadly danger—"is a consequence drawn by analogy with the earlier decision on self-defense under attack, the truth of which no one doubts."[1] Thus the first feature of casuistic method is the ordering of cases under a principle by paradigm and analogy.

MAXIMS

The second significant feature of classical casuistry is the use of moral "maxims" within a case. If the more general classification of cases rested on an unquestioned moral principle, such as a commandment of the Decalogue, more particular arguments invoked formulas drawn from traditional discussions and phrased aphoristically which served as fulcra and warrants for argument. The arguments about self-defense, for example, often turn on the maxims *vim vi repellere* and *moderamine inculpatae tutelae* ("force may be repulsed by force," "defense measured to the need of the occasion"). These particular maxims originated in Roman Law, were taken over into canon law, and were cited in Aquinas' argument for self-defense. In all three sources the maxims are said to derive from "natural law."[2]

In cases based on the Eighth Commandment, phrases from Scripture tended to dominate (e.g., "the mouth that lies kills the soul"), along with the definitions and dicta of St. Augustine, such as "a lie is a false sign with intent to deceive" or "to whose advantage or disadvantage the lie." Such maxims were, we may recall, the bread and butter of moral instruction in the Middle Ages and Renaissance; they were counted as important argumentative devices in all traditional rhetoric. They are also the kinds of phrases typically invoked by ordinary people when arguing a moral issue: "Don't kick a man when he is down" or "One good turn deserves another." These maxims are seldom further proved; their relevance is seldom explicitly demonstrated; yet they play an important role in the development of a moral argument. Laymann's influential interpretation of the Peace of Augsburg relied on the maxim, "What is not explicitly granted should be considered forbidden," in order to work out his complicated argument about the limits of religious toleration. Similarly, a Council of Theologians summoned to advise the Emperor Ferdinand II about making concessions to the Protestant Princes based their argument on the maxim, "A lesser evil can be tolerated to prevent a greater."[3]

CIRCUMSTANCES

Third, cases of progressive difficulty were constructed by the addition of complicating circumstances to the paradigm cases. The casuists drew on the traditional list of circumstances—"who, what, where, when, why, how and by what means." They asked, for instance, whether the facts that one's assailant is a person of authority in the state, that the goods stolen can be easily retrieved, that alternative ways to escape danger are available make any difference to the argument about the right to kill in defense of life or property. They also take note of the "conditions of the agent": does fear for one's life, for one's reputation, for one's goods, justify a lie? Does instant rage at an insult, or the passion of hot pursuit, excuse a fatal blow? The cases are filled with qualifications about greater or lesser harm, more or less serious injury, more or less imminent danger, greater or lesser assurance of outcome. These were the qualifications that Aristotle, Cicero, and the classical rhetoricians had taught aspiring orators, if they were to argue properly and carefully, under the heading of *Topics*. The casuists incessantly called these circumstances to attention; they insisted that "circumstances *make* the case" and inevitably modified moral judgment about it. Says the casuist Laymann, "after the arguments (concerning principle) have been made clearly and fully, then assessment is made by the person of good judgment, considering circumstances of time, place and person."[4]

PROBABILITY

Fourth, cases were qualified in terms of the "probability" of their conclusions. Each case would be noted either as "certain" or as more or less "probable" or as "thinly probable" (*tenuiter*) or as "hardly probable." This qualifying "note"—as later theologians came to call it—was the casuist's judgment about the strength of the arguments and the weight of the authorities advocating the opinion in question. Opinions in particular cases, beyond the paradigms, were rarely offered as necessary, conclusive or apodictic; rather, they were expressed as carrying more or less conviction, based on the intrinsic arguments and the extrinsic authorities. Any person seeking advice or absolution ought to be informed of this qualification in order that he might decide, on the basis of the assessed probability, how far to risk being morally in the wrong. The classic debate over probabilism centered on the prudential rules for making such choices; yet quite apart from that debate, all the casuists acknowledged that moral choices were usually more or less "arguable." Least susceptible of being argued against were the paradigm cases; the further one moved away from the paradigm, the more arguable—in terms of pro and con—the case became. It was not until late in the history of casuistry that there appears the concept of "an intrinsically evil act," the kind of act that under all conceivable circumstances would have to be judged as wrong.[5]

Once again, Father Daniel's refutation of Pascal includes an apposite comment:

> All will agree on a few basic principles, such as that a man should not use force to right a wrong if it can be righted by legal authority; but, this being supposed, a thousand difficulties of great importance arise which must be considered by canonists and theologians."[6]

The work of the casuists was precisely the analysis of complex cases in the light of "a thousand difficulties." Because that analysis moves further and further from the cases on which "all agree," its results inevitably will be marked by greater or lesser plausibility rather than certainty. The movement from paradigm through analogies, marked by slightly varying interpretations of accepted maxims, as applied to differing circumstances, gave the casuists a refined sensitivity to the manifold ways in which cases differed from one another. When advice was to be given to particular persons in particular situations, this sensitivity was a virtue. Only when it became generalized and exaggerated did it degenerate into a vice, "casuistry" in its modern pejorative meaning.

CUMULATIVE ARGUMENTS

Discussions about moral issues usually present arguments in support of the position advanced. In the history of casuistry, the Penitential Books had listed particular sins and recommended penances. The seriousness of these penances, in terms of inconvenience and hardship imposed upon the penitent, was an indication of the seriousness of the sin. However, these books rarely went beyond the citing of a scriptural or patristic text to justify the penitential verdict. The Confessional Books and Summas, which were influenced by scholastic theology, were more intent on offering justifications, though these are usually stated very briefly, usually by citing a maxim rather than constructing a formal argument. In the era of high casuistry the reasons justifying an opinion were explained more expansively. Yet the casuists still make relatively short arguments, usually offering several distinct kinds of reasons to support their conclusions: a scriptural text, a citation from canon law, an appeal to the virtue of charity or justice, and a prudential point might be set beside each other, with little effort to integrate them into a single coherent argument.

The conclusion that an opinion deserved to be ranked as "more" or "less" probable followed not by any rigorous logic—although the casuists are mindful, if not meticulous, about logic—but from the accumulation of many and varied supporting reasons. There is little resemblance to those forms of moral reasoning that seek to "deduce" a particular conclusion from a moral principle that serves as a universal premise. Rather, casuistical argument resembles the rhetorical and commonsense discourse that piles up many kinds of argument in hopes of showing the favored position in a good light. The "weight" of a casuistical opinion came from the accumulation of reasons rather than from the logical validity of the arguments or the coherence of any single "proof."

RESOLUTION

Finally, the casuists always concluded the analysis of a case with a resolution. They would close the case with advice about the moral licitness or permissibility of acting in one particular way or another. At this point the distinction between actions "speculatively probable but practically impermissible" sometimes appears (a distinction that Pascal ridicules as "vain").[7] The casuists recognized that one might be able to present a powerful speculative argument about a moral issue by abstracting from all circumstances of any particular case. Father Daniel, responding to Pascal's complaints on this point, defined "speculative" conclusions as those that "refer only to general principles, considering nothing but the principles and the connection this proposition has with the principle without regard to anything else." He goes on: "The object of moral science is practice. All conclusions that are not practical but merely speculative, are not properly moral conclusions: they are not decisions."[8] The casuists' intent was to come as close as possible to decision and action. They were obliged to resolve the case because in their view, acting "from a doubtful conscience" (that is, without reaching any conclusion about the morality of an act) was itself immoral.

Vividly aware that in morals, as in medicine, difficult cases can never be resolved by logical deductions leading to certain conclusions, they almost always presented their resolutions as "more or less probable." They would say, for example, "In these circumstances, given these conditions, you can with reasonable assurance act in such-and-such a way. By so doing, you will not act rashly or imprudently, but can be of good conscience."

To sum up, the method of casuistry involved an ordering of cases by paradigm and analogy, appeals to maxims and analyses of circumstances, the qualification of opinions, the accumulation of multiple arguments, and the statement of practical resolutions of particular moral problems in the light of all these considerations. Given these features, we can now offer our own definition of "casuistry" as being

> the analysis of moral issues, using procedures of reasoning based on paradigms and analogies, leading to the formulation of expert opinions about the existence and stringency of particular moral obligations, framed in terms of rules or maxims that are general but not universal or invariable, since they hold good with certainty only in the typical conditions of the agent and circumstances of action.

In these respects the casuists' ways of analyzing and resolving moral perplexities display their methodological kinship to the physician's ways of analyzing and resolving medical problems of clinical diagnosis. In both these practical fields the first need was for a reliable taxonomy of well-analyzed "type cases," which could serve as objects of comparison (or "paradigms") in dealing with fresh and more puzzling cases. And the ways in which the taxonomy was put to work had to respect the inevitable limits on the kinds of "certainty" available to human agents in any such field of practice. In morals and medicine alike, the most confident opinion about a particular case may subsequently be called in question in the light of fresh considerations. Even the most strongly supported (or "probable") of practical opinions can be presented only as the outcome of "presumptive," not "necessary" inferences; while the discovery of new facts about the circumstances of any particular case may always rebut, or force one to qualify, a former opinion about it.

The casuists' analyses were no more concerned than, say, common-law arguments or medical diagnoses with formal proofs of kinds that can be judged by anyone with an eye for "necessary connections." Historically, therefore, their arguments display genealogical links to the Aristotelian tradition of practical reasoning (*phronesis*). They were presented in well-defined forums and were required to carry conviction with an experienced professional audience. In these respects they were "rhetorical" analyses whose powers of persuasion depended not merely on their intrinsic content but also on the circumstances in which they were put forward: for example, on being advanced by "people of good judgment" (*phronimoi*), and on finding "reasonable and understanding hearers."

The rhetorical character of casuistical reasoning does not mean that the arguments of the casuists were dressed up to deceive a gullible public. On the contrary: if the opinion of a Cicero, an Aquinas, or an Azor on some moral issue carried more weight than those of lesser authorities, that was no more unreasonable than the fact that today physicians pay more attention to the clinical opinions of colleagues whose experience and judgment they have learned to trust than they do to those of the average, run-of-the-mill M.D. True, the "experts" in casuistry did not always have the richest firsthand experience of human life in all its perplexity. Then as now, the celibacy of the priesthood was a stumbling block to a popular acceptance of their rulings on sexual issues; but then, defense attorneys do not have or need firsthand experience as criminals either. In law and morals, reasonably enough, what matters most is an ability to recognize, in full subtlety and detail, the relevant features of any particular case—both "circumstances of the action" and "conditions of the agent"—and to present them as bearing on the present issue in terms that "speak to the condition" of the current audience.

As always in practical reasoning, casuistry offered limited scope for universal, invariable generalizations. If "high casuists" hesitated to universalize their judgments, or to say "never" when it was more correct to say either "well, hardly ever" or "never, in any circumstances we have yet considered," they were acting like Supreme Court justices who eschew *obiter dicta* and refuse to present opinions going beyond the facts of the immediate case, for fear that they may prejudice ("prejudge") issues that may yet arise in some future case, the detailed facts of which are not yet available for their consideration. Recall, for example, the reluctance of the Commission of Casuists to pronounce on the Pope's case of the German Contract.[9] For, it turns out, in practical morals as in common law the best we can do in the way of *generalizing* judgments is to formulate rules or maxims that are general in form but limited in practical scope: recognizing that these can be applied without question only in cases that are close enough to the "paradigm cases" in terms of which they were defined.

Beyond all necessary inferences and deductions from general rules, there thus lie other, more basic issues of moral and judicial *judgment* about just how close the facts of any particular case lie to the facts of the relevant paradigm. Just how close is "having your honor impugned" to "being robbed of your wallet," "hiding your religious faith from a hostile interrogator" to "lying to a loyal friend," or "putting up risk capital for a business venture" to "lending money to a neighbor at his time of need"? The kind of wisdom involved in answering questions of this kind is just the personal talent Aristotle described as practical wisdom, or *phronesis*. This does not demand only the capacity to learn general rules and to make valid deductions: it rests, rather, on having a feeling for or a grasp of what is *epieikes*—equitable, fair, fitting, or reasonable—given all the detailed circumstances of some particular practical situation.

For the casuists, then, moral wisdom was like any form of practical wisdom. It required one to understand not only the general rules, maxims, and principles of morality, but—even more important—to understand in what kinds of circumstances and to what types of cases they do or do not apply: not just rules, that is, but equity in the application of those rules—or, as Father Azor wrote, "grasping the equity of the case from the circumstances."[10] Insisting, by contrast, that all moral principles must be read as universal, invariable and free of exceptions, meant moving away from an "equitable" conception of practical morals, in one or other of two directions. Either it meant dismissing all those circumstances that might be used to justify "making an exception" in practice as lax and indulgent; or, setting aside all matters of practice in favor of more "speculative" issues, and turning ethical theory back into a system of "axioms and deductions."

The seventeenth-century critics of casuistry attempted to move in both directions at once. For a start, Pascal saw the casuists' readiness to make exceptions to moral principles, as and when exceptional conditions required this, as encouraging laxity toward the claims of morality at a time when the strictest observance was needed: in this respect, the casuists' *practice* struck him as deficient. At the same time, their failure to stand by conclusions that were plainly entailed by general principles that they themselves professed he found intellectually objectionable. To a man of mathematical genius, such indifference to logical consistency was surely a grave deficiency in their *theory*. Before long, the two criticisms were telescoped together: the best remedy for laxity in practical morals (it seemed) was to give it a more intelligible foundation in ethical theory; and so began a new phase in the history of moral philosophy, to which we shall be turning shortly.

Both criticisms, however, were overstated. To cover its practical limitations, first: in the minds of lay readers, the whole terminology of tutiorism and probabilism, probabiliorism and laxism, might well be open to serious misunderstanding. If moral issues were of grave importance, how could the casuists waste so much time quibbling about just how many (and just which) learned doctor must support a given opinion before it could be accepted as a guide to conscience? Many laypeople could now read and think for themselves, and the Protestants at least were taught to consult their own consciences in preference to a confessor; so how could they be asked to go against their own strongly held convictions on the basis of nothing more than a dubious balance of views among a handful of theologians? It was no wonder that such quibbling brought Catholic teaching into disrepute!

Yet that argument missed the point. Any moral theologian worth his salt knew that excess scrupulosity was almost as grave a threat to sound conscience as laxity. A laxist casuistry may put your con-science at ease, provided only that some case (however weak) can be made out in favor of your actions; and this certainly leaned in the direction of what our own contemporaries call "permissiveness." But a tutiorist casuistry will not allow your conscience to be easy unless you avoid all actions *against* which any case whatever can be made; and this has its own deficiencies. Those whose consciences are not open to counterarguments, or even to a clarification of ambi-guities, may, like some of the nuns of Port-Royal, easily fall into inflexibility or self-righteousness. The resolution of moral problems has no claim to be "reasonable" (let alone "rational") unless it goes beyond the immediate deliverances of an uncriticized Inner Voice.

This was why, in the end, the casuists' theoretical discussion came down to a choice between "probabilism" and "probabiliorism." When the authority of earlier casuists and moral teachers was appealed to in actual practice, was it enough to follow *any* respected doctor who had reflected deeply on a particular issue and had given a reasoned opinion? Or must one also satisfy oneself that, among all the reasoned opinions that were available in the teaching tradition, this particular one had the best "intrinsic" support, in being support-ed by the most compelling paradigms, analogies, and other relevant arguments? Unfortunately the casuists saw the probabilist and probabiliorist views as exclusive options, whereas they can be plausibly understood as alternatives for different situations. When faced with complex issues that you have no chance to reflect on yourself, accepting an opinion that appears reasonable from any sound doctor ("probabilism") may be prudent practical policy; but if you have time to undertake a fresh analysis of the issues, the other ("probabiliorist") course, which demands that you look for the sound*er* doctor and the *more* reasonable opinion, is surely preferable. Thus in the last resort, both "intrinsic" and "extrinsic" probabilities have to be considered.[11]

On either hand, of course, the analysis must be carried through with an eye to the *context* of the argument. Casuistical methods of reasoning, like all practical procedures, could either be used properly or be misused. But there was no way of telling which of these two things was happening by looking at the words of their arguments alone. Like the legal arguments of working attorneys, the arguments of practicing casuists were formulated and presented within an institutional framework; and their merits could be judged only by seeing how they fitted into that larger situation. The health of casuistry as a professional activity thus depended on the health of the institutions within which it operated. In any event, what did most to discredit it later was not its intellectual failings, which were corrected, but the Catholic Church's loss of its earlier institutional authority, which had given the high casuists a freedom to deal so confidently and clear-headedly with the vexed problems of moral practice as they arose.

Not only were the moral analyses produced by the casuists from the late fifteenth century on responsive to the changing social and historical needs of the time—for example, those arising out of the mercantilism and capital investment or European exploration and settlement of other continents. In many cases they remain even today a good starting point for practical analysis of urgent public issues. Anyone who discusses at all seriously the moral problems created by nuclear weapons, for instance, soon starts using the terminology of the casuists' analysis of the morality of War. In an ideal world it might have been enough to issue a blanket condemnation of all War, as such. In a world of human beings, and of States governed by human rulers who, unrestrained, did not need a Clausewitz to teach them that War is a continuation of Policy by other means, it was more constructive for casuists to think through in detail the question on what conditions and in what circumstances the use of military force as an instrument of policy went beyond the tolerable limits set, for example, by the morality of self-defense. Thus were formulated all those distinctions, between "combatants" and "noncombatants," and between the "necessary" and "needless," or "proportionate" and "disproportionate" use of force for legitimate state ends that still play a crucial part in all serious practical discussions either of nuclear or of non-nuclear war.[12]

Catholic moral teaching subsequently gained a reputation for being dry, inflexible, and dogmatic. But this reputation was the product of a later time and was most marked in those provinces where the influence of Augustine and the Jansenists remained at its strongest (e.g., where the priesthood was staffed from the Irish seminary at Maynooth whose faculty, during the long repression of Catholic education in Ireland, had been trained at Jansenist Louvain). Still, the consolidation of the Protestant denominations was a continued threat to the authority of Catholicism, and Pascal's charge of laxism had stung. From the mid-seventeenth century, too, the Catholic Church was on the defensive in many Protestant countries, and problems of religious authority were compounded by political hostility. Even after the seventeenth century, for instance, Catholicism was open to the same general suspicion among the English public that attaches nowadays to communism in the United States. In a country where politicians competed with one another in denouncing "Papists" or "the Whore of Rome," and claimed that the Papacy was planning to invade England and reconvert its population to Catholicism by force, innocent discussions of case morality could hardly expect a fair hearing. Even in Catholic countries such as France the Church tended to become associated with Royalism, and so was out of sympathy with the ideals of republicanism.

All of this led progressively to a politicization of religious loyalties, the tightening of discipline, and an adoption of new, harder line positions. Only at this late stage, for example, was the thesis that some types of action are wrong unconditionally, without any possibility of exceptions (*malum ex toto genere suo*), introduced into Catholic casuistry. In its days of confidence and success, the casuists had been able to respond to new situations and novel problems with flexibility and originality. At times this meant that the Church had to insist on the moral claims of the existing paradigms, even in the face of political pressure to the contrary. The pleas of Bartolomeo de

Las Casas on behalf of the indigenous peoples of Latin America, for instance, led the Pope to pronounce his ruling that Amerindians were human beings on a par with Europeans and must be respected as such. In consequence, despite all the hopes and wishes of the Conquistadores, the native population of Latin America was never formally enslaved.[13] (By an irony of history, the peoples of Africa found no such champion and never won the same protection from the Church.)

To return to the theoretical objections to casuistry, these reenacted the earlier differences between Plato and Aristotle. Those who regarded moral problems as essentially *practical*, within the scope of *phronesis*, saw unquestioned merits in the taxonomic mode of analysis. In exploring the reach of moral "paradigms" and "analogies" involved, one confronted issues of equity directly; and the method's possible misuse, by confessors who made unwarranted exceptions on behalf of the rich or powerful, was a small price to pay for those merits. As for the counterargument, that it was "logically inconsistent" to acknowledge a universal principle in general terms but then set it aside in "exceptional" cases, this carried weight only for those who denied or ignored Aristotle's claim that Ethics is not and cannot be a demonstrative Science, and for those who still hoped to turn the subject into a deductive theory or *episteme* the "axioms" of which were so many universal, invariable, and exceptionless moral rules.

For the professional casuists of the Middle Ages and Renaissance, this hope for an ethical *episteme* was illusory. The focus of their moral inquiries remained case analysis—classifying actions and circumstances into different species, and developing "moral taxonomies" rich and subtle enough to cover all the serious problems that typically arise in different sectors of human experience. They laid no claim to "wisdom" or insight into "truth." Rather, they were people who had shared in the common human experience but who were unusually practiced in thinking about and arguing through the issues that arise out of experience. Above all they were experienced in formulating practical resolutions of those issues. They acknowledged no "wholly irresoluble" moral problems, any more than physicians recognize "wholly untreatable" patients. There are, no doubt, terminal patients for whom little can be done beyond making them comfortable; but that is itself a proper kind of medical "treatment." So some moral cases are genuinely paradoxical, for which no resolution will be satisfactory. Likewise, there were moral choices that called for no especially subtle arguments because so little was at stake; yet even here the very decision *not* to rule on the issue was a "moral" one, indicating that the choice in question was indifferent.

In short, the casuists, like the civil and canon lawyers, formed a learned community with their own shared professional standards and procedures. (Often enough, indeed, lawyers and casuists might be the same individuals.) These standards controlled the kinds of arguments to which they could appeal, in matching specific issues of case morality with the accepted system of moral categories and distinctions. We cannot hope to understand the procedures of the casuists today, if we look at this "moral taxonomy" in the abstract, without considering also the ways in which it was applied to actual practical cases. Professional solidarity and intellectual understanding, which linked the high casuists during their years of greatest confidence and distinction, were twin aspects of a "form of life" that was undermined from the early seventeenth century on.

Then the schisms among the Protestant and Catholic churches—with the English Church poised awkwardly in the middle—thrust the whole debate into confusion. Catholic casuists were no longer generally seen as speaking "with authority" about moral problems; Anglicans, meanwhile, developed their own analytical casuistry; but the Calvinists, like the Jansenists, put responsibility for "conscience" and choice squarely on the individual believer. (Recall Pascal's injunction, "Follow God!") The result was a recipe for Babel.

We must be clear, however, where exactly this Babel was *located* and what it was *about*. So long as "moral" issues were addressed as collective, practical issues there was still room to set aside doctrinal conflicts and resolve them by resorting to the traditional procedures. Despite separation from Rome, for instance, Anglican casuists treasured the Catholic inheritance of "case morality" and the *ratio naturalis*. This kind of practical convergence is still possible today: it was no accident, for example, that members of the National Commission (about which we wrote earlier) so often arrived at shared opinions about their problems. The practical questions that the U.S. Congress had formulated as their terms of reference—for example, "On what conditions, if any, is it morally acceptable for prisoners to take part as subjects of biomedical research projects?"—helped (in Samuel Johnson's phrase) to "concentrate their minds wonderfully"; and in the course of addressing these practical issues, they developed a "casuistry" of biomedical and behavioral research using shared criteria by which to discriminate among research projects of morally distinct kinds.

As the commissioners tackled these practical tasks, their ability to arrive at more or less agreed resolutions became less and less of a mystery to them. Yet some onlookers saw this practical consensus as a fictitious product of political pressure, which glossed over serious conflicts on the doctrinal level: the commissioners (said these critics) just ignored their own very real differences of opinion and compromised their personal commitments for the sake of completing the allotted tasks. If they had only been more candid about their real ethical views, it would have been apparent to the public that they were a deeply divided group.[14]

Yet this objection merely brings us back to our original questions about the relationship between ethical theory and moral practice. And if we pursue this direction of argument, hard questions arise. What, then, should we say that anyone's "real" ethical views consist in? How are we to identify those views? Do we look and see what general moral maxims he announces for himself, or applauds when presented by others? Or are we to give greater weight to the practical attitudes he adopts in dealing with concrete cases of specific types in particular circumstances? So long as we place primary importance on people's public pronouncements of universal moral principle, or to their abstract and general philosophical theories, the contemporary ethical debate may appear pure Babel.[15] But as the commissioners' experience also showed, we do not have to take that route. For good Aristotelian reasons, the medieval tradition of casuistry gave priority to *concrete issues of practice* rather than to *abstract matters of theory*; and that alternative remains open to us today.

As we noted earlier, the casuists of the sixteenth and seventeenth centuries were people of their times, and some of their moral findings strike us as outrageous today. Still, the results of their work, preserved in the vast literature that they left us, are a treasure trove of material for philosophical ethics which is neglected by most philosophers, who find its concrete particularity too lacking in generality and theoretical analysis to contribute much (in their view) to a philosophical understanding of moral thought and practice. They deserve more attention, especially from those who are prepared to take seriously Aristotle's concern that we only generalize to the extent that is compatible with the subject matter in question.

PART VI

The Future of Casuistry

14

After *The Provincial Letters*

In the Catholic world casuistry survived Pascal's battering, but its life was not easy. Though cured of laxism, it began to show signs of senescence. From 1700 on it lost much of its analytic vigor and boldness of attack. Later Catholic moral theologians practiced a sound but somewhat dull variety of case analysis. For a further half-century the Jansenist controversy raged on. In France Jansenism briefly won some sympathy in royal and ecclesiastical circles, but successive royal and papal edicts finally destroyed it. In the field of morals the Jansenists won several small victories: for example, the Holy Office, in 1665 and 1666, condemned a list of laxist propositions drawn from casuists, most of them taken from the works of Thomas Hurtado, a non-Jesuit.[1] The Roman decrees were inspired by earlier censures from the University of Louvain—as always sympathetic to Jansenism—and from the University of Paris: some wordings from their censures were even incorporated into the papal condemnations.

During the pontificate of Pope Innocent XI (1676–1689), laxism was condemned even more severely. This Pope was attracted by the Jansenists' moral austerity and zeal and responded favorably to a request from some French bishops who were Jansenist sympathizers. (The petition to the Pope was composed by Nicole himself.) A decree of the Holy Office, issued in 1679, stigmatized as laxist sixty-five propositions drawn from the casuistical literature, and subsequent volumes of casuistry and moral theology customarily includ-

ed the text of these condemnations in their prefatory notes.[2]
Innocent XI also indicated to the Jesuits his hope that one of their
theologians who had written against probabilism might be elected
General of the Society. So in 1689 Father Thyrsus Gonzales de
Santilla, who had fought a lonely battle in favor of probabiliorism,
was elected General. Alexander VIII (1689–91) balanced the ledger
by condemning thirty-one rigorist propositions excerpted from
Belgian casuists.[3] So as the seventeenth century ended, the extremes
of high casuistry, laxism, and rigorism were chastened, and the casuists had been warned of the incautious use of probabilist methods.
But casuistry itself still stood and continued to serve the practical
need of confessors and counselors for guidance in the resolution of
moral problems.

The papal condemnations of laxism and rigorism had a double
effect: they purged casuistry of its excesses, but they also contributed to its demise as a vigorous discipline. As Charles Curran
has written, the decrees were "the most significant intervention up
to that time by the papal office in the area of moral theology, and
began a trend that has continued until contemporary times."[4]
Aware of this new Roman vigilance toward their teaching, casuists
and theologians now began to submit difficult points and cases to
the authorities in Rome for "official" opinions, and bishops moved
to settle disputes among the theologians by seeking definitive resolutions from Rome. Rome responded readily, and several depart-
ments of the Roman Curia began to issue *responsa*, notably the Holy
Office of the Inquisition and the Sacred Penitentiary. Although this
happened relatively rarely in the eighteenth century, the practice
became common in the nineteenth as the Vatican centralized its
authority in the face of a rising tide of democracy and revolution
across Europe.

These official *responsa*, prepared by the faculty and staff theologians of the various Roman universities, implicitly carried the
authority of the Pope, and this was enough to lend the opinion a
very weighty "extrinsic" probability. Indeed these responses, as
issued, seldom set out substantial arguments that could have provided some "intrinsic" probability to the rulings: to find these arguments the petitioner was advised to "consult the standard texts by
approved authors." For example, on 21 May, 1851 the Holy Office
issued a decree:

The Apostolic See is asked what theological note is to be applied to the following propositions: (1) a married couple may practice contraception for morally good motives; (2) this form of marital intercourse is not certainly against the natural law. The Holy Office answers: the first proposition is scandalous, erroneous and contrary to the natural law of marriage; the second is scandalous and implicitly condemned in proposition 49 of Innocent XI.[5]

The appearance of *responsa* such as these inhibited that free exchange of opinion which had inspired high casuistry. Certain limits were set; maxims were fixed in place and probabilities determined not by debate but by decree. In the nineteenth century popes began to use Encyclicals as a medium of teaching on moral matters, and in this form longer expositions of argument were presented to justify the teaching. Coming from the pen of the Pope, such arguments were in a sense "canonized," so moral theologians tended to pay them great respect while ignoring alternatives or counterarguments. They even refrained from criticizing these privileged lines of reasoning. The culmination of this centralization of authority in the moral sphere was the Encyclical *Humanae Vitae* (1968), in which Paul VI condemned all forms of birth control except abstinence as intrinsically evil; but because of the worldwide protests of many leading moral theologians and even of bishops, it was also the beginning of its decline.[6]

Within the world of Catholic moral theology, a serious theological critique of casuistry appeared. Initially put forward by the faculty of the University of Tübingen in the first half of the nineteenth century, it criticized casuistry as diverting attention from the moral teaching of the Gospels; as stressing sin rather than perfection; and as viewing the moral life as a matter of observing lower limits rather than of aspiring to the higher ideals of love and sacrifice. In ironic contrast to the Jansenist charge of laxism, this later critique accused casuistry of legalism.[7] Though repeated many times, this critique did little to impede the work of the casuists. Indeed, for many moral problems (e.g., the living wage, abortion, and warfare) some of the more cogent analyses have appeared in the last hundred years: beginning in the 1940s a group of American Jesuits regularly published excellent casuistical analyses in the scholarly journal, *Theological Studies*.[8] In general, however, most twentieth-century Roman Catholic casuistry has been a textbook exercise, purveyed in mechanical form to seminarians.[9]

Another reason for the demise of a vigorous casuistry within the Roman Catholic tradition was the application of the technique to matters of ritual and ecclesiastical discipline. Proper performance of ceremonial ritual was required for the validity of the sacrament; thus questions about the appropriate manner of wearing vestments and correct gestures became important. Similarly, church discipline required attendance at Sunday Mass, fasting during Lent, abstaining from meat on Friday. Problems were posed about how late one could arrive at Mass in order to fulfill one's Sunday duty, how much food constituted a permitted meal, whether frogs' legs were meat or fish. The application of casuistry to these questions, useful as it might be for scrupulous Catholics, sapped the strength of the method. Paradigm cases are hard to find; maxims are weak; grounding lies in obedience to rule rather than moral value. Casuistry easily slides into trivial sophistry.[10]

During the 1960s a slight renewal of interest in casuistry was stimulated as a result of the brief vogue of "situation ethics." Some theologians proposed that God's commands could be perceived only in the particular concrete "situations" of decision; others taught that moral obligations appeared not as general principles but as intuitions of what was the most loving act at any particular moment. This "situational" (or "existential") approach favored an ethics of cases, in which specific concrete situations demanded moral choice, and some authors even liked to describe it as a kind of "casuistry." On closer examination, however, many differences can be found between situation ethics and classical casuistry. Where the casuists had worked with a multitude of moral paradigms, principles, and maxims, situationists acknowledged no general principles, or only a single principle. (Although situationists acknowledged a role for maxims, these were to be viewed only as "guidelines.") Where the casuists had been attentive to "circumstances" as one feature of moral life among many others, situationists reduced the moral life to a bare succession of circumstances. The casuists analyzed novel cases by analogy with prior or paradigm cases: situationists focused on moral choices that were concrete but unique and isolated. So in 1956, Pope Pius XII condemned situationism as an acceptable approach for Catholic moral theology. In a brief but intense debate, casuistry was distinguished from situationism, while several situationist theses were quietly absorbed into conventional moral theology.[11] A parallel debate was stimulated among Protestant writers by

Joseph Fletcher's book, *Situation Ethics,* whose title seemingly gave the method its name.[12]

Echoes of the Tübingen criticism were heard again during the *aggorniamento,* the wave of renewal that swept the Church during the papacy of Pope John XXIII; and a new moral theology emerged from the theological and pastoral ferment of the Second Vatican Council. In this new moral theology casuistry has had little place. Among the moral theologians of the Catholic tradition, which originally provided its life and its nourishment, the practice of casuistry has today few practitioners and finds little sympathy.[13]

The enfeeblement of traditional Catholic casuistry after 1700 reflects the weakening of its institutional base. The vigor of debate among the high casuists, from 1550 to 1650, was enhanced by their professional independence and freedom to develop opinions grounded in the classical arguments they had inherited from Cicero, Augustine, and Aquinas.[14] From now on, intellectually speculative *Summas* were displaced by officially approved manuals of theology, and the work of theologians was hampered by a centralized ecclesiastical authority that eroded their autonomy. At the worst, this reduced their task to interpreting decrees and policies promulgated in Rome: the casuist's serious moral enterprise was transformed into a bureaucratic one of fitting all difficult problems of conduct into predetermined official categories.

How may we explain these changes in the institutional practice of the Catholic Church and the increasingly political atmosphere in which moral theologians had to work? Two historical events—the Protestant Reformation, and the French Revolution—first initiated, and later reinforced, these changes. During five or six hundred years, from Hildebrand to Luther, the spiritual and intellectual authority of the Church was largely unchallenged, and there was no reason for the Vatican to subject moral theologians to centralized control or their writings to scrutiny and censorship. In any event, it could hardly have done so even if it had wished: problems of communication and travel, along with the diffusion of political power in medieval Europe, made for a "collegial" cooperation between Rome and the provinces of the Church and among the different provinces. Nobody challenged the ecclesiastical primacy of the Pope; but, over doctrinal issues, his institutional leadership left him only *primus inter pares.* Theologians and other scholars did not have to check "official opinion" on issues in their professional fields, let alone defer to it. They could reach their own judgments freely, relying on the intellectual standards of their disciplines, and did not have to seek approval from people in Rome whose authority rested less on scholarly distinction than on their status in the hierarchy.

After the Reformation matters changed. During the sixteenth century the dominant position of the Catholic Church faced three challenges: the rise of a secular and vernacular culture, the spread of Protestantism, and the collapse of medieval cosmology.[15] The Church planned its counterattack in the mid-sixteenth century, at the Council of Trent, and the aftermath of the council was a "drawing together of the wagons" to fight off, and beat down, heresy and schism. The spiritual rivalry of the churches was now replaced by political hostility, intellectual competition by ideological confrontation.

In a newly unified France, the Duc de Guise and his brother, the Cardinal Archbishop of Strasbourg, led the Catholic League in a fight against the power of the Huguenot nobility. By the Edict of Nantes (1598) Henri IV imposed an interlude of religious tolerance; but after his assassination, Richelieu and his successors persuaded Louis XIII and Louis XIV to impose the Catholic religion by force. In fragmented Germany dozens of kingdoms, duchies, and free cities picked sides, until the outbreak of the Thirty Years' War (1618) turned this rivalry into a bloody conflict in which all parties treated each other with a murderous brutality.[16] In England, after the Anglican separation from Rome, Queen Mary's marriage to Philip of Spain, and the débacle of the Spanish Armada, led the English of all classes to identify the cause of the Anglican Church with that of nationalism. Charles I's execution, followed fifty years later by the expulsion of James II, destroyed the last political ambitions of the Catholic party and strengthened the general suspicion of "Popery."

A hundred years later, the French Revolution further intensified Catholic fears. During the long reigns of Louis XIV and Louis XV, the leaders of French Catholicism committed the Church to Royalism and so made it a natural target for critics of the régime. The spectacle of the revolution filled other countries with horror, at the Jacobins' bloodstained hands and their professed atheism alike. Alarmed by the new French Republic's anticlerical declarations, the Church recoiled into a defensive posture and took on a deeply conservative political color quite out of harmony with its best medieval traditions.

This phase in the history of the Catholic Church culminated in the pontificate of Pope Pius IX (*Pio Nono*) who encouraged a doctrinal and disciplinary inflexibility that was to last for several generations. Under Pius, for example, the First Vatican Council endorsed the dogma of papal infallibility, which despite its doctrinal limitations reinforced a centralized conformity in matters of faith and morals. The attempt has been made more recently, both at and since the Second Vatican Council (1962), to revive older, collegial patterns of Church discipline and doctrinal judgment. But especially in the moral realm, the Vatican today still adopts a centralized style of teaching, which meets with skepticism in the provinces, notably at the parish level. So, it appears, the tension between collegiality and centralization has not yet been fully resolved.

Pascal had explicitly challenged the credibility of casuistry: its practical vigor was sapped by institutional changes in, and social changes around, the Church. At the same time, the reputation of casuistry as a method of intellectual inquiry was implicitly called into doubt by the novel claims of the seventeenth-century system-atizers. During the sixteenth century the work of the humanists, from Erasmus to Michel de Montaigne and Francis Bacon, and of the natural philosophers, from Copernicus to Tycho Brahe and Johannes Kepler, generated an increasing skepticism about medieval cosmology and philosophy. Now, with the appearance in the 1630s of Galileo's *Dialogue Concerning the Two Great World Systems*, followed by René Descartes' *Discourse on Method*, the European intellectual world was entranced by the ideas of "system" and "method."

This movement, known at the time as "the new mathematical and experimental natural philosophy," culminated in the publication of Isaac Newton's *Philosophiae Naturalis Principia Mathematica* in 1687. That extraordinary treatise did for mechanics and astronomy—and, by implication, for the rest of physical science as well—what Euclid's *Elements* had done for geometry in antiquity. It put forward a new set of dynamical concepts, captured in three "Axioms, or Laws of Motion," by appeal to which (it seemed) all the varied phenomena of the natural world might eventually be explained in full mathematical detail. For the next two hundred years this remained an emblematic work, which scholars in all subjects took as a model of intellectual achievement, even to the point of idolizing it. From now on any discipline wishing to be accepted as a serious field of study, regardless of its subject matter, was expected to develop its own body of abstract, theoretical concepts and principles and to present them, if possible, in the form of an axiomatic system.[17]

In the fields of Law and Morality, the first great systematizer was Hugo Grotius (1583–1645). Grotius's treatise on the law of war, *De Iure Belli et Pacis* (1625), handles many of the same topics as did earlier authors such as Althusius, Vitoria, and Suarez. But Grotius also makes a deliberate attempt to reveal the "principles" of law, as

> in themselves manifest and clear, almost as evident as are those things which we perceive by the external senses.[18]

He makes frequent references to the virtues of mathematics, arguing that once the first principles of law are grasped as "axioms," they can form the basis for an entire deductive system of law. One modern commentator has written of Grotius:

> Like a mathematician, he proposed to withdraw his mind from every particular fact. . . . He intended to do for the law just what, as he understood the matter, was being done with success in mathematics.[19]

Grotius's systematizing tendency is particularly evident in his early and unpublished work, *De Iure Praedae*. This opens with a section called "dogmatica" containing a set of *axiomata, regulae,* and *leges;* which he then applies to the cases set forth in the following section, called "historica."

However, Grotius is still too close in spirit to his predecessors for him to make a complete break with the earlier scholastic and casuistical method. He is vividly aware that

> what Aristotle said is perfectly true: certainty is not to be found in moral matters in the same degree as in mathematical science.[20]

In discussing the just occasions for war, for instance, his treatment of "self-defense" surveys, in order, the classical cases that reveal the legitimacy and the limits of the defense against aggression. (He even includes a nuanced discussion of "killing for a slap".) Similarly, his analysis of truth-telling under the circumstances of war repeats the familiar casuistical analysis of the subject, although his introduction of the concept of "the right to know" makes it possible for him to give a more systematic account than is to be found in his predecessors. Still, with his interest in the creation of a deductive system of law, Grotius is only a "shadow" casuist for whom the old cases lurk in the background of his own more theoretical exposition.[21]

Samuel Pufendorf (1632–1694) idolized Grotius and set out to popularize him under the title of the "Father of Natural Law"; yet he explicitly disagreed with the master's concession to Aristotle about the uncertainty of moral matters.[22] He strongly believed that moral problems could be resolved by deduction from first principles. Like Grotius, he wrote an early work openly patterned on mathematical reasoning, *Elementorum Jurisprudentiae Universales Libri Duo* (1658). But again like Grotius, he reverted to casuistical reasoning when it came to dealing with substantive issues. Indeed, his principal work, *De Jure Naturae et Gentium*, has all the appearance of a book of high casuistry: after an exposition of the basic principles of law and morals, the chapters march through case after case. Nevertheless the ideal of system dominated Pufendorf's work and touched his many students, who carried it into their teaching of moral philosophy in the universities of Germany. Thomasius, for example, who acknowledged his dependence on Pufendorf, published a book with the suggestive title, *Fundamenta Juris Naturae et Gentium ex Sensu Communi Deducta* (*Foundations of the Law of Nature and of Nations Deduced from Common Sense,* 1704).

The philosopher who brought this concept of a "rational system of law" to perfection was Christian Wolff. An early biographer wrote of him,

He formulated a plan of making all philosophical knowledge into a true system in which conclusions would be drawn from principles and all propositions would be deduced one from the other by demonstrative evidence.[23]

Wolff's contribution to jurisprudence and ethics was a densely and closely reasoned deduction of moral rules and rights from the Idea of Perfection. A historian of philosophy says of Wolff:

Because of its comprehensiveness and its formal and orderly arrangement, his system was able to provide a school philosophy for the German universities . . . and dominated until the rise of Kantian criticism."[24]

The ideal of system slowly invaded even territories that had formerly been safe for casuistry. Even in the Jesuit colleges, where a balanced exposition of Aquinas and cases had earlier prevailed, the teaching of moral theology and philosophy began to be affected by the Cartesian demands for geometrical clarity and system. Although a pupil of the Jesuits, Descartes' attempt to have his books introduced as texts in the Jesuit colleges had been rebuffed: his old teachers harbored suspicions about the orthodoxy of his thinking and about the merits of his method. But Descartes had time on his side. By the end of the seventeenth century textbooks had begun to appear that bore the marks of his method; even "case books" were written in a form that presented casuistry itself in the guise of deductive system.[25] By the early eighteenth century, then, the dominance of case analysis as the accepted means of resolving moral problems had faded, to be outshone by the Enlightenment vision of a "rational system."

True, the emancipation of many thinkers, notably in Germany, from the ecclesiastical authority of Rome, made possible an approach to moral and legal matters that was freed from canon law and its casuistry. Both Grotius and Pufendorf deliberately built systems of natural law on a purely secular basis; meanwhile, Lutheran ethics cast doubt on claims for the resolution of moral problems by anyone other than the Christian, both sinner and justified. Casuistry was originally nourished by the practice of penance and individual confession, and this Protestants no longer maintained. By contrast, the advice of Lutheran pastors and theologians was at best a pale illumination of the individual Christian conscience, informed by the Word of the Gospel. So Protestant pietism and secular rationalism alike contributed to the temporary eclipse of casuistry.

15

Philosophy and the Springs of Morality

In moral philosophy as in law, nineteenth-century writers moved away from the taxonomic variety and discrimination of case methods toward universal, systematic ethical theories. As late as the 1860s, the basic ethics text at Cambridge University was *The Elements of Morality*[1] by the Master of Trinity College, William Whewell. This book is a secular version of a traditional moral theology text. It embodies discussions of such traditional cases as Cicero's grain dealer who conceals news of the approach of fresh supplies for a starving city so as to profit from a shortage while he can,[2] and it also includes separate sections on duties of distinct kinds, arising from family relationships, promises, and contracts or the general demands of benevolence. Whewell does not deduce all these obligations from any single universal principle, any more than Aristotle treated all kinds of *philia* as calling for the same modes of conduct. These different moral considerations make their distinct demands on us, and in practice, they can often be squared with one another only by the exercise of moral perception and discrimination.

During Whewell's tenure of the ethics chair at Cambridge, the name of the position was changed: the Knightbridge Professorship of Casuistical Divinity became the Knightbridge Professorship of Moral Philosophy. When Whewell was succeeded by Henry Sidgwick, the very goals of the subject also changed, and the theoretical ambitions about which Aristotle was so skeptical came back to life.

Sidgwick thought Whewell's account of morality sloppy. Offended by the untidiness of casuistical reasoning, he looked for methods of moral argument more rigorous than those that Whewell had used. As he wrote in old age,

> My first adhesion to a definite Ethical system was to the Utilitarianism of Mill: I found in this relief from the apparently external and arbitrary pressure of moral rules which I had been educated to obey, and which presented themselves to me as to some extent doubtful and confused; and sometimes, even when clear, as merely dogmatic, unreasoned, incoherent. My antagonism to this was intensified by the study of Whewell's *Elements* which was prescribed for the study of undergraduates in Trinity. It was from that book that I derived the impression—which long remained uneffaced—that Intuitional moralists [e.g., Whewell himself] were hopelessly loose (as compared to mathematicians) in their definitions and axioms.[3]

In his own book, *The Methods of Ethics*, Sidgwick set out to remedy these theoretical deficiencies of case morality, giving back to moral reasoning abstract theoretical foundations of kinds that the concrete and pragmatic procedures of casuistry apparently lacked.[4]

This does not imply that Sidgwick saw no use for case reasoning about particular moral issues. As a young Cambridge don he was supposed to take Holy Orders, but this went against his beliefs, and as a way of resolving this acute personal quandary, he composed a careful analysis of the resulting *casus* for himself.[5] Still, he was also convinced that moral philosophers should rise above the level of specific practical cases, and engage in a critical debate about more general or "fundamental" principles. The resulting theoretical inquiries dominated the English debate about moral philosophy until after the Second World War.

For a century, moral philosophy in Britain and the United States followed Sidgwick's example. From G. E. Moore, Ralph Barton Perry, and W. D. Ross, by way of Charles Stevenson, to John Rawls and R. M. Hare, philosophers discussed abstract theoretical issues in isolation from concrete problems, practical issues, and actual circumstances. They did not reflect on right actions of specific kinds, viewed with an eye to detailed circumstances or concrete situations: rather, they set out to define the abstract relaionships between, say, the "good" and the "right" in completely general terms.[6] Thus, when F. H. Bradley taught that people from different "stations" have distinct "duties," he conceded Arisotle's distinction about the varieties of *philia*, at least in point of theory; but the point was for him merely theoretical.[7] Likewise, when other philosophers offered examples to settle the issues that divided them (e.g., "If your duty is to return a borrowed book, is it sufficient to *set yourself* to return it, or must you *ensure* that it reaches the owner's hands?"[8]), their problems were not, in practical terms, serious: rather, they served as a new way of testing the intellectual merits of rival theoretical positions. This whole discussion accordingly took for granted just what Aristotle had been careful to call into question: namely, the assumption that moral reasoning and moral concepts can be—and should be—analyzed in universal and invariable terms.[9]

So Sidgwick's philosophical project, of putting Ethics on a clear, strict, and general basis, closer to that of mathematics, gave rise to problems. How could one accept it as a legitimate program for moral philosophy without ignoring (even contravening) the insights of Aristotle's *Nicomachean Ethics*? Aristotle put forward three sets of considerations to support his view that resolving moral problems does not call for appeals to theory, but for practical wisdom:

1. In any field of argument we can look only for such kinds of exactitude or necessity as the nature of the case allows; and the practical nature of Ethics makes it inappropriate to demand mathematical exactness or formal necessity.

2. Given the concrete concerns of moral practice, Ethics is never systematic in the way abstract theoretical disciplines such as geometry and planetary dynamics are.

3. The moral claims that arise in practical situations depend on the detailed circumstances of individual cases, to such an extent that Ethics rests on no invariable "axioms" or other strictly "universal" generalizations.

After Sidgwick, most English-speaking philosophers treated Ethics as a *theoretical* field of inquiry, in just the way Aristotle had declared inappropriate. They viewed specific circumstances or cases as relevant to their inquiries only if they had the power to probe or test matters of general theoretical doctrine.

The striking exceptions to these generalizations about moral philosophy since Sidgwick are the pragmatists, William James and John Dewey. William James was skeptical about the theoretical programs of the moral philosophers of his time—notably, about their aiming at a "system of truth"—and he was open-minded about the value of case reasoning in ethics. In particular, he adopted an experiential approach to ethics. As he said in an address, "The Moral Philosopher and the Moral Life," given before the Yale Philosophical Club,

> There is no such thing possible as an ethical philosophy dogmatically made up in advance. . . . There can be no final truth in ethics any more than in physics, until the last man has had his experience and said his say.[10]

In James's view three questions need to be addressed. These are the *psychological* question, about the historical origin of our moral ideas and judgments, the *metaphysical* question, about the very meaning of the words "good," "ill," and "obligation"; and the *casuistic* question, about the goods and ills that men recognize.[11] As to origins, some goods and ills (James concedes) "are explicable as signifying pleasures to be gained and pains to be escaped." But not all of them have this source; and it is to the credit of "the intuitionist school" that they avoid imposing a false unity on moral psychology.[12] As to the meaning of ethical terms, for James as for Aristotle, these words have multiple meanings and can be applied wherever conscious agents have dealings with one another or with the world.[13]

> They mean no absolute natures, independent of personal support . . . [and] have no foothold or anchorage in Being, apart from the existence of actually living minds.
> Wherever such minds exist, with judgments of good and ill, and demands upon one another, there is an ethical world in its essential features. . . . Whether a God exists, or whether no God exists, in yon blue heaven above us bent, we form at any rate an ethical republic here below.[14]

But James's views are most distinctive, when he comes to the final, "casuistic" question:

> Truth [in ethics] cannot be a self-proclaiming set of laws, or an abstract "moral reason," but can only exist in act, or in the shape of an opinion held by some thinker really to be found. . . . Various essences of good have been found and proposed as bases of the ethical system. . . . No one of the measures that have been actually proposed has, however, given general satisfaction. . . . No single abstract principle can . . . yield the philosopher anything like a scientifically accurate and genuinely useful casuistic scale.[15]
> No philosophy of ethics is possible in the old-fashioned absolute sense of the term. Everywhere the ethical philosopher must wait on facts. . . .

The philosopher is just like the rest of us nonphilosophers, so far as we are just and sympathetic instinctively, and so far as we are open to the voice of complaint. His function is in fact indistinguishable from that of the best kind of statesman at the present day. His books upon ethics, therefore, must more and more ally themselves with a literature which is confessedly tentative and suggestive rather than dogmatic. . . . Treated in this way ethical treatises may be voluminous and luminous as well; but they can never be final, except in their abstractest and vaguest features; and they must more and more abandon the old-fashioned, clear-cut, and would-be "scientific" form.[16]

However, William James's example was not widely followed, and a more "old-fashioned, clear-cut" program for moral philosophy kept its charms. Even after the Second World War, most philosophers in Britain and America viewed Ethics, and the "meaning" of moral terms, from a theoretical standpoint, and still insisted, as late as the 1950s, that substantive issues were not their business.[17] Moral philosophers, they claimed, are concerned with "meta-ethics": with the general character of moral judgments and attitudes, as such, not with the specific characters of their objects. It is their task to provide a sound constitutive account of how judgments and attitudes can be identified as "moral," and contrasted with, for example, matters of law or technique, politics or etiquette. The boundaries that separate law from morality, etiquette, or technique are conceptual not substantive; so it is not of any concern to philosophers whether a particular moral judgment has to do with someone being willfully cruel to a child or merely with someone who is wearing too brightly colored a tie. Their concern is not with the specific acts or objects that are the targets of moral judgments, but with the general meaning and function of moral judgments themselves.[18]

A few philosophers, such as Henry Aiken, continued to champion the approach of James and Dewey,[19] but the philosophical current has begun to flow in significantly new directions only recently. Alasdair MacIntyre's book, *After Virtue* repudiates the mid-twentieth-century "meta-ethical" tradition; and others who have written about medical ethics and related fields since 1960 have also been driven in more substantive directions.[20] Still, few have challenged head-on the central agenda of moral philosophy since Sidgwick. One of these rare exceptions is Bernard Williams: in his book, *Ethics and the Limits of Philosophy,* he denies that we can derive practical guidance about specific kinds of cases from purely general ("analytical") definitions of ethical concepts, of the kind typical of British philosophical ethics since Sidgwick and Moore; and he will not let moral philosophers off the hook by allowing them to disclaim responsibility for substantive moral positions. Instead he argues, philosophical ethics can make a practical contribution to the current moral debate only if it contents itself with a less ambitious program of inquiry and takes on well-defined and circumscribed problems.

Does this mean that Bernard Williams endorses any proposal to revive the methods of traditional casuistry? As he sees, this is one way in which his argument might be read. But Pascal's legacy is still powerful; and in response, he is as wary as any eighteenth-century preacher about the uncertain implications of casuistical reasoning. About the parallel between case law and case morality implicit in the casuists' methods of argument, for instance, he says:

> [This view] is encouraging to objectivist views of ethics, since the core cases are given in an understanding of . . . ethical terms, and their application to hard cases, though it is a contentious and ethically fraught matter [and it] is constrained by rational criteria of what is and what is not an adequate similarity to the core cases. There can be rational discussion whether a given extension of the term properly bears the spirit or underlying principle of its application to the core cases. . . .
>
> Arguments in this style are, in the Catholic tradition, known as arguments of casuistry (the unfriendly use of that term was a deserved reaction to devious uses made of this technique).[21]

So far, so good as a summary of the history presented in this book. But Bernard Williams has reservations:

> The trouble with casuistry, if it is seen as the basic process of ethical thought, is not so much its misuse as the obvious fact that the repertory of substantive ethical concepts differs between cultures, changes over time, and is open to criticism. If casuistry, applied to a given local set of concepts, is to be the central process of ethical thought, it needs more explanation.
>
> It has to claim that there are preferred ethical categories that are not purely local. They may be said to come from a theory of human nature. . . . They may be said to be given by divine command or revelation. . . . An exponent of the casuistical method could perhaps fall back simply on the idea that the categories we prefer are the ones we have inherited. This has the merit of facing an important truth, but it will not be able to face it in truth unless more is said about ways in which those categories might be criticized.

How well founded are these reservations, and how are we to meet them? One thing can be said at once: the "more explanation" for which he calls does not have to be given *from outside* the casuistical tradition, let alone in terms of abstract, general philosophical theory. As we saw, procedures for criticizing the core categories of moral practice are *built into* the established traditions of case reasoning in all civilizations and cultures. Questions about "ways in which those categories might be criticized" are, thus, not external to casuistry: they are part of casuistry's own agenda. Nor is the assumption that these categories are "not merely local" based on general or abstract arguments: it rests, rather, on the practical overlap between the ideas of Ciceronian ethics, Christian casuistry, Jewish rabbinics, and the Islamic *shariya*, and the methods of internal self-criticism that might bring them still closer in fact.

Nor do Bernard Williams's references to "human nature" and "cultural inheritance" rest on theoretical abstractions: rather, they remind us that living moral traditions have the capacity to respond to cultural variety and historical change without lapsing into dogmatic absolutism or naive relativism. No doubt, as he says, these important questions need more explanation. But, as in case law jurisprudence, that "more" can be dealt with, or decided, only in the context of the actual procedures of case argument which the traditions of practical moral reasoning themselves provide.

DEFINING THE SCOPE OF MORALITY

The effects of Sidgwick's work on subsequent moral philosophy are puzzling because they put us back where we were at the beginning of these inquiries—in a stand-off between two established modes of ethical argument: a *theoretical* mode, which rests on general rules or principles, and a *practical* mode, whose starting points are specific circumstances. These modes of thinking about ethical theory and moral practice are in competition, however, only if it is assumed that general ethical theories "entail" the correctness or incorrectness of particular judgments about specific practical problems; and there is no more reason to believe that this is the case in Ethics than it is in, say, Medicine.[22] To recall: taken by themselves, general biological theories do not *prove* that particular clinical judgments by practicing physicians are correct or incorrect. Nor can theoretical positions in moral philosophy *entail* solutions to particular practical problems. Each field of knowledge has its own kind of exactitude and necessity and calls for its own kinds of theory. So at this point we must ask what other roles there might be in Ethics for theoretical analyses, universal principles, and other kinds of abstract generalizations.

Three possibilities present themselves:

1. Philosophers may be concerned with "boundary drawing": that is, with defining and delimiting the respective scopes of law, technique, morality, and other practical enterprises.[23]
2. Second, they may be aiming at "redressing balances": that is, with criticizing their predecessors' analyses with an eye to problems that are currently prominent or urgent, for historical or social reasons.
3. Again, their goal may be to "make out a case for morality": presenting the central considerations and concerns of ethics so as to show their substantive (not formal) coherence, and help them to carry conviction.

Let us look at a few examples of these approaches taken from the history of moral philosophy, beginning in the late eighteenth century, with Immanuel Kant.

Even now some scholars still take Kant's "categorical imperative" principle to be intended as the primary axiom in a practical moral system: as requiring us to resolve moral problems in real-life situations by taking the facts of each case as "values" of the "variables" in his principle, and "deducing" solutions to our problems as its necessary consequences.[24] Yet such readings are surely anachronistic. Not for nothing does Kant call moral and other practical imperatives "maxims." In doing so he places himself in the practical tradition of Aristotle, Cicero, and the casuists, rather than the theoretical inheritance of Plato and the moral geometers. And that, indeed, is the right context in which to consider him. The illustrations he gives to explain the notion of "universalization," for example, parallel the examples used in Cicero's *De Officiis*,[25] whereas the terms in which he deals with the problem of equivocating in reply to questioners would at once be familiar to Augustine and the English Catholic recusants.[26] So we cannot see Kant, any more than Aquinas or Aristotle himself, as a philosopher who dreamed of turning Ethics into a formal branch of *episteme*.

True, in his early *Lectures on Ethics,* Kant did not sharply distinguish analyses of the philosophical foundations of ethics from substantive moral opinions.[27] But later, when he wrote his mature *Metaphysic of Morals,* he clearly acknowledged the difference between these two things; and as his analytical discussion went along, he broke off from time to time, to interject what he called "casuistical digressions" dealing explicitly with specific kinds of cases.[28] Given this distinction, we may ask: "Supposing that Kant's ethical theory is *not* meant to establish a body of axiomatic moral rules, or to establish a rational code of substantive morality, what purpose did philosophical ethics have for him?"

First and foremost one may say, Kant's theory of ethics is meant to map the frontiers of the moral realm by showing the differences between "moral" maxims and, for example, technical instructions or legal rules. The way in which he draws boundaries between law, technique, and morality displays a clear connection with Aristotle's corresponding questions about those between *episteme, techne,* and *phronesis.*

Medieval scholars did not find it so important to draw a hard and fast line between "moral" and "legal" issues, because the same set of institutions and professional clerics were then responsible for handling both kinds of problems. An eighteenth-century Prussian academic, by contrast, naturally found it crucial to mark off the realm of morality from that of political action; while a man of pietistic Lutheran upbringing naturally distinguished the realm of moral motivation from that of personal self-interest.[29] This was most urgent in Kant's time because the standard account of human motivation was "psychological egoism." On this account human beings are not *by nature* cooperative or altruistic but act always as "inclination" leads them to. So Kant needed strong arguments to persuade his contemporaries that it was morally important to hold "inclination" at bay and allow other people's interests equal weight with one's own.[30]

In this respect Kant's boundaries between morals, technique, and law were not as timeless as they first appeared. When he marked off *moral* reasons for acting from desires, wishes, and other "inclinations," he did so in terms his contemporaries already understood. No doubt his analysis of morality was intended to be "constitutive," showing what gives moral concepts and judgments a moral (not, e.g., a legal) *meaning*, rather than "substantive," showing what motives or actions are valuable *in fact*. No doubt also he hoped that his criteria for marking off "moral" reasons from reasons of self-interest, for example, had lasting validity and were not limited to the times in which he wrote.

Still, in deciding what aspects of moral conduct and motivation he should spell out explicitly, Kant's choices show the influence of his own historical context. Despite his emphasis on "intersubjective" rationality, the terms in which his position is stated take for granted received ideas about human nature typical of his time. Later generations, less skeptical than Kant about natural human altruism, find his insistence on pitting "inclination" against "respect for reason" needlessly sharp. So even within Kant's severe and self-conscious rational system of philosophy there is thus room for "rhetorical" elements: both because of the debts he owed to his predecessors in the rhetorical tradition, such as Aristotle and Cicero, Augustine and Aquinas, and also because his arguments were not wholly timeless but "spoke to the condition" of his contemporaries.[31]

REDRESSING THE CURRENT BALANCE

In the case of other philosophers, the larger context of their work is more directly relevant to their ethical views. Their philosophical ideas are not so easily separated from the social and cultural context, and they can be viewed historically as correcting imbalances and omissions that were the products not just of the internal philosophical situation but of contemporary cultural and social factors as well. We may illustrate this second possibility by discussing two figures 150 years apart. The first is Jeremy Bentham, the late eighteenth- and early nineteenth-century social critic and founder of utilitarianism, who was an adviser to reformers and constitution makers in many countries besides Britain.[32] The other is John Rawls, the Harvard philosopher whose book *The Theory of Justice* broadens our theory of *equity* to embrace, in calculations of social fairness, not just "equal" but—where appropriate—"compensatory" justice also.[33]

It is unusually hard to tell the theoretical aspects of Bentham's works from his practical concerns. His life was that of a man for whom "to think was to act." A master theorist, he was never interested in bare abstractions but was forever engaged in practical reform: inventing new designs for prisons, improving the ballot, and so on. So in presenting his "utilitarian" theory of ethics in *The Principles of Morals and Legislation* he was not involved in abstract and speculative "pure inquiry," nor was he offering a definition of "morality" to be discussed *sub specie aeternitatis*. His mind was centrally occupied by topical questions of social practice—especially about the ways in which legislators exercise responsibility in constitutional and representative systems of government.

Why were those questions so topical in Bentham's place and time? When the Hanoverians took over the throne of the United Kingdom, they did so with the consent of Parliament, in fulfillment of the constitutional ideals that had led to the expulsion of the Stuarts in 1689. And during the eighteenth century a new form of British monarchy began to develop, in which the king's former absolute authority over legislation and policy making was gradually eroded, to the benefit of ministers and Parliament.[34] In earlier times ministers had been the king's "servants" in fact, not merely in name. Parliament, likewise, was at most a channel by which the people were free to petition the monarch, not to impose their wishes on him. All the validation a policy needed was the assurance, "The King wishes it."[35] By Bentham's time liberal-minded people in Britain were no longer happy to accept "the King's wish" as law without more ado. In their eyes policy required deeper justification, so new arguments entered the discussion of laws, policies, and institutions. The question ceased to be "Who says?" and became "To what good?"; and the task of judging the merits of laws and policies fell increasingly to the people's elected representatives in Parliament.[36]

The virtues of representative government are so taken for granted nowadays that we forget what a radical and subversive idea it was two centuries ago. From the start the thesis that ordinary citizens are free to criticize the sovereign's decisions in moral terms,[37] or to subject the results of his actions to an ethical appraisal, was a revolutionary one; and this notion has still not been fully digested in some countries.[38] Taken in its social context, utilitarianism was not an abstract intellectual theory but a powerful political weapon. Jeremy Bentham's *Principles of Morals and Legislation* was not an analysis of "right" and "wrong," "good" and "bad" in abstract, general terms: rather, it showed how the happiness of citizens can be made relevant to legislative decisions about laws and policies, customs and institutions. In short, the book considered not "the principles of morality" *tout court* but the specific ways in which "moral principles" should direct a legislature's activity.

We can make a parallel point about Rawls' book. At first glance this is to be read as one more attempt (despite Aristotle's protests) to give a timeless, universal account of the central concepts of social ethics, justice, and fairness. Rawls is not a prominent crusader for social reform; so, unlike Bentham's *Principles*, his book does not carry a political message on its face, and we may naturally read his position in theoretical rather than in practical or political terms. But in doing so we once again run up against the chief difficulties that have faced our whole inquiry:

> What does Rawls tell us about the *intrinsic scope and limits* of his argument? What *specific kinds* of practical issues, cases, and circumstances does his analysis cover? And what exactly do his conclusions imply about those practical cases and issues?

It is less easy to answer these questions from *A Theory of Justice* than to answer the corresponding questions about Bentham. Nowhere does Rawls show how his theoretical novelties—the "original position," the "veil of ignorance," and so on—allow us to resolve practical problems that we could not deal with before.[39] So his arguments are closer to Kant's than to Bentham's, and his philosophical aims are more "constitutive" than they are political. No doubt current moral conceptions embody an ideal of *impartiality*,[40] and Rawls's notion of the "veil of ignorance" helps unravel the implications of this ideal.

Still, assuming that moral problems demand "impartiality" of one and the same kind, in all cases and situations alike, can lead us far astray; so Rawls does not escape from the need to answer Aristotle's questions.[41] There are, in fact, good reasons for thinking that the kind of "impartiality" embodied in Rawls's notion of the "veil of ignorance"—the belief that any truly *moral* argument has a form that will be equally powerful if all the names and identities of the parties to the issue are interchanged, so that whatever goes for Mr. A will, all else being equal, go for Ms. B or Baby C too—has only a limited relevance to moral practice.

In the actual affairs of life we acknowledge important differences between our moral relations with our families, intimates, and immediate neighbors or associates on one side and our moral relations with complete strangers on the other. In dealing with children, friends, and colleagues we expect—and are expected—to recognize their individual personalities and tastes and make allowances for these in our dealings with them; and we try our best to tailor our actions to our perceptions of their current moods and plans. In dealing with the bus driver, the sales clerk, the hotel barber, and other casual contacts, there is usually no basis for making these allowances and no chance of doing so. In transient encounters our moral obligations are limited, anonymous, and chiefly negative: namely, not to act offensively, violently, or deceitfully.

In "the ethics of strangers," accordingly, respect for *rules* is all, and the chances for *equitable discretion* are few and far between. By contrast, in "the ethics of intimacy" discretion is all and the relevance of strictly impersonal rules is much reduced. For some serious moral thinkers, indeed (notably Tolstoy) only the ethics of intimacy is properly called "ethics" at all. For them, impersonal matters of, for example, state policy fall outside the moral realm. This view may seem to us today exaggerated and extreme; but, if taken as a general theory of justice or morality, Rawls's view is just as extreme and exaggerated in the opposite direction.

In dealing with our casual acquaintances and unidentified fellow citizens, we may rightly make impartiality a prime moral demand; but among intimates a certain discreet partiality is only equitable, and surely not "immoral." By giving all his children exactly the same amount of time or attention and buying them all monetarily equivalent Christmas presents, regardless of their tastes, needs, and bents, a father shows not the clarity and purity of his ethical thinking, but rather, the confusion and insensitivity of his moral feelings. And while any system of philosophical ethics that appeals above all to universalization, impartiality, and similar considerations—and Rawls's "veil of ignorance" is only one of a family of similar accounts—may be wondrously *fair*, it will also be essentially an ethics of the relations between people who are strangers, not only to each other but to themselves.

It is a mistake, then, to generalize John Rawls's theory or assume that it applies equally well to moral issues of all kinds, in all contexts. Far from being a comprehensive account of all moral thinking or reasoning, this theory fails to acknowledge the specific features of interfamilial and similar relations (modes of *philia*) which make psychological perception, equity, and discretion morally indispensable, and focuses instead on those considerations that typically apply in relationships between strangers. Within the realm of political moral- ity—especially in a country committed to democratic proce- dures—"justice" may come very close to "fairness." In a family, business partnership, or other similar context, equity is the most important aspect of justice, and equating justice with fairness—let alone "equality"[42]—quickly becomes double edged.

So much for the moral issues that Rawls's theory does *not* cover: those in which equitable discretion outweighs anonymous prin- ciples. Suppose, then, that we look instead at the issues about which his account is most helpful and illuminating. One urgent and topical issue that Rawls's book was clearly addressing when it was first published is the problem of racial inequalities. It emphasized the need to accept a *compensatory* element in calculating what is "just, fair and right," which would not have had the same urgency for any other generation; and the relevance of his argument to disputes about "affirmative action" is too plain to be denied. The history of American racial discrimination showed that in the social aftermath of slavery, absolute equality of administrative treatment might not be a universally adequate measure of fairness, so that any account of moral philosophy that totally equated justice and equality failed even to meet the proper demands of the contemporary political situ- ation. By his timely extension of "justice" to include certain com- pensatory elements, Rawls spelled out a moral basis for the political reforms that were meant to undercut the social and economic lega- cies of North American slavery.

Key social concepts are always likely to be refined and redefined in response to economic and social changes. So today we can no more define the term "justice" out of Plato's *Republic* alone than Jeremy Bentham could base his account of the notion on Blackstone's *Commentaries* alone. Like Bentham's *Principles of Morals and Legislation*, John Rawls's *Theory of Justice* is a document the full mean- ing of which may be recognized only by paying attention to the con- text of its publication. Its author presents it as "the" theory of jus- tice—that is, as a uniquely correct analysis of a concept that is, by implication, *timeless* and *universal* —but instead it turns out to be both a product of its time and one that gives an account of justice that fits only certain specific kinds of cases. Rather than being time- less, it takes a historically developing concept of "justice" and extends it to meet the social and political needs of a new age. And rather than being universal in its scope, it illuminates only matters of "anonymous" morality —namely, the morality of general social and political issues—and throws no direct light on the other familiar problems of justice that arise between people, such as colleagues and family members, who are closely known to one another.

RHETORIC AND THE SPRINGS OF MORAL ACTION

If general, abstract theories in moral philosophy are read against their historical and social backgrounds, they will need to be understood not as making *comprehensive and mutually exclusive* claims but, rather, as offering us *limited and complementary* perspectives on the whole broad complex of human conduct and moral experience, personal relations, and ethical reflection. So interpreted, none of these theories tells us the whole truth (even the only fundamental truth) about ethical thought and moral conduct. Instead, each of them gives us part of the larger picture we require, if we are to recognize the proper place of moral reflection and discussion, ideas and rules, in the world of human interactions and in our relations to the larger scheme of things.

Keeping this point in mind, we can restate the contrast between the two traditional accounts of moral argumentation in new terms. As we saw at the outset, those who take a *geometrical* view of moral reasoning and put their faith in universal, eternal, and unchallengeable principles believe that such principles will provide "knockdown" arguments for demolishing their opponents' positions and so settling all moral disputes. On the more general philosophical level, correspondingly, they assume that all of these principles can be deduced from some comprehensive *super*principle that captures all essentials of moral action and reflection in a single formula.[43] So a "demonstrative" model of practical moral reasoning leads naturally on to an "axiomatic" view of theory in philosophical ethics.

By contrast, those who take a *rhetorical* view of moral reasoning see general rules and principles as bearing on limited classes of problems and cases alone. They do not assume that moral reasoning relies for its force on single chains of unbreakable deductions which link present cases back to some common starting point. Rather (they believe), this strength comes from accumulating many parallel, complementary considerations, which have to do with the current circumstances of the human individuals and communities involved and lend strength to our conclusions, not like links to a chain but like strands to a rope or roots to a tree. Meanwhile on the more general level, a "cumulative" view of practical moral reasoning goes naturally with the rejection of "axiomatic" theories of moral philosophy in favor of a more complex and pragmatic view of ethical theory.

In this respect John Dewey joined William James in looking beyond the traditional search for ethical "superprinciples" to the broader context of value judgments and the resolution of moral problems. Both of them saw the philosopher's task as being to lend credence and clarity to our moral ideas and habits of thought by setting them into their human and natural backgrounds. For Dewey as for Aristotle, the preoccupation with demonstrative arguments, deductive certainty, and fundamental "axioms" that was characteristic of general philosophy since René Descartes, and of moral philosophy since Henry More, had encouraged philosophers to abandon a concrete appreciation of particular circumstances in favor of an abstract understanding of general theories, and in so doing had enthroned *episteme* where *phronesis* ought to be. Instead of continuing the attempt to found ethics on axiomatic superprinciples, philosophers would do better to learn about the complexities of human life from the novelists and dramatists, statesmen, political reformers, and others who have reflected deeply on our actual experience.[44]

Ever since Descartes, Pascal, and More in the seventeenth century, especially since Sidgwick criticized Whewell's *Elements of Morality* for its illogical untidiness, philosophers have been drawn to the simpler of these two research programs for philosophical ethics. One of these looks for underlying axioms or superprinciples to provide the theoretical unity beneath the diversity of moral practice and experience. The other accepts the complexity and concreteness of moral experience at its face value, and assembles a composite and nuanced picture that can find room for all the distinct and separate ways in which moral problems arise, and are resolved, in the course of our individual and collective lives.[45]

If moral philosophers tend to be coy about mapping the complexity of practical experience, the same is not true of the moral theologians. Thus in texts on moral theology we find general theories of a third kind, which set out to make the leading features of moral thought familiar and convincing and so release the natural springs of moral action. Here we may consider, as one illustration, a modern (but pre-Vatican II) manual of Roman Catholic moral theology by Dom Odo Lottin.[46] Like earlier theologians, Father Lottin divides virtuous and sinful conduct into several specific types and discusses each of these separately, but he also deals with certain more general theoretical issues. In discussing these general points he takes particular judgments about specific actions and modes of conduct as a starting point and considers how those specific judgments look when related to other, broader notions and classifications. In one context, for instance, he classifies the modes of action *d'après les vertus Évangéliques*, in another context he discusses them *d'après le Décalogue*; in a third, *d'après le vertu de charité*, and so on. And aside from all these different headings and classifications of "deadly sins," "cardinal virtues," and the rest, he is ready to give our practical ideas about morality a doctrinal background and justification by finding for them scriptural warrant and authority, or presenting them as being many different expressions of the general maxims about "Christian love."

How far, then, are these theological discussions truly "theoretical"? Or is it pretentious to apply that term to them? Granted, although they are in comparatively general terms, the structure that they bring to the moral debate never takes it far away from the level of everyday conduct. Still they have two merits, which reflect their Aristotelian roots:

1. They avoid bringing more generality to such questions than the nature of the case permits. Rather than imply that all virtues share a single underlying justification, they see ethics as having multiple and complex contexts.

2. They present their "theories" not as mutually exclusive but as complementary. Instead of claiming that their accounts are logically inconsistent rivals, of which one alone is correct, they readily acknowledge that these accounts are parallel and rhetorically compatible alternatives.

If "theories" in moral theology were opposed to one another as a matter of *logic*, supporters of any one account would then be intellectually obliged to forswear all the others. But because the points at issue between them rest, rather, on considerations of *rhetoric*, the only question left to answer is, "What makes appeals to one of the accounts cogent and appropriate on one particular occasion, while appeals to another will carry more conviction on a second occasion?"

A full presentation of any system of moral theology will thus seek to relate morality not only to the central beliefs of the given religious denomination but also to a larger shared pattern of doctrine, embracing also associated ideas about virtue and character, nature and rationality. In practice theologians rarely have occasion to spell out "the whole story": in a particular situation, defined by different preoccupations, it is usually more effective (both rhetorically and rationally) to focus on those aspects of the complete account which illuminate what is at stake in the situation. But if it is sometimes appropriate to discuss moral conduct or maxims in terms of the deadly sins, that does not prevent the theologians from thinking about those issues at other times in terms of the cardinal virtues; nor will it stop them from appealing to scriptural authority on a third occasion, or linking moral issues with considerations about "human nature" or "right reason" on a fourth. These parallel discussions draw attention to distinct features of human experience, moral deliberation, and personal relations, as we know them in different human and natural circumstances, and so give us complementary rather than mutually exclusive insights.[47]

To sum up, in fields of concrete particular experience, such as ethics and clinical medicine, abstract universal questions rarely have unique answers. The philosopher's mission may be to reflect on different fields of experience in the most general *possible* terms; but this is not to say that he must do so only in *completely* general terms. Rather, in each fresh field of experience he must address the most general questions that are consistent with *the nature of the field*; and in ethics this means that the degree of generality we can aim at is limited.[48] Novelists and others may frame some rough moral generalizations about broad kinds of human actions and motives—for example, treachery or innocence—but except for a few authors such as Iris Murdoch, these rarely involve deep analytical or theoretical insight, and they often rise scarcely above the level of homespun maxims such as "Honesty is the best policy." Meanwhile problems of moral appraisal, merit, or obligation arise out of experience in actual practice on occasions and in ways that need to be looked at in all their relevant detail. Like the clinical judgment of a perceptive physician, moral wisdom (*phronesis*) "speaks to the condition" of a particular agent, acting in a specific situation.

Every well-founded ethical theory carries conviction on some occasions, in some circumstances, applied to problems of some kinds; but no theory has a monopoly in all situations or over all kinds of problems. Philosophical accounts of morality are thus complementary not opposed, in the way that Aristotle's *topoi* (rhetorical commonplaces and patterns of substantive argument) are complementary, not opposed. The objection to thinking of ethics as a "science," presented by pragmatic philosophers from Aristotle to William James, are as strong as ever. The dream of capturing all our moral ideas about good and bad character, right and wrong decisions, noble and base actions, or free and slavish societies in a single geometrical system is as much a delusion today as ever. What patterns of argument are appropriate in dealing with any particular kind of problem must nowadays, as always, be judged *contextually* with an eye to the specific case at issue.

It does not follow that in ethics we cannot hope to develop theories *of any kind*. The exact sciences have no monopoly on *theories*, nor do all theories take the form of deductive, quasi-geometrical *systems*. We shall, indeed, better recognize what kinds of theory moral reflection admits of by taking as our objects of comparison enterprises other than natural science. Consider, for example, how two attorneys may discuss what strategy to employ in arguing an injury claim before the court. One decision they need to make is what "theory" to follow in presenting the case to the judge or the jury:

> Given this particular fact situation, is it best to rely, say, on tort arguments, or should we make out our case on a contract or agency theory?

The choice between tort theory and agency theory is not the kind of all-or-nothing choice familiar in moral philosophy. We are not facing two rival accounts of civil liability for personal injuries, each of which claims to provide one and only one correct view relevant to *every* kind of injury case. Rather, the choice is plainly a topical one: to decide which among a number of possible but complementary standpoints one can most effectively use to present the facts of *this present* case.

No one questions that in some kinds of personal injury cases—for example, those alleging willful injury or negligence—tort theory is an appropriate framework for argument. Nor does anyone doubt that in some other kinds of cases, such as those in which the injury was caused by the actions of an employee, agency theory provides the more appropriate framework. In problematic or marginal situations, indeed, the choice of standpoint (or "theory") can be ambiguous. It is because of this ambiguity that such situations give rise to arguable "cases" at all. In such situations, then, one urgent question for a trial attorney is,

> Which of the available theories is the most cogent, and the most likely to carry conviction, in presenting the facts of the present case to this particular court?

In the field of law, accordingly, the "rhetoric" of any case—how it can be presented *most persuasively*—in no way conflicts with its "merits"—that is, the *rational strength* of the relevant arguments. In practical enterprises such as civil law, that is, the role of "theory" is, at one and the same time, *both rational and rhetorical*.

Far from being inescapably opposed, the claims of "reason" and those of "rhetoric" are therefore natural allies. In some situations rhetorical arguments may be criticized as distracting attention from the claims of rationality, but in other situations they can equally be used to ensure that "rational" claims obtain a proper hearing.[49] So, the practical question for our trial attorney is, "Which set of terms is the most persuasive vehicle for presenting clearly the legal merits of this case?" Any trial attorney who fails to present the legal merits of a case as persuasively as he knows how accordingly acts in a way that simultaneously fails both rationally and rhetorically.

If this is true in the field of law, however, why should it not be true in ethics also? Exercising moral judgment in particular circumstances and cases is surely a sufficiently similar enterprise to, say, practicing as a trial attorney for the two activities to share many of the same basic methods. Certainly when Aristotle sets ethics and rhetoric alongside each other, he does not imply that all moral discourse is *"merely* rhetorical"—that is, designed to persuade a hearer of things for which no sufficient reasons have been presented. Instead he insists on two points for which our own inquiries have given us strong support:

1. The patterns of argument (*topoi*) used in discussing and resolving moral difficulties are not so many rival intellectual theories, of which one and only one gives a universally correct general analysis of morality and moral reasoning. Rather, they are complementary practical theories, each of which is relevant to some specific types of moral problems.

2. Decisions about which practical theory, perspective, and pattern of argument will best allow us to resolve any particular problem

can only be made in the context and with an eye to the detailed circumstances of that particular problem.

On this reading the continued relevance of Aristotle's position is easy to illustrate. Anyone who is acquainted with such active fields of moral discussion as medical ethics soon realizes that "consequentialist" arguments (appeals to the prospective consequences, effects, or results of a problematic course of action) carry more weight in some kinds of cases than they do in others. The same holds for appeals to "patient autonomy"—that is, the rights of the sick to make crucial decisions about their treatment—or "professional scruples"—the right of any physician to abstain from medical procedures that offend their consciences, etc. All these appeals are persuasive, and carry conviction with informed hearers, only when the circumstances of the particular case create an appropriate occasion for an argument of that specific kind. In ethics as in law, particular patterns of argument depend for their force not on making comprehensive or mutually exclusive claims to *universality*; rather, their force comes from earning a place in the accepted armamentarium of moral arguments, when applied to a limited range of *particular* cases.[50]

In philosophical ethics and moral theology alike, in short, "moral theories" operate on a number of distinct levels. At one extreme, their appeal is one of intellectual aesthetics. Some philosophers, such as Henry Sidgwick, find practical ethics messy or untidy and welcome the formal elegance of an nicely framed ethical analysis. Sidgwick's preference was neither eccentric nor transitory: quite recently, in a similar spirit we find Jonathan Glover complaining about the "baroque complexity" of practical morals and invoking

the aesthetic preference most of us have for economy of principles, the preference for ethical systems in the style of the Bauhaus rather than the Baroque.[51]

But this aesthetic preference operates only on an intellectual level. If we allow our passion for simplicity and elegance to affect our moral decisions in practice, we risk errors of moral judgment similar to the clinical errors that Bernard Shaw pillories in his play *The Doctors' Dilemma*. His doctors do not base their medical judgments on examining the patient: instead they assume that his illness is the one in which they themselves specialize, and urge the corresponding treatment. Yet anyone suffering from serious illness rightly prefers a physician who takes his clinical condition as he finds it—complexities and all—and views with suspicion any specialist who lets his theories oversimplify his diagnosis.

Those who consider moral problems in practice likewise need to beware of oversimplifying their judgments on the basis of elegant but limited ethical theories. To quote the Fourth Lateran Council again,

> Let the confessor be discrete and careful, in the manner of an experienced physician . . . diligently inquiring about the circumstances of sinner and sin, so that he might understand what advice to give and what remedies to apply, using different experiments to heal the sick.[52]

Like the physician, who assembles a "full medical history" before he arrives at a confident diagnosis, the moral confessor is exhorted to delay any final judgment until it is clear that he has the "whole story" about the relevant circumstances of the actor and actions in question.

At the other extreme, general ethical theories have a power to touch our hearts as well as our brains: they act on us (in psychological jargon) "affectively" as well as "cognitively." Between appeals to natural reason, cardinal virtues, and scriptural authority, the operative differences are thus not ones of intellectual cogency alone. In different contexts, arguments of different sorts have power to carry conviction with us, win our allegiance, and mobilize our springs of moral action.[53] These two extremes are joined by a spectrum of cases that embraces many intermediate examples.

The term "utilitarianism," for instance, covers not merely one theory but a whole family of doctrines. On the theoretical level it refers to a *philosophical* theory, which relates our moral concepts to the results, outcomes, effects, or consequences of the actions that it analyzes. On a somewhat more practical level, another version of utilitarianism played a part in the history of *economics*. The "mathematical psychics" of Francis Edgeworth which fathered mathematical economics, for example, grew out of the philosophical utilitarians' "hedonic calculus," and G. E. Moore's ethical theory of "ideal utilitarianism" gave John Maynard Keynes the impulse to explore the theories of probability and economic good.[54]

At the practical extreme, the historical utilitarianism of Jeremy Bentham and his associates was frankly political: it underlay the program of constitutional and social reform on which much of nineteenth-century British liberalism was constructed. Like a skilled trial attorney, Bentham sought both to convince and to persuade: he offered voters and legislators powerful political arguments in the hope of moving them to act. Given his own severe tastes, the *Theory of Morals and Legislation* did not, perhaps, read much like a sermon in itself; but utilitarian arguments soon became the staple rhetoric of liberal reformers and politicians.

By contrast, at the theoretical extreme, the philosophical arguments of Immanuel Kant appear hardly at all context-dependent and rhetorical; yet even Kant "spoke to the condition" of his contemporaries. When he rejects *inclination* in favor of *respect for reason*, for instance, he endorses the standard eighteenth-century view that altruism is not an inborn part of human nature; and his claim to a uniquely "rational" account of morality is justified only if that denial is securely based. Although Kant's agenda for philosophy has an a priori character, his analysis of moral reasoning thus turns out to rest, like that of Aristotle or Aquinas, on factual assumptions about human nature. In choosing the terms he did to differentiate morality from expediency and self-interest, he was not, after all, making abstract, context-free statements whose meaning spans the intervening centuries without any need for historical interpretation. Rather, he was presenting a rhetorical case directed at reasonable eighteenth-century readers which questioned current theories about a moral *sentiment* and sought to rest the cogency of moral maxims on their *rational* merits instead. Regardless of its purity, therefore, Kant's moral theory (like Bentham's) served as a timely exaggeration by focusing attention on only those aspects of ethics that addressed the presuppositions of his time.

Finally, the terms we choose to discuss the most general issues in either moral theology or philosophical ethics influence the *spirit* in which we address the problems of moral practice and the priorities embodied in the ways we resolve those problems. Philosophers and theologians from different schools may share similar casuistical taxonomies. But viewing the *point* of ethics in general as directed, say, to "avoiding harming other people" is one thing, but it is another to see it as "fulfilling human nature"; while it is another again to regard it as "promoting welfare," or "acting as individual members of a virtuous community," or "doing God's Will." So when we deal with difficult cases, different *theoretical* approaches may still affect the marginal considerations that determine how we reconcile conflicting and ambiguous demands.

These theoretical differences imply different ways of thinking about the *point* of morality and relating our moral perception to a vision of humanity, and of the place of human beings in the natural world.[55] In our experience of moral and practical life what ultimately carries conviction, and activates our moral "springs of action," is not the assurance of necessary connections between moral propositions and concepts so much as our ideas about the possibilities of human life. These alone determine the framework of ideas and assumptions within which the maxims of practical ethics are seen as "making good sense," and only the ambitions that these visions generate can move us to give those maxims full weight.[56]

Throughout these inquiries we have noticed that philosophers who approach ethics from a formal direction and explain the strong and weak points of moral argument in analytical terms alone tend to narrow their views and focus attention on a limited class of considerations and cases. Their demand that moral arguments be seen (despite Aristotle's warnings) as "chains of propositions" leads them to assume that practical arguments, in morality or elsewhere, are "valid" or "invalid" in the same ways as the theoretical arguments of Euclidean geometry or mathematical logic. But if, instead, we heed Aristotle's advice to take a more substantive and practical approach to ethics, we can broaden our view and recognize in what multiple ways moral arguments are rooted in experience. Rather than being "chains" that pull or fail to pull in one direction at a time, moral arguments form "networks" whose multiple roots and inner connections give them—in the jargon of the electronic engineers—the "redundancy" they need if they are to be provided with effective strength in practice.

For three hundred years, from the 1660s to the 1960s, the central preoccupations of moral philosophy have been *theoretical*. The attention of philosophers was distracted from the riches that exist in the archives of traditional casuistry, as a source of material for reflections on substantive moral reasoning. Those philosophers who study the common law have always been familiar with the power that legal claims derive from historical precedents. But moral philosophers have not yet recognized what light the study of historical "cases of conscience" can throw on deeper issues of moral perception and judgment.

If we go back even to Coke or Clarendon, the history of Anglo-American common law has never despised "case studies." Indeed, one can scarcely make sense of the evolution or the meaning of tort concepts without tracing the key cases by which equitable resolution of personal injury suits gave rise, successively, to concepts of "negligence," and concepts of "strict liability." The parallel historical analysis of our moral conceptions is only now at its beginning; and even so, many moral philosophers are skeptical about its relevance to their central questions.[57]

Looking through the anthropological reports and historical documents, for instance, we might ask such questions as these:

> How far have current paradigmatic, or "type" cases, of, say, benefit and injury, veracity and falsehood, changed down the centuries?
>
> In what respects, if any, do such taxonomic changes refine people's moral conceptions and improve their moral discrimination? (Attitudes toward the treatment of children or animals are fruitful topics for such case studies.)
>
> To what extent are the variations in the conception of *honor*, say, from nation to nation to be found in other moral conceptions also? Or are some shared ideas about, for example, loyalty and treachery or cruelty and kindness within the family more widespread in the actual practices of different peoples?

Philosophers who adopt a "tough-minded" antihistoricist stand claim that these issues are irrelevant to their inquiries. However, anyone who sees the point of Aristotle's account of *ta eschata* ("ultimate particulars"), or who feels the force of the historical links and rhetorical parallels between the arguments of "common morality" and "common law," can find in the riches of the various casuistical traditions a valuable and largely untapped source of material for philosophical reflection and historical analysis. The prime ambition of this book is to counter the disregard of case argument as a fruitful method of practical moral reasoning, but it will be encouraging if it also stimulates among historians and philosophers an interest in the rich store of moral arguments that have survived from the casuistical tradition.

16

The Revival of Casuistry

Since the 1960s philosophers have paid much closer attention than before to specific questions about moral practice. The historical reasons for this change are complex and still partly obscure, but they had less to do with developments within philosophy than with the challenges to authority and expertise that were evident in many other areas of life at this time. During the early twentieth century people in Britain and the United States had taken for granted a broad consensus about basic values. The urgent questions, it seemed to them, were questions of efficacy: How can we best get done those things that we all agree ought to be done? During the 1960s this consensus vanished; and even professionals whose good intentions had earlier been unquestioned (first, physicians) found their integrity being called into question. So there began a discussion of issues in professional ethics—first in medicine, subsequently in business, law, and other fields—that has continued ever since.

The medical profession had slowly achieved a moral preeminence that almost ruled out debate about medical ethics. However, the theologian Joseph Fletcher did raise serious questions, not about physicians' morals but about the quandaries created by new advances in medical care, in his pioneering book, *Morals and Medicine* (1954). The discussion widened during the 1960s with the arrival of organ transplantation and the prospect of "genetic engineering." Another theologian, Paul Ramsey, produced his important book, *The Patient as Person*, in 1970. Two research centers—the

Institute for Society, Ethics and the Life Sciences at Hastings-on-Hudson, New York, and the Kennedy Institute for Bioethics at Georgetown University, were set up at about the same time. Then in 1974, stimulated by public outcry over abuses of human rights in medical experimentation, Congress established the National Commission for Protection of Human Subjects of Biomedical and Behavioral Research.

All of this activity had its effect on philosophical ethics, too. Looking at medical ethics, it seemed to philosophers that here was a field in which the practical merits of their theories might at last be tested.[1] During the first few years of the resulting discussions, they tended to take as their starting point the general, abstract concepts of philosophical theory: in their eyes medicine was just one more terrain on which to pursue their existing theoretical campaigns. Philosophical ethics had for long been discussed in terms that assumed that *facts* (how the world *actually is*) must be differentiated and decided separately from *values* (how we think the world *ought to be*). With the 1960s this older "fact/value dichotomy" was openly challenged, and a new concreteness and particularity entered moral philosophy. So as time went on, the significance and particularity of clinical issues were better appreciated. Still, taken by themselves, disputations between "consequentialists" and "deontologists," or between Kantians and Rawlsians, were not of much help in settling vexed practical issues, such as the question, "How much responsibility should physicians allow gravely ill patients (and their closest relatives) in deciding what treatments they shall undergo?" Philosophical *concepts* may be of help in clarifying the manner and terms in which these problems are stated.[2] But in the end the debate will always return to the particular situation of an individual patient with a specific medical condition, and the discernment that is needed to reach any wise (or even prudent) decisions in such cases goes beyond the explanatory or clarifying insights of even the best theories—whether scientific insights of molecular biologists or ethical perceptions of moral philosophers.

Meanwhile, the 1960s and '70s saw people enter the moral debates about medicine, legal practice, social policy, nuclear war, and half a dozen such problems from other directions as well. The twentieth century had, of course, seen earlier discussions about the morality of war, in particular of weapons of mass destruction. This debate was triggered by the bombing of the Basque city of Guernica during the Spanish Civil War of the 1930s, and it was renewed toward the end of the Second World War by people who had scruples about the indiscriminateness of Allied bombing attacks on the cities of Germany. A classic casuistic analysis of saturation bombing was written by the Jesuit moralist John Ford in 1944. (In this respect the dropping of the atomic bombs on Hiroshima and Nagasaki only gave questions that were already imperative a sharper edge.) During the 1960s the issues broadened with the bitterly contested American intervention in Vietnam; theologians and historians such as Paul Ramsay and Michael Walzer brought traditional "just war" theory to bear on these issues, and James Childress carried further the analysis of the morality of conscientious objection.[3]

Increasingly, then, over the last twenty years serious discussions of the moral problems that arise out of issues of social conscience and public policy have moved in a taxonomic direction. As in the days of Ciceronian and Christian casuistry, a feeling for the features of moral experience that led Aristotle to put ethics in the realm of *praxis* and *phronesis*, not *theoria* and *episteme*—the specificity of moral issues, the particularity of cases and circumstances, and the concreteness of the stakes for those individual human beings who are involved in them—has reentered the moral debate. Nowadays the moral problems of public policy are not merely stated in casuistical ways: they are also debated in the same taxonomic terms, and resolved by the same methods of paradigm and analogy, that are familiar to students of common law and casuistry alike.

By now, there should be no mystery about this fact. Like the clinical problems of individual patients whose medical conditions are marginal or ambiguous, the moral problems faced by agents in marginal and ambiguous situations always take them beyond the reach of universal principles and general theories, and require them to strike equitable balances between varied considerations in ways relevant to the details of each particular set of circumstances. Now that moral considerations once again take a central place in serious discussions of public issues, therefore, it is no accident when they are dealt with by the methods of "case morality."

Modern casuistry resembles its medieval and Renaissance precursors, in both substance and methods of argument, on several levels:

1.   Similar type cases ("paradigms") serve as final objects of reference in moral arguments, creating initial "presumptions" that carry conclusive weight, absent "exceptional" circumstances.

2. In particular cases the first task is to decide which paradigms are directly relevant to the issues each raises.

3. Substantive difficulties arise, first, if the paradigms fit current cases only ambiguously, so the presumptions they create are open to serious challenge.

4. Such difficulties arise also if two or more paradigms apply in conflicting ways, which must be mediated.

5. The social and cultural history of moral practice reveals a progressive clarification of the "exceptions" admitted as rebutting the initial moral presumptions.

6. The same social and cultural history shows a progressive elucidation of the recognized type cases themselves.

7. Finally, cases may arise in which the factual basis of the paradigm is radically changed.

We can illustrate each of these features in turn using examples from the current debate about different topics.

1. In ancient moral philosophy, such as Cicero and the Stoics, the type cases that were final objects of appeal or comparison in moral deliberation and argument (Aristotle's *eschata*) were such things as willfully using violence against innocent and defenseless human beings, taking unfair advantage of other people's misfortunes, deceiving others by lying to them, damaging the community by your disloyalty, and acting—in general—inconsiderately toward your fellows. This is still the case today. Taken in isolation, appeals to these type cases rarely resolve serious moral problems on the spot, because those issues that involve one single kind of issue can scarcely be regarded as problematic. Rather, these type cases are the markers or boundary stones that delimit the territory of "moral" considerations in practice.

If all we know about some particular action is, say, that it involves willful violence to a child, nothing more is needed to call it in question on moral grounds, as any willful violence to defenseless human beings is "presumably" wrong. In a few particular cases, of course, some additional facts about the actual circumstances may enable this challenge to be met and the presumption to be rebutted: we may be convinced that in this case the violence was a legitimate and well-earned act of punishment. Unless and until this is done, however, the "burden of proof" lies on anyone who wishes to excuse an action of this kind: other things being equal, willful violence against the weak is presumably wrong. Reference to the paradigm alone settles the case and justifies the moral judgment in a direct and unproblematic way. No complex moral argument is needed to demonstrate that child abuse is wrong.

2. In problematic situations, however, the first substantive task is to agree just which basic "paradigm" best fits the circumstances in question. This is not always as easy as the simpler cases suggest. For example, one deeply contested issue of medical ethics and public policy has to do with current practice in neonatal intensive care units. Using modern medical techniques, it is now technically possible to maintain the breathing of ever smaller premature infants, to a point at which they have a fair hope of surviving on their own. In itself this is a marvelous achievement, but it has its drawbacks. To begin with, the treatment itself has certain deleterious side effects and is presumably painful; and, even when the infants survive this ordeal, they may suffer severely handicapped lives. Some of these "salvaged" children have little chance to develop into independent human beings, and they need continual attention from their families and medical caretakers. Even at birth they are already like those terminally ill patients to whom we allow the option of declining further weeks of pain and powerlessness tied to mechanical life support systems: the difference being that that premature infant has no way of exercising the choice whether to struggle on or to let itself slip away.

In this situation some pediatricians believe in good conscience that they must exercise moral and technical discrimination in deciding when to resuscitate the premature infants and when, in an extreme case, it is more merciful to let the infant die as it inevitably would have done before neonatal intensive care was invented. So in these cases, the couplet from Arthur Hugh Clough's ironical poem, *The New Decalogue*—"Thou shalt not kill, but needst not strive/ Officiously to keep alive"—acquires a bitter and topical edge. Are pediatricians to "act to preserve life" or to "mercifully refrain"? Are they to understand the general medical duty of preserving life as covering premature infants who have barely begun life in the extrauterine world and whose chance of any but a short, painful and gravely handicapped existence is slight? Or may they, rather, exercise the same discrimination in the neonatal intensive care ward that they have learned to do with terminally ill geriatric patients?

This moral choice alone, surely, would be a painful enough burden for the pediatrician's conscience. Yet neonatologists are now being put in an even more difficult position because of the terms in which their quandary is discussed in the political arena and the way in which legislation and governmental regulation are being formulated and exercised. On top of the existing hard choice between lifesaving and mercy, those who do not initiate treatment can be charged with "child abuse." Congress has passed legislation that sets the problem of withholding care from the newborn under the general heading of child abuse and neglect. In a situation in which there were already conflicting moral claims, based on the two alternative type cases of "saving life by medical means" and "avoiding the prolongation of pointless suffering," the discussion is now more confused than before, with the introduction of the third paradigm—that of "child abuse."[4]

More than anything else, where a moral argument ends depends on where it begins. What view we take of clinical neonatology depends on which paradigm we see as carrying most weight. Is a comparison between pediatric practice and child abuse convincing? Or is that line of argument morally grotesque? And even if we stay with the original quandary, "How should one balance lifesaving against mercy?" there is still a choice of paradigm:

> Is an exceedingly premature infant, which can be kept breathing by mechanical means but has only the barest chance of living a normal life, morally closer to a normal neonate, whose life should be preserved at all cost, or to a terminally ill patient, whom one may spare further suffering by declining to put them on a life support system?

Recalling our historical review of casuistry, we see that the "choice of paradigm" was most problematic in the debate about usury. This debate is still topical. Usury was first condemned in situations in which, in a subsistence economy, neighbors took advantage of the misfortunes of the afflicted (notably, poor farmers and peasants) by charging interest on their loans and dispossessing them for nonpayment. Such moneylending threatened to disrupt primitive agricultural societies and was perceived as unfair, even cruel.[5] Taking any interest on loans thus acquired a bad name—the paradigm was "theft"—and any inclination to usuriousness came to be seen as a defect of personal character. Yet commerce, industry and finance could never have developed if no way had been found to answer this challenge.

How was that done? The problem was to allow for the differences between loans involving shared risks (investments) and those involving demands for excessive return (exploitation). In commercial loans, the parties are typically free of grave social or economic inequalities: in the absence of exploitation they avoid the reproach of "usuriousness." Thrifty investors were therefore judged against a different type case or paradigm from those of usurious moneylenders; and the vice of profiting from loans changed into a virtue. Did the Church, in this way, *change its mind* about the morality of usury? That is misleading: no one ever doubted that it was immoral to make loans to the needy so as to gain power over them; so no one had second thoughts about the immorality of exploitation. What the Church recognized was a new distinction, between those loans that *were* usurious, given that the interest charged was out of proportion to the risks of the enterprise, and those that *were not* usurious, as the profit was reasonable given the risks. This was not a change of mind about the morality of "usury" but a recognition that not all loans-at-interest are clear cases of "usury." The distinction made sense only by recognizing a new paradigm.

In the last few years, the debate about usury and exploitation has revived. Thus Islamic fundamentalists, in Iran and elsewhere, have renewed medieval objections to the charging of interest as part of a broader attack on Western influences, and look for alternative ways of financing commerce and industry that (in their eyes) do less violence to Islamic morality. They see international loans from Western governments and banks as essentially exploitive, but hope to find ways of retaining elements of capitalism within their domestic economies as instruments for fostering development within the family. So the medieval debate about clever new forms of contract, aimed at circumventing moral objections to interest, is being repeated in contemporary Islam, in the hope of squaring the needs of commerce with the traditional injunctions of the *Sharī'ya*.[6]

In Western countries in the early 1980s, high interest rates together with new investments instruments such as "money funds" led savers to expect risk-free, high-interest returns on their savings, and encouraged a revival of "usuriousness." Meanwhile the loans that international banks had made to poorer countries during the 1970s, with interest rates tied to market levels, proved more extortionate than anyone ever intended. So the classic contrast, between "moral" investing and "immoral" moneylending, acquired new relevance in the modern world, and the medieval question has taken on new life:

> "Which of these two templates best fits international lending: innocent investment, which shares the risks of others, or immoral exploitation, which takes advantage of needs and afflictions?"

3. Deciding what type case, or paradigm, best applies in any given circumstance is only the first step; two other harder sets of problems then have to be faced. The first set of problems derives from ambiguities that arise at the margins of all moral descriptions. We looked earlier at the historical example, namely, the permissibility of equivocating or perjuring oneself when interrogated by officials whose authority and *bona fides* were open to question. Sixteenth- and seventeenth-century Europe was full of examples: French Calvinists under Charles IX and Louis XIV, English Catholics under Queen Elizabeth, Anglicans under the Commonwealth knew from experience the conflicts and penalties associated with disapproved religious beliefs. They respected the general presumption against lying or equivocating under oath, but they also knew that exceptions might be made when the authority of an interrogator was in doubt or when the lines of questioning exceeded that authority.

> Is it a "lie" to conceal information for which the questioner has no business to ask? Does a sovereign whose agents harass subjects of unorthodox religious beliefs forfeit his normal claim to loyal obedience? When loyalties are divided, how is one to tell proper obedience from justified recusance, or legitimate evasions from downright lies?

This discussion, too, has contemporary relevance. Many people today confront the same moral problems as Huguenot and Marian recusants four centuries ago. Nowadays the problem turns on communal loyalty more often than on religious belief, and the ambiguities involved imply political, not theological challenges (although this modern distinction was certainly not clear at that time). In the sixteenth century one man's "loyal subject" was another's "damnable heretic": today one man's "freedom fighter" is another's "terrorist." These moral ambiguities are only aggravated by the obsolescence of the nation-state: minorities today too often justify lying and murder by appeal to the right of "self-determination," just when the traditional forms of nationalism have elsewhere lost their former claims. So in the realm of politics, moral presumptions remain as open to rebuttal as ever. In general terms, few deny the value of loyalty to civil society: in particular cases applying this general rule unambiguously is still as hard as ever. General rules whose "presumable" implications no one doubts give rise to bitter disputes as applied in "exceptional" cases simply because they are so ambiguous.

> The presumptions created by moral rules have undoubted force in normal cases; yet just *what* circumstances are normal, and *what* the exceptions? Are Arabs in Palestine, for example, morally obliged to respect political institutions set up by the Jewish authorities of Israel, any more than English Catholics were morally obliged to betray their priests to Queen Elizabeth's interrogators?[7]

As Aquinas and Azor well understood, changes in the "circumstances" may completely change the "moral species" of an action: even actions that are "right or wrong *absolute*"—that is, paradigmatically right or wrong, *in the normal case*—may be understandable, pardonable, or even justifiable, if the circumstances are sufficiently exceptional.[8] So, we ask, "Just how can we tell what circumstances are normal, and what are truly exceptional?"

4. The second set of problems that arises when general moral rules are applied to particular cases is no less familiar and just as hard to generalize about. They spring less from the ambiguities in the practical application of a single rule than from the fact that, in one and the same case, several rules may make claims on an agent. Early on the Christian casuists recognized that a single human action may be subject to moral claims, and have effects, of more than one kind. St. Gregory spoke of the paradox and proposed the choice of the lesser evil. St. Thomas formulated this into the "principle of the double effect."

To cite a modern application of the ancient principle of "double effect": an obstetrician diagnoses an ectopic pregnancy (i.e., a fetus developing within the fallopian tube). He knows that this condition could be fatal to the mother and so operates to remove that portion of the fallopian tube in which the fetus is growing. He saves the mother's life and allows the fetus to die. This kind of "indirect killing" of the fetus does not, in Catholic teaching, constitute a prohibited abortion. Certainly the death of the fetus is regrettable; but it is the undesired and unintended side-effect of saving maternal life.[9]

These cases of "double" (or rather "multiple") effect are only one subgroup from a larger group of practical moral problems. In these cases it is hard not to acknowledge the diverse moral claims that bear on an agent's decisions: these claims are usually easy to see and to state. The hard thing is to balance off several obligations whose conflicting claims make the relevant cases the moral tragedies they are. An obstetrician is subject to two professional claims: that he preserve a mother's life, and that he deliver her infant unharmed. In a normal delivery, the same action meets both claims: in a hard one the only way to meet one claim may be to act in ways that contravene the other. For him to do nothing would be to abdicate his professional responsibilities: instead, he must handle such conflicts of moral obligation as his conscience and technical knowledge, between them, best indicate.

In medical situations moral conflicts typically spring from the fact that clinical interventions have multiple consequences—some admirable, others regrettable—and we cannot always choose the good effects in ways that avoid the bad ones.[10] But not all conflicts of obligation take this form. Elsewhere one may have to choose between, for example, keeping a promise and preventing an injury—Cicero's history of "the noble Regulus"[11]—or else between the claims of country and family—Sartre's "resistance fighter."[12] Actions affect other individuals and groups in different ways: the problem is to decide whom it is least objectionable to harm.[13] Or moral claims arising from a promise have to be weighed against the likely effects of meeting those claims: the problem is then to judge what risk of harm warrants breaking how serious a promise.[14]

At this point we may recall the parallels between practical morals and clinical medicine. In generalizing about conflicts of moral obligation we face the same temptation to *personalize* problems of moral judgment that we met in discussing the nature of clinical understanding. Conflicts can be resolved, it is sometimes said, only if all individual human agents bring their experiences and emotions to bear on problematic situations in ways they can personally "live with." This approach to moral conflicts has as much (and as little) merit as the view that individual physicians treat difficult cases best by relying on personal experience and hunches. In each case personalizing the problem of conflict underlines the need to respect any differences between the opinions that different agents conscientiously hold; and that is a real merit. But it has a counterbalancing defect as well. It ignores the fact that the agents are not always the best people to weigh their own opinions about alternative courses of action. Agents may be as conscientious as you please, but their opinions will have value only if they are informed and experienced as well. Unreflective and inexperienced people sometimes live with ways of resolving moral problems that anyone would reject if only they had more—or had more reflectively considered—experience of life.

In this respect the tasks we face in everyday moral practice are truly practical, like those of medicine, and also share the tacit character that Michael Polanyi found in the practice of natural science.[15] The heart of moral experience does not lie in a mastery of general rules and theoretical principles, however sound and well reasoned those principles may appear. It is located, rather, in the wisdom that comes from seeing how the ideas behind those rules work out in the course of people's lives: in particular, seeing more exactly what is involved in insisting on (or waiving) this or that rule in one or another set of circumstances. Only experience of this kind will give individual agents the practical priorities that they need in weighing moral considerations of different kinds and resolving conflicts between those different considerations.

5. In ethics as in medicine, this "practical experience" is as much collective as personal. The priorities that have important roles in moral reflection and practice are, in part, outcomes of the lives and experiences of different individuals; but in part, they are also the products of each individual's professional, social background. One sadly neglected field of historical research is the history of ethics—not a mere record of successive doctrines and theories but an understanding of the ways in which moral practice, with its social, cultural, and intellectual contexts, has evolved over the centuries.[16]

All of the problems we have focused on—the ambiguities involved in matching moral terms to marginal cases, the scope of the "exceptions" that entitle us to "rebut" the presumptions created by general rules, and the difficulty of reconciling different considerations in case of moral conflict—have long and rich histories. Our ways of dealing with them are not reinvented by each individual agent. Like the procedures for resolving problems in common law, these "resolutions" are the products of long-term historical processes which embody the collective experience on which we draw in addressing difficulties that face us in our own day. As an illustration, let us look and see how we decide whether the use of violence by individuals or by agents of the state is morally permissible.

Current American attitudes toward this question are intelligible only if we recall their genealogy and see them as a phase of a much longer story. The debate about *nuclear war* extends the earlier just-war debate: even those who argue that a conflict between states in which nuclear weapons were actually used would not be a "war" in the former sense of that term—given that no legitimate goal of national policy can be achieved only at the price of nuclear violence—support this claim by appealing to traditional views about the "morally defensible" goals and methods of state violence.[17] Correspondingly, the widespread consensus that *torture* is not a morally acceptable instrument of state policy—a consensus the force of which is only confirmed by the hypocrisy of the words that many governments use to deny, conceal, or gloss over the abominable deeds of their authorized agents—is the historical outcome of long-standing experience by human societies, and the evolution of this consensus deserves closer attention.

In the area of individual violence, likewise, the moral issues facing us today are recognizable successors of older issues. Even the abortive attempts around the year 1600 to justify killing in defense of honor have their modern counterpart. True, the idolized object nowadays is not honor but *property*. In the suburbs of Los Angeles, for example, apartment blocks and private homes bear signs threatening intruders with "armed response."

> Do Los Angeles householders, then, believe that it is morally justifiable to shoot (or even kill) vagrants, trespassers, or lost strangers who come to the door late at night asking for directions?

The answer to that question is not wholly clear. Most of the householders involved probably have not reflected on the meaning of their own signs.[18] The phrase "armed response" is vague enough for them to gloss over its implications euphemistically, as national governments use phrases such as "vigorous interrogation" to gloss over torture. Some householders, again, would defend the threatening signs in the way the governments of nuclear powers defend their keeping nuclear weapons—as a "deterrence"—arguing that the purpose of these threats is to prevent them from ever being put into effect. Both in the state and the individual contexts, the moral force of such deterrence arguments is dubious, and their scope is very limited. In any case, the statistics of handgun ownership in the United States make it clear that many Americans take a light view of acts of violence when performed in the defense of "real property"; and enough innocent intruders are in fact killed each year to put the sincerity of the deterrence defense seriously in question.

If we place the "armed response" case alongside the earlier example of "killing in defense of honor" and ask how our own practices will appear to historians two hundred years hence, we may find the answers sobering. Does the sacrosanct integrity of household territory so deserve protection that it overcomes the moral presumptions against individual violence and makes it defensible to kill or wound trespassers and intruders? Or have we assumed attitudes toward property that our successors will find as self-serving, ridiculous, and rhetorically exaggerated as attempts to justify "killing for a slap" nowadays appears to us?

6. Historically the moral understanding of peoples grows out of reflections on practical experience very like those that shape common law. Our present readings of past moral issues help us to resolve conflicts and ambiguities today, and our present experience will provide arguments for those who succeed us. In both common law and common morality problems and arguments refer directly to particular concrete cases; and they share a common casuistical ancestry, dating from a time when there was not yet any sharp line between law and morality.[19] In both fields, too, the method of finding analogies that enable us to compare problematic new cases and circumstances with earlier exemplary ones, involves the appeal to historical precursors or precedents that throw light on difficult new cases as they occur.

This method can provide positive guidance only if the precedents are close enough for a positive decision. Otherwise the claims of charity or equity demand an openness to novelty and a readiness to rethink the relevance and appropriateness of older rules or principles. This does not mean questioning the *truth* of those principles: they will remain as firm and trustworthy as ever, as applied to the "type cases" out of which they grow and to which they paradigmatically refer. It means only that historical novelties—social, cultural, or technological—may compel us to rethink not only the precise scope of such legal notions as *liability* and *injury* but also the exact scope of moral concepts and rules. Occasionally, we may even encounter situations so radically novel that the current corpus of rules, principles, precedents, and considerations not only *does not* but *cannot* give us definite guidance in dealing with the problems they pose.

We saw how Christian casuists modified earlier moral analyses in response to the new situation created by commerce and industry. Despite the Catholic Church's hostility toward usury, the resulting novel financial activities overcame earlier moral objections to the giving of loans at interest. During the second half of the twentieth century our moral traditions have had to be most actively reconsidered less in the financial realm than in the fields of family relations and sexuality; and it is there that we find the most striking new precedents and paradigmatic cases. These days—except out of intellectual desperation or fanatical dogmatism—few people would claim that earlier teachings give us all the guidance about family life and sexual morals that we need in our own situation. Over the last forty years we have rethought the moral basis of sexual and family relations not merely in general terms: now we also face some specific new problems that go as far beyond the earlier problems of family life and sexuality as the financial activities of the early capitalists went beyond traditional experience with loans and interest.

Given twentieth-century increases in life expectancy, availability of reliable birth control methods, and other changes—social and economic, technical and psychological—what difference do all these developments make to ideas about family and sexual relations? We shall not discuss that specific question fully here, but one thing at least is clear. In those countries where these broader changes have become securely established, middle- and professional-class people now accept patterns of householding and sexual conduct quite unlike those approved of forty years ago or more. At times the widespread tolerance of couples "living together," before or outside marriage, suggests that Western liberal societies are changing to a system of "marriage by stages," like those traditional forms that some African Catholic bishops defended at the General Synod of Catholic Bishops in Rome in late 1985.[20] Similarly, although official Roman Catholic teaching still opposes all "artificial" methods of birth control, both the practices of the laity and the pastoral attitudes of the Catholic parochial clergy are more tolerant, complex, and nuanced.[21]

The discriminations and distinctions embodied in the current sexual morality of Western Europe and North America do not represent any radical break with earlier moral considerations and attitudes. Rather, they reflect changes in the "qualifications," "exceptions," and "rebuttals" to which older rules are regarded as now subject. Nothing at the heart of the so-called sexual revolution, for instance, weakens traditional moral objections to sexual relationships that are unloving and exploitive, or to promiscuity that is divorced from true human affection. Indeed, in its constructive aspects the rethinking of

sexual morality and family life over the last thirty or forty years has
no more broken with earlier traditions of moral reflection than the
debate about nuclear weapons has cut us off from all the experience
embodied in the traditional analysis of the preconditions for a just
war. Rather, it refines a traditional analysis of sexuality and family
life further, in the light of new developments in society, technology,
and psychology.[22]

7. So far we have reviewed the substance and methods of casuistic reasoning, referring to their application to current issues. We
noted how paradigm cases create presumptions that carry conclusive weight, in the absence of exceptional circumstances. We commented on the manner in which a progressive clarification of exceptions through history may allow rebuttal of the initial moral presumptions. Now, however, we must go further and examine the
occasional situation in which the very factual underpinnings of the
presuppositions are challenged by technical or social changes. The
factual structure of the paradigm itself is, in some sense, demolished. This presents the most radical problem to ethical reasoning:
the case is literally unprecedented and so defies resolution in terms
of existing categories and generalizations. A striking illustration is
the casus presented several years ago by Professor Baruch Brody.[23]

> John has been married for eight years and is the father of three chil-
> dren. Even before his marriage he had suffered from identification
> with the other sex. Increasingly, however, he finds his male role unac-
> ceptable, and he now seeks hormone therapy and sex-change surgery
> to become a female. His wife objects, arguing that she is incapable of
> managing her family alone and is unwilling to live with him if he
> undergoes the surgery and therapy. John is unwilling to forgo the
> surgery and therapy.
>
> As John's physician, may you begin the hormone therapy at his
> request? Do you need the prior consent of his wife? If the therapy
> and surgery are completed, with or without her consent, will John still
> be married to his wife?

This case raises many intriguing issues and may provoke different moral responses from the reader. For our purposes, we shall
pick out for comment only one of the issues, leaving the rest (with
regret) untouched. The point we shall focus on is the following:

> The medical and surgical procedures of "sex change" undercut some
> of the most basic *factual* assumptions about the married state.
> Specifically, both the idea and the institution of "marriage" take it for

granted that any marriage initially contracted between a man and a woman will remain, for so long as it lasts, a marriage between a man and a woman. When we face the possibility of a marriage in which, say, the husband turns into a woman, issues arise about which neither the legal nor the moral precedents can give us clear or unambiguous guidance.

The final question posed in the scenario (namely, "After the sex change, will John still be married to his wife?") raises questions for both law and ethics. Although the two sets of questions are closely related, they may be separated and addressed one at a time. The legal contract of "marriage" establishes and endorses a relationship that confers on the two parties rights and obligations of several kinds. Morally speaking, a marriage normally implies intimacy: most often, though neither necessarily nor exclusively, including sexual intimacy. Legally, it normally involves a pooling of economic interests, assets and obligations, and so carries with it, for example, the right to be taxed jointly. The termination of any marriage requires us to consider both its legal and its moral consequences: both of them bear on the question, "On what conditions is the marriage at an end?" The moral significance of John's proposed sex change lies in his implied withdrawal from normal matrimonial intimacy, more specifically from sexual intimacy; and this prospective withdrawal prompts the question,

Is the original contract of marriage automatically *voided*? Or does it become *voidable* at the wife's insistence?

If the issue is stated in these particular terms, our moral and legal traditions are rich in relevant guidance. First, the absence or termination of sexual intimacy does not by itself void a marriage because any marriage carries with it also legal or moral rights and obligations of other kinds: familial, custodial, and fiscal. In some cases questions about marriage are easily separated from questions about sex: for instance, merely because elderly couples do not intend (or are unable) to have sexual relations, they are not debarred from marrying. Still, whenever the sexual character of a marriage is basically changed, the question of mutual consent is a morally weighty one. (If, say, one partner to a previously sexual marriage wishes to begin living celibately for religious reasons, it is morally relevant to ask if the other partner willingly consents to this change.)

With these considerations in mind, the short answer to the question, "Will John still be married to his wife after the sex change?" is "*yes*." Despite any loss of intimacy between John and his wife, and whether or not she gave formal consent to the surgery, they will initially remain married *at least* until one or the other petitions for a change of status and a court makes alternative provisions for the other aspects of the marriage: notably, to protect the interests of the children. In any Anglo-American jurisdiction, no doubt, the wife should easily obtain a decree ending the marriage on grounds of the sex change *if and when* she so petitions. But until that has happened, the marriage will remain a legal fact.

All the same, circumstances only slightly different from those stated here may raise a more extreme problem. What will the position be, either legally or morally, if the wife is content to remain married to John and even to resume sexual intimacy *after* the sex change? In the absence of any petition from the parties to the marriage, has any court the power—indeed, *ought* it to have the power—to terminate the marriage arbitrarily? Surely it will be on safe ground only if the original marriage was already invalid, as being, say, incestuous or bigamous. Given only this one factual modification, John and his wife can apparently stay married, in a lesbian union, with legal endorsement.

In light of this consequence, some readers will find it natural to ask the next question along the same line of development:

> If in those circumstances the law would be obliged to agree to *continuation* of a marriage between partners of the same sex, what then becomes of all the arguments against the *contracting* of marriages between partners of the same sex?

This final problem forcefully confronts fundamental questions about practical reasoning over moral issues. It is not a matter of working with rules, principles, generalizations, or other warrants, the force of which we have already acknowledged but whose relevance to the current case is, to some extent, problematic. Now it is no longer clear how the basic categories we worked with hitherto can be applied: the factual assumptions that provide their "backing" have been undercut, thereby putting the validity of these categories in question.

After a sex change, the everyday presuppositions built into the term "marriage" (notably, the assumption that the partners to a marriage contract have permanent and definite genders) are so deeply undercut that this term, as it stands, no longer covers all the relevant practical problems. We must now ask ourselves what its moral force is, in future, to be. Recall the pattern of analysis outlined in chapter 1:

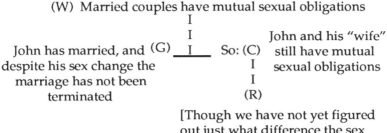

(W) Married couples have mutual sexual obligations

John has married, and (G)   So: (C) John and his "wife" still have mutual sexual obligations
despite his sex change the
marriage has not been
terminated   (R)

[Though we have not yet figured out just what difference the sex change *ought* to make]

The trouble in this case is no longer (as in conflicts of obligation) that the argument involves *too many* acceptable "warrants." The available concepts and generalizations have now failed us, as it is unclear whether John and the woman he married are still to be called a "married couple." So long as the factual assumptions built into the everyday use of the term "marriage" continue to hold without further clarifications or agreed understandings, we have no way of resolving the moral problems created by the sex-change surgery without going beyond the existing conceptions of what "marriage" implies.

If, after the surgery, John and his wife stay together *as lovers,* are we to say that they are still "a married couple"? The only possible answer to that question is surely "yes and no." Custodially, on the one hand, the matrimonial home will be kept alive and the couple's care of the three children will continue as before: sexually, on the other hand, their new relationship is one that society has not hitherto accepted as "matrimonial." At least in this class of cases, which was created *de novo* by modern medical technique, some hitherto unquestioned generalizations and rules about sexual life and family relations have lost their previously clear meaning.

Within a tradition that is committed to serious moral reflection, we have only one effective way of resolving the difficulty. Instead of letting ourselves be hypnotized by the terms and rules that have, quite properly, shaped our thought and practice about such matters up to now, we need to look beneath them to the substantive issues that underlie them and so return directly to the deepest sources of moral concern.

> Forget about "marriage," in the normal sense: that is beside the point in this case. If John and his wife stay together after his sex change, how can the deeper purposes of marriage be best provided for? In particular, in order to meet the interests of the children, can we not regard their parents' marriage as continuing just as before? Or are we so afraid of the larger consequences of sanctioning a lesbian union in this special case, that we must guard ourselves against them by dissolving the present marriage arbitrarily, against the wishes of the two partners?

Respecting the demands of basic moral concepts, considerations, and rules is fine and admirable so long as their applicability to new cases is clear, meaningful, and unambiguous. The accepted "backing" for these rules and concepts (or for the general "warrants" this acceptance implies) can certainly not be called into question without good reason. But we have to reconcile ourselves to the fact that the conditions of human life are always changing and that from time to time new historical circumstances are liable to put us in situations of moral embarrassment where we can no longer continue relying on the "common sense" and "common morality" that have served us more or less well hitherto, and are forced to reconsider the goals of moral life and reflection at a deeper level.

Using these historical and topical examples from both "older" and "newer" casuistry as our raw material, we may now summarize what they showed us about the structure and workings of practical moral argument. To return to the general points from which we started:

1. The final objects of reference in moral arguments are certain type cases or paradigms: these give rise to the "initial presumptions" that carry weight in the absence of "exceptional" circumstances.

A case in which one moral consideration alone carries any real weight and fits the circumstances without doubt or ambiguity—a case in which, say, an angry father is thrashing his child without good cause—is one in which the initial presumption stands unquestioned: "It's simply wrong for him to thrash the child so violently, and that's that!" In these circumstances, this one and only one weighty consideration can be expressed in the form of a general rule, or "warrant," and the absence of exceptional factors means that the action cannot be excused or extenuated. In this case the rule warrants an inference that is as near to a straight geometrical deduction as a practical moral argument ever gets:

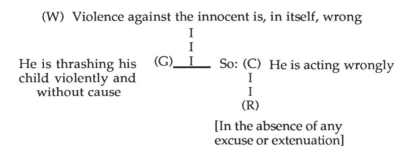

(W) Violence against the innocent is, in itself, wrong

He is thrashing his
child violently and
without cause

(G)   So: (C) He is acting wrongly

(R)

[In the absence of any
excuse or extenuation]

This is the case because (and only because) the situation is unambiguous, and displays only one relevant feature that carries moral weight.

This lack of ambiguity, however, also ensures that the case is one in which no real moral problem arises: one that we label as *unprob-lematic*. So the claim that any particular moral argument is "demonstrative," that its conclusion follows with "geometrical" certainty, implies that the case in question is "unproblematic." Conversely, if a case is one in which the moral claims involved are genuinely *problematic*, that is a sure indication that there is *no way of resolving those problems* "demonstratively" and "geometrically." Truly problematic cases, we saw, are of three types. Two of these are familiar and straightforward: they are concerned with ambiguous and marginal cases. The third is more perplexing, involving those occasional—but unavoidable—circumstances in which our basic moral categories are called into question.

To start with the two familiar types of cases:

2. In problematic cases the first task is to decide what "type cases" bear on (or might decide) the issues they raise.
3. Problems of a first kind arise when the type cases fit current problem cases ambiguously, and the presumptions they create are therefore open to serious challenge.

4. Problems of a second kind arise when two or more type cases apply to the same case in conflicting ways, and we have to decide between them.

Until we have seen which type case, or paradigm, the facts of the present case most closely resemble, there may be several possible rules, warrants, and arguments, any one of which would be demonstrative, or conclusive, in the absence of the others. The choice is not between one, formally valid inference and other, formally incoherent ones: it is between several formally valid inferences, one of which—given the substantive facts of the case—provides *the most relevant and applicable* way of dealing with the case. So the pattern of a successful argument must acknowledge the multiple possible considerations. For instance, in a marginal case:

(W) Borrowed objects should be returned after use

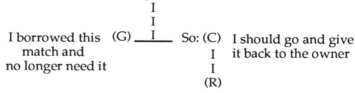

I borrowed this   (G) ___I___   So: (C) I should go and give
match and   it back to the owner
no longer need it   (R)

Except that
A used matchstick is
hardly worth the
trouble of returning

Or, in an ambiguous case—

(W) Borrowed objects should be returned after use

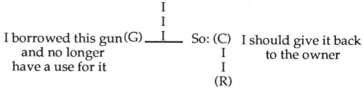

I borrowed this gun (G)___I___   So: (C) I should give it back
and no longer   to the owner
have a use for it   (R)

Except that
The owner threatens to shoot
his neighbor the moment he
gets the gun back

In morally problematic cases the solidity of the basic arguments, and the relevance of the warrants, thus depend on substantive judgments. In the first case the question is whether someone who "lends" a neighbor a match really expects to have it returned after use: in the second case, the question is what relative weight one should allow the two relevant considerations—the obligation to return a borrowed gun, and the duty to avoid being a party to violence or homicide.

How far are these substantive judgments about ambiguities and margins similar in all cultures and periods? That brings us to the next two sets of issues.

5. The history of moral practice at different times and in different cultures reveals a progressive clarification of the "exceptions" that can be admitted as rebutting the basic moral "presumptions";

6. The same historical record also shows progressive extension and elucidation of the type cases (or "paradigms") associated with those presumptions.

We discussed at particular length the examples of usury, equivocation, and the defense of honor. But we could have illustrated these historical and anthropological points just as well by considering different people's ways of thinking about and treating, for example, young children or animals.

At any stage in the development of a people and culture, experience brings them to adopt certain general opinions about the *scope*, *force*, and *relative priority* of different kinds of moral considerations. For example, "Just how conscientious does one need to be in returning borrowed objects when their monetary or sentimental value is negligible?" There is room for a *de minimis* doctrine in morality, quite as much as in law. Likewise, "Under precisely what exceptional circumstances should we think twice about returning borrowed objects at the earliest possible moment?" A little "common sense," we might say, is all that you need when you hesitate to return a borrowed gun if its owner is enraged. (People who fail to see the importance of these marginal issues are likely to be criticized as, for example, "being overscrupulous" or "having a weird sense of timing.")[24]

As we move from period to period these understandings change. Every new generation brings fresh nuances to its reading of basic moral categories, rules, and warrants: each draws in subtly different ways the lines dividing half-truths from downright "lies," joking and horseplay from "insults" and "assaults," "serious" promises from "frivolous" ones. Among different cultures and periods the range of variation is greater in some kinds of cases than in others. Ways of dealing with such centrally moral issues as violence, bodily harm, and veracity tend to be less labile and variable than ideas about marginal, class-based issues such as "honor."

In particular, cultures vary in the range of application they allow to moral claims among the members of the community. In some, those people who lie outside your extended family are not regarded as "protected persons" when it comes to, say, theft and lying. Obligations of veracity and fidelity do not apply in the case of strangers but have a force within the family that they never have outside its boundaries. This does not mean that in different cultures people take *formally* different moral arguments seriously. But it makes all the *substantive* difference in the world, in practice, who qualifies as belonging to the family for moral purposes and who does not.[25]

To return to the central theme of this whole investigation:

> 7. Practical moral reasoning today still fits the patterns of topical (or "rhetorical") argumentation better than it does those of formal (or "geometrical") demonstration.

Those who are involved in practical reasoning about moral issues soon meet the first two sets of problems that "the newer casuistry" inherits from its progenitor: ambiguities that arise at the margins of application of moral terms, and conflicts that arise between different moral claims. The sex-change example adds one further class of substantive problems: those that arise, very occasionally, when historical changes in our social relations, technical resources, and psychological understanding undercut the factual presuppositions of our earlier moral concepts and positions and force us to rethink our ideas more fundamentally.

All three kinds of problems share one common feature. There is no straightforward way of elucidating the modes of reasoning by which they are resolved so long as we continue to assume that moral reasoning must be formal and demonstrative or else not "rational" at all. Demonstrative reasoning, of the theoretical kind that leads to *episteme*—the knowledge exemplified for classical Greeks by geometrical "theorems" and "proofs"—has the kind of rigorous "validity" and "necessity" it does only because it operates *within* a system of concepts whose practical applicability and relevance are not for the moment in doubt. To recall, it is in precisely this respect that all theoretical arguments are *abstract*: their relevance to real-life instances and concrete situations has been set aside, and we are free to focus solely on relations *internal to* the theory concerned. But if we think for only a moment about the kinds of reasoning that are involved in moral practice, we remember all the things that prevent moral arguments from being "abstract" or "demonstrative" in the same ways as formal, mathematical arguments, and so make "moral knowledge"—to use that contested phrase—a matter of practical wisdom rather than one of theoretical comprehension.

It is not that practical arguments about the substantive relevance of moral considerations to particular cases are less "reasonable" or "rational" than formal demonstrations within deductive theories. Still less is it to imply that moral argumentation is based only on "personal" preferences or "subjective" matters of taste about which people are free to have their own idiosyncratic opinions. Most of the features that prevent practical reasoning about moral issues from being purely "formal" or "theoretical" hold good equally of practical reasoning about issues in clinical medicine; and despite their concrete particularity, no one would regard clinical judgments in medicine as based merely on "matters of taste." Rather, the outcome of our inquiry confirms what Aristotle taught long ago: that ethical arguments have less in common with formal analytic arguments than they do with topical or rhetorical ones. They are concerned not with theoretical relations *internal to* a system of concepts but with relating and applying those concepts *outwardly*, to the world of concrete objects and actual states of affairs.

The arguments used in topical and rhetorical discussions (we saw) conform to patterns quite different from those that govern axiomatic or other formal demonstrations. The general inferences they embody support "presumable" rather than "demonstrable" conclusions. These presumptions may be as strong as you please, but they are always subject to two kinds of qualifications, each of which is reflected in one of our sets of moral problems. To begin with, presumptive conclusions can have "certitude" only when the relevance of the concepts or terms involved is not in doubt. When the cases in question are marginal or exceptional, so that there is active doubt, the presumptions may be rebutted. ("Is corporal punishment 'cruelty to children'? Is it morally acceptable to paddle your little boy? That depends . . .") Further, parallel arguments often point to different presumptions the practical implications of which have to be reconciled. In this respect conflicts of obligation are once again a special case of practical problems generally, and the same "judgment call" may be required in any enterprise that brings several general concepts to bear on any particular concrete case or set of circumstances.

The presumptive, rebuttable character of moral conclusions does not, of course, mean that they can be disputed capriciously. In practice the most serious and prolonged ethical debates in the history of Western culture and society have been directed at questions concerning whether or not to recognize some new "exceptions" to a general moral rule. (The dispute about the moral permissibility of killing in defense of honor is again a classic example.) This, of course, was what the probabilism debate within casuistry was about. "Intrinsic" authority of an argument bore on the strength of the argument to rebut a presumption; extrinsic authority on the reputation for practical wisdom which the author of the argument enjoyed in the community of casuists. The debate over probabilism lost its course because, instead of examining closely the nature of arguments and of practical reasoning, it turned to excoriation of laxist opinion. Arguing that some novel kind of case ought to be accepted as a legitimate exception is not *in itself* "lax" or permissive. If the new case resembles a familiar class of exceptions, well and good: charges of "laxity" carry weight only when the counter-arguments have to strain after an acceptable interpretation.

Meanwhile public moral debate continues to focus on the question of how far we may enlarge the range of recognized exceptions, or how far we should shrink it. To every "permissive" argument, for admitting more exceptions to some general moral rule and so making it less rigorous, there corresponds an equally vehement "strict constructionist" plea for tightening up the application of earlier exceptions. The real issue, then, is not "rigidity *versus* permissiveness." We would all argue for strictness in certain cases and about some issues and for tolerance in other cases or about other issues. Those who tolerate new patterns of sexual and family life and are ready to enlarge the range of exceptions to moral injunctions in that area tend to reject some of the exceptions that would be allowed by other, more conservative injunctions: for example, condoning the use of guns in defense of the territorial integrity of one's home. Those who argue most strongly for the unqualified sanctity of life in the case of human embryos, conversely, tend to view capital punishment as a legitimate exception to that same principle. Cries of "Permissiveness!" are thus rhetorical in the popular sense of that word: they are heard chiefly in political contexts, against new patterns in, say, sexual relations, when they might just as easily be turned against tolerance of, for example, unrestricted handgun ownership.

True moral perception or "discernment" lies in the ability to see how and when strictness is the better course, how and when the deeper wisdom lies in tolerance of exceptions; and that ability once again requires not an abstract grasp of theoretical relations but constructive reflection about the practical lessons of concrete experience. Finally, in our third set of problematic cases, illustrated by the consequences of John's proposed sex-change surgery, all of this holds good even more surely. There the source of the problems is more radical: namely, that the circumstances of the cases in question contain elements for which all our previous experience makes no provision.[26]

Some people may still find our position in this book ambiguous. For, they ask, how far does "the new casuistry" *contradict* the traditional view of moral practice as applying universal principles from ethical theory to practical cases? Is not its actual task, rather, to match these principles to particular situations, so making itself (in the words of a recent essay by the philosopher John Arras) the "necessary complement to any and all moral theories that would guide our conduct in specific situations"?

> So long as we take some general principles or maxims to be ethically binding, no matter what their source, we must learn through the casuist's art to fit them to particular cases. But on this gloss of "casuistry," the most hidebound deductivist, not to mention the more subtle partisans of reflective equilibrium, would have to count as casuists. So defined, casuistry might appear to be little more than the handmaiden of applied ethics.[27]

Our position surely has more substance than this. One conclusion for which we argue in this book is, certainly, the one stated here: namely, the claim that *casuistry is unavoidable*. If taken alone, this is so weak a conclusion that no moral theologian or philosopher with abstract tastes and theoretical inclinations could lose any sleep over it: if it were all we had set out to establish, we would indeed be making much ado about very little. So that first conclusion must be distinguished from a second, stronger claim—namely, that *moral knowledge is essentially particular*, so that sound resolutions of moral problems must always be rooted in a concrete understanding of specific cases and circumstances.

Arras formulates this second claim as follows:

> Instead of focusing on the need to fit principles to cases, this [second] interpretation [of casuistry] stresses the particular nature, derivation, and function of the principles manipulated by the new casuists. Through this alternative theory of principles, we begin to discern a morality that develops, not from the top down as in Roman law, but rather from case to case (or from the bottom up) as in the common law. What differentiates the new casuistry from applied ethics, then, is not the recognition that principles must eventually be applied, but rather a particular account of the logic and derivation of the principles that we deploy in moral discourse.[28]

"Henceforth," he concludes, "I will reserve the term 'casuistry' for this 'common law ethics' model."[29]

These two claims are distinct. One can perfectly well argue for the first, weak claim without being committed to the second, stronger one. In this book, however, we are advancing *both* claims. The stronger account sees the primary locus of moral understanding as lying in the recognition of *paradigmatic examples* of good and evil, right and wrong: the typical cases of, for example, fairness or unfairness, cruelty or kindness, truth-telling or lying, whose merits and shortcomings even a small child "knows at a glance."[30] In the history of culture and society, and in the child's own growing up also, this moral discernment has to be applied to new and more complex cases with progressively greater refinement: sometimes in ways that are truly discriminating, deepening and enriching our perception of human relations, obligations, and needs, sometimes in more sophisticated ways, which cloud our perception and confuse our judgment. Either way, the *locus* of judgment still remains the specific case, the concrete problem, the particular set of circumstances. These are the *elements* that constitute a given "moral" issue, just as, within the traditions of the common law, the corresponding elements constitute a "legal" issue.

On the second account, the core of moral knowledge is not found in accepting universal propositions such as "Cruelty is wrong." Cruelty is a basic "wrong," just as willful wounding is a basic "tort," so that proposition can go without saying. Rather, moral knowledge consists in the ability to put our moral discernment to work, cultivate an eye for subtle and far from obvious considerations, which may be morally crucial in difficult situations. That ability is not the "cognitive skill" of learning to make ever-more-powerful "ethical deductions." Instead, it is a matter of our affective sensibility: learning what novel factors and circumstances we should look out for, and be responsive to, as the range of our moral experience extends.[31]

If the resolution of moral problems depends more on the practical understanding of concrete cases than it does on the theoretical grasp of abstract connections, why then has a *geometrical* model, the point of which is to illustrate the formal merits of theoretical arguments, had such an appeal in the essentially *practical* field of Ethics? If moral arguments are practical, so that moral wisdom is *phronesis*, not *episteme*, how can people still think of ethical theories as the foundations of some "moral geometry"?

The answer to those questions is that, in many circumstances, the appeal to a geometrical model of argument itself has a powerful *rhetorical* effect. When particular cases call for reemphasizing strict principles and for holding pretended "exceptions" at arm's length, this model underlines the moral considerations concerned and helps to discredit all counterarguments in favor of relaxing those principles. So the deductive model itself can be a "rhetorical trope" in the service of the rigorist cause.

Certainly Blaise Pascal's own arguments functioned in this way. Pascal was not only a mathematician himself: he was also a contemporary of such geometrically minded philosophers as René Descartes (1596–1650) and Baruch Spinoza (1632–1677). Aside from the intrinsic charms of the rigorist position for a man of Pascal's character, in a country riven by the Wars of Religion and the assassination of Henri IV, it need not surprise us that rhetorical tropes modeled on mathematics not only attracted Pascal personally but also carried conviction with his readers.[32] By contrast, his Jesuit opponents were committed to the humane traditions of the earlier rhetorical argument: their methods were subtle, but they were essentially nonmathematical and so unconvincing to anyone who was predisposed to equate *rigor* with *formal necessity*.[33]

Carried away by the power of these mathematical tropes, Pascal's readers (and finally Pascal as well) lost sight of the fact that his attack on the Jesuit casuists in *The Provincial Letters* had been purely rhetorical. That meant that it was unclear whether Pascal himself was arguing as a *casuist*, defending rigorist positions against laxist Jesuits and their allies; or whether he was claiming to have found a way to discredit casuistical arguments of all kinds on the ground of their *mathematical* inadequacy. Misled by his irony, Pascal's successors took the quasi-mathematical force of his "rigorist" arguments as entitling them to reject "case reasoning" of all kinds in the realm of morals and ethics.

In retrospect one thing is clear. Considered for their rational force, not their rhetorical power, rigorist arguments are no more demonstrative or purely formal than are laxist arguments. It is not, for example, the case that rigorist arguments have "necessary" conclusions whereas laxist arguments are only "presumptive." Both styles of argument have presumptive conclusions, and they differ only in the ease with which those presumptions can be rebutted. For laxists, these conclusions can be set aside when *one and only one* reputable authority is found who presents a contrary opinion; for rigorists, they retain undiminished force and authority unless the circumstances are *unanimously* seen as changing the nature of the case. Neither interpretation can exempt moral conclusions from all possible reconsideration, as it would do if those conclusions were established "necessarily." Rigorists know, as well as laxists do, that exceptional cases occasionally turn up in which even the strongest moral presumptions can be set aside.

This misunderstanding of Pascal's arguments has its legacy today in the tendency for public debates about moral issues to lapse into a deadlock between rival sets of principles, each advocated by moral zealots whose enthusiasm edges toward spiritual pride.[34] However, when the matters for discussion are as pressing as they have been during the last twenty years, people find themselves forced to address the practical, specific, concrete nature of moral issues and the deliberation for which they call. And once this has happened, the exigences of practical life fortunately lead the people involved to adopt, for their own purposes, a new casuistry that—in the nature of things—reinvents the methods of the old.

17

Epilogue: Conscience and the Claims of Equity

In the opening pages of this book we recounted the troubles of the group of Roman Catholic nuns who rallied to the support of vice-presidential candidate Geraldine Ferraro in 1984. With advice from several moral theologians, they issued a public statement endorsing her position on abortion. This position, they claimed, adhered "to the principles of moral theology, such as probabilism, religious liberty and the centrality of informed conscience."[1] A reincarnate casuist from the high era of the discipline would recognize at least two of these "principles of moral theology." Although he might not be accustomed to the phrase "religious liberty," the terms "probabilism" and "informed conscience" would have a familiar ring. He would approve of using these terms in public debate over a moral matter. But in all likelihood he would be somewhat puzzled by the meaning the Sisters attached to these terms.

By this point in our discussion the casuists' meaning of "probabilism" and the crucial role this concept played in classical casuistry should now be clear. The Sisters displayed a vague familiarity with that traditional meaning, without appreciating the essence of the notion; the ecclesiastical authorities who reprimanded them unfortunately suffered the same shortcoming. As we have shown, it is certainly true that the tradition allowed one to decide that some particular act was moral or immoral, if one could discover some authoritative "probable opinion" in support of that personal decision. In the first instance, however, that "opinion" was never the opinion of the agent making the decision, but the opinion of "accepted doctors" based upon sound "intrinsic reasons." Furthermore the probable opinion did not cover an entire generic class of actions (e.g., homicide, warfare, or abortion) but referred to a particular subtype of such actions (e.g., killing in a specific set of circumstances).

The agent faced with the decision must make a specific choice about a particular action. The detailed circumstances of the action may be unique and unrepeatable; in considering its morality the decider will look for opinions about other actions in situations as similar as possible to his own. These opinions may carry a certain "probability," based on the reputation of their author and the intrinsic argument, but the final decision how to act must rest not on a probability but on the moral certitude of the informed conscience. While honoring "probable opinions," Catholic moral theology has never tolerated acting in doubt. On the contrary, the very usefulness of the "reflex principles" that engendered probabilism lay in their application to the resolution of practical doubt.

The Roman Catholic debate over the killing of a fetus is a long one. Many "probable opinions" appear in that long history. For example, the moral status of the fetus, its being or becoming human, has been interpreted in many different ways, and the implications of those different interpretations about the morality of killing the fetus have given rise to different probable opinions.[2] In addition, circumstances surrounding the killing of a fetus have generated other probable opinions: for example, "Does the fetus that poses a threat to the physical life of the mother become, for the purpose of moral analysis, an unjust aggressor?"[3] In recent years the permissibility of destroying fetal life to save maternal life has been accepted as a probable opinion if that killing is "indirect": that is, an unavoidable and unintended side effect of an act that is immediately directed at saving the mother from a pathological condition, as in cancer of the uterus or invasion of the fallopian tubes by ectopic pregnancy.[4]

In their statement the Sisters wrote, "Direct abortion, even though tragic, can be a moral choice." In these words they blended classic casuistry with contemporary personalism. The distinction between a "direct" and an "indirect" abortion is a special case of the distinction established by Aquinas, in the context of his analysis of homicide, and long used by the casuists to clarify the intention and the object of actions. But the idea that an abortion may be "tragic" arises, rather, from a twentieth-century view of the moral life, which sees right and wrong actions in light of the burdens and sorrows of human existence in the world. On this modern view, the fact that a wrong action is tragic helps to absolve or excuse the agent from guilt; for the casuists the tragedy of an action was not in itself relevant to its moral evaluation.

It is in this mélange of moral evaluation and personal anguish that the Sisters' use of the classical notion of "conscience" departs from the casuists' view. For them the intensely personal and existential character of moral choice represents "the centrality of informed conscience." For the casuists, by contrast, informed conscience might be intensely personal, but its primary concern was to place the individual agent's decision into its larger context at the level of actual choice: namely, the moral dialogue and debate of a community. Conscience was "knowing together" (con-scientia). The dialogue and debate consisted in the critical application of paradigms to new circumstances, but those "paradigms" were the collective possession of people—priests, rabbis or common lawyers or moral theologians—who had the education, the opportunity, and the experience needed to reflect on the difficulties raised by new cases and to argue them through among themselves. So "liberty of conscience" never meant the right to take up a personal moral position that ran in the face of the general agreement of reflective scholars and doctors: rather, it meant that when the outcome of the collective debate left room for differences of opinion in marginal or ambiguous cases, it was for each individual to resolve those residual ambiguities in accordance with the dictates of his or her heart and convictions.

In the debate about abortion, as elsewhere, the extreme positions are presented publicly using techniques of persuasion, not rational discussion. Proponents of unqualified "liberty of conscience," or "the right to choose," sometimes talk as though every pregnancy poses the same ambiguous or marginal problems, so that the people involved can in all cases claim the right to decide in individual ways. Equally, the proponents of an embryo's unqualified "right to life" sometimes talk as though the moral status of every pregnancy were an open-and-shut matter, and as though no pregnancy could ever be the occasion for moral ambiguity or other difficulties. The very existence of a human zygote creates, for them, moral claims that can never be overridden by the most urgent counterclaims: all

abortions, they imply, are mortally sinful and morally evil, criminal-
ly actionable and humanly unforgivable, in the same way and for
the same reasons.

It may seem that there is no room for mediation between these
two rhetorical extremes. Yet just as undiscriminating appeals to "liberty of conscience" exaggerate the amount of room for disagreement
that usually exists in actual cases, so too indiscriminate denunciations of "the evil of abortion" or proclamations of "the woman's
right over her own body" conceal the need—even here—to look at
different kinds of cases with an eye to the real and relevant differences among them. The fact that significant distinctions can be
drawn among specific kinds of cases embraced within the moral
genus, "abortion," is clear from considerations of two distinct sorts.
Looking at the problem in biological terms, it is not enough to
remark that a zygote is a living human entity, as if no other facts
about the embryo or fetus had any bearing on the issue. During the
nine months from implantation to birth, the embryo develops in
ways that are relevant to the nature of its moral standing and the
strength of its claims; and it requires a certain obstinacy or obtuseness to deny that *any* morally significant differences exist between a
newly formed zygote and a fetus in the eighth month. The
ancients—like many modern mothers—were impressed by "quickening," which was the traditional point of division after which the
fetus was thought of as an independent being. Anatomical precursors of the nervous system are formed early in embryonic development, but the capacity for "sensation" seems to develop much later;
whereas the mother's bonding to and attitude toward the fetus
change as the months go by in ways that are still not fully understood.

Only people whose minds are too firmly made up to reconsider
the complexities of the abortion issue can say in advance that none
of these changes has any possible relevance to the matter. In half a
dozen ways at least the Catholic tradition of pastoral theology was
always responsive to such differences. The zygote, as such, was
never recognized in practice as a full *person*. Early miscarriages are
occasions for grief but do not call for a religious burial; and even
with a stillbirth, it has never been obligatory to baptize the issue of a
delivery unless it has reached the stage of being clearly and visibly
an infant.

To go further, we cannot leave the casuistry of abortion without
asking the question, "What practical consequences are supposed to

follow from different possible moral judgments about this issue?" No one, surely, can doubt that in the best of all worlds there would be no occasion for abortion to be considered, let alone performed; or that, as a counsel of perfection, abortion is best avoided. But as always, this is only one of a dozen distinct consequential questions. In the cure of souls, as well as personal charity, we know that sometimes the decision for an abortion is, at the very worst, *deeply regret-table but understandable*—certainly not *unforgivable*, to say nothing of *damnable*.

This, indeed, may be all that the American Sisters had in mind when they declared that having an abortion may sometimes be "a *moral* choice." Not that for them, any more than for their opponents, having an abortion is in itself a positive moral achievement: only that before we take a "principled" stand toward particular cases of abortion, charity and equity require that we be informed about the circumstances of the particular case.

As for the further proposal that participation in any abortion should be made a criminal offense, this proposal is not justified by producing only analytic syllogisms of the form,

> Willfully terminating the life of a human being is murder;
> Early abortions willfully terminate the lives of zygotes;
> Zygotes are human beings;
> So, even early abortions are murder.

It raises also profound questions of jurisprudence and public policy about the extent to which, and the conditions on which, good purposes are served by bringing the judicial processes of the State to bear on the most painful and personal aspects of the lives of the citizens. In deciding such matters, points of pure principle make great slogans; but the demands of personal discernment and the practice of the confessional place upon us other more serious moral demands; and, in confronting difficult and often bitterly grief-laden problems, we need all the institutional support we can find.[5]

The unanswered question then is, How can there be a renewed casuistry in a culture where the crucial institutions do not exist? The recent revival of casuistical debate that we studied in chapter 16 showed us how individuals, mostly academics, have been returning to the idea that case analysis can yield insight into moral problems, and also that certain institutions still have the capacity to maintain a coherent moral discussion in the modern world—for example, the Roman Catholic Bishops of the United States who have, almost unwittingly, returned to a traditional mode of reflecting on moral problems. These revivals of interest in case ethics are not in themselves equivalent to a full-scale renewal of casuistry. Such a renewal calls for more than a grasp of the intellectual methods of casuistry; it requires institutions that provide the locus for and lend support to the uniquely casuistical way of approaching moral problems.

Some of the needed institutions seem to have come into existence in one area of modern life at least: namely, medicine and health care. In the opening pages of this book we described the National Commission for the Protection of Human Subjects of Biomedical and Behavioral Research, and suggested that the methods of that Commission were, in fact and unknown to itself, a "casuistry" of human experimentation. That Commission had a successor, the President's Commission for the Study of Ethical Problems in Medicine and in Biomedical and Behavioral Research, which has studied such problems as the definition of human death by brain criteria, the withholding or withdrawing of life supporting medical technology, and screening for genetic defects. Several other bodies have been established by various Federal agencies of the United States government to make recommendations about the ethical problems posed by modern medicine and health care.

These official groups are unique: each has had to find its own way of analyzing problems and offering recommendations for public policy in ethical matters. They provide an institutional skeleton for casuistry; but we say only a skeleton, because they could not work unless there were a body of public interest, expert scholarship and professional support. All of these have come into existence. In 1970, at the very beginning of the concern about ethical issues in medicine, one of the pioneer scholars, the theologian Paul Ramsey, wrote:

> Medical ethics today must, indeed, be casuistry; it must deal as competently and exhaustively as possible with the concrete features of actual moral decisions of life and death and medical care. But we can no longer be so confident that the "resolution" or "solution" will be forthcoming.[6]

Another pioneer of the bioethics movement, Daniel Callahan, suggested why a new casuistry might not work:

The only kinds of ethical systems I know of which make it possible to reach specific conclusions are those of an essentially deductive kind, with well established primary and secondary principles and a long history of highly refined casuistry. The Roman Catholic scholastic tradition and the Jewish responsa tradition are cases in point. Unfortunately, systems of that kind presuppose a whole variety of cultural conditions and shared world views which simply do not exist in society at large.[7]

Still, in bioethics, the institutions capable of supporting casuistry have come into being. A number of scholars in philosophy, theology, law, and medicine have become interested in the problems of medical ethics and have devoted attention to the analysis of various issues. They have published their work and debated over various points. They meet frequently in various settings. Two centers of research were established in the 1970s, The Hastings Center and The Kennedy Center for Bioethics, both of which have fostered scholarly analysis and debate. Thus there have come into being modern analogues of the *clerici* and the *universitates*.

More, however, is needed. The world of medicine and health care is a world presided over by physicians; the profession of medicine has an ancient ethical tradition, and maintains powerful control over the education, research, and practice of physicians. If the profession of medicine had not listened and participated, the casuistry of medical ethics would have been vaporous. Scholars in medical ethics are invited to speak at important medical meetings, to act as consultants to medical societies, and to publish in medical journals. They are appointed as professors in medical faculties and attend when hospital physicians make their rounds of patients.

The cases that appear in the casuistry of medical ethics are real; their moral implications are important to those who care for patients. As in the earlier period, one important product of this debate has been the recognition of new "type cases" or "paradigms." In some areas of discussion—for example, decisions to forgo life-sustaining treatments with dying patients or the patient's right to refuse medical treatment—the considerations central to effecting decisions about situations are well understood and widely accepted.[8]

The profession of medicine is also influential in the political and legal world. The interest of federal and state agencies in ethical issues of medicine and health care is not abstract: governmental policies touch moral issues very closely. When we consider current government policies concerning funding of expensive procedures such as heart transplantation, care of the elderly, and abortion, it is difficult to see where politics and morality divide. A casuist of the high era would hardly be surprised at this interpenetration of the ethical and the political; but moderns are accustomed to separating morals and politics, just as they separate church and state. Yet the casuistry of medical ethics is now heard every day in the halls of government and the offices of the bureaucracy. National and state commissions are established, "ethicists" are named to advisory committees, and moral philosophers testify before legislatures and boards.[9]

Similarly, the courts have found themselves forced to judge cases of kinds never before heard in American legal forums. The Karen Ann Quinlan case was the first in which a judge had to decide whether or not the continuation of technological life support procedures was legally mandatory. Many other cases have followed. These issues have strained the standard jurisprudence of tort and contract. So new collaborations have been necessary between legal scholars and ethicists, and from these collaborations have come recommendations for statutes about the definition of death, "living wills," and "durable powers of attorney."

Finally, all of this takes place in an environment of intense public concern. The media cover dramatic events, such as the implantation of the artificial heart, with unremitting attention. Articles appear in popular magazines and newspapers almost daily. Debates are held on television. Books on bioethics enjoy steady sales. Lectures are widely attended by the public. Individuals raise questions about these issues with their doctors. Thus in the world of medicine and health care, institutions for the support of casuistry have come into being. The institutions of medical casuistry have developed a life of their own.

These institutions are not neatly designed; they are somewhat ramshackle, yet they allow a reasonable conversation, an effective debate, to go on about new types of cases. A small group of *clerici* (the so-called ethicists) bend their minds to describe cases accurately and analyze them acutely. Their work is fostered by the medical, legal, and governmental agencies that recognize the importance of their analyses but also contribute the viewpoints and constraints of the "real world." So the academic debates of the ethicists are forced into the real world of professional and policy actuality, and all of this is done under the eye of a public that realizes that these issues may touch their personal lives.

When we set out the central problems for this book in the Prologue, we remarked how the demand for rigorous and universal moral principles, which has inspired much of the recent debate about moral issues, generates by reaction an equally extreme cultural relativism. "Absolute principles" appear so attractive today partly because of the continuing power of that "quest for certainty" about which John Dewey wrote.[10] Not that it needed Dewey to teach us the weakness of absolutism: Aristotle himself saw that ethics contains no *essences* and that there is accordingly no basis for geometrically rigorous *theories* in ethics. Practical reasoning in ethics is not a matter of drawing formal deductions from invariable axioms, but of exercising judgment—that is, weighing considerations against one another. It is a task not for clever arguers but for the *phronimos* (or "sensible practical person") and the *anthropos megalopsychos* (or "large spirited human being").[11]

So by rhetorically abusing casuistry *as a whole*, Pascal went too far. It was all very well to attack the Jesuit casuists at the French court for being too ready to make exceptions in favor of rich or high-born penitents: that no doubt made a point. But in making this a reason for rejecting case methods in moral discussion completely, he set us a lasting bad example. When discretion is abused, the first step is not to eliminate the occasion for exercising discretion and impose rigid rules instead: rather, it is more appropriate to ask how matters might be adjusted, so that discretion can be exercised more equitably and discriminatingly.

In closing, let us record our own votes against Pascal and in favor of the casuists and the Talmudists. We need not go as far as Leo Tolstoy did, arguing that an ethics modeled on law rather than equity is no ethics at all. But we may recognize that a morality built from general rules and universal principles alone too easily becomes a tyrannical, disproportioned thing, and that only those people who have learned to "make equitable allowances" for the subtle individual differences among otherwise similar circumstances have developed a true feeling for the deepest demands of ethics.

The *abuse* of casuistry—not the misuse of case methods in moral argument, but the insulting scorn to which they have been subject since Pascal attacked the Jesuits in *The Provincial Letters*—has thus been almost entirely unjustified.

By ignoring the insights of the casuists and rejecting their use of moral discernment for a more principled but grossly simplistic approach to moral issues, we do humanity a disservice that has produced bitter fruit. During the last twenty-five years many people felt an understandable need to criticize *permissiveness*, and it is not surprising if their rhetoric recalls the seventeenth-century attacks on laxism. But by now we have had enough of these denunciations and can look at the other face of the picture. Whatever weakness there may have been in a readiness to make, and allow, exceptions to general moral rules, the spectacle of *principled dogmatism*—legalism without equity, and moralism without charity—has never been a pretty sight either. No doubt the casuists had their faults; but they were, in our view, faults on the right side.

Every serious tradition of moral thought and practice embodies legends and stories which put in a nutshell the view of conduct shared by its reflective, responsible participants. In the Jewish tradition, a story is told of the great Rabbi Hillel. One day, Hillel was taking a bath, when an importunate student asked him, "Tell me, Rabbi: is it possible to recite the whole of the Law while standing on one leg?" Hillel replied, "Do unto others as you would have them do unto you—all the rest is commentary. Now go and study the commentary." And in their lighter moments, Catholic moral theologians, too, talk about the distinguished Father Tanqueray, who spent a lifetime writing treatises on the subject which became ever more concise. He started in his thirties with a seven volume *Summa* of moral theology, then moved, decade by decade, through a five volume *Digest* in his forties to a three volume *Compendium*, a one volume *Manual*, and finally a slim *Medulla* (or "kernel") *Theologiae Moralis* in his seventies. In his extreme old age, he was asked whether the essentials of Christian ethics could be summarized even more briefly: he took some paper and wrote a single sentence from St Augustine, *Ama, et fac quod vis*—i.e., "Love, and do what you will."

At the end of the day, then, all reflective moral traditions keep it in mind that the kernel of moral wisdom consists, not in a hardline commitment to principles which we accept without qualification, but in understanding the human needs and relations that are nurtured by a life of reflective moral action. With that preoccupation, the practical task is to apply general moral rules, and other ethical considerations, to new and more complex sets of circumstances, in ways that respect these human needs.

A Catalogue of Casuists

An exhaustive list of casuists and their work is impossible to compile. First, there were many of them and, of these, many did not issue their work in printed books. Second, the class of "casuist" is not clearly demarked. Many scholars devoted their major efforts to case analysis; many others, who were primarily theologians or canon lawyers, occasionally commented on cases. The following catalogue is a sample, including the most prominent names in the history of casuistry, as well as some minor figures. Readers of *The Provincial Letters* will miss Becanus, Petau, Annat and a few others frequently cited by Pascal's "Good Father." These men were Jesuits—one of them, Petau, a splendid patristic scholar—but they wrote little in the field of moral theology. Readers of *The Provincial Letters* will also miss some of the bizarre names listed by the "Good Father" in Letter V. After a recitation that includes "Achoker, Dealkozer, Bizozeri, et al," Pascal exclaims, "Oh Father, were all these men Christians?" Of this list, Krailsheimer writes,

> The most famous, and brilliant thrust [of sarcasm] is the ca-
> cophonous litany of Jesuit authorities offered at the end of the Fifth
> Letter as replacement for the outmoded Fathers of the Church. Here,
> as elsewhere, Pascal deftly distorts some names, rearranges them to
> produce the maximum sound effect and, of course makes sure that
> there is no Frenchman among them. (Krailsheimer, *op. cit.*, p. 21)

This catalogue is not as colorful, nor as cacophonous as Pascal's list,
but it is more accurate. All the authors are verified from Hurter's
Nomenclator Litterarius or Sommervogel's *Bibliothèque de la Compagne
de Jésus*, the standard bibliographical references for Roman Catholic
and Jesuit authors, respectively. A more complete list can be found
at "casuistique," in *Dictionnaire de Théologie Catholique* II–2, col
1871–1875. Asterisks indicate works consulted by the authors.

Acolea, Martin *Diana Coordinatus* (Lyon, 1667)

* Alain of Lille (+1203) *Liber Poenitentialis* (c.1200)

Alloza, John, S.J. (1598–1666) *Flores Summarium Seu Alphabetum
Morale omne fere conscientiae casus* (Lima, 1665)

Alvarez, Diego, S.J. (+1618) *Decisio Casuum Conscientiae
Occurentium In Articulo Mortis* (Seville 1604)

* Ames, William (1576–1633) *De Conscientia, Ejus Jure et Casibus*
(1630)

* Amort, E. (1692–1775) *Dictionarium Casuum Conscientiae*
(Avignon 1762)

* Antoninus of Florence (1389–1459) *Summa Moralis* (Florence,
1460?)

————*Summula Confessorum* (Venice 1480)

* Astesanus de Asti (+c.1330) *Summa Astesana* (Venice, 1468)

* Azpilcueta, Martin (1492–1586) *Enchiridion Sive Manuale
Confessariorum et Poenitentium* (Rome 1573)

* Azor, John, S.J. (+1603) *Institutionum Moralium In Quibus
Universae Quaestiones Ad Conscientiam Recte Aut Prave Factorum
Breviter Tractantur* (Rome 1600)

* Bartholomaeus de Pisa (+1347) *Summa Pisana* (c.1473)

* Bauny, Etienne, S.J. (1564–1649) *Theologia Moralis* (Paris, 1640–1645)

——*Somme des Péchés* (Paris 1630)

Baxter, Richard (1614–1691) *Christian Directory or Summ of Practical Theology and Cases of Conscience* (1673)

Bertolotti, G., S.J. *Sylloge Casuum* (Rome 1893–1897)

Berardi, E *Casus Conscientiae* (Padua 1885–1895)

Benedictus XIV, Pope (1675–1758) *Casus Conscientiae* (Venice 1782–1788)

Bouquillon, Thomas (1842–1902) *Theologia Moralis Fundamentalis* (Brussels 1890)

Bucceroni, G., S.J. *Casus Conscientiae* (Rome 1897)

Burgo, John de (+1386) *Pupilla Oculi* (Strasbourg, 1516)

* Busenbaum, Herman, S.J. (1600–1668) *Medulla Theologiae Moralis Facili et Perspicua Methodo Resolvens Casus Conscientiae ex Variis Probatis Auctoribus Concinnata* (Munster 1645)

Cagnazzo, John, O.F.M. (+1521) *Summa Tabiena vel Summa Summarum de Casibus Conscientiae* (1517)

* Caramuel-Lobkowitz, John, O.Cist. (1606–1682) *Theologia Moralis Ad Prima Eaque Clarissima Principia Reducta* (Louvain, 1645)

* Carletti, Angelus, O.F.M. (Clavasio) *Summa Angelica* (c.1476)

Castro Palao, Ferdinand (1581–1633) *Tractatus Operis Moralis* (Lyon 1631)

* Concina, Daniel, O.P. (1687–1756) *Theologia Christiana Dogmatico-Moralis* (Naples 1772–75)

Cotonio, Anthony, O.F.M. (1613–1682) *Summa Diana* (Anvers 1656)

* Davis, Henry, S.J. *Moral and Pastoral Theology* (London 1935)

* Diana, Anthony, O.Theat. (1585–1663) *Resolutiones Morales* (Venice, 1635)

* Escobar y Mendoza, Anthony, S.J. (1589–1669) *Liber Theologiae Moralis Viginti Quatuor Societatis Jesu Doctoribus Resertus* (Lyons, 1644)

* ———*Universae Theologiae Moralis Receptiores Absque Lite Sententiae Nec Non Problematicae Disquisitiones* (Lyons, 1652–1663)

  Filliucci, Vincent, S.J. (1566–1622) *Quaestionum Moralium De Christianis Officiis in Casibus Conscientiae* (Lyons 1622)

  ———*Synopsis Universae Theologiae Moralis* (Herbipoli 1626)

  Funez, Martin, S.J. (1560–1611) *Speculum Morale Et Practicum in Quo Medulla Omnium Casuum Conscientiae Continentur* (Cologne 1610)

* Genicot, Edward, S.J. (1856–1900) *Casus Conscientiae Propositi Ac Soluti* (1901)

  ———*Theologia Moralis Institutiones* (1896)

  Gobat, George, S.J. (1600–1679) *Alphabetum Quadruple Quo Plus Clx Casibus Factis Non Fictis Resolvuntur* (Constance 1672)

  ———*Operum Moralium Libri Tres* (Venice 1698)

* Gury, Jean-Pierre, S.J. (1801–1866) *Compendium Theologiae Moralis* (Lyon, 1850)

* ———*Casus Conscientiae In Praecipuas Quaestiones Theologiae Moralis* (Ratisbon, 1865)

  Illsung, John, S.J. (1632–1695) *Arbor Scientiae Boni Et Mali Sive Theologia Practica Universa De Bono Et Malo Morali* (Dillingen, 1693)

  Henriquez, Henry (+1608) *Theologiae Moralis Summa* (Venice 1591)

Hurtado, Thomas (1589–1659) *Tractus Varii Resolutionum Moralium* (Lyon 1651)

Iorio, T. *Casus Conscientiae* (Naples, 1858–60)

Iturriaga, M., S.J. (1728–1819) *Dissertationes in Morales Quaestiones* (Assisi 1794–1796)

* Lacroix, Claude, S.J. (1652–1714) *Theologia Moralis Antehac Ex Probatis Auctoribus Breviter Concinnata* (Cologne 1707–1714)

Lamet, A *Dictionarium Casuum Conscientiae* (Venice 1761)

* Laymann, Paul, S.J. (1574–1635) *Theologia Moralis* (Munich 1625)

———*Theologiae Moralis Compendium Absolutissimum* (Lyon 1631)

* Lehmkuhl, August, S.J. (1834–1918) *Casus Conscientiae* (Fribourg 1902–1904)

———*Theologia Moralis* (Fribourg 1883)

* Lessius, Leonard, S.J. (1554–1623) *De Justitia Et Jure Caeterisque Virtutibus Libri Quatuor* (Louvain 1605)

* Ligouri, Alphonsus, C.S.S.R. (1696–1787) *Medulla Theologiae Moralis R.P.H. Busenbaum Cum Adnotationibus Per R.P. Alphonsum de Ligorio Adjuntis* (1748)

———*Praxis Confessarii* (1748)

———*Theologia Moralis Juxta Methodum R.P. Hermanii Busenbaum* (1757)

———*Homo Apostolicus* (1759)

* Lugo, John de, S.J. (1583–1660) *Responsorium Moralium Libri Se* (Lyon 1651)

———*De Justitia Et Jure* (Lyon 1642)

Maldeus, John (1563–1633) *Tractatus de Restrictionum Mentalium Abusu* (Antwerp 1625)

Marc, Clement, C.S.S.R. (1831–1887) *Institutiones Morales Alphonsianae* (Rome 1891)

Merkelbach, Benedict, O.P. (1871–1942) *Summa Theologiae Moralis* (Paris 1931–33)

————*Quaestiones Pastorales* (Liege 1936)

Molanus, John (+1585) *Theologiae Practicae Compendium* (Cologne 1585)

* Molina, Louis, S.J. (1536–1600) *De Justitia Et Jure* (Conchae 1593–1600)

Moura, A. *Examen Theologiae Moralis Medullam Omnium Casuum Conscientiae* (Douai 1625)

* Noldin, Jerome, S.J. (1838–1922) *Summa Theologiae Moralis* (Innsbruck 1902)

Oviedo, John, S.J. (1670–1757) *Succus Theologiae Moralis* (Mexico City 1754)

* Palazzini, Paul *Casus Conscientiae* (Vatican City 1953)

————*Dictionarium Morale et Canonicum* (Rome 1962–68)

* Perkins, William (1558–1602) *Whole Treatise of Cases of Conscience* (Cambridge, 1606)

* Peter the Cantor (+1197) *Summa de Sacramentis et Animae Consiliis* (c.1191)

Pisè, Marcellus *Theologiae Moralis Encyclopedia* (Paris 1637–1641)

* Pontas, John (1638–1728) *Dictionarium Casuum Conscientiae* (Luxembourg 1731)

Potesta, Felix, O.F.M. *Examen Ecclesiasticum in Quo Universae Materiae Morales Omnesque Fere Casus Conscientiae Excogitabiles Solide et Perspicue Resolvuntur* (Venice 1720)

* Priero, Sylvester de, O.P. (+1523) *Summa Sylvestrina vel Summa Summarum* (Strasborg 1516)

* Prummer, Dominic, O.P. *Manuale Theologiae Moralis* (Barcelona 1946)

* Raymond, Pennafort, O.P. (1175–1275) *Summa de Paenitentia* (c.1225)

   Regnault, Valery, S.J. (1545–1623) *Theologia Practica et Moralis* (Cologne 1653)

   ———*Praxis Fori Poenitentialis Ac Directionem Confessarii* (Lyon 1616)

   ———*Compendaria Praxis Difficiliorum Casuum* (Lyon 1618)

   ———*De Prudentia Et Caeteris in Confessario Requisitis* (Lyon 1610)

   ———*Tractatus de Officio Penitentis* (Lyon 1618)

* Robert of Flamborough (1135–1219) *Liber Poenitentialis* (c.1210)

   Ricci, D. *Casus Conscientia* (Mutinae 1881)

* Sa, Emmanuel, S.J. (1530–1596) *Aphorismi Confessariorum ex Doctorum Sententiis Collecti* (Venice 1595)

* Sanderson, Robert (1587–1663) *De Obligatione Conscientiae* (1660)

   ———*De Juramenti Promissorii Obligatione* (1647)

   Sayrus, G., O.S.B. *Thesaurus Casuum Conscientiae* (Venice 1601)

   ———*Flores Decisionum Sive Casuum Conscietiae* (Venice 1601)

* Sanchez, Thomas, S.J. (1550–1610) *Opus Morale In Praecepta Decalogi Seu Summa Casuum Conscientiae* (Madrid 1613)

   Soto, Dominic, O.P. (1494–1560) *Commentarium in Quartum Sententiarum* (Venice 1570–1598)

   ———*De Justitia Et Jure* (Salamanca 1553)

————*Reflectio de Ratione Tegendi et Detegendi Secretum* (Brixiae 1582)

* Suarez, Francis, S.J. (1548–1617) *Tractatus de Legibus et de Deo Legislatore* (Coimbra 1612)

————*Defensio Fidei Catholicae et Apostolicae Adversus Anglicanae Sectae Errores* (Coimbra 1613)

Tamburini, Thomas, S.J. (1591–1675) *Expedita Juris Divini, Naturalis et Ecclesiastici Moralis Expositio* (Venice 1662)

————*Methodus Expeditae Confessionis* (Rome 1647)

————*Explicatio Decalogi* (Venice 1654)

Tanner, Adam, S.J. (1571–1632) *De Justitia et Jure* (Ingolstadt 1609)

Tanquerey, Adolph, S.S. (1854–1932) *Synopsis Theologiae Moralis* (Baltimore 1902)

* Taylor, Jeremy (1613–1667) *Ductor Dubitantium or The Rule of Conscience in All Her General Measures Serving as a Great Instrument for Determination of Cases of Conscience* (1660)

Tournely, Honoré (1658–1729) *Tractatus de Universa Theologia Morali* (Paris 1743–50)

Toledo, Francis, S.J. (1532–1596) *Summa Casuum Conscientiae* (Cologne 1600)

Valentia, Gregory, S.J. (1551–1603) *De Discernenda Humanorum Contractuum Justitia et Injustitia* (Ingolstadt 1577)

Vasquez, Gabriel, S.J. (1549–1604) *Commentaria in II–II Summa Theologia Sancti Thomae Aquinatis*

Vega, Christopher, S.J. (+1672) *Casos Raros De La Confesion* (Valencia 1656)

* Vermeersch, Arthur, S.J. (1858–1936) *Theologiae Moralis Principia, Responsa, Consilia* (Rome 1921)

* Vitoria, Francisco, O.P. *Relectio de Indis et de Jure Belli* (Salamanca 1539)

Viva, Dominic, S.J. (1648–1726) *Cursus Theologico-Moralis* (Pavia 1712)

——*Opuscula Theologico-Moralis* (Pavia 1721)

Voit, E., S.J. (1707–1780) *Theologia Moralis ex Solidiis Probatorum Auctorum Principiis et Variorum Casuum Fictorum et Factorum Resolutionibus* (Wurzburg 1750)

* Zaccaria, Francis, S.J. (1714–1795) *Theologia Moralis* (1755?)

Notes

PROLOGUE: THE PROBLEM

1. *New York Times*, 4 Aug., 11 Sept., 1984.

2. Ibid., 13 September, 1984.

3. Ibid., 5 August, 1984.

4. Ibid., 7 October, 1984.

5. *Summa Theologiae*, II–II, q. 64, a. 8, ad 2, and *Commentarium in III Sententiarum*, d 3, q. 5, a. 2, solutio. See also John Connery, *Abortion: The Development of the Roman Catholic Perspective* (Chicago, 1977), chap. 7.

6. Kristin Luker, *Abortion and the Politics of Motherhood* (Berkeley, 1984).

7. Ibid., chap. 8, pp. 194 ff.

8. See L.W. Sumner, *Abortion and Moral Theory* (Princeton, 1981), for an attempt to construct a middle position between "pro-choice" and "pro-life."

9. Alexander Pope, *The Rape of the Lock*, v. 22.

10. A. Brunetière, "Une Apologie Pour La Casuistique," *Revue des Deux Mondes* (January 1885): 200.

11. Pascal, *The Provincial Letters*, Letter XI.

12. S. Levinson, "A Symposium Review," *The Nation* 2 Sept. 1978.

13. Kenneth Kirk, *Conscience and Its Problems, An Introduction to Casuistry* (London, 1927), p. 125.

14. The reports of the commission were published by the Department of Health, Education and Welfare of the United States government from 1975 to 1978. For a discussion of the commission's methods of argument, see the paper by Stephen Toulmin in the collection of case studies, *Scientific Controversies*, ed. H. T. Engelhardt, Jr., and A. L. Caplan (Cambridge, Eng., 1985). On a *completely* general level, it is true, the members of the commission were able to share certain agreements—for example, as to the principles of autonomy, justice, and beneficence. But these shared notions were too comprehensive and general to underwrite specific moral positions. The National Commission did issue a statement of general principle, but it was composed only after the commissioners had worked through their problematic cases casuistically. See *The Belmont Report: Ethical Principles and Guidelines for Protection of Human Subjects of Biomedical and Behavioral Research* (Washington, D.C., 1978).

1. THEORY AND PRACTICE

1. Plato, *Timaeus* 53C-55C. On the role of the young Theaetetus in solving this Pythagorean problem, see A. E. Taylor, *A Commentary on Plato's Timaeus* (Oxford, 1928), 358-359. See *Theaetetus* 142A-148E.

2. See Plato's *Republic* 524D-531C; Aristotle, *Posterior Analytics* I, xii-xiv, 77a-79b, and his books on specific scientific topics.

3. Aristotle, *Eth. Nic.* (*Nicomachean Ethics*) VI, iii-vii.

4. *Ibid.*, VI, vii, 1141b19. The opinion that chicken is "good to eat," in the aternative sense of "tasty" is, of course, another matter.

5. Ibid., VI, ii, 1139ab.

6. Ibid., VI, viii, 1142a.

7. See the *Prologue* to this volume.

8. These notions became the basis of much later "Platonism," in its many and varied forms. Whether Plato himself is really committed to the view is less clear, but the starting points for this development can certainly be seen in, for example, the *Timaeus, 90B–D.

9. The idea of truth and certainty "flowing" in one or another direction within a network or system of propositions was developed by Imre Lakatos to distinguish between alternative doctrines in the philosophy of science: see, e.g., *Criticism and the Growth of Knowledge* (Cambridge, 1970).

10. This pattern for analyzing practical arguments is presented in Stephen Toulmin, *The Uses of Argument* (Cambridge, Eng., 1958), and also in

Stephen Toulmin, Richard Rieke, and Allan Janik, *An Introduction to Reasoning* (New York, 1983).

11. In their turn, behavioral and social sciences blend theoretical and practical goals and methods in other (sometimes even inextricable) ways.

12. The word *explanation* is used here for an account of underlying processes and mechanisms. In a weaker sense of the term, of course, one may still speak of clinical facts being "accounted for," and even "explained," when they are subjected to preliminary statistical analysis, even before their underlying mechanisms have been investigated.

13. There have, of course, been historical periods during which physicians saw the relationship between theory and practice in more formal terms: consider the iatrochemical and iatromechanical schools of the seventeenth century, as discussed by Lester King, *The Philosophy of Medicine* (Cambridge, Mass., 1978), chaps. 4 and 5.

14. Augustine, *Morals of the Catholic Church*, chap. 28.

15. See Henry Denzinger and Adolf Schönmetzer, *Encheiridion Symbolorum Definitionum et Declarationum de Rebus Fidei et Morum*, edn. xxxiii (Rome, 1965), #2813: this standard manual is hereafter referred to as *D-S*.

16. Kirk, *Conscience and Its Problems*, pp. 108–109.

2. THE ROOTS OF CASUISTRY IN ANTIQUITY

1. Significantly, until recently colloquial English contained no word for a professional "expert" in ethics. Even now the complete *Oxford English Dictionary* mentions the word "ethicist" without offering a definition: its entry simply reads "ethics + ist"!

2. See, e.g., K. J. Dover, *Greek Homosexuality* (Cambridge, Mass., 1978). One may recall also the case of Pericles' ward, Alcibiades, who was ridiculed for having, while drunk, knocked the phallus off the Hermes in the public street: *Cambridge Ancient History*, IV, chap. 2.

3. J. W. Jones, *Law and Legal Theory of the Greeks* (Oxford, 1956).

4. On Hecateus, see Pauly-Wissowa, *Realencyclopädie der classischen Altertumswissenschaft* (Stuttgart, 1912), Reihe I, vol. VII, pp. 2667–2750: also see, Herodotus, *Histories* II: 143.

5. Xenophanes, fragment 15: see Kathleen Freeman, *Ancilla to the Pre-Socratic Philosophers* (Oxford, 1948), p. 22.

6. An ambiguity arises. Are we to *equate* the philosophers' principles with these basic "entities"? Or are the principles just theoretical *statements* about those entities? The classical debate did not always make this clear, and Greek grammar made it easy to confuse "objects" and "events," "truth"

and "existence." Recall the notorious problem about "false beliefs" that figures in several of Plato's dialogues (e.g., the *Theaetetus*). Ancient Greek allowed one to omit the copula (*is*) from simple sentences. The utterance, "Bald Socrates" might, as in modern English, serve as a noun phrase used to point to an existing person, or as a complete statement, used to assert that "Socrates is bald." Conversely, "Red-haired Socrates" might be taken *either* to make a false assertion (since Socrates' hair was not in fact red) *or else* to point to an *un*actual, *non*existent person. On this second reading the mystery then was, "How can we possibly grasp the 'nonexistent fact' seemingly pointed to by a false utterance?"

7. The marriage of ontology and geometry never went far beyond planetary astronomy. For Plato the task of developing geometrical constructions to explain the motion of the planets across the stars was the paradigmatic example of "saving appearances": it remained the crucial task for the scientific theorists of late antiquity, as in the work of Claudius Ptolemy, around A.D. 150.

8. Dover, *Greek Homosexuality*; see also Arthur W. H. Adkins, *Merit and Responsibility* (Chicago, 1960).

9. In classical Greek, *ethos* is the standard word for "custom" and *ethikos* means merely "customary." The same is true of Latin *mos* and *moralis*, from which English "morality" words are derived. The etymological question is how, when, and for what reasons the words "ethical" and "moral" ceased to refer only to the "customary" and came to indicate rather the "obligatory."

10. This account of early Roman law, especially the development of legal "rules," relies heavily on the excellent book by Peter Stein, *Regulae Iuris* (Edinburgh, 1966).

11. The pontiffs' function as mediators is reflected in the very etymology of the Latin words *pontifex* and *pontificare*: these derive from the phrase, *pontem facere* (i.e., "make a bridge"). The exact significance of this title was a matter of dispute even in antiquity: it may have had something to do with the responsibility of the pontiffs for the bridges across the river Tiber, around which the city grew. See Pauly-Wissowa, *Realencyclopädie*, supp. vol. XV, esp. pp. 334–341.

12. See Stein, *Regulae Iuris*, pp. 26, 80–82, 124–127.

13. Hence arose the notion of a common "law of the peoples," or *ius gentium*, which was to play an important part in the medieval analysis of the shared moral and legal ideas of different nations and cultures. In Imperial Rome supervision of the codification of these different local bodies of law was the special concern of the *praetor peregrinus*, or "praetor for foreigners."

14. Carried over into nineteenth-century England, the resulting separation of courts of law and courts of equity is familiar to readers of Dickens's novel *Bleak House*.

15.   Jacob Neusner, ed., *Understanding Rabbinic Judaism* (New York, 1974), p. 1.

16.   Ex 18:20.

17.   A form of Talmudic reasoning that employed "casuistical" reasoning, in the sense of subtle arguments and precise distinctions, was known as "pilpul," meaning "sharp as pepper." Although known in ancient times, it was popular in seventeenth and eighteenth-century rabbinical schools, particularly in Poland.   It was criticized in terms similar to those directed against Catholic casuistry as "twisting the plain truth by hairsplitting." Its strongest critic in the late eighteenth century was Elijah ben Solomon Zalman, the Gaon of Vilna. *Encyclopedia Judaica* (Jerusalem, 1971), vol. 13, pp. 526–527.

18.   These are only one example of the kinds of local adjudicative tribunals—formal and informal—by which conduct in many fields of human activity used to be regulated.   "Courts of limited jurisdiction" were one victim of the nineteenth-century administrative changes in the Anglo-American legal system inspired by Bentham, John Austin, and the utilitarian reformers.   See, e.g., H. W. Arthurs, *Without the Law: Administrative Justice and Legal Pluralism in 19th-Century England* (Toronto, 1985).   See also H. Berman, *Law and Revolution* (Cambridge, Mass.: 1983), Part II.

19.   See chapter 4.

20.   Gal 3:28.

21.   Alexander's "cosmopolitan" ideals—the very word dovetails the *cosmos*, or natural universe, with the *polis*, or human society—was taken up by the Stoics, who developed it for educated Romans of the later Republic and early Empire.   In this later form, it survived to influence Kant's moral theories, and the modern French practice of treating anyone from *les pays Francophones* who masters French culture as "French."

22.   On Gorgias, see M. Untersteiner, *The Sophists* (Oxford, 1954).

23.   Aeschylus, Fragment 302N, *Tragicorum Graecorum Fragmenta*, ed. B. Snell (Göttingen, 1971), vol. 1; Aristotle, *Eth. Nic.* II, 2.4, 1104ᵃ.

24.   Plato, *Republic*, bk. VII, 517d.

25.   Aristotle, *Eth. Nic.* I.vi.11 ff, 1096ᵃ-1097ᵃ.

26.   Ibid. I.iii.1–4, 1094b.

27.   Ironically, some moral theologians today criticize Aristotle's ethics as "essentialist" because they wrongly take him to be committed to the very "moral essences" about which both they and he himself were rightly skeptical.   See, e.g., Charles Curran, *Directions in Fundamental Moral Theory* (Notre Dame, 1985), pp. 151–158.

28. The English word "prudence" is derived from Latin *prudentia*, which is the word Cicero and other Roman authors used to translate *phronesis*: see, e.g., chapter 3. Despite the scholarly practice of translating the Greek word *phronesis* by the English *prudence*, the "practical wisdom" called for in, say, clinical medicine has little to do with "prudence" in the modern colloquial sense of the word—that is, "cautious, calculating foresight." As both "prudence" and "wisdom" have irrelevant overtones in modern English, it is hard to find an exact English equivalent to Aristotle's term. See P. Aubenque, *La Prudence chez Aristote* (Paris, 1963).

29. Aristotle, *Eth. Nic.* VI. v.1–4, 1140a–b; xiii.1–6, 1144b.

30. Ibid., VI. vii.7, 1141b.

31. Ibid.

32. Ibid., VI. viii. 9,1142a.

33. Ibid.

34. This condensed passage from the *Ethics* has caused translators and scholars difficulty, perhaps because they read the analogy between ethical and mathematical "perception" as intended to be closer than Aristotle meant it to be. For, he added, *phronesis* in Ethics is different in kind (*allo eidos*) not just from sense perception but from mathematical perception also; and in this way he took back some implications of what he had said just previously. Our reading takes the word *eschaton* as covering what we earlier called "a paradigmatic case." See, e.g., the paper by David Wiggins, "Deliberation and Practical Reasoning," in *Essays on Aristotle's Ethics*, ed. Amélie Ochsenberg Rorty (Berkeley, Los Angeles, London: 1980), pp. 221–240.

35. Aristotle, *Eth. Nic.*, II.ii.3–4, 1104a.

36. Ibid., I. vi.11–16, 1096b–1097a.

37. Ibid.

38. Ibid., V.x, 3–7, 1137b.

39. Aristotle, *Nicomachean Ethics*, ed. W. D. Ross (Oxford, 1924).

40. Aristotle, *Eth. Nic.*, III. i, 16 ff, 1111a.

41. Aristotle, *Rhetoric* I, 1, 1355b15.

42. Ibid., I, 4, 1359b10 ff.

43. Ibid., II, 21, 1395a1–5: compare *Eth. Nic.* I. iii.1094b–1095a.

44. Aristotle, *Topics* III, chaps. 1–6.

3. CICERO: PHILOSOPHER, ORATOR, LEGISLATOR

1. Marcus Tullius Cicero, *De Officiis*, trans. Walter Muller (Cambridge, 1913); H. A. Holder, *De Officiis Libri Tres*, Introduction, Analysis and Commentary (Amsterdam, 1966).

2. Plato, *Republic* I, 331e; Gorgias, *Double Arguments*, in *The Sophists*, p. 179; Aristotle, *Eth. Nic.*; Cicero, *De Officiis* III, 95.

3. M. Janet, quoted in R. Thamin, *Un Problème moral dans l'antiquité: étude sur la casuistique Stoîcienne* (Paris, 1884), p. 275.

4. See M. J. Buckley, "Philosophical Method in Cicero," *Journal of the History of Philosophy* 8 (1970):143–154; L. Mahieu, "Ciceron Moraliste," *Mélanges de Sciences Religieuses*, 5 (1948), 89–108.

5. J. M. Rist, *Stoic Philosophy* (Cambridge, 1969); J. M. Rist, ed., *The Stoics* (Berkeley, 1978).

6. P. Milton-Valente, *L'Ethique Stoîcienne chez Ciceron* (Paris, 1956); M. Pohlenz, "Antikes Fuhrertum: Cicero De Officiis und das Lebensideal des Panaitios," *Neue Wege zur Antike* 2 (1934); M. Van Straaten, *Panétius: sa vie, ses écrits et sa doctrine* (Amsterdam, 1946); G. Nebel, "Zur Ethik des Poseidonius," *Hermes* 34 (1939).

7. On these distinctions see Rist, *Stoic Philosophy*, chap. 6. The meaning of these terms was a matter of dispute among the ancients and still is among modern scholars.

8. Cicero, *De Officiis* III, 14.

9. *De Republica* III, 33. In *De Officiis* I, 31, Cicero defines the Natural Law in simpler terms: "the foundation of justice, namely, to refrain from harm and to serve the common good."

10. Cicero, *De Officiis* I, 59.

11. Ibid., I, 32.

12. Ibid., I, 59.

13. Ibid., I, 147.

14. Ibid., III, 8.

15. Ibid., III, 35.

16. Ibid., III, 18.

17. Ibid., III, 38; Plato, *Republic* III, 359C.

18. Cicero, *De Officiis* III, 89.

19. Ibid., III, 29–31.

20. Ibid., III, 51–57.

21. Ibid., III, 99–113.

22. Stanley Bonner, *Education in Ancient Rome* (Berkeley, 1977); G. Kennedy, *The Art of Rhetoric in the Roman World* (Princeton, 1972); and idem, *The Art of Persuasion in Greece* (Princeton, 1963).

23. Marcus Tullius Cicero, *De Inventione* trans. H. M. Hubbell (Cambridge, 1949); idem, *De Oratore*, trans. E. W. Sutton and H. Rackham,

(2 vols.) (Cambridge, 1967–1968). On the pervasive influence of *De Inventione*, see G. Kennedy, *Classical Rhetoric and Its Christian and Secular Tradition* (Chapel Hill, 1980).

24. Cicero, *De Inventione* I, 34.

25. Ibid., I, 7; *De Oratore*, 14, 45; 36, 126. Aristotle, *Rhetoric* I, 9.

26. Cicero, *De Inventione*, I, 9.

27. Ibid., I, 77.

28. Ibid., I, 46.

29. Ibid., I, 57; see Aristotle, *Prior Analytics* II, 26, 70a, 10.

30. Ibid., II, 150.

31. *Brutus* 78, 271. On the topics as commonplaces, see J. M. Lechner, *Renaissance Concepts of the Commonplace* (New York, 1962).

32. Cicero, *De Inventione* I, 100–106.

33. Cicero, *De Oratore*, 33, 119.

34. Cicero, *De Inventione* II, 159–174.

35. Bonner, *Education in Ancient Rome*, pp. 173-175.

36. See Richard McKeon, "Rhetoric in the Middle Ages," *Speculum* 17 (1942):1–32; H. Caplan, "Classical Rhetoric and the Medieval Theory of Preaching," *Classical Philology* 28 (1933):73–96; J. W. O'Malley, *Praise and Blame in Renaissance Rome: Rhetoric, Doctrine and Reform in the Sacred Orators of the Papal Court 1450–1521* (Durham, 1979); and F. de Dainville, *L'éducation des Jésuites* (Paris, 1978), chap. 2.

4. CHRISTIAN ORIGINS

1. Mt 19:16–22; Dt 5:6–21.

2. Lk 9:57–62.

3. Mt 19:3–12; 12:1–14; 15:1–20.

4. Mt 5:17–48; Mt 16:24.

5. Rudolf Schnakenberg, *The Moral Teaching of the New Testament* (New York, 1965). The great study of the rabbinic background of the New Testament is H. Strack and P. Billerbeck, *Kommentar zum Neuen Testament aus Talmud und Midrash* (Munich, 1928).

6. Gen 9.

7.   Acts 15:1–29. Rabbinic tradition acknowledged the Noachic Law, certain laws imposed on Adam and all "The Sons of Noah" by God before the revelation of Sinai. These were said to be (1) not to worship idols, (2) not to blaspheme, (3) to establish courts of justice, (4) not to kill, (5) not to commit adultery, (6) not to rob, and (7) not to eat flesh cut from a living animal. See Tosef 'ab Zarah, ix, 4; Sanhedrin, 56 seq. E. Benamozegh, *Israël et l'humanité* (Paris, 1961).

8.   I Cor 10:19-11:33; 8:1–13.

9.   I Cor 5, 6, 7, 11. Yves Congar, "St. Paul's Casuistry," in *Priest and Layman* (London, 1967); W. D. Davies, *Paul and Rabbinic Judaism* (London, 1970).

10.   Mt 19:23.

11.   R. Thamin, *Une Problème morale dans l'antiquité* (Paris, 1884), p. 290. See F. Murphy, "Background to a History of Patristic Moral Thought," *Studia Moralia* I (1962):49–85. E. Osborn, *Ethical Patterns in Early Christian Thought* (Cambridge, 1976); C. N. Cochrane, *Christianity and Classical Culture: A Study of Thought and Action from Augustus to Augustine* (Oxford, 1940).

12.   Lactantius, *Institutiones Divinae*, 5, 15–18, citing Mt 23:12, "he who humbles himself shall be exalted."

13.   Ambrose, *De Officiis Ministrorum*, III, iv, citing Mt 26:52. On this work, see T. Deman, "Le De Officiis de St. Ambroise dans l'histoire de théologie," *Revue des Sciences Philosophiques et Théologiques* 37 (1953):409–424; and J. Gaffney, "Comparative Religious Ethics in the Service of Historical Interpretation: Ambrose's Use of Cicero," *Journal of Religious Ethics* 9 (1981):35–47.

14.   Mt 19:16–22.

15.   M. Spanneut, *Le Stoïcisme des pères de l'Eglise* (Paris, 1957).

16.   On Augustine's moral teaching, see J. Mausbach, *Die Ethik des Heilige Augustine* (Freiburg, 1929), and B. Roland-Gosselin, *La Morale de St. Augustine* (Paris, 1925).

17.   Job 40:17.

18.   Gregory the Great, *Moralium Libri*, XXXII, chaps. 16–20, 28–40. We are indebted to Alan Donagan for adverting us to this text, which he discusses in his book *The Theory of Morality* (Chicago, 1977), p. 144. On the notion of the perplexed conscience, see also Aquinas, *Summa Theologiae* I–II, q. 19, a. 6; *De Veritate*, q. 17, a. 4; Bernard Haering, *The Law of Christ* (Westminster, Pa., 1964), I: 156 ff.

19.   Gal 3:28; 6:4.

20. *Institutiones Divinae*, I, 9.

21. The Council of Calcedon (451), refuting the heresy that Christ had only one nature (monophysitism), declared Christ to be "one person and subsistence . . . in two natures." The Christian philosopher Boethius (475–525) defines "person" as "an individual substance of rational nature" (*De Persona* III). See S. Schlossmann, *Persona und Prosopon im Recht und im Christliche Dogma* (Darmstadt, 1968).

22. *Penitential of Bede* in J. T. McNeil and H. M. Gamer, *Medieval Handbooks of Penance* (New York, 1938), p. 223.

23. *Pastor of Hermes* IV, I. On the early history of the doctrine and practice of penance, see O. D. Watkins, *A History of Penance*, 2 vols. (London, 1920); B. Poschmann, *Die Abendländische Kirchenbusse im Ausgang des Christlichen Altertums* (Munich, 1928); and R. C. Mortimer, *The Origins of Private Penance in the Western Church* (Oxford, 1939).

24. Council of Cabillonense (A.D. 813), cited in A. Van Hove, *Prolegomena* (Rome, 1945), p. 295. On the Penitential Books, see Ludwig Bieler, *The Irish Penitentials* (Dublin, 1963), and McNeil and Gamer, *Medieval Handbooks of Penance*.

25. Cummean III, 8–11 in Bieler, *The Irish Penitentials*, p. 110. There is a notable similarity in form and even in content between the Penitential literature and some of the civil law from the same period and cultural milieu. See Katherine Drew, *The Burgundian Code* (Philadelphia, 1949) and *The Lombard Laws* (Philadelphia, 1973). Alexander Murray notes another similarity: "A comparison of the earliest Irish and Celtic penitential codes with the astonishingly similar Brahmin Codes has led to the conclusion that these penitential tariffs were an amended Christian version of long pre-Christian legal customs shared by the Indo-European peoples. The analogy between the penitential tariffs and the Wergeld system of Western German kingdoms may be one of the reasons why the Irish system made headway." "Confession in the Middle Ages," lecture delivered at University College Dublin, 13 January, 1983.

26. Ibid., XI, 29, p. 133; see also text of the preface to the Bigotan Penitential in Bieler, *The Irish Penitentials*, p. 199.

27. Grove of Victory 2, in Bieler, *The Irish Penitentials*, p. 69.

28. *Penitential of Burchard*, 40, in McNeil and Gamer, *Medieval Handbooks of Penance*, p. 329.

29. Bigotan Penitential, Preface, in Bieler, *The Irish Penitentials*, p. 199. The text from Abbot Cassian is found in his *Collationes*, 19, 7. On the doctrine of medical methodism, see Ludwig Edelstein, *Ancient Medicine* (Baltimore, 1967).

5. THE CANONISTS AND CONFESSORS

1. The present summary of demographic and social change in Europe from 1050 to 1250 draws heavily on the much fuller treatment of the subject in Harold J. Berman's fascinating and illuminating book, *Law and Revolution: The Formation of the Western Legal Tradition* (Cambridge, Mass., 1983).

2. *Unam Sanctum* 18 Nov., 1302; *D–S*, #870–875; see W. Ullmann, *Medieval Papalism* (London, 1949).

3. Berman, *Law and Revolution*, pp. 127ff.

4. Ibid., p. 129.

5. Ibid., p. 251. Henry Lea, *The Duel and the Oath*, ed. E. Peters. (Philadelphia, 1974); J. W. Baldwin, "The Intellectual Preparation for the Canon of 1215 against Ordeal," *Speculum* 36 (1961): 613-636.

6. Berman, *Law and Revolution*, pp. 129 ff.

7. Ibid., p. 130.

8. Because the words "moral" and "ethical" both meant *customary*, they originally implied that individual actions must normally conform to collective practices and expectations.

9. Berman, *Law and Revolution*, pp. 256, 531.

10. Ibid., p. 222.

11. See, for example, Noonan's *Bribes*, chapters 5-11.

12. Aquinas, *Summa Theologica* I, q. 19, a. 6, ad 1. See "absolvo" in R. J. Deferrari, *A Lexicon of St. Thomas Aquinas* (Baltimore, 1948).

13. Berman, *Law and Revolution*, p. 142.

14. Ibid., pp. 74–75.

15. David Knowles, *The Evolution of Medieval Thought* (New York, 1962), pp. 80–81: compare Berman, *Law and Revolution*, pp. 161–162.

16. This is the phrase used in Islam to cover Jews, Christians, and Muslims alike, as all of them accepted the sacred status of the Old Testament.

17. See Aquinas' treatise on the natural law, *Summa Theologiae* I–II, q. 90–97, especially the remarks on the *jus gentium*, Q. 95, a. 4, ad. 4; Cicero, *De Republica*, 3.22.33, *De Legibus* I, 6, 18–19.

18. For a fascinating discussion of this whole matter, see the essay by Robert Gordis, "A Dynamic Halakhah: Principles and Procedures of Jewish law" in *Judaism*, vol. 28 (1979), pp. 263–82; and also the vigorous series of

seventeen responses to that essay in the next number of the quarterly, *Judaism*, vol. 29 (1980), pp. 4–109. The most uncompromising restatement of the Orthodox view is the response by Rabbi J. David Bleich, pp 30-37.

19.   In Islam the expression *shari'a* ("the way") designates the comprehensive form of personal and social life proper to the Faithful. *Shari'a*—literally "the path toward water"—is the holy law of Islam revealed in the words of Qur'an and in the traditions about the deeds and words of the Prophet and in the consensus of the community of Islam. In a narrower sense, *shari'a* refers to the external forms of ritual and social conduct to be observed by all Muslims. From the earliest era of Islamic religion (seventh or eighth century A.D.) leaders and teachers expounded and interpreted these obligations. Gradually, as theology and jurisprudence developed within the Arabic civilization, personal and subjective interpretations coalesced into a discipline and body of knowledge; and various schools of thought placed different emphasis on different factors—for example, the importance of tradition, the role of logical reasoning, the nature and origin of obligation, or the exact content and stringency of the law. Whatever their particular emphases, Islamic scholars agreed that all human obligation is rooted in the Will of Allah, that Allah's Will is inscrutable, that human will—conditioned and free at the same time—is bound to follow the Divine Will, and that human reasoning may determine how the inscrutable Divine Will is to be followed Within the context of these apparently contradictory theological positions, an elaborate moral/legal system was worked out that covered ritual, social, political, judicial, and economic activities.

It became customary to rank the stringency of obligations according to a fivefold scale: (1) duties whose performance was obligatory, (2) meritorious or recommended acts, (3) permitted or indifferent acts, (4) reprehensible acts, and (5) forbidden acts. The precise application of these categories, however, is a subject of continuing debate among the *mufti*. Given that Allah's Will is inscrutable, and given that human beings live in a present world still marred by sin and ignorance, it is not possible to observe the law perfectly. The law in its perfection is intended only for the ideal community of Islam: for the pious of this world it is a cause for confession of frailty, as well as having an educational and inspirational value. Thus Allah permits humans to find exceptions and use strategies (*hiyal*) for "evasion" of the law. There are always ways in which the strict letter of the law can be considered to have been observed, even though the means used in doing so are devised outside the law.

There is ample room for "casuistry" within this system. Those learned in the law [the *mufti*] are charged with interpreting how any particular requirement found in the Qur'an or tradition is to be applied in particular cultural and personal circumstances. Logical deduction and analogical reasoning [*fikh*] are accepted techniques in this interpretation. As an example, President Bourguiba of Tunisia was reported in the *New York Times* for 12 June 1983 as proposing that Tunisians invoke the exception from the obligation to fast during the month of Ramadan recognized in the case of people who are at war, since "Tunisia is at war against economic underdevelopment, and Ramadan slows the pace of economic and administrative life." Again, on 28 June 1983, the Grand Muftî of Jerusalem issued a *fatwâ* stating that any pious Muslim could, with moral justification, assassinate President Assad of Syria because, by expelling the leader of the Palestine Liberation Organization, Yassir Arafat, from Damascus, he had revealed himself to be evil and the cause of the death of many faithful.

So in Islam we recognize both the features of religious jurisprudence that are found in Catholic casuistry: the interpretative application of laws and rules in changed or special circumstances by use of analogical reasoning, and the readiness to devise forms of conduct that can be designated as "exceptions" to the strict letter of the law.

See F. Rahman, *Islam* (New York, 1966), chaps. 4 and 6; J. Schacht, *An Introduction to Islamic Law* (Oxford, 1964); and *Journal of Religious Ethics* 2, no. 2 (Fall 1983).

20. Gratian, *Concordantia Discordantium Canonum* P.I, D.1, in *Corpus Juris Canonici*, ed. A. Richter and A. Friedberg (Leipzig, 1922). The quotation from Isadore of Seville is from *Etymologies* v, 2, 1. On this famous text, see M. Villey, "Source et portée du droit naturel chez Gratien," *Revue de Droit Canonique*, 4 (1954):50–64. A brilliant summary of the complex and little-known history of canon law can be found in Berman, *Law and Revolution*, chaps. 4–6.

21. Stefan Kuttner, *History of Ideas and Doctrines of Canon Law in the Middle Ages* (London, 1980), p. 13. See also, for the general history, G. Le Bras and J. Gaudemet, eds., *Histoire du droit et des institutions de l'Eglise en Occident* (Paris, 1955–1958) 3 vols.

22. Ep 4:13, PL 83, 901.

23. Prom. PL 161, 50A; Letter 214, PL 162, 218.

24. Letter 250, PL 162, 256; Letter 16, PL 162, 29.

25. Isadore of Seville, Letter 4, 13 (PL 83–901). Ivo of Chartres, *Panormia*, Preface (PL 161, 50A), Letters 214 (PL 162, 218), 250 (PL 162, 256), 16 (PL 162, 29). See J. Salgado, "La methode d'interpretation du droit en usage chez les canonistes," *Revue de l'Université d'Ottawa* 22 (1951):201–213; 23 (1952):23–35.

26. Cicero, *Topics* IV, 23.

27. Aristotle, *Eth. Nic.* V. x. 3–7, 1137b.

28. Kuttner, *History of Ideas*, p. 15; Hostiensis, *Summa* I, 5.

29. Kuttner, *Repertorium der Kanonistik (1140–1234)* (Vatican City, 1937), citing the *Summa Parisiensis*, c. xviii, q. ii. This definition of *casus* is similar to the definition of *regula* in Roman Law: "a rule is a short statement which

briefly relates a matter." (*Dig.* 50.17): see P. Stein, *Regulae Juris* (Edinburgh, 1966). In Gratian's *Decretum* the more classical rhetorical term *causa* is used to describe the particular case.

30. Peter Cantor, *Summa de Sacramentis et Animae Consiliis*; Ed. See J. A. Duganquier, *Analecta Medievalia Namurcensia*, vols. 4, 7, 11, 21 (Namur, 1950–1972), III: 220. For a comprehensive study of Peter Cantor and his times, see J. W. Baldwin, *Masters, Princes and Merchants*, 2 vols. (Princeton, 1970). The general studies of the Confessional Books are J. Dietterle, "Die 'Summa Confessorum seu de Casibus Conscientiae' von Ihren Anfängen an bis zu Sylvester de Prieras," *Zeitschrift für Kirchengeschichte* 24 (1903), 25 (1904), 26 (1905), 27 (1906), 28 (1907); and P. Michaud-Quantin, *Sommes des casuistiques et manuels de confession au Moyen Age* (XII–XVI) (Louvain, 1962).

31. Alain of Lille, *Liber Poenitentialis*, ed. J. Longère, 2 vols. (Louvain, 1965), I: 27; II: 19.

32. Thomas of Chobham, *Summa Confessorum*, ed. F. Broomfield (Louvain, 1968), III, ii, q. 1-2.

33. Baldwin, *Masters, Princes and Merchants*, I: 19. The work of Robert Courson exists only in manuscript, except for a portion edited by V. Kennedy, "Robert Courson on Penance," *Medieval Studies* 7 (1945):330–378.

34. Robert of Flambrough, *Liber Poenitentialis*, ed. J. J. F. Firth (Toronto, 1971).

35. Michaud-Quantin, *Sommes des casuistiques*, p. 35.

36. E. Dublanchy, "Casuistique," *Dictionnaire de Théologie Catholique* II, c. 1872.

37. Raymond of Pennafort, *Summa de Poenitentia*, ed. X. Ochoa and A. Diez (Rome, 1976), I, x.

38. IV Council of the Lateran, *D–S*, #812–814. On the Albigensian heresy, see R. Foreville, *Lateran I-II-III-IV* (Paris, 1965); and H. Warner, *The Albigensian Heresy* (New York, 1967). This is the religious doctrine so vividly portrayed in Le Roy Ladurie's *Montaillou* (New York, 1978).

6. THE THEOLOGIANS

1. F. Vandenbroucke, *La Morale monastique du XIᵉ au XIVᵉ siècle* (Louvain, 1966); J. T. Welter, *L'Exemplum dans la littérature religeuse et didactique du Moyen Age* (Geneva, 1973); *Florilegium Morale Oxonense*, ed. C. H. Talbot (Louvain, 1956); *Moralium Dogma Philosophorum*, ed. J. Holmberg (Uppsala, 1929).

2. Peter Abelard, *Ethica seu Scire Teipsum*, ed. D. E. Luscomb (Oxford, 1971); Roger Bacon, *Philosophia Moralis*, ed. F. Delorme and E. Massa (Turin, 1953).

3. Luscomb, *Ethica*, p. xix.

4. Aquinas, *S.T.* I–II, q. 1, a.7, ad 2; Odo Lottin, *Morale fondamentale* (Tournai, 1954), p. vi. On the history of theological ethics, see Dom Odo Lottin's magisterial *Psychologie et morale aux XIIe et XIIIe siècles*, 6 vols. (Gembloux, 1942–1954) and, more briefly, T. Deman, *Aux Origines de la théologie morale* (Paris, 1951).

5. St. Thomas Aquinas was a systematic theologian rather than a casuist, but he shows himself to be a passable casuist on occasion—for example, his analysis of the vexed problem of multiple benefices (*Quodlibetales*, VIII, a. 13) and the question whether a judge should convict on public evidence a man whom he privately knows to be innocent (*S.T.* II–II, q. 67, a. 2). T. Deman comments on Aquinas's analysis of the benefice problem, "Eclaircissment sur Quodlibetales VIII," *Divus Thomas* 38 (1935): 42–61.

6. Ro 2:15.

7. *Digest* I, i, i; *Decretum* D I. The most concise history of the concept of natural law is A. P. d'Entrèves, *The Natural Law* (London, 1970). A more ample study is F. Fluckiger, *Geschichte der Naturrechts* (Zurich, 1954).

8. O. Lottin, "Le Droit naturel chez St. Thomas d'Aquin et ses prédécesseurs," *Psychologie et Morale*, II: 71–100.

9. *S.T.* I–II, q. 91, a. 1.

10. Aquinas, *S.T.* I–II, q. 94, a. 1. On Aquinas' theory of natural law, see Joseph Fuchs, *The Natural Law* (Dublin, 1965), and D. O'Connor, *Aquinas and the Natural Law* (London, 1967); G. Grisez, "The First Principle of Practical Reason: Commentary on S.T. I–II, 94," *The Natural Law Forum* 10 (1965):168–201.

11. Aquinas, *S.T.* I–II, q. 95, a. 4; *Commentarium* in *V Ethica* I, 12. See R. A. Armstrong, *Primary and Secondary Precepts in Thomistic Natural Law Teaching* (The Hague, 1966).

12. Aquinas, *S.T.* I–II, q. 94, a. 4, ad 6; in *V Ethica* I, 16.

13. Francisco Suarez, *De Lege et de Deo Legislatore* (Oxford, 1944) II, vi, 174.

14. Timothy Potts, *Conscience in Medieval Philosophy* (Cambridge, 1980), p. 1.

15. Ro 2:16.

16. Jerome, *Commentarium in Ezechiel*, 25, 22, cited in Potts, *Conscience in Medieval Philosophy*, p. 80. The reference to Plato is *Republic* IV, 463B–441B. The words *synteresis, synedesis,* and *synderesis* have a somewhat different meaning, each of which medieval theologians exploit; *synderesis* finally becomes the most general word equivalent to "conscience." See C. Pierce, *Conscience in the New Testament* (London, 1953). See also Lottin, *Psychologie et morale*, II: 103–350.

17. Peter Lombard, *Sentences*, I–II, chaps. 1–3 in Potts, *Conscience in Medieval Philosophy*, pp. 90–93; Philip Chancellor, *Summa de Bono, de Conscientia*, in ibid., pp. 94–109.

18. Aquinas, *Quaestiones Disputatae de Veritate*, Qq. 16–17, in ibid., pp. 122–136.

19. Potts, *Conscience in Medieval Philosophy*, pp. 55–60. For a modern Thomistic interpretation of the doctrine of conscience, see Philip Delhaye, *The Christian Conscience* (New York, 1968).

20. Cicero, *De Officiis* I, 43.

21. Chancellor, *Summa de Bono*, III, 1, 259–264. The image of the charioteer is from Plato's *Phaedrus*, 246-256.

22. Aquinas, *S.T.* I–II, q. 47, aa. 1–16. On Aquinas' teaching, see T. Deman, *La Prudence* (Paris, 1949). The Aristotelian concept of *phronesis* is expounded in chapter 2 of this volume.

23. Aquinas, *S.T.* I–II, q. 47, a. 15; q. 49, a. 7, ad 1–2; q. 49, a. 8, ad 3.

24. Boethius, *De Differentiis Topicis* (Migne, *Patres Latinae*, 64, 1205); Cicero, *De Inventione* I, 6; *Topica* 21, 80; Quintillian, *Institutiones* III, 5, 17. See J. Gründel, *Die Lehre von Umständen der Menschlichen Handlung im Mittelalter* (Munster, 1963).

25. Cicero, *De Inventione* I, 24–28; *De Rhetorica* 7.

26. Aristotle, *Eth. Nic.* III 1, 1110b30–1111a18.

27. Aquinas, *S.T.*, I–II, q. 7, a. 3.

28. *Decretum* L5, D40; St. John Chrysostom, *In Mattaeum*, 40, 21; pseudo-Augustine, *de Vera Poenitentia*, chap. 14; Huggucio, *Summa in Decretum*, ad c 5, D40. See D. Robertson, "A Note on the Classical Origins of 'Circumstances' in the Medieval Confessional Literature," *Studies in Philology* 43 (1946): 6–14.

29. Abelard, *Ethica*, chap. 7; Aquinas, *S.T.*, I–II, q. 7, a. 2; Albertus Magnus, *Quaestiones in Ethica*, cited in Gründel, *Die Lehre von Umständen*, p. 507; Cicero, *De Inventione* I, 34. On Abelard's doctrine, see Lottin, "La problème de la moralité intrinsique d'Abelard à St. Thomas d'Aquin," *Psychologie et morale* II: 421–465.

30. Aquinas, *S.T.* I–II, q. 18, aa. 10–11; *Quaestiones Disputatae de Malo*, q. 2, a. 4, ad 13; in *IV Sententiarum* 33, 1, 1.

7. SUMMISTS AND JESUITS

1. The general historical studies of the authors we are about to discuss are E. Dublanchy, "Casuistique," *Dictionnaire de Théologie Catholique* (Paris, 1932), II-2, cols. 1859–1877; T. Deman, "Probabilisme," in ibid., XII, cols.

418–619; P. Michaud-Quentin, *Sommes de casuistiques et manuels de confession au moyen age* (Louvain, 1962); J. Dietterle, "Die Summa Confessorum Sive de Casibus Conscientiae: Von Ihren Anfängen an bis zu Sylvester de Prieras." *Zeitschrift für Kirchengeschichte* 24 (1903), 25 (1904), 26 (1905), 27 (1906), 28 (1907); J. Theiner, *Die Entwicklung der Moraltheologie zur Eigenständigen Disziplin* (Regensburg, 1970).

2. Cajetan, *Summula Peccatorum* (1523), preface; R. Fumus, *Summa Armilla*, (1550) dedication; François Rabelais, *Gargantua and Pantagruel* III, chaps. 39–44. None of the fourteenth- and fifteenth-century summas and none of the books of "high casuistry" have benefited from a scholarly modern edition. Although published in innumerable editions, copies are difficult to come by and the dates and proper sequence of editions difficult to ascertain. The Bodleian Library at Oxford University and the Woodstock Library, Georgetown University, were invaluable resources for these works.

3. All of these distinctions can be found in the classical summas, such as *Angelica* or *Sylvestrina*, under the entry "Peccatum" or "Actus Humanus." They can be found in any modern work on moral theology, such as Häring, *The Law of Christ*. All of these distinctions bear on the nature of sin. Critics of casuistry often note the apparent preoccupation of casuistical authors with sin or, as one of them said, "moral pathology" (T. Slater, *Manual of Moral Theology*, New York, 1931, preface). Still, as Dom Lottin comments, "although moralists tend to speak of the distinction of species and number only with respect to sin, the discussion is equally applicable to morally good acts." *Morale fondamentale* (Tournai, 1954), p. 60.

4. Michaud-Quentin, *Sommes de casuistiques*, p. 110.

5. See T. Tentler, *Sin and Confession on the Eve of the Reformation* (Princeton, 1977).

6. Council of Trent, Session XIV, chap. 5 in *D–S*, #1679, #1707; and see Henry Jedin, *A History of the Council of Trent* (St. Louis, 1957). The decree made official a teaching that had been common among theologians for several centuries: for instance, Jean Gerson (1363–1429) *De Arte Audiendi Confessiones*. "The confessor should know all sins by species and number just as a learned physician knows illnesses" (*Oeuvres complètes*, Paris, 1971), VIII: 11.

7. Owen Chadwick, *The Reformation* (Grand Rapids, 1965); John Dolan, *The History of the Reformation* (New York, 1965).

8. The cultural, social, and economic history of the era during which casuistry flourished is related in detail in the studies of Fernand Braudel, *The Mediterranean and the Mediterranean World in the Age of Philip II*, trans. S. Reynolds, 2 vols (New York, 1973), and *Civilization and Capitalism 15th–18th Centuries*, 3 vols. (New York, 1981).

9. Francisco Vitoria *Relectio de Indis et de Jure Belli*, trans. E. Nuys (Washington, 1917); Francisco Suarez, *Defensio Fidei Catholicae et Apostolicae*

Adversus Anglicanae Sectae Errores, in *Selections from Three Works of Francisco Suarez,* trans. G. C. Williams (Oxford, 1944). See B. Hamilton, *Political Thought in Sixteenth-Century Spain: A Study of the Political Ideas of Vitoria, De Soto, Suarez and Molina* (Oxford, 1963); R. Bireley, *Religion and Politics in the Age of the Counterreformation* (Chapel Hill, 1981).

10. Theiner, *Die Entwicklung der Moraltheologie,* p. 24. One author characterizes the artistic and literary style of the era as naturalistic, marked by virtuosity in use of time and space, influenced by classical antiquity, and notes: "the fleeting glance, the momentary gesture, the changing aspects of nature tell of transience, mutability and time's swift flight . . . in the hands of Rubens, Poussin and Bernini, the 'allegory of truth revealed by time' becomes one of the classic features of Baroque art" (J. R. Martin, *Baroque,* New York, 1977, p. 8). The urge to describe casuistry in these terms is hardly resistible.

11. Jonathan Glover, "It Makes No Difference Whether I Do It or Not," *The Aristotelian Society,* Supp. vol. 49 (1975):183.

12. Antoninus, *Summa Moralis* (1460), I, c. 373; see D. Hay, *The Italian Renaissance and Its Historical Background* (Cambridge, 1977).

13. William Banger, *A History of the Society of Jesus* (St. Louis, 1972). An example of the pejorative use is found in G. Calebresi's *A Common Law for the Age of Statutes* (Harvard, 1982), "judicial interpretation that would make the proverbial Jesuit blush" (p. 1).

14. J. Spence, *The Memory Palace of Matteo Ricci* (New York, 1984); J. Correia-Alfonso, *Letters from the Mughal Court: The First Jesuit Mission to Akbar* (1580–1583) (St. Louis, 1981); G. Dunne, *A Generation of Giants: The Story of the Jesuits in China in the Last Decade of the Ming Dynasty* (London, 1962).

15. Ignatius of Loyola, *The Spiritual Exercises,* trans. Louis Puhl (Chicago, 1952). See Hugo Rahner, "Discernment of Spirits," in *Ignatius the Theologian* (New York, 1968), and Michael Buckley, "The Structure of Rules for Discernment of Spirits," *The Way,* supp. vol. 20 (1973):19–37.

16. G. de Bruès, *Dialogues: A Critical Edition with a Study in Renaissance Scepticism and Relativism,* ed. P. P. Morphos (Baltimore, 1953); R. H. Popkin, *The History of Scepticism from Erasmus to Spinoza* (Berkeley, 1979).

17. *Constitutio Societatis Jesu* IV, 5; *Ratio Studiorum,* "de casibus" (1591); *Institutum Societatis Jesu* II, 586; *Epitome* IV, viii, 372. These major documents are available in English in *The Constitutions of the Society of Jesus,* trans. G. Gans (St. Louis, 1972) and the *Ratio Studiorum of 1599,* trans. A. Farrell (Washington, 1970).

18. *Ratio Studiorum* of 1599. "Rules of the Professor of Cases of Conscience." The title of this office was changed to Professor of Moral Theology in the revised *Ratio Studiorum* of 1832.

19.   On the teaching of moral philosophy and theology in the Society of Jesus, see Theiner *Die Entwicklung der Moraltheologie,* and A. Schimberg, *L'Education morale dans les collèges de la Compagnie de Jésus en France* (Paris, 1913). On the influence of casuistry on one famous Jesuit pupil, Calderón, see P. Pring-Mill, "La Casuistica como factor estructurizante en las comedias de Calderón, *Iberomania* 14 (1981):60–74.

20.   H. Hurter, *Nomenclator Litterarius Theologiae Catholicae,* 5 vols. (Innsbruck 1903–1913) III: 353–355, 590–603, 880–896, 1175–1202.

21.   F. Hofmann, *Moraltheologische Erkenntnis und Methodenlehre* (Munich, 1963); B. Häring and L. Vereeke, "La Theologie morale de St. Thomas d'Aquin à St. Alphonse de Ligouri," *Nouvelle revue theologique,* 77 (1955): 673–692.

22.   F. Dainville, *L'Education des Jésuites: xvie–xviie siècles* (Paris, 1978); F. Donnelly, *Principles of Jesuit Education* (New York, 1934).

8. TEXTS, AUTHORS, AND METHODS

1.   Martin Azpilcueta, *Enchiridion Sive Manuale Confessariorum et Poenitentium* (Rome, 1573; Lyon, 1582).

2.   E. Dunoyer, *L'Enchiridion Confessariorum del Navarro* (Pamplona, 1957), p. 123.

3.   Azpilcueta, *Manuale Confessariorum,* chap. xv, p. 101; xvii, p. 323; xiv, p. 239. For Navarrus' contribution to the doctrine of usury, see M. Grice-Hutchinson, *The School of Salamanca* (Oxford, 1952).

4.   Dunoyer, *L'Enchiridion Confessariorum,* p. 128.

5.   Juan Azor, *Institutionum Moralium in Quibus Universae Quaestiones ad Conscientiam Recte aut Prave Factorum Breviter Tractantur* (Rome, 1600–1611).

6.   Ibid., I, xviii, pp. 43-44 (Cologne, 1602).

7.   Ibid., III, ii, pp. 102 f.

8.   Jean Gury, quoted in "Azor," *Dictionnaire de Théologie Catholique* (Paris, 1922), I, col. 2653. The word "classical" is properly applied: the first pages of many volumes of casuistry contain lists of authors "of the first rank (*primae classis*)," "of the second rank," and so on, designating their standing in the casuistic world.

9.   Antonio Escobar y Mendoza, *Liber Theologiae Moralis Vigintiquatuor Societatis Jesu Doctoribus Resertus* (Lyon, 1644); *Universae Theologiae Moralis Receptiores absque Lite Sententiae necnon Problematicae Disquisitiones* (Lyons, 1652–1663). See A. Gazier, *Blaise Pascal et Antonio Escobar* (Paris, 1912), and P. Weiss, *P. Antonio Escobar y Mendoza als Moraltheologe in Pascal's Beleuchtung und in Lichte der Wahrheit* (Freiburg in Bresgau, 1911).

10. Hermann Busenbaum, *Medulla Theologiae Moralis Facili et Perspicua Methodo Resolvens Casus Conscientiae ex Variis Probatis Auctoribus Concinnata* (Munster, 1650).

11. Alphonsus Ligouri, *Theologia Moralis Juxta Methodum Medullae Hermanii Busenbaum* (Bonn, 1748).

12. Antonio Diana, *Resolutiones Morales*, 10 vols. (Palermo, 1629–1654).

13. D. Prummer, *Manuale Theologiae Moralis* (Barcelona, 1946), p. 226.

14. Martin de Acolea, *Diana Coordinatus* (Lyon, 1667); Antonio Cotonio, *Summa Diana* (Anvers, 1656).

15. T. Deman, "Probabilisme," *Dictionnaire de Théologie Catholique* XIII, col. 491.

16. Juan Caramuel-Lebkowitz, *Theologia Moralis ad Prima Eaque Clarissima Principia Reducta* (Louvain, 1645). This energetic character wrote many books on many subjects. The titles of two reveal the spirit of the author: *Pandoxion Physico-Ethicon: Opus Pugnax et Contentiosum Non Solum Philosophiis et Theologiis necnon Canonistis, Legistis, Sed Mediciis et Mathematicis Utile et Necessarium* (Campania, 1668), and *Apologema pro Antiquissima et Universalissima Doctrina de Probabilitate contra Novam, Singularem, Improbabilemque Prosperi Fagnanii Opinationem* (Lyons, 1658).

17. Dunoyer, *L'Enchiridion Confessariorum*, p. 126.

18. See Paul Althaus, *The Ethics of Martin Luther* (Philadelphia, 1972). One classic example of casuistry in the Lutheran tradition was the *Theologia Casualis* (1680) of Johann Adam Osiander; William Ames' *De Conscientia, ejus Jure et Casibus* (1630) was equally popular in the Calvinist tradition. Karl Barth writes a stinging critique of casuistry as "an encroachment on man's action under the command of God, a destruction of Christian freedom . . . the casuist sets himself on God's throne, distinguishing good from evil." *Church Dogmatics* (Edinburgh, 1961), III (4): 7–19.

19. H. McAdoo, *The Structure of Caroline Moral Theology* (London, 1949); T. Wood, *English Casuistical Divinity during the Seventeenth Century* (London, 1952); E. Rose, *Cases of Conscience: Alternatives Open to Recusants and Puritans under Elizabeth and James I* (Cambridge, 1975); and C. Slights, *The Casuistical Tradition in Shakespeare, Donne, Herbert and Milton* (Princeton, 1981).

20. "An Advertisement Touching the Controversies of the Church of England," *Letters and Life of Francis Bacon*, ed. J. Spedding, 7 vols. (London, 1861–1872) I: 92. On Bacon's problem of conscience, see John Noonan, *Bribes* (New York, 1984), chap. 12.

21. "Epistle Dedicatory," in William Perkins, *Whole Treatise of the Cases of Conscience* (1606), pp. 3–4. The modern edition is *English Puritanist: His Pioneer Works in Casuistry*, ed. T. Merrill (Niekoop, 1966).

22. Robert Sanderson, *De Juramenti Promissorii Obligatione* (1647); *De Obligatione Conscientiae* (1660). It is interesting to note that William Whewell, who was to abandon the word "casuistical" in the title of the Knightbridge Chair, edited Sanderson's *Works* in 1854. The quotation from Izaak Walton is from "Life of Dr. Sanderson" (1678), *Lives* (London, 1951), p. 281.

23. Jeremy Taylor, *Ductor Dubitantium or The Rule of Conscience in All Her General Measures, Serving as a Great Instrument for Determination of Cases of Conscience. Whole Works,* ed. R. Heber (London, 1850), preface. Taylor goes on: "We cannot be well supplied at the Roman storehouses, for though there the staple is, and many excellent things exposed to view, yet we have found the merchants to be deceivers and the wares too often falsified."

24. *De Juramenti Obligatione,* 6, in *Works of Robert Sanderson,* ed. William Jacobson, 6 vols. (Oxford, 1854), IV: 331.

25. Ibid., 3, 4.

26. Taylor, *Ductor Dubitantium,* preface.

27. George Herbert, *A Priest to the Temple* (1652), chap. V.

28. Wood, *English Casuistical Divinity,* p. 137.

29. Taylor, *Ductor Dubitantium,* Preface.

30. Ibid., XII, IV, 2.

31. Wood, *English Casuistical Divinity,* p. 36.

32. Kenneth Kirk, *Conscience and Its Problems,* p. 203.

33. C. Hill, *The Century of Revolution, 1603–1714* (Edinburgh, 1961), p. 244. It is also worth noting that, at the end of the century, a vigorous movement for "reformation of manners"—that is, Sabbath breaking, drunkenness, swearing—swept England. Such movements are usually rigorist and thus have little sympathy for a casuistry that recognizes exceptions and excuses.

34. Vernon Bourke, *History of Ethics* (Garden City, N.Y., 1968), p. 137. Henry More corresponded with that other geometrically minded philosopher, René Descartes, and also influenced Isaac Newton. As he wrote, "I will take from the storehouse of the soul certain principles which are immediately true and needing no proof, but into which almost all moral doctrine is plainly and easily resolved even as a mathematical demonstration is resolved into common axioms." *Enchiridion Ethicum* (1667), 3, 2. Henry Sidgwick considered More one of his intellectual progenitors: see his *Outlines of the History of Ethics* (1886), p. 300, and chapter 15 in this volume.

35. William Whewell, *Lectures on the History of Moral Philosophy in England* (London, 1852), p. 9.

36. Henry Sidgwick, *The Methods of Ethics* (London, 1874); on Sidgwick's work, see J. B. Schneewind, *Sidgwick's Ethics and Victorian Moral Philosophy*

(Oxford, 1977). One historian of Victorian England has noted, "schematic solutions had always been a Victorian specialty—everything from ethics to biology had been tabulated, subdivided and classified." Jan Morris, *Farewell the Trumpet: An Imperial Retreat* (London, 1978), p. 59.

37. G. A. Starr, "From Casuistry to Fiction: The Importance of the *Athenian Mercury*," *Journal of the History of Ideas* 27 (1967):17–32; and *Defoe and Casuistry* (Princeton, 1971). Dear Abby and Ann Landers, then, are the descendants of the casuists and, on occasion, would do their ancestors proud. For example, Dear Abby answered "a question of ethics with regard to abortion: to whom is the family physician more responsible, the parents or the teenager?" with a proper casuistic analysis of the complex relationship between the parties (*San Francisco Chronicle*, 18 October, 1985).

38. Slights, *The Casuistical Tradition in Shakespeare*; Starr, "From Casuistry to Fiction,"; also A. E. Malloch, "John Donne and the Casuists," *Studies in English Literature* 2 (1962):58; D. Cathcart, *The Doubting Conscience: Donne and the Poetry of Moral Argument* (Ann Arbor, 1975).

39. Bartolomeo Medina, *Expositio in Summae Theologiae Partem*, I-II, q. 19, a. 6. This brief sentence spawned an enormous literature. See de Blic, "Medina et les origines du probabilisme," *Ephemerides Theologiae Louvainensis* 7 (1930):46–93, 264–291. The most readily available explanation of the doctrine can be found in Häring, *The Law of Christ* I: 169–189. The most scholarly essay is T. Deman, "Probabilisme," *Dictionnaire de Théologie Catholique* XIII, i, cols. 417–619. A massive study, quite biased against probabilism, is I. Dollinger and F. H. Reusch, *Geschichte der Moralstreitigkeiten in der Romisch-Katholischen Kirche seit den 16 Jahrhundert*, 2 vols. (Nordlingen, 1889). A more favorable study, but limited to the prehistory of the doctrine, is J. Ternus, *Zur Vorgeschichte der Moralsysteme von Vitoria bis Medina* (Paderborn, 1930). The distinction between epistemological probability and the statistical probability known to modern science is traced in I. Hacking, *The Emergence of Probability* (Cambridge, 1975).

40. Pascal, *The Provincial Letters*, Letter V, p. 81. All page references here to Pascal's *Provincial Letters* will be to A. J. Krailsheimer's translation (London and Baltimore, 1967).

41. Quoted in Deman, "Probabilisme," col. 502.

42. Alexander of Hales, *Summa Theologiae* II, 2, 3, 2. See O. Lottin, "Le tutiorisme morale du XIIIᵉ siècle," *Psychologie et Morale* II: 354–417.

43. Aquinas, *Summa Theologiae* II–II, q. 70, a. 2. See A. Gardiel, "La Certitude probable," *Revue des sciences philosophiques et théologiques* 5 (1911):441–485. The Latin "probabilis" also means "provable."

44. Medina, *Expositio in Summae Theologiae Partem*.

45. See T. N. Tentler, *Sin and Confession on the Eve of the Reformation* (Princeton, 1977). "Confessor shopping" was a common phenomenon, par-

ticularly for persons engaged in morally problematic activities, such as business involving the paying and charging of interest. See chapter 9.

46. Gabriel Vasquez, *Commentaria in II-II*, LXII, iv. These two components of a probable opinion persist into modern law. For example, the *Book of Approved Jury Instructions* of the State of California (1977) requires the judge to instruct a jury that has heard expert witnesses, "in resolving conflict in the testimony of expert witnesses, you should weigh the opinion of one expert against another. In doing this, you should consider the qualification and believability of each witness, the reasons for each opinion and the matter on which it is based."

47. Thomas Sanchez, *Opus Morale* I, ix, 7; Caramuel, *Theologia Regularis* VI.

48. Caramuel, *Theologia Regularis*, 1.; Escobar y Mendoza, *Universae Theologiae Moralis*, I, Praeloquium, c. 23.

49. Pascal, *The Provincial Letters*, Letter V, p. 84.

50. *Decretales* 129, 8. A list of 211 maxims or rules of this sort appears in the *Digest of Justinian* at Title 50.17. See Berman, *Law and Revolution*, pp. 137–139, for a discussion of their import and origin. Similar lists of maxims can be found in many books of casuistry, for example, F. Zacharia, *Theologia Moralis ad Quaedam Generalia Axiomata Redactae*, included in later editions of C. Lacroix's influential *Theologia Moralis* (1707–1714).

51. Franciso Suarez, *De Bono et Malo Humanorum Actuum*, XII, 4–5.

52. Paul Laymann, *Theologia Moralis* (1625), I, 1, 5.

53. D. Prummer, *Manuale Theologiae Moralis* (Fribourg, 1927), I: 217.

54. Vasquez, *Commentaria in II–II*, D. 62, 6; 63, 2–3; 64, 2–4.

55. Dunoyer, *L'Enchiridion Confessariorum*, p. 126.

56. Deman, "Probabilisme," col. 496.

57. Pascal, *The Provincial Letters*, Letter V, p. 81.

58. Deman, "Probabilisme," col. 517.

59. See A. Eberle, "Das 'Probabile' bei Thyrsus Gonzales als Grundlage Seines Moralsystems," *Theologische Quartalschrift* 127 (1947):295–331. Among the early Jesuit critics of probabilism were Paul Comitolus, *Responsa Moralia* (1609); Andrew Bianchi *De Opinionum Praxi Disputatis* (1642); Francis Rabello, *De Obligationibus Justitiae, Religionis et Charitatis* (1608); and even, perhaps, the great Robert Cardinal Bellarmine (see Deman, "Probabilisme," col. 498). Two generals of the society, Claude Acquaviva, in 1613, and Mutius Vitelleschi, in 1617, wrote official letters warning about the teaching "of less solid doctrine" in moral matters, but the recipients, being good probabilists, favored freedom and continued to support the doctrine.

60. Quoted in Deman, "Probabilisme," col. 527.

61. This twentieth-century reprise of the debate can be found in T. Richard, "Théories de la certitude morale," *Revue Thomiste* 28 (1923):157–178, 194–205; E. Brisbois, "Pour la probabilisme," *Ephimerides Theologiae Louvainenses* 13 (1936):80–94; M. Rolland, "La fondament psychologique du probabilisme," *Nouvelle revue théologique* 63 (1936):351–364. A modern edition of the work of John of St. Thomas recently appeared: *Tractatus de Signis: The Semiotic of John Poinsot*, ed. J. N. Deely and R. A. Powell (Berkeley, 1985).

62. *De Opinione Probabili* (Rome, 1665), n. 109–111; Deman, "Probabilisme," cols. 509–510.

63. Fagnanus, *De Opinione Probabili* (1665), 109–111, cited in Deman, "*Probabilisme*," cols. 509-510; John Henry Newman, *A Grammar of Assent* (London, 1870).

64. See R. M. Hare, *Moral Thinking: Its Levels, Method and Point* (Oxford, 1981).

65. Deman, "*Probabilisme*," col. 534. The Roman Decrees can be found in *D–S*, #2021–2065; 2101–2168; 2301–2332.

66. Alphonsus Ligouri, *Theologia Moralis* I, 1, 2. See P. Raus, "St. Alphonse et les variations de son système morale," *Nouvelle revue théologique* 55 (1928):241–265, 334–352, and D. Capone, "Dissertazione e Note di S. Alfonso sulla Probabilità e la Conscienza," *Studia Moralia* 1 (1963): 265–343; 2 (1964): 89–155; 3 (1965):82–149. The similarity between probabilism and equiprobabilism was hotly debated by moral theologians in the nineteenth century. A. Ballerini, *De Morale Systemate St. Alphonsi Ligouri* (Rome, 1863); L. Le Bachelet, *La Question Ligourienne* (Paris, 1899). Brief and accurate definitions of "tutiorism," "probabilism," "probabiliorism," and "equiprobabilism" can be found in the *Dictionary of Christian Ethics*, ed. James Childress and John McQuarrie (New York, 1986).

PART IV: THREE SAMPLES OF CASUISTRY

1. Bernard Williams, *Ethics and the Limits of Philosophy* (Cambridge, Mass., 1985), p. 96.

2. Claude LaCroix, *Theologia Moralis* (1707), II, iv, ii, citing in agreement Azor, Suarez, Laymann, and Fillucci. He notes that it is particularly sinful to eat *matzos*.

3. Alphonsus Ligouri, *Theologia Moralis* (1763) IV, iii, ii, iii, citing in agreement Navarrus, Lessius, DeLugo, Laymann, and Tanner. Torture, allowed in Rome (though Ulpian considered it a foolish method for ascertaining truth; *Digest* 48:18), was condemned by the Synod of Christian Bishops in Rome, A.D. 384. It was revived in order to supplant the Ordeal

in the twelfth century. The Roman Inquisition had elaborate codes of ethics that stated the conditions and limits of torture (Torquemada, 1484; Edict of Inquisitor Valdes, 1561). That staunch opponent of judicial torture, the Italian jurist Beccaria, published his *Crime and Punishment* in 1764, the year after Ligouri's work just quoted. A papal decree of 1816 abolished torture as an inquisitorial method. See A. Jonsen and L. Sagan "Torture and Medical Ethics," in *The Breaking of Bodies and Minds*, ed. Eric Stover and Elena Nightingale (New York, 1985), and Edward Peters, *Torture* (Oxford, 1985).

4. *D-S* #2039; Ligouri, *Theologia Moralis* I, III, iv, i, ii, citing H. Busenbaum and Lessius. On the history of this question, see S. Sullivan, *Killing in Defense of Private Property* (Missoula, 1976), chap. 2.

5. The best historical review of the sexual ethics of the Roman Catholic Church is John Noonan, *Contraception* (Cambridge, Mass., 1965). The concept of a "sin mortal by its entire nature" (*mortale ex toto genere suo*) was introduced as late as the eighteenth century by the Jesuit casuist Claude LaCroix in *Theologia Moralis*, IV, II, I, 199, to designate a moral issue in which there was no "small matter" that could constitute a venial sin, as, for example, theft of a few pennies from a rich man would be. All sins would be mortal unless excused by a defect in knowledge or voluntariness. The concept was extensively used in sexual ethics but hardly anywhere else. The earlier "probable" doctrine that allowed for "small matter" in sexuality (e.g., a casual glance at beautiful breasts exposed in the fashionable gowns of the time), was condemned by Pope Alexander VII (*D-S* #1140). Since that time, Catholic moralists have maintained that any sexual pleasure sought outside matrimony is sinful *ex toto genere suo*. See Häring, *The Law of Christ*, III, 2, 3; A. Meier, *Das Peccatum ex Toto Genere Suo Mortale* (Regensburg, 1966); M. Kleber, *De Parvitate Materiae in Sexto* (Regensburg, 1971); B. Doherty, *The Sexual Doctrine of Cardinal Cajetan* (Regensburg, 1966).

6. R. Brandt, *Ethical Theory* (Englewood Cliffs, N.J., 1959), p. 73; see R. Firth, "Ethical Absolutes and the Ideal Observer," *Philosophy and Phenomenological Research* 12 (1952):317–345.

9. PROFIT: THE CASE OF USURY

1. The best introductions to the vast literature on the history of the usury problem are those by John Noonan, *The Scholastic Analysis of Usury* (Cambridge, Mass., 1957), and Benjamin Nelson, *The Idea of Usury*, 2d ed. (Chicago, 1969). The classic study is F. Schaub, *Der Kampf Gegen den Zinswucher, Ungerichten Preis und Unlautern Handel in Mittelalter: Von Karl dem Grossen bis Papst Alexander III* (Freiburg im Breisgau, 1905).

2. Deut. 23:19–20.

3. Saint Jerome, *Commentarium in Ezechiel* VI:18. St. Thomas Aquinas adopts this interpretation: "We are to understand that to take interest from any man is simply evil, because we ought to treat every man as our neigh-

bor and brother, especially in the State of the Gospel whereunto we are all called." *S.T.* II–II, q. 78, a. 1, ad 2. Another influential patristic text, St. Ambrose, *De Tobia*, XV, 15, allowed taking interest from one's enemies in warfare. The rabbinical commentary on the texts from the Old Testament (Dt 23:19; Ex 22:21; Lv 19:33, 25:35) is extensive. See J. Hejcl, *Das Alttestamentlische Zinsverbot* (Fribourg, 1907).

4. Council of Nicea, Canon 15.

5. Cited in Noonan, *The Scholastic Analysis of Usury*, pp. 15–16.

6. *Decretum* II c.14, 4.

7. *In Lucam* 6:35.

8. *Sententiarum Liber III*, D. 37, c. 3.

9. Paucapalea, *Summa*, c. 14, q. 3. The relevant passages in Roman law are *Digest* 44:7; *Institutiones* 3:14. Aquinas notes this etymological argument, which had become commonly accepted among theologians, but places little reliance on it (*S.T.* II–II, q. 78, a. 2, ad 5).

10. Bonaventure, *De Decem Praeceptis*, 6, 19.

11. Aquinas, *S.T.* II–II, q. 78, a. 1; *De Malo*, q. 13, a. 4. The passages from Aristotle are *Eth. Nic.*, V.5, 1133a, and *Politics* I.9, 1257b.

12. Aquinas, *S.T.*, II–II, q. 78, a. 2 ad 5; *Glossa Ordinaria*, c. 14, q. 3, c. 3; *Digests* 17:2; *Institutiones* 3, 25, 2; Pope Gregory IX, "Naviganti" (c. 1227), in *D-S* #823. On the evolution of commercial law (*lex mercatoria*) in the Middle Ages, see Berman, *Law and Revolution*, chap. 11.

13. Noonan, *The Scholastic Analysis of Usury* p. 152.

14. Hostiensis, *Summa* V, 8. See Noonan, *The Scholastic Analysis of Usury*, chap. 5. On the economic and social effect of these "titles," see J. Gilchrist, *The Church and Economic Activity in the Middle Ages* (London, 1969).

15. Noonan, *The Scholastic Analysis of Usury*, pp. 103–108.

16. Ibid., p. 225. Antoninus, *Summa Moralis* II, q. 1.

17. M. Grice-Hutchinson, *The School of Salamanca* (Oxford, 1952). The economics of the age are vividly described in the works of Fernand Braudel, *Civilization and Capitalism* 3 vols. (New York, 1981).

18. Noonan, *The Scholastic Analysis of Usury*, p. 100.

19. Ibid., chap. 10; *Summa Angelica* "usuria"; on Eck's role, see Heiko Obermann, *Masters of the Reformation* (Cambridge, 1981).

20. James Broderick, *The Economic Morals of the Jesuits* (London, 1934), p. 124.

21. Ibid., p. 149.

22. Ibid., p. 124. Father Polanco was the author of the first book of casuistry to be produced by a Jesuit. See chapter 7 this volume.

23. Ligouri, *Theologia Moralis* III, v, 3, 7. John Calvin taught that usury was only that level of interest that was harmful to the borrower; a just return on investment was morally licit. *De Usuris, Opera* X, ed. G. Baum, E. Cumitz, and E. Reuss (Brunswick, 1863–1906), cols. 248–249. This teaching had a considerable influence on Protestant views toward business, as Tawney noted in *Religion and the Rise of Capitalism* (London, 1926). The Catholic authors, Charles du Moulin (1500–1566) and Scipio Maffei (1675–1755), and Cardinal Cesar of Luzerne espoused a similar position (see Noonan *The Scholastic Analysis of Usury*, chap. 19). One of the last defenders of the medieval thesis was the nineteenth-century Irish priest Jeremiah O'Callahan, whose quixotic story is told in Nelson's *The Idea of Usury*, pp. 124–132.

24. See Fernand Braudel, *The Wheels of Commerce*, vol. 2 of *Civilization and Capitalism* (New York, 1981).

25. Pascal, *The Provincial Letters*, Letter VIII, p. 121.

10. PERJURY: THE CASE OF EQUIVOCATION

1. Pascal, *The Provincial Letters*, Letter IX, p. 140. The ethics of truthtelling and keeping secrets is thoroughly explored in Sissela Bok's two books, *Lying, Moral Choice in Public and Private Life* (New York, 1979) and *Secrets, On the Ethics of Concealment and Revelation* (New York, 1984). The most complete history of the Catholic teaching is J. Dobszynski, *Catholic Teaching about the Morality of Falsehood* (Washington, D.C., 1948).

2. Aristotle, *Eth. Nic.* IV.7, 1127ab; Plato, *Republic* III, 389b.

3. Cassian relates the sheer pragmatism of the Abbot Joseph, a holy anchorite (*Collations* XVII, 8: see Kirk, *Conscience and Its Problems*, pp. 188–192). St. Augustine's anger was kindled by St. Jerome's suggestion that St. Paul had deliberately lied about his disagreement with St. Peter (In Gal 2; St. Augustine, Letters 28, 30, 75, 82, 180). Clement of Alexandria, Origen, and John Chrysostom are said to have permitted lying for good purpose (see Dobszynski, *Catholic Teaching*, pp. 16 f).

4. Augustine, *De Mendacio*, chap. 6. *De Mendacio* was probably prompted by St. Augustine's irritation at St. Jerome's exegesis of Galatians 2:11, while *Contra Medacium* was written in refutation of the Priscillianists. Augustine was dissatisfied with the arguments he devised in *De Mendacio*, considering them too obscure, but in the end he allowed the book to circulate in hope that "it might arouse the love of truth in its readers" (*Retractions*, chap. 1). The case of refusal to lie in order to protect the innocent was based on an actual event—a certain Bishop Firminus, "firm in name, firmer in willpower," underwent torture because "he could neither lie nor betray" (*De Mendacio*, chap. 13).

5. *De Mendacio*, chap. 25. Augustine does concede that a "jocose" lie, a mere pleasant falsehood stated in jest, is not a sin, but he suggests that "souls striving for perfection" would avoid such frivolity, a position that led medieval monastic rules to outlaw joking (*De Mendacio*, chap. 2; Rule of St. Benedict, chaps. VI, VII). See the wonderful debate over laughter in a monastery in Umberto Eco's *The Name of the Rose* (New York, 1980), pp. 130–132. The severity of the Augustinian position may not have dominated penitential practice. For example, the Old Irish Penitential (c. 800) visits perjury with seven years' penance, and even little boys who perjure themselves to hide a companion's misdeeds are given one year on bread and water. "But if anyone utters falsehood deliberately without doing harm, three days in silence . . . anyone who utters falsehood whereof good results by giving a false description of a man's enemies or by carrying messages of peace between disputants or by rescuing a man from death, there is no heavy penance if it is done for God's sake" (McNeill and Gamer, *Medieval Handbooks of Penance*, pp. 162–163).

6. Aquinas, *S.T.* II–II, q. 110, a. 3, ad 4. Aquinas refers here to Augustine, *De Mendacio*, chap. 10, but adds the words "by a certain dissimulation."

7. Raymond of Pennafort, *Summa de Paenitentia* I, x. Pennafort's treatise is largely a commentary on Gratian's *Decretum* II, c. 22, which discusses perjury in view of the case of a bishop whose archdeacon refuses obedience because the bishop had unknowingly sworn to a falsehood.

8. *Summa Sylvestrina*, "Mendacium," 5; "Juramentum," 3.2. On the importance of the question about plague, see Carlo Cipolla, *Faith, Reason and the Plague in 17th-Century Italy* (Ithaca, N.Y., 1979).

9. Domenico Soto, *De Ratione Tegendi et Detegendi Secretum* (1582), XIII. The great Cardinal Cajetan rejected the mental restriction (in II–II, q. 89, a. 7, ad 4).

10. *D-S* #814. See B. Kurtscheid, *A History of the Seal of Confession* (St. Louis, 1927).

11. Navarrus, *In Decretales* II, c. 22, q. 5. The text refers to Gregory the Great, *Moralia in Job*, xxvi, 7, but apparently Gratian or some other commentator added the maxim-like phrase, "Intention should not be made to serve the words, but words the intention."

12. Azor, *Institutionum* I, x, iv; III xiii, iii.

13. For example, F. Suarez, *De Religione* V, iii, 9–10, and L. Lessius *De Justitia et Jure*, I, xlii, 47, favors the thesis of Navarrus, whereas Laymann, *Theologia Moralis* IV, 3, 13 and DeLugo, *De Fide* IV, 62–63, disapprove. The majority of casuists seem to have sided with the latter (see A. Vermeersch, "Restriction Mentale," *Dictionnaire apologetique de la foi catholique* (Paris, 1922), IV, cols. 967–982.

14. This story is told dramatically in Evelyn Waugh's *Edmund Campion* (Oxford, 1935). On the general background of this issue, see J. Bossy, *The English Catholic Community 1570–1850* (London, 1976) and P. Holmes, *Resistance and Compromise* (Cambridge, 1981). Many original documents of the era are collected in the two books edited by Philip Caraman, *The Other Face: Catholic Life under Elizabeth* (London, 1960) and *The Years of Siege: Catholic Life from James I to Cromwell* (London, 1966).

15. W. Haugaard, *Elizabeth and the English Reformation* (Cambridge, 1968), p. 327. On the "Bloody Question," see P. Hughes, *The Reformation in England* (London, 1954), III: 352–356.

16. William Perkins, *The Reformed Catholike* (1589), p. 346. This passage is cited in Rose, *Cases of Conscience*, the most complete history of the problem of truth-telling faced by Catholics and Puritans in that era. Rose notes that Perkins relied on Molanus, *Theologiae Practicae Compendium* (1590), v, 86–87, a passage that is, in fact, more subtle than Perkins admits.

17. State Papers 12.279.90, cited in Rose, *Cases of Conscience*, p. 83.

18. State Papers 14.18.16, cited in ibid., p. 90.

19. *Macbeth* II, iii; IV, ii. For commentary on these passages, see A. L. Rouse, *The Annotated Shakespeare* (New York, 1974), III: 414.

20. Holmes, *Resistance and Compromise*, p. 133; Rose, *Cases of Conscience*, p. 83.

21. P. Holmes, *Elizabethan Casuistry* (Catholic Record Society, 1981), J2, p. 52.

22. Ibid., J5, p. 54.

23. Ibid., L17–19, p. 71.

24. Ibid., L26, pp. 76–77. The use of Navarrus at the Douai-Rheims seminary is attested to in T. F. Knox, *Douai Diaries* (London, 1878), p. 28.

25. H. Garnet, *A Treatise of Equivocation or Against Lying and Fraudulent Dissimulation* (1595), ed. D. Jardine (London, 1851), pp. 9–12. On the background of this work, see P. Holmes, *Resistance and Compromise*, pp. 134–136. See also C. Devlin, *Robert Southwell* (London, 1956) and P. Caramen, *Henry Garnet and the Gunpowder Plot* (London, 1964).

26. Garnet, *A Treatise of Equivocation*, pp. 15–17.

27. Ibid., p. 54.

28. Ibid., p. 55.

29. Ibid., p. 64.

30. Ibid., p. 83.

31. Ibid., p. 92.

32. Ibid., pp. 104–105.

33. Robert Persons, *Discourse against Taking the Oath* (1606), Stonyhurst MS, cited in Holmes, *Resistance and Compromise*, p. 124.

34. Persons, *A Treatise Tending toward Mitigation* (1607), cited in Holmes, *Resistance and Compromise*, p. 124.

35. Hugo Grotius, *De Jure Belli et Pacis*, III, chap. 1; Immanuel Kant, "On the Supposed Right to Lie for Altruistic Purposes," in *Kant's Critique of Practical Reason and Other Works on the Theory of Ethics*, ed. T. K. Abbott (London, 1927.) One of the most sensitive discussions of the problem of equivocation is that of Cardinal Newman, who comments on Ligouri's acceptance of broad mental restriction, "in this department of morality, much as I admire the high points of the Italian character, I like the English rule of conduct better. . . . casuistry is a noble science but it is one to which I am led neither by my abilities nor my turn of mind." The "English rule" would have been followed by Samuel Johnson, who, Newman asserted, would have knocked down the inquiring murderer. *Apologia Pro Vita Sua* (London, 1880), chap. V and note G., pp. 244, 306, 310.

36. Robert Sanderson, *Works* V, 17–36. See C. Slights, *The Casuistical Tradition*, pp. 43–59.

37. Pope Innocent XI, *Condemnation of Laxist Doctrine* (1679), *D-S* #1176–1178; T. Sanchez, *Opus Morale* III, VI, 15; ibid., 9; Lessius, *De Justitia et Jure* II, XLII, 9, 48.

38. Arthur Vermeersch, "Restriction mentale," *Dictionnaire apologétique de la foi catholique* IV, cols. 967–982, at 973. See also Father Vermeersch's "De Mendacio et Necessitatibus Commercii Humani," *Gregorianum* 1 (1920): 11–40, 425–474; and Kenneth Kirk's gentle criticism in *Conscience and Its Problems*, note G, pp. 399–404.

11. PRIDE: THE CASE OF THE INSULTED GENTLEMAN

1. Pascal, *The Provincial Letters*, Letter VII, p. 105.

2. Justin Martyr, *Apology* I, 16, 3; Origen, *Contra Celsum* III, 7. On the early Christian teaching, see B. Schoph, *Das Totungsrecht bei den Frühchristlichen Schriftstellern* (Regensburg, 1958). The ancient rabbinic teaching on the sanctity of life is expressed in the saying "whoever preserves a single person is considered to have preserved a whole world; whoever destroys a single person is considered to have destroyed a whole world." Avoth Rabbi Nathan 31:2. See Baruch Brody, *Abortion and the Sanctity of Life* (Cambridge, Mass., 1975), and the issue of *Journal of Medicine and Philosophy*, "Medical Ethics from a Jewish Perspective," vol. 8 (1983):207–328.

3. St. Ambrose, *De Officiis* III, c. 4; Cicero, *De Officiis* III, 89.

4. St. Augustine, *Letters*, Letter 47, "Ad Publicolam."

5. Ibid., Letter 153, "Ad Macedonium."

6. Ibid., Letters 100, 139. On Augustine's just war teaching, see Roland Bainton, *Christian Attitudes toward War and Peace* (New York, 1960), chap. 6. The persistence of this ambivalence is notable even in the U.S. Bishops' Pastoral on nuclear war, *The Challenge of Peace* (1983). One commentator writes, "in the document the two traditions open to Catholics—pacifism and just war—are joined in such a way that they corrupt each other. . . . The two traditions derive from and foster . . . different patterns of moral reasoning and lead to different practical resolutions." James Finn, "Pacifism and Just War: Either or Neither," in *Catholics and Nuclear War*, ed. P. Murnion (New York, 1983), p. 143.

7. Cicero, *Pro Milone* 4; *Digests* IX, 2, 45, 4.

8. Synod of Grove of Victory, in Bieler, *Irish Penitentials*, p. 69; Ex 22:12.

9. *Corrector of Burchard* V, I, 14, in McNeill and Gamer, *Medieval Handbooks of Penance*, p. 325.

10. "Significasti," *Decretales* X, 5, 12, 18; "Si furiosus," *In Clementinam* V, 4, I; "Interfecisti," *Decretales* X, 5, 12, 2. On this development, see Shaun Sullivan, *Killing in Defense of Private Property* (Missoula, 1976). On the history of the cases of the monks defending themselves, see Berman, *Law and Revolution*, pp. 190–194.

11. Aquinas, *S.T.* I-II, q. 64, a. 7. On "double effect," see Joseph Mangan, "An Historical Analysis of the Principle of Double Effect," *Theological Studies* 10 (1949): 40–61, and Richard McCormick and Paul Ramsey, *Doing Evil to Achieve Good* (Chicago, 1978).

12. The rabbinic interpretation, in such texts as Baba Kaha 79b, Pesahim 2b, Yoma 85a, Mekhilta Ad Ex 22:2, and Sanhedrin 72a, are explained in B. Jackson, *Theft in Early Jewish Law* (Oxford, 1972). Texts from Roman law are "Furem Nocturnem" from the *Lex Cornelia* (76 B.C.), *Dig.* 28.8.9; "Si Pigniore," *Dig.* 47.2.56, and "Itaque," *Dig.* 9.2.4. The Canon "Si Perfodiens" is found in *Decretales Greg. IX, De Homicidio* V, 12, 3.

13. Raymond of Pennafort, *Summa Paenitentialis*, II, 1, 3.

14. Sullivan, *Killing in Defense of Private Property*, p. 27. See also L. Martines, ed. *Violence and Civil Disorder in Italian Cities* (Berkeley, 1972).

15. Panormitanus, *Commentaria in Libros Decretalium* Ad Significasti; *Summa Sylvestrina*, "Bellum" 2.1.

16. J. Azor, *Theologia Moralis* III, 2, 1, 14-16.

17. L. Lessius, *De Justitia et Jure* II, 9; Pascal, *The Provincial Letters*, Letter VII, p. 112. Kant discusses this distinction in his essay, *On the Old Saw that*

"It May Be Right in Theory, But It Won't Work in Practice" trans. E. Ashton (Philadelphia, 1974). Recently the United States Supreme Court considered, and rejected, the claim that honor is analogous to property; in *Paul v. Davis* (424 U.S. 693; Supreme Court 1155, 1976).

18.   Escobar y Mendoza, *Theologia Moralis* I, VII, 48; Laymann, *Theologia Moralis* III, iii, 3.

19.   Pascal, *The Provincial Letters*, Letter VII, p. 112.

20.   De Lugo, *Responsorium Morale* I, 9, 2, 80; Pascal, *The Provincial Letters*, Letter VII, p. 112. Father Tanner's writings (e.g., *De Justitia et Jure*, 1609) were not available to verify his remark, but he was resident at the Jesuit College of Ingolstadt, Austria, where many a haughty Habsburg soldier must have been stationed, so it is not hard to consider the attribution accurate. (Spanish *superbia* and Austrian *Gemütlichkeit* probably did not mix.) Recall, also, the words of another proud officer, Othello: "He who steals my purse, steals trash. . . He that filches my good name makes me poor indeed" (*Othello* III, iii). For a modern discussion of honor and reputation as moral goods, see Michael Walzer, *Spheres of Justice* (New York, 1983), chap. 11.

21.   Pope Innocent XI, Condemnation of Laxist Doctrines *D-S* #2130.

22.   Ligouri, *Theologia Moralis* III, iv, 1.

23.   Concina, *Theologia Christiana* VII, xvi–xvii.

12. CASUISTRY CONFOUNDED: PASCAL'S
CRITIQUE

1.   Our page references are to Blaise Pascal, *The Provincial Letters*, trans. Alban Krailsheimer (London and Baltimore, 1967). The critical edition of Pascal's works is L. Brunschvicq, P. Botroux, and F. Gazier, eds., *Oeuvres de Blaise Pascal* 14 vols. (Paris, 1914–1923). For a general biography, see Jean Chevalier, *Pascal* (London, 1930).

2.   On Jansenism, its theology, and the history of the controversy, see Nigel Abercrombie, *The Origins of Jansenism* (Oxford, 1936).

3.   L. Laporte, *La Doctrine de Port Royale* (Paris, 1952). On the *parti devot*, see Louis Cognet,"Ecclesiastical Life in France," in *The History of the Church*, eds. H. Jedin and J. Dolan (London, 1981), vol. VI.

4.   John Bossy,"The Counter-Reformation and the People of Catholic Europe," *Past and Present* 47 (1970): 51–70.

5.   Cited in ibid, p. 64.

6.   A. de Meyer, *Les Premières controverses Jansénistes en France* (Louvain, 1919), p. 383.

7.   A. Krailsheimer, Introduction, *The Provincial Letters*, p. 20. Antonio Escobar y Mendoza, *Liber Theologiae Moralis Viginti Quatuor Societatis Jesu*

Doctoribus Resertus (1644). See chapter 8. It is said that the good Father Escobar, to the end of his days, was puzzled by Pascal's attack; see "Escobar y Mendoza," *Dictionnaire de théologie Catholique* V, 1, cols. 520–521.

8.   Pascal, *The Provincial Letters*, Letter XII, p. 190.

9.   A. Brunetière,"Une apologie pour la casuistique," *Revue des deux mondes* 67 (1885): 213.

10.   Krailsheimer, Introduction, *The Provincial Letters*, p. 20. On Pascal's rhetoric, see P. Topless, *The Rhetoric of Pascal: A Study of His Art of Persuasion in the Provinciales and the Pensées* (Leicester, 1966).

11.   James Broderick, *The Economic Morals of the Jesuits*, p. 99.

12.   Pascal, *The Provincial Letters*, Letter V, p. 77.

13.   Ibid.

14.   Ibid., Letter XIII, p. 205.

15.   Ibid., Letter XVI, p. 257.

16.   Ibid., Letter XI, p. 177.

17.   Ibid., Letter XI, p. 170.

18.   *Oxford English Dictionary*,"casuistry."

19.   Pascal, *The Provincial Letters*, Letter X, p. 161.

20.   Daniel Concina, *Theologia Christiana-Dogmatica Moralis* (1772–1775), passim. See chapter 11.

21.   On this general problem, see James Gustafson, *Theology and Christian Ethics* (Philadelphia, 1974), chap. 2.

22.   See Anthony Levi, *The French Moralists* (Oxford, 1964).

23.   Pascal, *Pensées* #748. Paragraphs in the *Pensées* will be numbered here according to the edition of Louis Lafuma, *Blaise Pascal, Pensées sur la réligion et sur quelques autres sujets* (Paris, 1953), trans. J. Warrington (London, 1960).

24.   Pascal, *Pensées* #295. In a short essay, "Conversation with M. de Saci on Epictetus and Montaigne," Pascal compares and contrasts the Stoic and the Skeptic. The former is correct in disciplining his passions, the latter in revealing the inability of human reason to attain truth. Both are unsatisfactory guides, for neither humbles himself before the corruption of human nature and the absoluteness of God. See *Great Shorter Works of Pascal*, trans. E. Caillet and J. Blanknagel (Philadelphia, 1968).

25.   Pascal, *Pensées* #246.

26.   Ibid., #402.

27. Ibid., #433. On the Jansenist teaching on grace, see Abercrombie, *The Origins of Jansenism*, Pt. I.

28. Pascal, *Pensées*, #300.

29. Ibid., #405.

30. Ibid., #125: see also, "Without Jesus Christ and without Scripture. . . we cannot teach sound morality" (#380); "The whole company of casuists cannot give certitude to an erring conscience" (#844).

31. Ibid., #214. In a revealing jotting, Pascal notes,"Sceptic, geometer, Christian: doubt, assurance, submission" (#355).

32. Ibid., #343.

33. E. Baudin, *Études Historiques et critiques sur la Philosophie de Pascal*, Vol. III, *Sa Critique de la casuistique et du probabilisme morale* (Neuchatel, 1947), p. 132.

34. See John McNeill, *A History of the Cure of Souls* (New York, 1951), and Benjamin Nelson, "Self-Images and Systems of Spiritual Direction in the History of European Civilization," *The Quest for Self Control: Classical Philosophies and Scientific Research*, ed. S. Z. Klausner (New York, 1965).

35. Kirk, *Conscience and Its Problems*, p. 162.

36. Broderick, *The Economic Morals of the Jesuits*, p. 55. Pere Annat's retort was quickly translated into English by the Jesuit Martin Grene as *An Answer to the Provincial Letters Published by the Jansenists under the Name of Lewis Montalt against the Doctrine of the Jesuits and School Divinities Made by Some Fathers of the Society in France* (Paris, 1659). (Lewis Montalt was one of Pascal's *noms de plume*.) Father Grene says of the author of the *Provincial Letters* (p. 63), "he handles divinity like a stage-player." *The Provincial Letters* had appeared in English as *Mysteries of the Jesuits*, translated by J. Davis, in the year following their original publication.

37. Letter of Father General Goswin Nickel to Father Renault, Provincial of Paris, 18 February, 1659, quoted in Broderick, *The Economic Morals of the Jesuits*, p. 59.

38. "Daniel," *Dictionnaire de theologie Catholique* IV, col. 104. See J. Steinman, ed., *Les Provinciales: Résponse aux provinciales par Père Daniel* (Paris, 1962).

39. Broderick, *The Economic Morals of the Jesuits*, p. 115. Detailed but divergent comparisons of these two authors are given by K. Weiss, *P. Antonio Escobar y Mendoza als Moraltheologe in Pascal's Beleuchtung und im Lichte der Wahrheit* (Freiburg, 1911), and A. Gazier, *Pascal et Escobar* (Paris, 1912).

40. Escobar, *Liber Theologiae Moralis* III, ii, 163.

41. Pascal, *The Provincial Letters*, Letter VIII, p. 123.

42. Lessius, *De Justitia et Jure* (1605) II, 16, 1.

43. Pascal, *The Provincial Letters*, Letter XII, p. 191.

44. Kirk, *Conscience and Its Problems*, pp. 207-208.

45. Pascal, *The Provincial Letters*, Letter VI, p. 91.

46. Abercrombie, *The Origins of Jansenism*, p. 252.

47. H. Stewart, ed., *Les Provinciales* (Manchester, 1920), p. xxxv.

48. Broderick, *The Economic Morals of the Jesuits*, p. 66. The term *morale géometrique* recalls Spinoza, who was a contemporary of Pascal. Despite great differences, they represent ethical viewpoints with interesting similarities. Professor David Daube suggests that the modern meaning of "compromise" (namely, "coming to agreement by partial surrender of principles") is a product of the Jansenist-Jesuit dispute. He writes, ". . . evidently it is a product of Jansenism with its rigorous anti-Jesuit stance. The Jansenist school condemned not simply immorality—everybody did that—but more specifically a pragmatic give-and-take attitude to fundamental values." See D. Daube, "Compromise," *The Juridical Review*, December, 1983.

49. Deman, "Probabilisme," col. 517.

50. Pascal, *The Provincial Letters*, Letter IV, p. 61.

51. C. A. Saint Beuve, *Causeries du Lundi* (Paris, 1853), IX, 291. For an interesting reading of *The Provincial Letters* by another great literary figure, see Hilaire Belloc,"An Analysis of *Les Lettres Provinciales*," *Studies* 9 (1920):355–373.

13. THE ACHIEVEMENT OF CASUISTRY

1. G. Daniel, *Entretiens de Cléanth et Eudoxe* (1694), p. 358.

2. The current debate about terrorism arises at the edge of traditional cases about self-defense and turns on these same maxims. Was the American bombing of Libya "self-defense," as President Reagan claimed (*New York Times*, 15 April, 1986)? What should be the degree of "clarity and certitude" about the actual perpetrators of aggression that Mr. Schultz believes can justify retaliation (*New York Times*, 1 January, 1986)? Why does Mr Weinberger object to "indiscriminate response" (ibid.)? The official American policy on retaliation endorses "judicious employment of force"—that is, *moderamine inculpatae tutelae* (*New York Times*, 1 March, 1986). But there is no reason to believe that Messrs. Reagan, Schultz, and Weinberger, or the White House Task Force on Terrorism, have ever read Azor or Lessius. See B. Netanyahv, *Terrorism: How the West Can Win* (New York, 1986).

3. Birely, *Religion and Politics*, pp. 81, 172.

4. *Th. Mor.* III, 3, 3, 2. Bartlett's *Familiar Quotations* attributes the often-quoted phrase, "Circumstances alter cases," to an obscure American author, Thomas Haburton, in his book, *The Old Judge* (1849), but it must certainly have had more venerable origins.

5. See Footnote 5, pg. 379.

6. Daniel, *Entretiens*, p. 356.

7. Pascal, *The Provincial Letters*, Letter VIII, p. 197.

8. Daniel, *Entretiens*, pp. 358, 363.

9. See chapter 9.

10. *Institutionum* I, xviii, 43–44.

11. Strictly speaking, this is as true in the natural sciences as it is in ethics. The more complex and detailed the contents of Science become, the less a working scientist can check for himself every single idea or result on which his own work depends. Instead, he must often accept as "established" many opinions that merely *seem* to him all right, relying on the knowledge that they carry the support and authority of professional colleagues whom he trusts. This "professional support and authority" is what the casuists called *extrinsic* probability, as contrasted with *intrinsic* probability, which can be provided only by the scientist's own direct evidence and calculations.

12. The Catholic Bishops of the United States, as well as the Anglican Bishops of the United Kingdom, have brought just war concepts to the analysis of nuclear warfare: see, e.g., *The Challenge of Peace: God's Promise and Our Response* (Washington, D.C., 1983) and *The Church and the Bomb* (London, 1982). The Methodist Bishops of the United States, although disagreeing with the Catholic Bishops about the morality of deterrence, also make use of a just war argument: see *In Defense of Creation: The Nuclear Crisis and a Just Peace* (1986). The Methodist document comments that just war concepts are "the foundations of the critique of nuclear war. . . [but] the logic of the tradition ultimately discredits nuclear deterrence as a morally tenable position" (*New York Times*, 26 April 1986). For a casuistical analysis of nuclear war, see Joseph Nye, *Nuclear Ethics* (New York, 1986). Recall also our discussion of self-defense in chapter 11.

13. Bartolomeo de Las Casas, *Defense against the Persecutors and Slanderers of the People of the New World Discovered across the Seas* (1552). De Las Casas engaged in a public *casus* with his opponent Juan Genes de Sepulveda before a commission of theologians convened by the Council of the Indies in Madrid, August 1550. See Lewis Hanke, *All Mankind Is One* (De Kalb, Ill., 1974).

14. Recall the discussion of the commission's methods of argument in the collection of case studies edited by H. T. Engelhardt, Jr., and A. L. Caplan, *Scientific Controversies* (Cambridge, Eng., 1985).

15. See Alasdair MacIntyre, *A Short History of Ethics* (New York, 1966), and *After Virtue* (Notre Dame, 1981).

14. AFTER *THE PROVINCIAL LETTERS*

1. *D-S* #2021–2065.

2. Ibid., #2102–2167.

3. Ibid., #2301–2332.

4. Charles Curran, *Directions in Fundamental Moral Theology* (Notre Dame, 1985), p. 222. See also Charles Curran and Richard McCormick, eds., *Readings in Moral Theology II: The Magisterium* (New York, 1952), and John Todd, *The Problem of Authority* (Baltimore, 1962), especially the chapters "Historical Development of Authority in the Church" by Yves Congar, "The Problem of Authority in the 16th and 17th Centuries" by B. McGrath, and "Authority in Morals" by Elizabeth Anscombe. Also, G. J. Hughes, *Authority in Morals: An Essay in Christian Ethics* (Washington, D.C., 1985).

5. *Decree of the Holy Office*, 21 May, 1851: *D-S* #2791–2793. A decree of April 1853 condemns the use of the contraceptive condom as *intrinsice malus*, in *D-S* #2795. This *responsa* is, of course, of great moment in the subsequent debate about birth control. See John Noonan, *Contraception* (Cambridge, 1965).

6. Pope Paul VI, *Humanae Vitae*, 29 July, 1968, para. 14: "Every action which either in anticipation of the conjugal act or in its accomplishment, or in the development of its natural consequences, proposes, whether as an end or a means, to render procreation impossible is to be excluded as a licit means of regulating birth." The reaction of many moral theologians to this papal statement was the first significant dissent from Roman moral teaching in two hundred years. See C. Curran and R. Hunt, eds., *Dissent in and for the Church: Theologians and* Humanae Vitae (New York, 1969). For the story behind the Encyclical, see Robert Kaiser, *The Politics of Sex and Religion* (Kansas City, 1985).

7. See E. Hirschbrech, *Die Enwicklung der Moraltheologie in Deutschen Sprachgebiet* (Klosterneuberg, 1959). The leading theologians of the Tübigen School were J. M. Sailer (1751–1832) and J. B. Hirscher (1788–1865). The work of F. Linsenmann (1835–1898), *Lehrbuch der Moraltheologie* (1878), was the most widely used product of this school. A leading Jesuit theologian, J. Mausbach, responded to the critics of casuistry while admitting its limitations in *Die Katholische Moral, Ihre Methoden,Grundsätze und Aufgabe* (Köln, 1902).

8. "Notes in Moral Theology," in the journal *Theological Studies*, published by the Jesuit seminary at Woodstock, Md., now at Georgetown University. Many of these essays are collected in C. Curran and R. A. McCormick, eds., *Readings in Moral Theology*, 4 vols. (New York, 1979, 1980, 1982, 1984).

9. See, for example, the periodical *The Casuist*, published from 1906 to 1917 and again in 1924–1925 under the editorship of J. McHugh, or Father Francis Connell's books, *Father Connell Answers Moral Questions* (Washington, D.C., 1959), and *More Answers to Today's Moral Questions* (Washington, D.C. 1965).

10. A glance at any 19th- or 20th-century manual of moral theology will confirm this trivialization of casuistry. In Henry Davis, *Moral and Pastoral Theology* (New York, 1952), for instance, 281 of the 474 pages of the book are taken up by Treatises XII-XX on the administration of the sacraments.

11. Instruction of the Holy Office, 2 Feb., 1956, "De ethica situationis," D–S #3918–3921. See J. C. Ford and G. Kelly, *Contemporary Moral Theology* (Westminster, Md., 1955), I, chaps. 7–8; J. Fuchs, *Situation und Entscheidung* (Frankfurt, 1952); R. Gleason, "Situational Morality," *Thought* 32 (1957): 533–558.

12. Joseph Fletcher, *Situation Ethics* (Philadelphia, 1966). A vigorous repudiation of situationism came from Paul Ramsey, *Deeds and Rules in Christian Ethics* (Edinburgh, 1965). The debate is reviewed in G. Outka and P. Ramsey, *Norm and Context in Christian Ethics* (New York, 1968) and criticized in James Gustafson, "Context versus Principle: A Misplaced Debate in Christian Ethics," *Harvard Theological Review* 58 (1965):171–202.

13. For a balanced review of recent Catholic opinion, see E. Hamel, "Valeur et limites de la casuistique," in *Loi Naturelle et loi du Christ* (Paris, 1964).

14. See chapter 13, this volume.

15. In John Donne's poem, *An Anatomy of the World* (1610–1611), in which he recorded how "new Philosophy calls all in doubt," all these different changes are deplored equally.

16. See, most recently, Geoffrey Parker, *The Thirty Years' War* (London, 1986).

17. The influence of this ideal of theory and method on other sciences, notably the behavioral and social sciences, is a familiar and depressing story.

18. *De Jure Belli et Pacis*, Prolegomena #39. This comment is of interest for two reasons. It echoes Aristotle's remark, discussed in chapter 2, about the "perception" that we have of the "ultimate moral particulars" that are the final objects of reference in ethics. Yet at the same time, it seems to anticipate Descartes' own criteria of "clarity and distinctness" as sources of *certainty* in philosophy.

19. G. H. Sabine, *A History of Political Theory* (New York, 1961), p. 425. *De Jure Belli et Pacis*, II, 23, 1.

20. *De Jure Belli et Pacis*, II, 23, 1.

21. *De Jure Belli*, II, 1 and III, 1. Father Coplestone, however, says, "I do not think that one ought to lay great stress on Grotius' place in the movement of philosophical thought characterized by emphasis on deduction, an emphasis due to the influence of the success of the mathematical sciences . . . [although] he did not escape that influence." See F. C. Coplestone, *A History of Philosophy* (New York, 1952), III, pt. 2, p.146. See also E. Dumbauld, *The Life and Legal Writings of Hugo Grotius* (Norman, Okla., 1969).

22. *De Jure Naturae et Gentium* I, 2, 9–10.

23. J. H. Formey (1757), quoted in the introduction to *Jus Gentium*, ed. J. B. Scott, in the series "Classics of International Law" (Oxford, 1934), p. xvii.

24. F. C. Coplestone, *A History of Philosophy* (New York, 1969), VI, pt. 1, p. 135. When we turn to Immanuel Kant himself, we shall find that he is still capable of working within the casuistical tradition. Reacting against the rationalism of Wolff, we shall see, Kant holds the idea of a comprehensive "axiomatic system" of ethics at arm's length. Thus in dealing with specific cases, like Grotius and Pufendorf before him, Kant turns away from all axiom systems and introduces "casuistical digressions" into his argument. In this respect he shows his debt to the rhetorical tradition, by which his own ways of thinking, and even some of his examples, link him back ultimately to, for example, Cicero.

25. Dainville, *L'Education des Jésuites*, pp. 372–378; G. Sortais, "La cartésianisme chez les jésuites au dix septième et aux dix heutième siècles," *Archives de Philosophie* VI (1929):36 ff.

15. PHILOSOPHY AND THE SPRINGS OF MORALITY

1. William Whewell, *The Elements of Morality Including Polity* (Cambridge, 1846).

2. See chapter 3.

3. This passage comes from a memoir found among his papers after his death and printed in the preface to the sixth edition of *The Methods of Ethics*, prepared by E. F. Constance Jones in 1901.

4. *The Methods of Ethics*, 1st ed., (London 1874). Note Sidgwick's reference to the "axioms and definitions" of "the mathematicians," and recall his acknowledged debt to the seventeenth-century Cambridge Platonist, Henry More. See also chapter 8, note 33.

5. See J. B. Schneewind, *Sidgwick's Ethics and Victorian Moral Philosophy* (Oxford, 1977), pp. 40–52. Peter Winch writes an interesting essay on

Sidgwick's "calculus of action" in which he contrasts the philosopher's demand for ethical universalizability with the moral dilemma of Captain Vere in Melville's novel *Billy Budd*. *Ethics and Action* (London, 1974), chap. 8.

6.   See, among others, Ralph Barton Perry, *The General Theory of Value* (New York, 1926); G. E. Moore, *Principia Ethica* (Cambridge, 1903), and *Ethics* (London and New York, 1912); W. D. Ross, *The Right and the Good* (Oxford, 1930); Charles L. Stevenson, *Ethics and Language* (New Haven, 1944); John Rawls, *A Theory of Justice* (Cambridge, Mass., 1971); and R. M. Hare, *The Language of Morals* (Oxford, 1952).

7.   Compare F. H. Bradley, "My Station and Its Duties," in *Ethical Studies* (London, 1876; 2d ed., Oxford, 1927).   Notice also Bradley's comments on casuistry: "The vice of casuistry is that, attempting to decide the particulars of morality by the deduction of reflective understanding, it at once degenerates into finding a good reason for what you mean to do" (*Ethical Studies*, 2d ed., p. 197), whereas "it is not the business of moral philosophy to tell us what in particular we are to do" (ibid, p. 193).

8.   Compare Ross, *The Right and the Good*, and C. D. Broad, *Five Types of Ethical Theory* (London, 1930).

9.   See chapter 2.

10.   *The International Journal of Ethics* (April 1891), as reprinted in *The Writings of William James*, ed. John J. McDermott (Chicago, 1977), pp 610–629. This passage comes from pp. 610–611.

11.   Ibid., pp. 611.

12.   Ibid., pp. 613–614.

13.   Ibid., pp. 616–617.

14.   Ibid., pp. 618–619.

15.   Ibid., pp. 619–621.

16.   Ibid., pp. 625–626.

17.   For historical accounts of English moral philosophy during this period, see the books by Geoffrey Warnock, *Contemporary Moral Philosophy* (London, 1967) and Mary Warnock, *Ethics since 1900* (Oxford, 1960).

18.   One of the present authors (S.E.T.) cosponsored a graduate class in Ethics at Oxford University in the early 1950s in which the discussion focused largely on precisely this question: whether, and on what conditions, we could ever describe, for example, "wearing the wrong colored tie" as *morally* offensive.   Are the possible applications of the term "moral" limited in substantive ways?   Or are the essential limits merely formal?   In the course of the seminar, Kurt Baier not surprisingly argued (as his book, *The Moral Point of View*, did later) for defining "moral" in substantive terms.   In

contrast, Philippa Foot at that time supported a formalist position, of a kind one would currently associate more readily with, for example, Richard Hare.

19. See, for example, Aiken's *Reason and Conduct* (New York, 1962), esp. chap. VIII: "The Concept of Moral Objectivity."

20. We return to these substantive discussions in chapter 16.

21. Bernard Williams, *Ethics and the Limits of Philosophy* (Cambridge, Mass., 1985), pp. 93–99. The passage discussed here comes from pp. 96–97.

22. See the general discussion in the last part of chapter 2.

23. See, for instance, M. J. Detmold, *The Unity of Law and Morality* (London and Boston: 1984), and G. Wallace and A.D. M. Walker, eds., *The Definition of Morality* (London, 1970).

24. Kant, *Groundwork for the Metaphysics of Morals*, trans. H. J. Paton, II, 53–57, and *Metaphysics of Morals* II, "The Doctrine of Virtue." A few recent philosophers have even tried to go Kant one better, hoping to find principles that provide more reliable and universal "decision procedures" for dealing with practical problems in ethics. For example, Alan Gewirth offers his "principle of generic consistency" as entailing correct answers to all the moral questions that can arise in any set of practical circumstances whatever: see his book, *Reason and Morality* (Chicago, 1978).

25. Kant, *Groundwork for the Metaphysic of Morals* (tr. H.J. Paton), II, 53–57, and *The Metaphysics of Morals* II, "The Doctrine of Value." See also W. I. Matson, "Kant as Casuist," *Journal of Philosophy* 51 (1954):855–860.

26. See chapter 10.

27. *Lectures on Ethics,* trans. L. Infield (New York, 1963). In their actual contents these lectures have a strongly medieval tone: see, e.g., "Duties toward the Body in Respect of Sexual Impulse" and "Crimina Carnis," pp. 162–171.

28. *The Doctrine of Virtue,* trans. Mary Gregory (New York, 1964). To cite two of these casuistical digressions: "One may not act contrary to the natural end of sexual intercourse, i.e. preservation of the race, but [he asks] may o ɔ use the sexual power without regard to that end?" (p. 425). Again, "Can we at least justify, if not extol, a use of wine bordering on intoxication, on the grounds that it enlivens the company's conversation and encourages frankness?" (p. 427). Not surprisingly, Kant was not inclined to countenance an exception in either case. He explains the place of casuistry: "Ethics, because of the play room it allows in its imperfect duties, inevitably leads judgment to pose the question of how a maxim should be applied in particular cases; and since the answer gives us another (subordinate) maxim, we can always inquire again after a principle for applying this maxim to cases that may come up. And so ethics falls into casuistry, which has no place in the doctrine of law. Thus casuistry is neither a science nor a

part of a science, for in that case it would be dogmatics, and it is not so much a doctrine of how to discover something as rather practice in the proper way of seeking truth. Hence it is woven into ethics only in a fragmentary way, not systematically (as a part of ethics proper would have to be) and is added to ethics only as scholia to the system" (*The Doctrine of Virtue*, p. 73–74).

29. The contrast between "rational motives" and "psychological causes" was of fundamental significance to Kant because of its connections with his central philosophical contrast between the world of causal *phenomena* and that of rational *noumena*. In addition, brought up as a Lutheran pietist, Kant will have had imprinted in his memory the dichotomies in terms of which Luther, and all Lutheran preachers, described the moral life: spirit and flesh, gospel and law, grace and sin. This theology of "the two realms" might easily have been transmuted in his thinking into the philosophical dichotomy between the two realms of *noumena* and *phenomena*, autonomy and heteronomy.

30. For the eighteenth-century debate about "reason" and "inclination," or psychological egoism, see, e.g., L. A. Selby Bigge, *British Moralists*, 2 vols. (Oxford, 1897).

31. Cultural historians may wonder why people in eighteenth-century Europe found psychological egoism so convincing a theory of motivation, and why they rarely acknowledged the altruistic components in human nature. In this, no doubt, the theoretical charms of egoism were reinforced by other less intellectual factors. But for our present purposes, the latter "nontheoretical" influences need not be placed in the foreground.

32. Not least, Simon Bolivar, the "liberator" of Venezuela and other South American nations.

33. John Rawls, *A Theory of Justice* (Cambridge, Mass., 1971).

34. This is a capsule description of a process that continued, slowly but more or less continuously, over a good two hundred years. For the many qualifications it requires, see, e.g., the essay by David Carradine, "The British Monarchy, 1820–1977," in *The Invention of Tradition*, ed. E. Hobsbawm and T. Ranger (Cambridge, Eng., 1983). Even in Queen Victoria's time the sovereign was occasionally tempted to act over the head of Parliament; and there was a lesser "constitutional crisis" just before the First World War, over David Lloyd George's proposal to limit the powers of the House of Lords by requiring the King to pack it with Liberal party supporters.

35. The standard Anglo-Norman formula used in Britain was, and remains, *Le Roy le veult*.

36. The most notable of the reformers who put the social program of the Benthamite utilitarians into practice was Edwin Chadwick, whose famous *Enquiry* into the sanitary conditions of the British working poor (1842) led to the passage of the pioneer piece of social legislation in modern times: the Public Health Act of 1848.

37. In the Middle Ages the actions of sovereigns were not immune to moral criticism, but it was only men of spiritual authority—bishops, popes, and saints—who did the actual criticizing. See, for instance, Aquinas' treatise on the morally acceptable use of political power, *De Regimine Principis*. In war a soldier might, for example, disobey an order to kill prisoners for moral reasons; but in explaining these reasons, he was not criticizing the general policy he had flouted but rather excusing his disobedience. One of the serious disputes in high casuistry was over the moral legitimacy of tyrannicide, a position condemned by the Jesuit General Aquaviva on 6 July, 1610, two months after the assassination of Henry IV of France. See Franklin Ford, *Political Murder* (Cambridge, Mass., 1985), pp. 150–157, 180–184. The Catholic tradition on severance of obedience to a ruler was reasserted recently by the Catholic Bishops of the Philippines: "A government that assumes or retains power through fraudulent means has no moral basis. . . . If such a government does not correct the evil it has inflicted upon the people, then it is our serious obligation as a people to make it do so" (*New York Times*, 14 Feb., 1986).

38. One can argue, for instance, that Russia has never fully internalized a "liberal" political philosophy. Both Tolstoy and Solzhenitsyn are scornful of representative institutions: these they see merely as giving scope for self-seeking scoundrels to grab power for themselves, as in the satirical picture of the *zemstvo* meetings in Tolstoy's *Anna Karenina*. The best they seem able to hope for is a sovereign who will act as a benevolent autocrat: that is, as a more pious version of, say, Louis XIV.

39. The nearest John Rawls comes to a discussion of practical morals is in his treatment of civil disobedience in *A Theory of Justice*, chap. VI, pp. 363–394, esp. p. 364.

40. See also Rawls's essay, "Two Concepts of Rules," *Philosophical Review* 64 (1955):3–32.

41. See Rawls, *A Theory of Justice*, chap. 3. On the dangers of exaggerating the moral significance of "impartiality" see, e.g., Stephen Toulmin, "Equity and Principles," *Osgoode Hall Law Journal* 30, no. 1 (1982): 1–17, or "The Tyranny of Principles," *Hastings Center Report* (August 1981). On the problems raised by one of the cornerstones of theoretical ethics—that of the "impartial observer"—see H. D. Aiken, "Concept of Moral Objectivity."

42. On the distinction between equity and equality, see Toulmin, "Equity and Principles," note 46.

43. For a fuller discussion of the role proposed for these "superprinciples" and an alternative account of the place of "theories" of moral philosophy, see the essay by Stephen Toulmin, "Principles of Morality," in *Philosophy* 28 (1953).

44. Recall, for example, the address by William James, "The Moral Philosopher and the Moral Life," quoted earlier (see note 10), and John

Dewey's books, *The Quest for Certainty* (New York; 1929) and *Human Nature and Conduct.* See also the useful collection, *The Moral Writings of John Dewey,* ed. J. Gouinloch (New York, 1976). For a useful commentary on the differences between the pragmatists' view of "experience" and the account modern philosophers have inherited from Descartes and Locke, see J. J. McDermott's commentaries in his editions of James and Dewey and his essay, "Pragmatic Sensibility: The Morality of Experiences" in J. De Maris and R. Fox, *New Directions in Ethics* (New York, 1986) pp. 113–134.

45. Without flogging a dead horse, we may recall the shift within early nineteenth-century German jurisprudence, from the grandiose intellectual ambitions of C. F. Wolff to the historical vision of Savigny and his successors, and the influence that Savigny in due course exerted on the rise of sociological jurisprudence in the United States. In the field of law practical necessity thus imposed a shift away from the Platonic oversimplifications of the eighteenth century to a more modest and historically informed approach. But in ethics no such practical considerations carried weight with philosophers before the rise of "medical ethics" in the 1950s and '60s (see chapter 16). On the work and influence of Savigny, we are indebted to an unpublished dissertation by Dr. Roger Michener of Princeton University.

46. Dom Odo Lottin, *Morale fondamentale* (Paris and Tournai, 1954). For other approaches by Christian theologians, see, e.g., Häring, *The Law of Christ,* and James Gustafson, *Ethics from a Theocentric Point of View,* 2 vols. (Chicago, 1981, 1983).

47. Moral theologians are not exempt from the inclination to look for "universalizing" theories of ethics. For instance, Gerard Gilleman proposed that charity might serve as the unique organizing principle of moral theology: see *Le Primat de la charité en théologie morale* (Louvain, 1952). Dom Odo Lottin disagreed, insisting that at the very least, both rationality and charity must be accepted as fundamental to moral deliberation. See Lottin, *Morale fondamentale,* pp. 234–240.

48. Recall the discussion in chapter 2.

49. Nor is this true only in practical enterprises and arguments. In the natural sciences also, apprentice research workers quickly learn how to write papers in the forms that are currently acceptable for publication in, say, *The Physical Review* or the *Quarterly Journal of Microbiology.* No one, of course, refers to this as training in the "rhetoric" of science; but this is for reasons of status, not of substance. Most moral philosophers do not care to admit the rhetorical character of their ethical arguments: similarly—not to say *a fortiori!*—few scientists are willing to acknowledge that a successful scientist must be not merely a sound mathematician and a skilled experimenter but also a bit of a rhetorician.

50. As an example of the primary moral "argument forms" used in clinical medicine, see Albert R. Jonsen, Mark Siegler, and William Winslade, *Clinical Ethics,* 2d ed. (New York, 1986).

51. J. Glover, "It Makes No Difference Whether I Do It or Not," *Proceedings of the Aristotelian Society,* Supp. Vol. 49 (1975):183. Compare chapter 7, note 11.

52. IV Lateran, *D-S* #814

53. Compare *The Writings of William James,* pp. 628–29: "In the interests of our own ideal of systematically unified moral truth, therefore, we, as would-be philosophers, must postulate a divine thinker, and pray for the victory of the religious cause. . . . [But] our postulation of him after all serves only to *let loose in us the strenuous mood"* (italics added).

54. F. Y. Edgeworth, *Mathematical Psychics: An Essay on the Application of Mathematics to the Moral Sciences* (London, 1881); and see J. M. Keynes, "My Early Beliefs," in *Two Memoirs* (London and New York, 1949).

55. This is true even of the aging Kant, whose vision of Humanity and Nature was shaken by the experience of living through the French Revolution. In a late eschatological essay, *Das Ende aller Dinge,* written in 1794, we find him rethinking the practical significance of his separation of *noumena* from *phenomena.* The French example seemed to give fresh hope that the rational (*noumenal*) demands of morality might, after all, be politically embodied in the causal (*phenomenal*) world of state power!

56. For a rare philosophical discussion of "vision" as a moral concept, see Stanley Hauerwas's book, *Vision and Virtue* (Notre Dame, 1974).

57. Notice how few of those who have pioneered such historical studies have been moral philosophers by profession. Michael Walzer's book *Just and Unjust Wars* is frequently pointed out as the example of the newer casuistry, but he disclaims being a philosopher. Noonan is a lawyer.

16. THE REVIVAL OF CASUISTRY

1. Just as moral philosophy was in danger of losing touch finally with moral experience, the needs of clinical medicine intervened to drag it back into the realm of practicality. For a fuller discussion, see Stephen Toulmin, "How Medicine Saved the Life of Ethics," *Perspectives in Biology and Medicine* 25, no. 4 (Summer 1982): 736–750.

2. This point is most explicitly stated in Richard Hare's paper, "Can the Moral Philosopher Help?" in *Philosophical Medical Ethics,* ed. S. M. Spicker and T. S. Engelhardt (Dordrecht and Boston, 1977), esp. pp. 52–59. "The main—perhaps the only contribution of the philosopher to the solution of these problems [in medical ethics] is clarification of the logical properties of tricky words like wrong, and the establishment of canons of valid argument It is my belief that once issues are throughly clarified in this way, the problems will not seem so perplexing . . . and, the philosophical difficulties having been removed, we can get on with discussing the practical difficulties, which are likely to remain serious" (p. 52). On the contrast between a

medical ethics that is theory based and one that is case based, see A. R. Jonsen, "Casuistry and Clinical Medicine," *Theoretical Medicine*, 7 (1986), 65–74, and Lawrence McCullough, "Methodological Concerns in Bioethics," *Journal of Philosophy and Medicine* 11 (1986):17–39.

3.   John Ford, "The Morality of Obliteration Bombing," *Theological Studies* 5 (1944):261–309.   Paul Ramsey, *The Just War: Force and Political Responsibility* (New York, 1968); Michael Walzer, *Just and Unjust Wars: A Moral Argument with Historical Illustrations* (New York, 1977); James Childress, *Civil Disobedience and Political Obligation* (New Haven: 1971). Compare also chapter 11, note 6.

4.   For a full presentation of the moral issues at stake in neonatology, see Jeff Lyon, *Playing God in the Nursery* (New York, 1985). The "Baby Doe" rules are found in Child Abuse and Neglect Prevention and Treatment Program, *U.S. Code of Federal Regulations*, 1340 *Federal Register*, 15 April, 1985.

5.   This is only one of the current interpretations of the hostility toward usury and interest taking. Some historians take the analysis further, or read the whole matter differently: see, e.g., Benjamin Nelson's *The Idea of Usury* (Chicago: University of Chicago Press, 1949), which explains this hostility by reference to the closeness of kinship in subsistence economies. In his view the making of loans at interest among neighbors typically runs up against the demands of familial loyalty, and so causes unacceptably bad relations in the community.

6.   A. Udevitch, *Partnership and Profit in Medieval Islam* (Princeton, 1970).

7.   Posing this question is in no way an "anti-Israeli" gesture: many honest and perceptive Israelis are quite aware of the problem here stated.

8.   See chapter 6.

9.   T. Bouscaren, *The Ethics of Ectopic Operations* (Milwaukee, 1943); and see R. McCormick and P. Ramsay *On Doing Good to Avoid Evil* (Chicago, 1978). See also chapter 11, note 11.

10.   This problem echoes in the most ancient of medical maxims: benefit or, at least, do no harm. See A. R. Jonsen, "Do No Harm," *Annals of Internal Medicine* 88 (1977), 827–830.

11.   See chapter 3.

12.   J. P. Sartre, *L'Existentialisme est une humanisme*, trans. B. Frechtman (New York, 1947), pp. 28–33.

13.   This is the moral issue in many "affirmative action" debates: for example, the famous *Bakke* case about the criteria for admission to medical school. See the philosophical analysis by Thomas Nagel, "Equal Treatment and Compensatory Discrimination," *Philosophy & Public Affairs* 2 (1973): 349–361.

14.   The classic illustration is the *Tarasoff* case, in which a psychologist's duty of confidentiality to his patient had to be weighed against the desirability of warning the patient's fiancée that he was potentially violent, and even homicidal. *Tarasoff v. Regents of the University of California* (1976, 17 Cal. 3d 425; 131 Cal. Rptr. 14, 551, p2d, 334). See also William Winslade, "After Tarasoff: The Therapist's Liability and Patient Confidentiality," in *Law and Psychiatry*, ed. L. Everstein (New York, 1986).

15.   M. Polanyi, *Personal Knowledge* (Chicago, 1958).

16.   There have been a few distinguished contributions to this field of study: notably, Arthur Adkins's and Kenneth Dover's studies of Greek practical morality, and John Noonan's histories of moral practices, *Contraception* and *Bribes*. But there has been no single-minded and collaborative attack on the subject such as there was, after 1945, on problems in the history of the natural sciences. (Foundations, please note!)

17.   Recall, e.g., Walzer, *Just and Unjust Wars*.

18.   To be fair, they put up the signs because many insurance companies charge lower premiums to those householders who employ security agencies and let the public know of the fact. Still, the houseowners themselves are surely responsible for the nature and consequences of those actions.

19.   Among contemporary moral philosophers, Alan Donagan has done most to explore the parallels between these two fields. Indeed, it was with him that one of the authors (S.E.T.) first recalls discussing "common morality," in the sense in which the phrase is used here, back in 1974. Donagan's own book, *The Theory of Morality* (Chicago, 1977), treats morality in more abstract and general terms than we have done here, but it adopts something of the same standpoint as we have done toward the role of tradition in practical moral reasoning.

20.   As described in reports on the proceedings of the Synod in at least some editions of the *New York Times*, during the last week of November and the first week of December 1985.

21.   For a recent sounding of lay opinion and practice, consider the results of the poll taken by the *New York Times* and CBS to measure "The Views of American Catholics" on these issues, as printed in the *New York Times* for 25 November, 1985.

22.   Sigmund Freud's discoveries and arguments have been seen as posing, in the field of sexual morality, the same kind of crucial challenge that the atomic bomb did to traditional ideas about the morality of war.

23.   See *The Hastings Center Report* (August 1981):8–13.

24.   The casuists were familiar with a maxim very similar to the maxim *de minimis non curat lex*: namely, *parvum pro nihilo reputatur*, which could be used to argue that even though formally an act were of a serious nature, its

material aspects may be of such little moment that the act, as a whole, cannot be considered serious. Thus Thomas Aquinas writes, "An act may be imperfect on the part of its object, which on account of its smallness could be considered as nothing, as Aristotle says in *Politics*, Book III" (*S.T.* I–II, q. 18, a. 4). Aquinas' reference to Aristotle is probably mistaken for *Physics* II.5, "A small distance is like no distance at all." Clearly judgments about what particularly constitutes "great or small matter" in this connection are themselves subjects for casuistical discussion and determination. See, e.g., O. Lottin, *Morale fondamentale*, pp. 279–281.

25. We need to accept such anthropological reports, and understand their basis, before any questions of approval or disapproval arise, because the cultures in question have a level of development different from our own. In Western Europe and North America, by contrast, it has—for better or for worse—been a rhetorical concern of moral philosophers over the last two hundred years to advocate the universalization of moral arguments: that is, the equal application of all moral rules to all *human* beings alike—even, in the case of supporters of "animal rights," all *sensitive* beings alike. See, e.g., Tom Regan, *The Case for Animal Rights* (Berkeley and Los Angeles, 1983).

26. We here use an extreme illustration of a more general point. Evidently we might have relied instead on the case of investment interest, in which it is again true that the previous moral category of *usury* "made no provision" for the new kind of case. Alternatively, we might have cited the examples referred to earlier from the history of tort law, in which the category of "injury through negligence" was introduced into a situation in which "willful injury" had been the paradigm. Similarly, we now face a situation in which the issue of "informed consent" to medical treatment may call for a new paradigm. As Marjorie Schultz argues ("From Informed Consent to Patient Choice; a New Protected Interest," *Yale Law Journal* 95 [1985]:219–299), neither the categories of tort nor those of contract law properly match the considerations that arise in the physician-patient relationship. So it may well happen that future textbooks of common law will include a novel chapter on damages arising from physician-patient and other similar professional relationships. If this happens the chapters in question will be relevant to our understanding of "common morality" as well as common law.

27. John D. Arras, "Methodology in Bioethics: Applied Ethics versus the New Casuistry" (presented at the Institute for the Medical Humanities of the University of Texas, Galveston, forum on "Bioethics as an Intellectual Field," 1986).

28. Ibid., one *caveat*. If Harold Berman is right, this reading of Roman law, as proceeding "from the top down," applies to the way in which Roman law was formalized and taught in the schools of medieval Europe, not to the way it was developed and deployed in the law courts of Imperial Rome. (Recall our discussion of Berman's *Law and Revolution* in chapter 5.)

29. There is some irony in the phrasing of this conclusion. We showed, in the historical chapters of this book, that "common law" and "common morality" share a casuistical ancestry; but if one studies the practice of spiritual and temporal authority in medieval Europe, it can be hard to know when a particular issue is perceived, by our standards, as *moral* and when as *legal*. In this case, the phrase "common law ethics" is pleonastic and would better be written in the form "common law/ethics."

30. These type cases, to recall, correspond to the "ultimate particulars" (*ta eschata*) of Aristotle's *Nicomachean Ethics*: that is, those moral instances that serve as the final objects of comparison in moral argument, which we have (he argues) a basic capacity to "recognize at sight" for what they are.

31. At this point we may once again refer, in passing, to the parallels between *moral* understanding of human problems and *clinical* understanding of medical problems. Both of these are learned by broadening and deepening our range of "experience," not by mastering additional algorithms and other "intellectual" skills.

32. Closer attention still needs to be paid to the relationship of the new intellectual movements of the early seventeenth century, both to the "general crisis" about which Eric Hobsbawm, Hugh Trevor Roper, and other English historians have recently written, and to the spiritual problems that arose in the aftermath of the Reformation and Counter-Reformation.

33. One thinks, for example, of the Jesuit, Matteo Ricci—who was, like Pascal, a mathematician and physical scientist—leaving Lisbon in 1578 to spend his life in the missionary field in China. He took with him the rhetorical methods for dealing with substantive issues into which he had been trained in Europe—his so-called memory palace—and, on his arrival in Peking, reequipped it with new furnishings better suited to the culture he found there. For a Jesuit of his time it was the substantive furniture of the mind that mattered most, rather than its formal architecture. See the account of Ricci's life and thought in Jonathan Spence, *The Memory Palace of Matteo Ricci* (Cambridge, Mass., 1984).

34. Recall, for instance, our remarks about the abortion debate in the Prologue.

EPILOGUE: CONSCIENCE AND THE CLAIMS OF EQUITY

1. *New York Times*, 7 October, 1984.

2. See J. Diamond, "Abortion, Animation, and Biological Hominization," *Theological Studies* 36 (1975): 305–324; C. Tauer, "The Tradition of Probabilism and the Moral Status of the Early Embryo," *Theological Studies* 45 (1984): 3–33. John Connery, *Abortion: The Development of the Roman Catholic Perspective* (Chicago, 1977); John Noonan, "An Almost Absolute

Value in History," in *The Morality of Abortion*, ed. J. Noonan (Cambridge, Mass., 1970).

3. J. Creusen, "Le fetus, injuste aggresseur?" in *Miscellanea Vermeersch* (Rome, 1935). There was also a vigorous debate in the nineteenth century over whether craniotomy constituted direct or indirect killing. See Connery, *Abortion*, chap. 13, 14. That it was "indirect" was a "probable opinion," quashed by a decree of the Holy Office, 31 May, 1884.

4. L. Bouscaren, *The Ethics of Ectopic Operations* (Milwaukee, 1944). See L. W. Sumner, *Abortion and Moral Theory* (Princeton, 1981). It is worth noting that after Sumner expounds the "right to life" and "right to choose" as principles, he moves into a casuistical discussion to show how both positions must be interpreted as practical arguments. See, in particular, his analysis of Judith Jarvis Thompson's well-known essay "A Defense of Abortion," in *The Rights and Wrongs of Abortion*, ed. M. Cohen (Princeton, 1974), pp. 65–73.

5. The best general discussion of the relation between abortion and public policy remains Daniel Callahan, *Abortion, Law, Choice and Morality* (New York, 1970).

6. *The Patient as Person* (New Haven, 1970), p xvii.

7. D. Callahan, "Bioethics as a Discipline," *Hastings Center Studies* I (1973): 72. Note that in this essay Callahan mistakenly describes casuistry as "essentially deductive," a description we have in this book been at pains to undercut.

8. Jonsen, Siegler, and Winslade, *Clinical Ethics*, 2d ed.

9. See, e.g., A. Jonsen, "A Concord of Medical Ethics," *Annals of Internal Medicine* 80 (1974):657–8.

10. Dewey, *The Quest for Certainty*.

11. Aristotle's "large spirited person"—misleadingly though usually translated as "great souled man,"—is the hero of his *Nicomachean Ethics*. The key characteristic of such a person is the ability to act on behalf of a friend, not out of any kind of self-interest, but from an understanding of the friend's own needs, wishes, and interests—the *phronimos* with feelings.

Name Index

Abelard, Peter, 122, 133
Abraham, 125
Acolea, Martin de, 156
Adrian, pope, 207
Aeschylus, 59
Alain, of Lille, 118-119
Albert, the Great, 129-130, 134, 139, 183
Alexander, of Hales, 165
Alexander, of Macedon, 58, 63, 84
Alexander VII, pope, 12, 174-175, 179
Alexander VIII, pope, 175
Ambrose, bishop of Milan, 94, 96, 141, 218-219
Ames, William, 160
Angelicus, 201
Annat, Pere, 243
Antigone, 75
Antipater, of Tarsus, 81-82
Antoninus, archbishop of Florence, 145, 186-187, 223
Apollodorus, 132
Aquaviva, Claudius, 149
Aquinas, St. Thomas, 4, 109, 111, 123, 126-127, 129, 131, 133-135, 139-140, 148-149, 154, 172, 174, 184-185, 197, 221-222, 251, 253, 258
Aistophanes, 51
Aristotle, 25, 36-37, 42, 48, 51, 53, 61-74, 84-85, 87-88, 101, 110, 116, 122, 126, 129, 131-134, 141, 148, 165, 168, 184, 195, 242, 254, 257, 259, 263, 265
Arnauld, Antoine, 232-233, 235

Arnauld, Mere Angelique, 232
Arnauld family, 232-233, 235, 246, 248
Augustine, of Hippo, 45, 87, 95-96, 101, 120, 126, 131, 133, 148, 196-197, 204, 213, 218-219, 222, 232, 251, 253, 262
Austin, John, 52
Azor, Juan, 153-155, 159-160, 201, 207, 224-225, 258-259
Azpilcueta, Martin. *See* Navarrus

Bacon, Francis, 159
Bacon, Roger, 122
Basil, Saint, 191
Baxter, Richard, 160
Becanus, Martin, 226
Becket, Thomas à, 107
Bede, Venerable, 97
Bentham, Jeremy, 74
Bérulle, Pierre de, 239
Beuve, Saint, 248
Boethius, 131-132
Bok, Sissela, 13-14
Bonaventure, Saint, 184
Boniface VIII, pope, 103
Boniface XII, pope, 169
Bossuet, Jacques benigne, 239
Bourdalue, Louis, 239, 248
Broderick, Father, 244, 247
Burgo, John de, 140
Busenbaum, Herman, 155-156, 248
Butler, Joseph, 163

Cagnazzo, John, 140
Cajetan, Cardinal Thomas de Vio, 140,
    153, 164, 173, 202
Calderón de la Barca, Pedro, 147
Calvin, John, 158-159, 232
Campion, Edmund, 201, 203
Cantor, Peter, 119, 168
Caramuel-Lebkowitz, Juan, 156, 168,
    248
Carletti, Angelo, 140
Carneades, 77, 94
Cassian, Abbot, 100
Charlemagne, emperor of the Franks, 102
Charles I, king of England, 160, 211
Charles II, king of England, 160
Charles V, Holy Roman Emperor, 144-145
Chrysippus, 76
Chrysostom, John, 133
Cicero, Marcus Tullius, 54, 71, 74-75, 77,
    82, 84, 88, 94, 101, 111, 116, 119, 122,
    126-127, 131-134, 165, 168, 218, 229,
    242, 251, 254, 258
Clausewitz, Karl von, 261
Clavasio, Angelus de, 188, 190
Clement, of Alexandria, 93-94, 141
Clement V, pope, 221
Concina, Daniel, 226-227, 238
Constantine, emperor of Rome, 55
Cotonio, Antonio, 156
Cudworth, Ralph, 163
Cyprian, Saint, 93

Daniel, Gabriel, 243, 252, 254, 256
Darwin, Charles, 64
David, 125
Defoe, Daniel, 164
De Las Casas, Bartoloméo, 262-263
Deman, T., 172, 247
Demosthemes, 51
Descartes, René, 110, 147-148
Diana, Antonio, 156, 248
Diodotus, 76
Diogenes, of Babylon, 81-82
Donne, John, 164

Eck, John, 188-189
Elizabeth I, queen of England, 203-204
Escobar y Mendoza, Antonio, 168, 225,
    235-236, 240, 244-245
Euclid, 25, 27-28
Euripides, 59, 74
Ezekiel, 128

Fagnanus, Prosper, 172, 174
Ferdinand II, Holy Roman Emperor,
    145, 253
Ferraro, Geraldine, 1

Fugger family, 189
Fumus, Bartoloméo, 141

Garnet, Henry, 205, 207-211
Gerson, John, 223
González, Thyrsus de Santilla, 172
Gorgias, 60-61
Gratian, 114-115, 119, 124, 133, 183, 200
Gregory I, pope, 95-96, 200
Gregory VII, pope, 103, 107
Gregory IX, pope, 221
Gregory XIII, pope, 152
Grotius, Hugo, 211
Gury, Jean, 155

Hallier, François, 235
Hare, R.M., 174
Hauranne, Jean Duvergier de, 232
Haywood, Jasper, 189
Hecateus, 49
Hecato, of Rhodes, 80
Henry II, king of England, 107
Henry VIII, king of England, 159
Herbert, George, 161
Hermagoras, of Temnos, 71, 83-84, 88, 132
Herodotus, 49
Hildebrand (Pope Gregory VII), 103
Hobbes, Thomas, 162
Horace, 52
Hostiensis, 186
Huguccio, of Pisa, 133
Hurter, H., 346

Ignatius, of Loyola, 138, 146, 148, 152
Innocent XI, pope, 174, 226
Irnerius (Guarneri), 104
Isadore, of Seville, 115
Ivo, of Chartres, 115-116

James I, king of England, 145
Jansen, Cornelius, 231-232, 239, 246
Jefferson, Thomas, 71
Jerome, Saint, 128, 182
Jesus Christ, 91-92, 96, 115, 198, 208,
    217, 239-240
John, of Fribourg, 139
John, of St. Thomas, 173
Johnson, Samuel, 264
Judah, Rabbi, 56
Justinian, emperor of Rome, 104, 114,
    124

Kant, Immanuel, 174, 196, 211
Kirk, Bishop Kenneth, 16, 46, 162-163,
    243, 246
Knightbridge, John, 160
Krailsheimer, Alban, 345-346

Lactantius, 94
Laymann, Paul, 170, 209, 225, 253-254
Leo the Great, pope, 182
Lessius, Leonard, 151, 190, 214, 225-227, 244-245
Ligouri, Alphonsus, 156, 175, 193, 226
Locke, John, 163
Lombard, Peter, 122-136, 183, 185
Louis XIV, king of France, 232-233
Lugo, John de, 151, 190, 209, 226-227
Luker, Kristin, 5
Luther, Martin, 140, 143, 157-158, 188

Maine, Henry, 52
Martyr, Justin, 218
Matthew, Saint, 118
Mazzolini, Sylvester, 140, 198, 201, 224, 245
Medina Bartoloméo, 164-166, 169-170, 175
Mill, John Stuart, 174
Milo, 219
Milton, John, 164
Molière (John Baptiste Poquelin), 147
Molina, Louis, 151, 190, 232, 235
Montaigne, Michel de, 148, 240-241
More, Thomas, 163
Mortimer, R. C., 163
Moses, 56

Navarrus (Martin Azpilcueta), 142-143, 150, 187, 200-202, 205, 207-209, 211-212, 214, 224, 227, 245
Newman, Cardinal John Henry, 162, 174
Nickel, Goswin, 243
Nicole, Pierre, 233, 235, 246-247
Noah, 58
Noonan, John, 185, 187-188
Nouet, Pere, 243
Nyder, Jean, 153

O'Connor, archbishop, 1
Orestes, 84
Origen, 218
Ovid, 122

Panaetius, 76-79
Panormitanus, 223
Pascal, Blaise, 11-15, 20, 90, 110, 143, 148, 155-157, 161, 169, 171-172, 177-178, 194-195, 216, 225-227, 231-247, 252, 254, 256, 259, 262, 264
Pascal, Jacqueline, 233
Paul, Saint, 58, 92, 96, 101, 124-125, 128, 205, 222
Paulus, 219
Perkins, William, 159-160, 205

Persons, Robert, 203, 210
Peter, of Poitier, 119
Peter, Saint, 217
Philip, the Chancellor, 128-130
Pickering, Thomas, 159
Pirot, Georges, 243
Pius V, pope, 152, 203
Plato, 25, 48, 51, 58, 60-63, 66-67, 70-71, 73-74, 80, 83, 110, 126-127, 130, 148, 263
Plutarch, 122
Polanco, Juan, 150, 190
Porto, Rodrigo da, 152
Posidonius, 76-77
Pythagoras, 25, 27

Quintillian, 87, 123, 131-132

Rabelais, François, 141
Raymond, of Pennafort, 120, 139-140, 197, 223
Regulus, 75, 82
Renault, Father, 243
Richelieu, Cardinal Armand Jean de Plessis de, 232
Robert, of Courson, 119
Robert, of Flambrough, 119
Ross, W. D., 69
Rufus, Musonius, 94

Saint Beuve, C. A., 247
Saint-Cyran, Abbé de, 232, 247
Sales, François de, 239
Salisbury, Lord Robert Cecil, 205
Samson, 125
Sanchez, T., 168, 195, 214
Sanderson, Robert 160-161, 163, 212
Santoconcordio, Bartoloméo de, 140
Seneca, 122
Shaftsbury, Anthony Ashley Cooper, 163
Shakespeare, William, 164, 205
Sidgwick, Henry, 12, 163
Silvius, 226
Sinnigh, John 172
Sixtus V, pope, 152
Smith, Adam, 71
Socrates, 48, 52, 59, 61-62, 75
Solomon, 125
Solon, 101
Sophocles, 51, 59
Soto, Dominico, 153, 164, 199, 202, 208-209, 224
Southwell, Robert, 207, 209
Spinoza, Baruch, 62
Suárez, Francisco, 127, 144, 151, 169-170, 173-174

Tanner, Adam, 226
Taylor, Jeremy, 160-161, 163, 242
Tertullian, 13
Theaetetus, 25, 62
Thomas, of Chobham, 119
Thrasymachus, 59
Toletus, Cardinal Francesco, 150-151, 189

Ulpian, 124
Urban III, pope, 182

Vasquez, Gabriel, 167, 170, 237
Vincent de Paul, 234, 239
Virgil, 52, 122
Vitoria, Francisco, 144

Voltaire (François Marie Arouet), 147, 234

Walton, Izaak, 160
Walzer, Michael, 13-14
Ward, Father, 205
Whewell, William, 163
William, of Auxerre, 125
Williams, Bernard, 177-179
Wycliff, John, 158

Xavier, Francisco, 151

Zaccaria, Francis, 251
Zeno, 76

Subject Index

Abortion, debate on, 1-5, 304-305, 333-337

Absolutism, 2-7, 111-112. *See also* Universal principles

Accepted and Problematic Opinions in Moral Theology (Escobar), 235-236

Accidental causes, 127

Actions, moral: circumstances and (*see* Circumstance, doctrine of); discrimination in, 96-100; evaluation of, 134; intention and, 117, 122; intrinsically evil, 254; prudent, 123, 130-131; realms of, 144; timeliness of, 60; voluntary, 132; wickedness of (*see* Sin)

Act of Supremacy (1559), 203

Advantage, personal, common good and, 79-81, 83 ·

Aequitas canonica concept, 114, 116

After Virtue (MacIntyre), 283

Against Lying (Augustine), 196

Agency theory, 297

Agnosticism, 62, 148

Agony columns, English, 163-164

Albigensians, 120

Altruism, 287-288

Ambiguities, moral, 311. *See also* Moral dilemmas

Amplifications, 86

Analogy, casuist method and, 86, 251-252

Anglican Church. *See* Church of England

Apatheia, 76

Apology for the Casuists Against the Calumnies of the Jansenists (Pirot), 243

Arbitration, Roman law as, 52-54

Argument, ethical: casuistical, 245; chains of propositions in, 302; circumstance and, 134; classical rhetoric and, 60-61, 73, 83-84, 87-88, 258; confirmation in, 85-86; context of, 261, 326; cumulative, 255-256; deterrence and, 315; double, 60; geometrical model of, 331; maxims in, 51, 73-74, 87, 253; presumptive conclusions in, 332; probable (*see* Probabilism); proper topics, 86; relevant, 72; theoretical vs. practical, 285-286

Atheism, French, 274

Athenian Mercury, The, 163

Athenian(s): abstract vs. practical wisdom, 58-74; ethical discussion and, 47-52; Macedonian domination of, 63. *See also* Rhetoric

Augustinus (Jansen), 232

Authority, religious, 52. *See also* Canon law

Axioms: Cicero and, 80-81; fundamental, 295; invariable, 109, 341; of motion, 275

Banking, 113. *See also* Interest, on loans
Bankruptcy, 245
Baroque period, 145-146
Behavioral research. *See* Bioethics
Bible, maxims from, 118, 130, 182, 198.
    See also New Testament; Old
    Testament
Bibliothèque de la Compagne de Jésus
    (Sommervogel), 346
Bigotan Penitential, 100
Bioethics, 16-19, 305, 334-339. *See also*
    specific issues
Birth control, Catholics and, 271, 317
Blameless defense, 227
Bologna, University of, 103, 106
Book of Deuteronomy, usury and, 182
*Book of Moral Theology Woven out of
    Twenty-Four Doctors of the Society of
    Jesus, The* (Escobar), 235
Breve Directorium (Polanco), 150
Buddhism, 50
Byzantium, 55

Calvinists, 158, 232. *See also* Puritans
Cambridge University, Chair of
    Casuistical Divinity at, 160
Canonists, 113-121. *See also* specific
    works
Canon law, 107, 133; canon lawyers (*see*
    Canonists); diversity of sources,
    114-115; English casuists and, 161;
    equity and, 114, 116; gloss, 114,
    116-117; vs. personal conscience, 1-3;
    private confession and, 117-118.
    See also specific canons
Case(s), moral: chains of, 245; circum-
    stances of (*see* Circumstance, doc-
    trine of); of conscience (*see* Cases of
    conscience); equivocation, 195-215;
    medieval case law, 107; moral max-
    ims and, 252-253; ordering of, 153;
    paradigmatic, 108, 252, 307-308,
    317-322; pride, 216-227; probability
    of conclusions in, 254; problematic,
    323; resolution of, 256; self-defense,
    219-221; taxonomy of, 17, 47-74,
    251-252, 257; usury, 181-194
Case analysis method, 251, 263-364;
    canon law and, 114-117; confession-
    al books and, 120; Jesuit education
    in, 149-150; patristic, 93-100. *See
    also* Case(s); Casuistry
Cases of conscience, 127-131; Bacon
    and, 159; equiprobabilism, 175;
    great cases, 144; moral philosophy
    and, 303; of power, 158; in prose,
    164

Casuistic method. *See* Case analysis
    method
Casuistry, 11, 137-151; Aquinas' doc-
    trine, 123; argument in (*see*
    Argument, ethical; Rhetoric);
    Baroque period, 145; canon law
    antecedents, 114-119; century of
    maturity in, 142; Christian, 57,
    79-80, 89-136; cultural variety and,
    177-178, 284-285; current issues
    and, 307-318; definitions of, 11-12;
    education in, 149-150; as explicit
    procedure, 101; geometrical certain-
    ty vs., 110, 275-277; high period of
    (*see* High casuistry period); institu-
    tions needed for, 337-338; laxism
    and, 15, 157, 246-248, 259-260,
    269-270; literature and, 90, 94-100,
    118 (*see also* specific works); method
    of (*see* Case analysis method);
    Pascal's attack on, 169, 238, 341; as
    practical exercise, 242-244; primi-
    tive Christianity and, 91-100; proba-
    bilism and, 164-175; professional
    practice and, 101; revival of,
    304-332; samples of, 177-178;
    Summas, 137-151, 157, 242 (*see also*
    specific works); theological critics
    of, 248-249; theoretical objections to,
    263; theory of, 250; twentieth-centu-
    ry Catholic, 271
Casuists: approved authors, 177;
    Belgian, 271; catalogue of, 345-353;
    as counselors to rulers, 145;
    English, 157-164, 206-207, 264;
    Jesuits as, 146-151; laxist, 246-248;
    of Middle Ages, 122-136; patristic,
    93-100; professional cadre of, 113,
    250, 258, 264; as rationalists,
    240-241, 278; summists, 139-151.
    See also Casuistry; specific persons,
    works
Casus. See Case(s)
Categorical imperative, 174, 286
Causa, defined, 132. *See also* Case(s);
    Circumstance, doctrine of
Certitude, moral, 162, 165, 174; geo-
    metrical, 110; kind of knowledge
    and, 65-66; limits on, 257; locus of,
    16-20, 65; practical, 18; probable,
    171-172; Reformation and, 148
Child abuse, 307-309
*Christian Directory or Summ of Practical
    Theology and Cases of Conscience*
    (Baxter), 160
Christianity: Anglican, 157-164; canon
    law, 101-121; casuistical tradition

in, 57, 89-136; Church Fathers, 93-96, 124; common morality in, 239-240; confessors, 101-121; origins of, 91-100. *See also* Moral theology; Roman Catholic Church; specific doctrines

Church Fathers, 93-96; natural law and, 124. *See also* Canon law; specific persons

Church law. *See* Canon law

Church of England: break with Roman Catholic Church, 158-159; moral education in, 161; Prayer Book, 203; Puritan wing of, 158-160

Church of Rome. *See* Roman Catholic Church

Circumstance, doctrine of, 108, 123, 131-136, 250; Aristotle and, 71, 134-136; casuist method in, 154, 253-254; Ciceronian hexameter, 132, 134; equivocation and, 202; ignorance of, 129; Pascal on, 246

Cistercian Convent of Port-Royal, 233

Civil law: common, 4, 209-210, 303; Low countries, 24-245; medieval, 108, 110, 117; moral issues and, 48-49; probabilism and, 169-170; as profession, 54; rhetorical theory in, 298; Roman (*see* Roman law)

Clergy, 93-96; Canonists, 113-121; as class, 102-103; education of, 103, 106, 131, 142-143, 149-150, 206-207, 213. *See also* Casuists

Code of Justinian, 104

Code of Noah, 58

Code of rules, 5-11. *See also* Rules

Codex Juris Canonci. See Canon law

Codex Juris Civilis. See Civil law

College of Pontiffs, 52-55

Commandments: casuist method and, 251; counsels of distinction and, 95; counsels of perfection and, 95; treatises on, 154. *See also* Sin

Commentaries (Blackstone), 292

Commerce, 113; corporations, 103; German contract, 188-190, 258; nation-states and, 193; partnerships, 185-186. *See also* Interest, on loans

Common law: abortion and, 4; common morality and, 18, 303, 330; equivocation and, 209-210; Roman, 54. *See also* Civil law

Conditions of the agent, 253-254, 258

Confession, 97; annual requirement, 121, 139; confessors, 101-121; equivocation and, 202; inviolability of, 200; manual for, 152-153; paradig-matic case of, 213-214; private, 117, 143; probabilism and, 167; public, 98; questions, 119. *See also* Penance

Confessional Books, 117-121, 242, 255

Congregational churches, 158

Conscience, 1-3, 11; Aquinas on, 123, 128-129, 250; erroneous, 165; excess scrupulosity, 260; natural law and, 127; Paul's letters on, 92; perplexed, 95; practical certitude of, 17, 166, 171; social, 306; ultimate act of, 135. *See also* Cases of conscience

Constantinople, 102

Constitutions of Clarendon, 107

Contracts, German, 188-190, 258. *See also* Commerce; Usury

Conversations Between Cleander and Eudoxius (Daniel), 243

Corporation, church as, 103

Corpus Juris Romani, 104-105. *See also* Roman law

Corrector of Burchard, 220

Council of Ancyra, 93

Council of Elvira, 93

Council of Jerusalem, 217

Council of Nicea, 182

Council of Trent, 143, 146, 190, 274

Counseling, casuistry as, 242

Counter-Reformation, 111, 151

Courage, Cicero on, 87

Courts: Anglo-Saxon, 110; ecclesiastical, 105-108, 162; folk, 108; principles of jurisprudence, 169-170, 174; Roman, 52, 54. *See also* Civil law

Credit. *See* Loans

Cultural relativism, 5-6, 49-50, 177-178; argument and, 284-285, 326; extreme forms of, 61

Customary law, 52, 54. *See also* Common law

Death, brain criteria for, 338

Debate, special field of, 74

Decalogue, 91, 125, 154, 217, 252

De Conscientia, ejus jure et casibus (Ames), 160

Decretum poenitentiae sunt arbitrariae (Gratian), 114-116, 119, 124, 133, 183, 220-221

Deduction, in reasoning, 85; Descartes and, 278; from invariable axioms, 341

Deeds. *See* Actions, moral

Defense: blameless, 227. *See also* Self-defense

Defensio Fidei Catholicae adversus Anglicanae Sectae Errores (Suárez), 144-145

De Inventione (Cicero), 84, 87
De Iure Belli et Pacis (Grotius), 276
De Jure et Justitia (Society of Jesus), 151
De Jure Naturae et Gentium (Pufendorf), 277
De Justitice et Jure (Lessius), 244
De Mendacio (Augustine), 196, 213
De Obligatione Conscientiae (Sanderson), 160
De Officiis (Cicero), 75, 77-79, 94, 286
De Officiis Ministrorum (Ambrose of Milan), 94
De Oratore (Cicero), 84
De Rhetorica quae supersunt, 87
Deterrence arguments, 315
De Vera et Falsa Poenitentia, 119
Diagnosis, medical, casuist method and, 257
Dialogue Concerning the Two Great World Systems (Galileo), 275
Diana Coordinatus (de Acolea), 156
Dictionnaire de Théologie Catholique, 346
Die Meistersinger von Nurnberg, 102
Digest (Justinian), 114, 116, 124
Digest (Tanqueray), 342
Dilemmas. *See* Moral dilemmas
Diplomacy, Jesuits and, 146-148
Discernment, moral, 9-10, 62, 342; Jesuit, 151; judicial, 54; novel cases and, 329
Discourse against Taking the Oath, A (Persons), 212
Discourse of Conscience (Perkins), 159
Discourse on Method (Descartes), 275
Dissimulation, 202
Divine grace, doctrine of, 99, 232-236, 240
Divine law. *See* Canon law
Divorce, Jewish law of, 91
Doctors' Dilemma, The (Shaw), 299
Dogmatism, principles, 5-11, 262, 342
Dominican Order, 139, 165, 171
Douai-Rheims, English Seminary of, 206-207
Double Arguments (Gorgias), 60
Double effect principle, 221-312-313
Doubt, moral, 165, 170. *See also* Probabilism
Ductor Dubitantium (Taylor), 160
Durable powers of attorney concept, 340
Duty, conflict in, 79-80

Ecclesiastical law. *See* Canon Law
Economics, 151; emerging science of, 193; usury case, 181-194; utilitarianism in, 300

Ecumenical Councils. *See* specific councils
Edict of Milan, 218
Edict of Nantes, 234, 274
Education, moral: English, 160-161, 206-207; Jesuits and, 146-150; medieval, 103, 106, 131; summists and, 142
Efficacy, 304
Elementorum Jurisprudentiae Universales Libri Duo (Pufendorf), 277
Elements (Euclid), 50, 275
Elements of Morality, The (Whewell), 279-280
Enchiridion Confessariorum et Poenitentium (Navarrus), 142, 150, 152-153, 207
England: Act of Supremacy, 203-204; casuistry in, 157-164; Church of (*see* Church of England); Engagement Oath, 211-212; Jesuit mission to, 203, 207
English Prayer Book, 203
Enlightenment, 278
Enthymemes, 73-74, 85
Epieikeia, Aristotelian, 116
Episteme, vs. *phronesis*, 58-74
Equiprobabilism, 175
Equity: canonical, 110, 114, 116; compensatory justice, 288; defined, 68; discernment and, 9; ethics modeled on, 341; law vs., 53-55; rules and, 259; social relations and, 290-292
Equivocation, 195-215; biblical examples and, 198; English Catholics and, 203-213; Garnet on, 207-210; Latin, 197; mental reservations and, 201-203, 207-208, 211-215; Persons on, 210-211; Raymond on, 197-198; Soto on, 199-200; two types of, 208
Ethic(s): abstract exactitude theory, 12, 62; Aristotelian, 64, 109; axiomatic vs. taxonomic approach, 109; case method of, 12, 16 (*see also* Case analysis method); Christian, 90-91, 104, 108, 158; circumstances and (*see* Circumstance, doctrine of); code of rules approach, 6-11; common law model, 4, 209-210, 303, 330; culturally diverse, 5-6, 49-50, 61, 177-178, 284-285, 326; *de minimis* doctrine, 325; dilemmas of (*see* Moral dilemmas); distinctive features of, 67; eternal vs. circumstantial, 2; general considerations, 67; of intimacy, 291; Kant's theory of,

286-288; law vs., 107; medical (*see* Medical ethics); medieval, 101-121; meta-ethics, 12, 283; in Middle Ages, 123; moral practice and, 265; in nineteenth-century theories, 279-313; philosophical foundations of, 50; principles of (*see* Principles); professional, 13, 304; public debates about, 1-3, 337-341; reasoning in (*see* Moral reasoning); rhetoric and (*see* Rhetoric); situational, 61, 272-273; of strangers, 291; as theoretical field, 19, 279-283
Ethica seu Scire Teipsum (Abelard), 122
Ethics and the Limits of Philosophy (Williams), 283
Europe: commercial markets, 193; creation of, 113; medieval, 100-121
Examples, in moral conflicts, 73-75. *See also* Case(s)
Existentialism, ethics and, 272
Experience, value of, 313-314
Experimentation, on human subjects, 17, 305, 308-309, 334-335, 338
Experts: authority of, 168; in casuistry. *See* Casuists
Expositio Praeceptorum Decalogi (Nyder), 153
Extrinsic probability, 167-169, 173

Fairness, 10. *See also* Equity
Falsehood. *See* Lying
Family relations, paradigmatic cases, 317-322
Fetus, killing of, 308-309, 334-335. *See also* Abortion
Formal proofs, 72, 110, 241, 275-277
Foundations of the Law of Nature and of Nations Deduced from Common Sense (Thomasius), 277
France: atheism in, 274; French Revolution, 111, 273-274; Jansenists in, 231-249; toleration of non-Catholics, 233-234
Free choice, 128
Friendship, casuistry and, 69
Fundamentalism, 111-112

Gargantua and Pantagruel (Rabelais), 141
Generalizations, moral, 8, 258
Genetic engineering, 304
Georgics (Virgil), 52
German contract, 188-190, 258
Germany, religious schisms in, 274
Gloss, canonical, 116-118
Good, eternal, universal form of, 62, 67

Gospels. *See* New Testament
Grace: fall from, 125; Jansenist-Jesuit controversy on, 232, 234-236; nature of, 99; Pascal on, 240
Grammar of Assent (Newman), 174
Great Britain. *See* England
Greece. *See* Athenians
Gunpowder Plot, 204, 206, 210

Halakhah, 57
Hastings Center, 339
Health care, modern casuistry institutions and, 338-341. *See also* Medical ethics
Heresy, 96, 120
Hermits of St. Augustine, 139
High casuistry period: achievements of, 260-265; antecedents to, 124, 137-151; demise of, 270; sample cases, 177-178; theoretical fault of, 238
Holy Living (Taylor), 242
Holy Office of the Inquisition, 200, 243, 270-271
Holy Scripture. *See* Bible
Honor, defense of, 224-227
Humanae Vitae, 271
Humanists, 147, 275
Human nature: paradox of, 240; taxonomy of behavior, 142
Human subjects, research on, 16-19, 264, 305, 308-309, 334-335, 338
Hypotheses, 84, 132. *See also* Case(s)

Ideal forms, Plato on, 61
Impartiality, ideal of, 290-291
Index of Forbidden Books, 243
Individual, distinctiveness of, 97
Induction, 85
Infidels, casuists on, 178
Informed conscience: abortion and, 333-334; cases of (*see* Cases of conscience); centrality of, 2-3; community and, 335
Injustice, 10, 54-55, 201. *See also* Equity
Inquisition, 200, 243, 270-271
Institutionum Moralium (Azor), 153-156, 159
Institutio Oratorica (Quintillian), 87, 123
Insurance contracts, 191-192
Interest, on loans: commercial loans, 191-193; defined, 191; German contract, 188-190; paradigmatic case, 191, 309-310; partnerships and, 185-186; theory of, 188; usuriousness of (*see* Usury)
Interpretation, Pascal on, 246

Intrinsic probability, 173
Investments, interest and, 191-193, 310
Islam: Quar´an of, 111-112; sharîya, 285;
    usury and, 310

Jansenists, casuistry and, 172, 231-249,
    269; on grace, 232, 234-235; ideals
    and, 246-247; moral teachings of,
    239; Pascal and, 246-247
Jesuits, 138, 171; casuistical books,
    150-151; classical rhetoric and, 88;
    Constitution of, 149; distaste for,
    160; education of clergy, 146-150;
    English Mission of, 203, 207; on
    German contract, 189-191; Jansenist
    controversy, 232-239; Pascal on,
    12-15, 161, 248. See also specific per-
    sons, works
Judaism: case ethics in, 14; Gentiles
    and, 111-112; Halakhah, 57; killing
    and, 217; legal vs. moral issues, 107;
    moneylending and, 184-185;
    Rabbinic, 55-58; Reform, 112
Judges. See Jurisprudence
Judgment, moral, 18, 67; conscience
    and, 1-3, 11, 129; generalizing of,
    258; knowledge required for, 165;
    locus of certitude, 16-20, 65; phrone-
    sis vs. episteme, 58-74; probable certi-
    tude, 166, 171; problems of moral
    practice, 108-109
Jurisdiction, legal and equitable, 54
Jurisprudence: canonical, 105-108, 162;
    general principles of, 169-170, 172,
    174; Roman, 51-55, 104-108; tort the-
    ory, 297; torture and, 178. See also
    Civil law
Justa defensio, 145
Just and Unjust Wars (Walzer), 13
Justice: absolute, 60; Cicero on, 87;
    compensatory, 170, 288, 292-293;
    equity and, 10, 68; Platonic ideal,
    110; procedures and, 105; rules and,
    9-10; social life and, 126

Kathormata, 76
Kennedy Center for Bioethics, The, 339
Key for Catholicks to Open the Juggling of
    the Jesuits (Baxter), 160
Killing: Augustine on, 218-219; casuist
    definition of, 251; common good
    and, 22; honor and, 224-227; proper-
    ty and, 222, 224, 227, 315-316
King John (Shakespeare), 164
Knowledge, moral, 331; abstract vs.
    practical, 58-74; Aristotle on, 63-64;

    locus of certitude, 16-20, 65; Plato
    on, 62
Koran, 111-112

Lateran Councils: II, 182; III, 182-183;
    IV, 100, 105, 120, 139, 143, 200, 300
Law(s): principles of, 276-277; universal,
    2-4, 10, 104. See also specific erc. type
Lawful Manner of Answering to
    Questions of Going to Church, A, 205
Laws of Henry the First, 110
Laxism, 157; papal censure of, 269-270;
    Pascal's critique of, 12-15, 165,
    231-249; remedy for, 259-260
Lectures on Ethics (Kant), 287
Legalism, 271
Lettres Provinciales, Les (Pascal), 11, 15,
    90, 143, 164, 227, 231-249, 332, 342,
    346
Liberal arts education, 103, 106, 131,
    146-147, 206-207
Liber Penitentialis (Alain of Lille), 119
Liber Penitentialis (Robert of Courson),
    119
Liber Theologiae Moralis Vigintiquatuor
    Societatis Jesu Doctoribus Resertus
    (Escobar), 155
Life, defense of. See Self-defense
Life support medical systems, 338-340
Literacy, Medieval European, 102-103
Literature, casuistical, 143; Anglican,
    157-164; confessional, 96-100, 123,
    133, 220, 242, 255; medieval unity
    in, 111; textbooks, 150. See also spe-
    cific works
Litigation, friendly concord vs., 110
Living wills, 340
Loans. See Interest, on loans
Locus of certitude, 16-20, 65
Logic, ethics and, 73, 75
Loyalty, communal, 311-312
Lutherans, 278
Lying: Augustine on, 196-197, 201;
    casuist definition of, 251; deceptive
    prevarication, 208; English
    Catholics and, 203-213; maxims
    and, 253; mental reservation and,
    202; primordial falsehood, 211;
    Raymond on, 197-198; sin of, 98-99.
    See also Equivocation
Lying (Bok), 13

Macbeth (Shakespeare), 205
Manichean heresies, 96
Marriage: assumptions about, 318-321;
    matrimonial law, 105

Mathematics, 110: existence of God and, 241; formal proofs, 72; as intellectual model, 47-52, 275-277

Maxims: Aristotle's use of, 73-74; casuist method and, 252-253; confessional books and, 118; general, 8; Greek, 51; Kant on, 286; laws and, 54, 169; medical, 100; Scripture and, 161; in training in rhetoric, 87

Mediation, English courts, 110

Medical ethics, casuistry and, 13, 250-251, 257, 304-305, 337-341; consequentialist arguments, 299; current casuistry of, 337-341; double effect principle, 312-313; *kairos*, 60; rhetorical adjustments, 72-73; spiritual healing and, 100, 121

Medieval era, 101-121; canonists, 113-121; ethical approach in, 109; Roman law and, 104-105; skepticism in, 275; synchronic vs. diachronic morality, 112; theologians of, 122-136

Medulla (Tanqueray), 342

Medulla Theologiae Moralis (Busenbaum), 156, 248

Mental reservation doctrine, 210; broad, 202-203, 209, 213-214; Catholic condemnation of, 214-215; Engagement Oath and, 212; Navarrus and, 207-208, 211

Meta-ethics, 12, 283

Metaphysic of Morals (Kant), 287

Method, idea of, 275. *See also* Case analysis method

Methodism, 100

Methods of Ethics, The (Sidgwick), 12, 280

Middle Ages, rhetorical theories, 87-88. *See also* Medieval era

Militancy, religious, 144, 200, 243, 270-271

Mishnah, 56

Missions, 146-147, 206-207

Molinism, 232

Moll Flanders (Defoe), 164

Monasteries, 96-97

Money: casuistry and, 244; nature of, 184; value of, 192. *See also* Usury

Moral certitude. *See* Certitude, moral

Moral competence, 62

Moral dilemmas: in ancient literature, 75; casuistry's role in, 96, 242-243; 337; fitting action, 78; lying and, 196-197; practical resolution of, 256-257; revival of interest in, 13; taxonomies and, 14, 17

Moral doctrine, 123; economics and, 181. *See also* Ethics; specific doctrines

Moralia (Gregory the Great), 200

Morality: case (*see* Case analysis method); *de minimis* doctrine in, 325; general theories of, 163; Jansenist view of, 247; natural law and, 78, 80-82, 113, 124-127; practical, 108-109; theoretical differences, 302. *See also* Ethics

Moral opinion, formulation of, 72-73, 216. *See also* Ethics

Moral philosophy: academic, 163-164; ideal of system in, 277, 279; objections to casuistry, 13-15, 17; penitential books and, 96-100; practical philosophy vs., 285-286; probable argument in, 78; rhetoric and, 87-88; temporality of theory in, 293; theoretical, 302-303; in twentieth century, 283, 304; universal rules and, 2-4, 13, 104, 279

Moral practice. *See* Actions, moral

Moral probabilism. *See* Probabilism

Moral psychology, 163; intuitionist school, 282; treatises on, 173

Moral reasoning: case vs. abstract morality, 280; Cicero on, 85; first principle of, 126; geometrical view of, 50, 110, 241, 275-277, 293; logic of, 173; moral philosophy and, 163; natural law and, 126-127; rhetorical view of, 293; temporal account of, 59. *See also* Ethics; Moral theology

Moral rules. *See* Rules, moral

Morals and Medicine (Fletcher), 304

Moral taxonomies. *See* Taxonomies, moral

Moral theologians, 14

Moral theology: Anglican, 157-164; approved manuals, 273; Calvinists, 158-159; Canonists, 113-121; Christian disputes, 1-5, 96, 231-249; complementary theories in, 295-299; cultural relativism and, 49-50; Jesuits and, 150-151, 235; medieval, 122-136; moral action and, 294-295; political atmosphere in, 107-108, 273-274; as practical art, 143; probabilism and, 164-175; scholastic, 103, 106, 242; secular versions, 1, 275, 279. *See also* Moral reasoning

Moral Theology of the Jesuits Faithfully Extracted from Their Books, The (Itallien and Arnauld), 235

Moral tutiorism, 241

Moral wisdom, 61, 72. *See also* Practical wisdom

Moral Works (Pascal), 195
Moral writing. *See* specific authors, works
Mores, Roman, 107
Mosaic law, 125
Motive, sin and, 133
Murder. *See* Killing

National Commission for the Protection of Human Subjects of Biomedical and Behavioral Research, 16-19, 264, 305, 338
Nationalism, 113, 145, 311
Nation-states, 113, 193
Natural law: common good and, 81-82; doctrine of, 123-128, 250; maxims from, 253; of Stoics, 76-78; right action and, 80; theological appeals to, 113
Natural philosophy movement, 275
Natural reason, Middle Ages and, 124-137
Natural sciences, analytic reasoning in, 64; Newton's effect on, 275
New Decalogue, The (Clough), 308
New Testament, 94; canon law and, 114-116; equivocation and, 198; self-defense and, 221; usury and, 182
Nicomachean Ethics (Aristotle), 6, 67, 69-71, 73, 123, 130-133, 281
Noachic law, 92
Nomenclator Litterarius (Hurter), 346
Northern Rebellion (1569), 204
Novel: as case, 164, 316; moral generalizations in, 296
Nuclear war, 314

Oaths, 82-83; of allegiance, 207-212; Engagement Oath, 212; equivocating under, 198, 209-210, 311; nature of, 212; oath-helpers, 105; sin of perjury and, 98-99; of supremacy, 203
Old Testament: on equivocation, 198; saints of, 125; on usury, 182
On Duties (Cicero), 75, 77-79, 94, 286
On Duties (Panaetius), 79
On Lying (Augustine), 196
On the Confession of Princes (Acquaviva), 147
On the Origins, Sources and Excellence of Casuistic Theology (Zaccaria), 251
Ontology, Greek, 50
Opinion: doubt vs., 165-166; expert, 168; of physicians, 72-73; probable (*see* Probabilism); ranking of, 255-256
Opportune time, doctrine of, 60-61
Oratory, 83-84; classical topics, 86, 254; doctrine of circumstances, 131. *See also* Rhetoric

Order of Friars Minor (Franciscans), 139
Order of Preachers (Dominicans), 139, 165, 171
Original sin, 125, 232
Pacis Compositio, 145
Panormia (Ivo of Chartres), 115-116
Papal infallibility, dogma of, 275
Paradigm cases, 251-252, 259; complicating circumstances to, 253, 321-323; as locus of judgment, 330; probabilism and, 254; taxonomy of, 257; valid inferences in, 324-325
Paradoxes, moral, 93-94, 263
Parens patriae doctrine, 55
Partnerships, legitimacy of, 185-186
Pastoral care, canon law and, 118
Pastoral writing, 96. *See also* specific authors, works
Pastor of Hermes, 98
Patient as Person, The (Ramsey), 304
Patres Ecclesiae, 93-100
Patristic casuistry, 91-100; Church Fathers, 93; nature of Jesus and, 96; penitential books, 96-100; sin doctrine, 97; taxonomy of moral action, 100; writings on prudence, 130
Pawnshops, 192
Peace of Augsburg, 253
Pelagian heresies 96, 125
Penance, 97, 119; determination of, 157; justification of, 255; monetary, 99; repentance and, 98
Penitential Books, 133, 255; idealism in, 242; on murder, 220; primitive casuistry and, 96-100. *See also* specific books
Penitential of Burchard, 99
Penitential of Cummean, 98
Pensées (Pascal), 231, 240
Pentateuch, 56-57
Perfection, idea of, 277
Periodicals, popular casuistry in, 163-164
Peripatetics, 75
Perjury. *See* Equivocation; Lying
Perplexed conscience, 95
Persecution, English Catholics and, 204-213
Personal relationship (*philia*), 69-70
Phaedrus (Plato), 130
Philosophiae Naturalis Principia Mathematica (Newton), 275
Philosophia Moralis (Bacon), 122
Philosophy: fact-value dichotomy, 305; ideal of system in, 276-278; pagan, 47-74. *See also* Moral philosophy; Natural law; Practical wisdom

Phronesis. See Practical wisdom
Physical sciences, 64, 66, 241, 274-275
Planetary geometry, 50. *See also*
    Mathematics
Poetry, casuistry in, 164
Politics: church, 104; Greek classical,
    59-60; medical ethics and, 339-340;
    medieval, 107-108; vs. moral issues,
    48-49, 274-275; as science, 151; uni-
    versal principles of, 51
Pontiffs, 52-54, 174-175, 271, 275. *See
    also* Roman Catholic Church
Positive law, 52
Possession, principle of, 169-170
Practical experience, collective, 314
Practical wisdom (*phronesis*), 19; current
    casuistry problems and, 13-20,
    304-332; vs. *episteme*, 53, 58-74; gener-
    alizations and, 62, 169, 258-259; prac-
    tical philosophy, 71-72, 110, 126; prac-
    tical theology, 139
Pragmatists, 281-283
Predestination, 232
Presbyterian Church, 158
Prescriptivity, 174
President's Commission for the Study
    of Ethical Problems in Medicine and
    in Biomedical and Behavioral
    Research, 338
Presumptive conclusions, 327-328
Pretence, 207
Prevarication. *See* Lying
Pride, case example of, 216-227
Priests. *See* Clergy; Roman Catholic
    Church
Primordial falsehood, 211
Principles: absolutism in (*see* Universal
    principles); conflict of, 8, 140; discre-
    tion in, 68; double effect, 312-313;
    exceptions, 250; first, 276-277; gen-
    erality of, 62, 168, 258-259; Greek's
    search for, 50; natural law doctrine
    and, 135; Pascal on, 241; practical,
    169; reflex, 170, 173-174, 251, 334;
    superprinciple, 293-294
Principles of Morals and Legislation, The
    (Bentham), 289, 292
Probabiliorism, 260-261
Probabilism, 1, 3, 82; abortion debate and,
    333-334; argument and, 132; dispute
    over, 12-15, 90, 148-149, 155, 161-162,
    167-168; doctrine of, 138, 237; as formal
    theory, 251; intrinsic vs. extrinsic prob-
    ability, 167-170; killing for a slap case,
    216-227; Medina's thesis, 164-167,
    169-170; novel cases and, 328; papal
    decrees and, 174-175, 271; Pascal's cri-

tique of, 165, 171, 216-217, 231-247,
    245; pastoral challenge to, 171; ranking
    of opinions in, 255-256; rules for,
    170-171, 254; Suárez and, 169
Probability, intrinsic vs. extrinsic,
    167-170
Probable opinions, doctrine of, 138, 237.
    See also Probabilism
Promises, 82-83, 212
Promulgation, principle of, 169-170
Proof, formal, 72
Property, defense of, 222, 224, 227,
    315-316
Propositions: chains of, 302; papal con-
    demnation of, 174-175; probable,
    166
Prose, casuistry in, 164
Protestants: consolidation of, 262; oaths
    and, 203, 207-212; pietism, 278;
    Reformation and, 110, 143-144, 148,
    157-158, 232, 273-274. *See also*
    Church of England
Proverbs, Greek, 51
Prudence, doctrine of, 123, 130-131;
    prudent understanding, 67-68
Psychological egoism, 287
Psychology, moral, 163, 173, 282
Public policy, medical ethics and,
    339-340; modern casuistry, 1-19,
    304-332. *See also* Politics
Pupilla Ocula (John de Burgo), 140
Puritans, 158, 160
Pyrrhonism, 240

Quaestio, 123
Questiones (Aquinas), 126
Qur'an, 111-112

Rabbinic casuistry, 56-57. *See also*
    Judaism
Racial inequalities, 292
Rape of the Lock (Pope), 12
Rationalism, 76, 240-241; *ratio naturalis*,
    112; secular, 278
Ratio Studiorum, Jesuits, 149-150, 154
Reality, time and, 61-62
Reason. *See* Moral reasoning
Reasonable justification, 78
*Reasoning about Revealing and
    Concealing Secrets* (Soto), 199
Rebuttal, of presumptions, 168, 328, 332
Recusants, 204, 209
Reflex principles, 170, 173-174, 251, 334
Reformation: casuistry and, 110,
    143-144, 148, 157-158; Counter-
    Reformation, 111, 151
Regnans in Excelsis (Pius V), 203

Relativism, ethical, 2-6; cultural, 49-50; moral practices and, 112; situation ethics, 61, 272-273; of Sophists, 62, 66
Relectio de Indis et de Jure Belli (Vitoria), 144
Religious liberty, 2-3, 162, 253, 274
Renaissance, 145
Repentance, doctrine of, 97, 118, 143
Representative government, 289
Republic (Plato), 59, 61, 292
Research, on human subjects, 16-19, 264, 305, 308-309, 334-335, 338
Reservation. *See* Mental reservation doctrine
Resolutiones Morales (Diana), 156
Resolutions, practical, 263
Revelation, immutable law and, 115, 125
Rheims, English Seminary at, 206-207
Rhetoric: case method and, 257-258; classical, 6, 71, 74, 83-88; doctrine of circumstances, 131; ethics and, 298; geometrical certainty vs., 110; hypotheses, 84 (*see also* Case(s)); Jesuits and, 151; maxims, 253; Middle Ages, 123; reason and, 298; Sophists and, 60-61
Rhetoric (Aristotle), 73
Rhetorica ad Herrenium (Cicero), 87
Rights and welfare, of research subjects, 16
Right to life. *See* Abortion
Robinson Crusoe (Defoe), 164
Roe v. Wade, U.S. Supreme Court, 4, 16
Roman Catholic Church: abortion disputes in, 1-5; Anglican break with, 158-159; bishops of, 52-55, 317, 338; canon law, 113-121; casuistry evolution in, 106-121; centralized style of, 275; common morality, 111-112; courts, 104-108; discipline and, 1-3, 272; dogmatism in, 262; English Catholics, 203-204; General Synod, 317; local councils, 98; moral taxonomy and, 14; Protestant regimes and, 144-145, 203-212, 273-274; reform in, 143, 146; Sacred Penitentiary, 152; supreme pontiff, 55, 275; as transnational institution, 101-102; twentieth-century casuistry, 271, 338; on usury, 181-194
Roman Empire, 54-55; Alexander and, 58; rhetoricians and, 83
Roman law (*Corpus Juris Romani*): collective wisdom in, 52; customary law and, 54; on interest, 185-186; maxims, 253; medieval codification of, 104-106; on interest, 185-186; persons of, 96; reliance on rules, 54; roots of casuistry in, 47; on self-defense,

219-221; as taxonomic system, 104-108. *See also* Civil law
Roxana (Defoe), 164
Rules: awareness of, 170; of customary conduct, 61; ethics of strangers, 291; exceptions, 328-329; inferences from, 258; of jurisprudence, 169-170, 172; law without, 153; moral code of, 6-11; vs. moral value, 272; nuances, 325-326; of probabilism, 170-171, 254; presumptions created by, 311-312; real-life application of, 9; Roman law and, 54; self-interpreting, 8

Sacraments, ritual and, 272
Sacred Congregation for Religious and Secular Institutes, 2
Sacred Penitentiary, 270
Saints, stories of, 122, 125
Salvation, natural law and, 124-126. *See also* Grace
Science, universal laws and, 64, 66, 241, 274
Scripture. *See* Bible
Self-defense, 117; Aquinas on, 221-222; canons on, 216-227; Grotius on, 276; maxims, 253; morality of, 90, 262; property and, 222, 224, 227, 315-316; Roman law and, 219-221; social status and, 223-227
Self-love, 240-241
Seven Deadly Sins, 251
Sexuality: casuists on, 178-179; paradigmatic cases, 317-322
Simony, 165
Sin: circumstances of, 99, 133-134; doctrine of, 97-98, 143; moral vs. venial, 141, 161; nature of, 118, 123; omission vs. commission in, 141; original, 135, 232; sexuality and, 178-179. *See also* Confession; Penance
Situation ethics: classical casuistry vs., 272-273; extreme forms of, 61
Situation Ethics (Fletcher), 273
Skepticism, 77, 148, 171
Social class: abortion and, 5; self-defense and, 223-227
Social practice, 289
Social relations: familial, 317-322; friendship, 69; moral duties of, 79
Societas, legitimacy of, 185
Society of Jesus. *See* Jesuits
Sociology, 5-6, 151
Sophistry, 60; abuse of rhetorical methods in, 73; agnosticism and, 62; casuistry as, 238; central claim of, 68
Spanish Armada (1588), 204, 274

Spectator, 163
Speech: Cicero on, 84; vs. intention, 200-201. *See also* Rhetoric
Spiritual Exercises (Loyola), 148, 242
Stasis theory, 83-84
Statutes. *See* Civil law
Stoicism: Christian ethos, 94; Cicero and, 76; good vs. evil in, 77, 141; moral wisdom and, 78, 130; self-discipline in, 239
Summa (Tanqueray), 342
Summa Angelica (Carletti), 140, 153
Summa Armilla (Fumus), 141
Summa Astesana, 139-140
Summa Casuum Conscientiae (Toletus), 150
Summa Confessionalis (Antoninus), 186
Summa Confessorum (John of Fribourg), 139
Summa Confessorum (Thomas of Chobham), 119
Summa de Poenitentia (Raymond of Pennafort), 120, 139
Summa de Sacramentis et Animae Conciliis (Peter Cantor), 118-120
Summa Diabolica, 143, 157
Summa Diana (Cotonio), 156
Summae Sylvestrina et Angelica, 146
Summa Metrica, 141
Summa Moralis (Antoninus), 186
Summa Pisana (Bartoloméo de Santo Concordio), 140
Summa Rudium, 141
Summa Summarum (Mazzolino), 140
Summa Sylvestrina (Mazzolino), 140, 153, 198, 223
Summa Tabiena (Cagnazzo), 140
Summa Theologiae (Aquinas), 123, 164
Summa Theologica (Aquinas), 134, 139, 149-150
Summists, 139-151, 157, 198-199, 242. *See also* specific authors, works
Summula Peccatorum (Thomas de Vio Cajetan), 140
Syllogisms, 73
Synderesis vs. *conscientia*, 128-129
Synod of the Grove of Victory, 220
System, ideal of, 275-278

Talmuds, 56-57
Tatler, 163
Taxonomies, moral, 14, 69; action and, 100; in antiquity, 47-74; high casuist cases, 251-252; human behavior and, 142; type cases, 257
Teacher, The (Clement of Alexandria), 94
Temperance, Cicero on, 87
Ten Commandments. *See* Commandments

Theft, loans as, 191; usury as, 182
Theologiae Moralis (Tanqueray), 342
Theologia Moralis ad Prima Eaque Clarrissima Principia Reducta (Caramuel-Lebkowitz), 156
Theological Studies, 271
Theology: Calvinists, 158-159; cultural relativism and, 49-50; medieval, 122-136; patristic, 93-100, 130; as practical art, 143; scholastic, 146-151, 242. *See also* Moral theology; specific persons
Theory of Justice, The (Rawls), 288, 290-292
Theory of Morals and Legislation (Bentham), 301
Theses, 84-85. *See also* Case(s)
Thirty Years' War, 145, 274
Timeliness, of acts, 60
Tolerance, religious, 2-3, 162, 253, 274
Toleration Act, 162
Topics (Aristotle), 74
Torah: evolving, 112; Talmuds of, 56-57
Tort theory, 297
Torture, 93, 178, 315
Treason, English Catholics and, 206-207
Treatise of Equivocation, A, 207
Treatise Tending toward Mitigation, A (Persons), 210
Truth: concealing of (*see* Equivocation); confidentiality of confession and, 213; physical tests of, 105; probable, 166; system, 281; universal, 61-62
Truth-telling: casuistry of, 201, 214; doctrine of, 195-215; English Catholics and, 204; morality of, 90; paradigm of confessional 200; war and, 276. *See also* Equivocation; Lying
Tutiorism, 241, 260
Type cases. *See* Paradigmatic cases

Ultimate particulars, 66
Understanding, prudent, 67-68
United States Supreme Court, 4, 16
Universae Theologiae Moralis (Escobar), 245
Universal principles, 2-4, 104; case method vs., 19-20; Greeks and, 50, 54, 59, 61-63; religious fundamentalism and, 111-112; role of, 174, 286; science and, 64, 66, 241, 274; tyranny of, 5-11, 341
Universalizability, 174
Universal reason, 54
Usury, 145; Aquinas on, 184; case of, 181-194; choice of paradigm, 309-310; doctrine, 153; German contract and, 188-190; Islam and, 310; permissible, 187

Utilitarianism, 81, 288-289; principle, 174; types of, 300-301

Values: challenges to, 158; secular vs. religious, 145-146; systems, 5-6
Vatican. *See* Roman Catholic Church
Vatican Councils, 275. *See also* specific council
Veil of ignorance, 290-291
Violence, morally permissible, 178, 314-315. *See also* Self-defense
Virtue: Aristotelian scheme, 122; cases and, 160; complex contexts of, 295; four cardinal, 78, 87, 130

Vows, natures of, 82-83, 212. *See also* Oaths

War: casuists on, 13, 261-262; just war concept, 219, 306, 314-315; law of, 276; moral debates on, 305-306
Whole Treatise of Cases of Conscience (Perkins), 159
Wisdom: Aristotle on, 65; Cicero on, 87; of experts, 168; practical (*see* Practical wisdom)
World views, 5-6

Zealots, 5-11, 111-112. *See also* Absolutism

Designer:	U.C. Press Staff
Compositor:	Vicky Jo Varner
Text:	10/13 Palatino
Display:	Palatino
Printer:	Vail Ballou
Binder:	Vail Ballou